MENTAL HEALTH PRACTICE AND THE LAW

MENTAL HEALTH PRACTICE AND THE LAW

Edited by

Ronald Schouten, MD, JD

Department of Psychiatry

Harvard Medical School

Law & Psychiatry Service

Massachusetts General Hospital

Boston, MA

OXFORD

UNIVERSITY PRESS

Oxford University Press is a department of the University of Oxford. It furthers
the University's objective of excellence in research, scholarship, and education
by publishing worldwide. Oxford is a registered trade mark of Oxford University
Press in the UK and certain other countries.

Published in the United States of America by Oxford University Press
198 Madison Avenue, New York, NY 10016, United States of America.

© Oxford University Press 2017

CIP data is on file at the Library of Congress
ISBN 978–0–19–938710–6

9 8 7 6 5 4 3 2 1

Printed by Webcom, Inc., Canada

CONTENTS

CONTRIBUTORS

Catherine Ayoub, EdB, MN, RN
Boston Children's Hospital
Law & Psychiatry Service
Massachusetts General Hospital
Boston, Massachusetts

Scott R. Beach, MD, FAPM
Psychiatrist, Avery Weisman Psychiatric
 Consultation Service
Massachusetts General Hospital
Associate Program Director, MGH/
 McLean Adult Psychiatry Residency
Assistant Professor of Psychiatry, Harvard
 Medical School
Boston, Massachusetts

Rebecca W. Brendel, MD, JD
Director, Masters of Bioethics Degree
 Program
Harvard Medical School
Center for Law, Brain, and Behavior
Massachusetts General Hospital
Boston, Massachusetts

Alec Buchanan, PhD, MD, FRCPsych
Associate Professor
Department of Psychiatry
Yale School of Medicine
New Haven, Connecticut

Philip J. Candilis, MD, DFAPA
Director, Forensic Psychiatry
 Fellowship
Saint Elizabeths Hospital/Dept. of
 Behavioral Health
Washington, DC
Clinical Professor of Psychiatry
George Washington University School of
 Medicine and Health Sciences
Howard University College of Medicine
Adjunct Professor of Psychiatry
Uniformed Services University of Health
 Sciences

Steven K. Hoge, MD, MBA
Columbia-Cornell Forensic Psychiatry
 Fellowship Program
Columbia University
New York, New York

Gary Jacobson, MD
Department of Psychiatry
Massachusetts General Hospital
Boston, Massachusetts

Robert Scott Johnson, MD, JD
San Francisco Psychiatry
San Francisco, California

Reena Kapoor, MD
Associate Professor
Department of Psychiatry
Yale School of Medicine
New Haven, Connecticut

Robert Kinscherff, PhD, JD
William James College
National Center for Mental Health and
    Juvenile Justice
Petrie-Flom Center for Health Law
    Policy, Biotechnology,
    and Bioethics
Harvard Law School
Boston, Massachusetts

Kimberly D. Kumer, MD, USAF, MC
Medical Director
Mental Health Flight
86 MDG (Medical Group)
Ramstein Air Base, Germany

Matthew Lahaie, MD, JD
Fellow in Forensic Psychiatry, Law, and
    Psychiatry Service
Massachusetts General Hospital
Clinical Fellow, Harvard
    Medical School
Boston, Massachusetts

Ariana Nesbit, MD
Cambridge Health Alliance
Harvard Medical School
Cambridge, Massachusetts

Jennifer L. Piel, JD, MD
Assistant Professor and Associate
    Psychiatry Residency Program
    Director

Department of Psychiatry and Behavioral
    Sciences
University of Washington
Staff Psychiatrist
VA Puget Sound Health Care System
Seattle, Washington

Debra A. Pinals, MD
Director, Program in Psychiatry,
    Law and Ethics
Clinical Professor of Psychiatry
University of Michigan
Ann Arbor, Michigan

Marilyn Price, MD
Harvard Medical School
Law & Psychiatry Service
Massachusetts General Hospital
Boston, Massachusetts

Phillip J. Resnick, MD
Professor of Psychiatry
Case Western Reserve University School
    of Medicine
Cleveland, Ohio

Navneet Sidhu, MD
Saint Elizabeths Hospital
Washington, DC
Northcoast Behavioral Healthcare
Cleveland, Ohio

Matthew Soulier, MSD
Associate Professor
Department of Psychiatry and
    Behavioral Sciences
University of California Davis Medical
    Center
Sacramento, California

MENTAL HEALTH PRACTICE AND THE LAW

/// 1 /// BASICS OF THE LAW AND LEGAL SYSTEM

RONALD SCHOUTEN

For most clinicians, the word "law" conjures up a set of rules that govern how things work. Those rules are regarded as set and predictable, even if there is some variation in their operation under specific circumstances. For example, the law of gravity reliably predicts that what goes up must come down, although in operation there may be some variation in how the law plays out (e.g., the rate of descent can be influenced by various factors). The laws that are the stuff of the legal system similarly define how things should work, but they are even more open to variation because the fundamental underlying rules are subject to interpretation (and at times, reinterpretation) and their application is largely dependent on specific facts and circumstances.

The openness of the law to interpretation and its variable application under specific circumstances lead to a lack of absolute uncertainty and a lack of clarity, which can cause great consternation to clinicians. This is especially true when clinicians encounter legal requirements and constraints that seem to interfere with their efforts to care for patients. A clinician who asks two attorneys what the law requires in a given situation may get slightly (or markedly) different answers. Law students know that "It depends" is often the best answer when asked a question in class about what the decision should be in a given case. Lawyers are referred to as "counselors at law" because their job is to advise their clients rather than tell them what to do. There is often no clear-cut answer to a legal question, and the lawyer must advise the client of the risks and benefits of pursuing a given course of action. Clinicians trained in the scientific method may be justifiably frustrated when told that there is no definitive answer to a legal question.

The reason that the law is open to interpretation is that its multiple components (i.e., statutes, regulations, and case law decisions) arise from different jurisdictions and are constantly interacting as they are applied to an almost infinite variety of facts. The law is a living thing that changes over time in response to developments in society's attitudes, beliefs, and needs. The concepts of psychotherapist–patient privilege (discussed in chapter 9) and informed consent (discussed in chapter 5) did not exist in early English common law but are essential aspects of modern clinical practice. Their development was a result of legislative action and judicial decisions reflecting changes in society.

The law is defined by legal principles and the application of those principles to the facts of a given case. For example, in civil commitment cases, the general legal principle is that a person can be involuntarily confined only if he or she poses a risk of harm to self or others. (See chapter 2 for a detailed discussion of civil commitment.) The facts of each case must be examined to see whether they fulfill the criteria for commitment. Does Mr. J., who is brought to the emergency department by police officers, pose a substantial risk of harm by virtue of his mania, grandiosity, and refusal to take medication?

This process of evolving interpretation and individual case application results in less certainty than many would hope to find in a legal system that supposedly governs society and guides the behavior of its members. But by the same token, it introduces flexibility that allows for growth and changes in societal beliefs and mores and also maximizes the opportunity for justice to be done in individual cases.

FUNDAMENTAL CONCEPTS

Clinicians who want to understand the legal system and its impact on clinical practice will benefit from an understanding of the following concepts and principles.

The Law

At the simplest level, the law is a system of agreed-on rules that allow a society to optimize how it functions by providing advance notice of how individuals are expected to behave, a process for resolving disputes, and a system of disincentives (usually in the form of penalties) for violating those rules.[1]

This system of rules has several sources. Natural laws are those considered to be inherent in nature, universal, and reflective of basic human ethical values. Prohibitions against theft, murder, and cheating are considered natural laws. Natural law was the basis for ecclesiastical law and has been the subject of much debate among legal philosophers. Humankind learned early on that reliance on natural laws was not wholly dependable in protecting society from those willing to ignore natural laws in the pursuit of their own interests or satisfaction. The result of this recognition was a system of positive laws. The earliest type of positive law was case-based law, in which elders in the community were asked to recall how the community had made decisions on similar matters in the past and to apply that experience to the conflicts presented to them. Before written records became available, this judge-made case law was passed down in the form of oral narratives. With the development of writing and manuscripts, the decisions of judges became a matter of record that could be referenced rather than relying on the memories of those asked to act as judges. As new fact situations arose, judges were challenged to apply old principles to them, and the law regarding given issues evolved as the judges established new principles. This case-based, or judge-made, law came to be known as the common law.[1-3]

The other type of positive law is generated by governmental entities in the form of pronouncements by monarchs or passage of laws by legislative bodies. In modern times, positive laws can take two forms. Statutes are laws enacted by legislative bodies for the purpose of enforcing principles of natural law or establishing other civil obligations or criminal prohibitions. State legislatures, for example, adopt statutes that define the crime of murder and the penalties for that crime.

The most fundamental law in societies that use them is the constitution, which provides a general framework defining the rights of the citizens and powers and responsibilities of government. All 50 states have constitutions, as does the United States as a whole. The U.S. Constitution, ratified in 1788, consists of seven articles that establish the branches of the federal government and their roles and powers and address the relationships and admission of states, the Constitution as the supreme law of the land, and the ratification process. The first 10 amendments to the Constitution, collectively referred to as the Bill of Rights, were ratified in 1791. They are listed in Table 1.1.

TABLE 1.1. The Bill of Rights

Amendment 1:	Freedom of Religion, Press, Expression; Rights of Assembly and Petition
Amendment 2:	Right to Bear Arms
Amendment 3:	Housing of Soldiers
Amendment 4:	Search and Arrest Warrants
Amendment 5:	Rights in Criminal Cases, including Due Process
Amendment 6:	Rights to a Fair Trial
Amendment 7:	Rights in Civil Cases
Amendment 8:	Bails, Fines, and Punishments
Amendment 9:	Rights Retained by the People
Amendment 10:	Powers Retained by the States and People

The amendments establish basic rights and protect those rights from encroachment by the federal government. The Fourteenth Amendment, ratified in 1868, extends the protection of those rights from violation by the states. Amendments of particular importance to clinical practice are discussed in this chapter. Canada has both a constitution and the Canadian Charter of Rights and Freedoms, which is analogous to the Bill of Rights.

Regulations are policies and procedures issued by administrative agencies that have been delegated the authority to write and enforce the regulations that make a statute operative. This area of the law is referred to as administrative law. For example, in many states, the legislature passes statutes that govern the licensing of clinicians, and those statutes include provisions establishing licensing boards. The licensing boards, rather than the state legislature, adopt regulations governing the practice of the professions and enforce those regulations. State legislatures enact statutes that set out the criteria for civil commitment, but state departments of mental health develop regulations that govern the details of how those statutes are to be applied, such as the criteria for licensing inpatient psychiatric facilities and requirements for seclusion and restraint.

Administrative law can also include administrative hearings at which allegations of regulatory violations are heard by administrative law judges or a panel of regulators appointed to the board of the regulatory agency. For example, violations of the National Labor Relations Act (which protects the right to organize unions, ensures fair union representation elections, and prohibits unfair labor practices) are first heard by an administrative law judge, whose decisions can be appealed to the National Labor Relations Board. The decisions of the board can, in turn, be appealed to the federal courts.[4]

Types of Laws

There are two basic types of laws: civil and criminal. Broadly speaking, criminal laws are those that relate to offenses against society, while civil laws concern conflicts between individuals or those that otherwise do not fall within the criminal law. In early history, no distinction was made between civil and criminal law. While Roman law recognized that distinction, English law before the Norman invasion did not, even though countries on the continent of Europe had done so. This led to a brutal form of justice in medieval England: the perpetrator of the accidental or intentional death of another person had to pay compensation to the victim's family, or that family was within its rights to take the life of the perpetrator or one of the perpetrator's family members. This violent approach to justice gave rise to the phrase "Buy off the spear or bear it."

The lack of a distinction between civil and criminal law in England ended in the late Middle Ages. Certain crimes were deemed to be offenses against the state, as embodied by the monarch, and to be "boteless"—so offensive to society that the accused could not pay money to avoid a penalty.[5] These boteless crimes—murder, rape, treason, theft—became the basis for the establishment of criminal law.

Criminal acts are punishable by fines, incarceration, or in some cases, death (i.e., capital punishment). Civil wrongs are punishable by fines, payment of monetary damages if another party has been injured, or an order to take or desist from certain actions. The last form of relief is referred to as injunctive relief, as one party is enjoined from engaging in certain behavior or is required to do something. For example, if Mr. A. builds a fence that prevents sunlight from reaching Mr. B.'s garden, destroying his crop of prize-winning flowers, Mr. B. can pursue relief in the form of monetary damages equal to the value of the destroyed crop, an injunction ordering Mr. A. to take down the fence, or both.

Jurisdictions

Laws vary from place to place, reflecting political boundaries and the preferences of the population in a given area. The distinct areas to which specific bodies of laws apply are referred to as jurisdictions. In the United States, the jurisdictions are divided between federal and state, reflecting the fact that certain matters (both civil and criminal) are covered by the Constitution and by federal statutes, regulations, and case law, while the remainder fall under those same sources of authority belonging to the states. In addition, each state is a separate jurisdiction, with the laws of one state having no authority in another, even if the states share a border. Similarly, Canada has both federal and provincial laws.

The Structure of the Court System and the Notion of Judicial Precedents

State and federal jurisdictions follow the same general model for their court systems, with the primary division between trial courts and appellate courts. Disputes between parties are decided in trial courts. These can be civil cases, in which one person sues another for monetary damages, or criminal cases, in which the prosecution seeks to convict a defendant. There are two separate functions to be fulfilled in a trial. The trier of fact must first assesses the credibility of the witnesses and the relative strength of the arguments and then decide whether the moving party (the plaintiff in a civil case or the prosecution in a criminal case) has met its burden of proof and won the day. In a jury trial, the jury serves the role of trier of fact, while the judge serves as the trier of law, with overall responsibility for ensuring the fairness of the proceedings and making decisions regarding applicable legal principles, procedures to be followed, and admissible evidence. Trials without juries, in which judges serve as both the trier of law and the trier of fact, are called bench trials.

Regardless of whether the case is being heard in a bench or jury trial, the trier of fact must reach a decision based on a standard of proof that is specific to the type of case and the degree of harm that will be caused if the defendant is incorrectly held civilly or criminally liable. In civil cases, such as personal injury cases in which only money damages are in question, the standard is a preponderance of the evidence. This means that the allegations are more likely than not true. In criminal cases, in which the penalty involves incarceration or other serious consequences, the prosecution must prove its case beyond a reasonable doubt. A standard of clear and convincing evidence is used when the potential harm from a wrongful decision is greater than in a civil case but less damaging than in a wrongful criminal conviction. As discussed in chapter 2, the U.S. Supreme Court has held that, at a minimum, the standard of clear and convincing evidence must be used in civil commitment cases. The rationale is that civil commitment constitutes confinement that encroaches on a person's liberty interests, but it is less harmful than criminal confinement because the purpose is treatment rather than punishment.

Depending on the jurisdiction, trial courts may be divided on the basis of function, the potential import of the case, or both. Trial courts in Massachusetts, for example, include the District Courts and the Superior Court. The major distinction between these two is based on the size of the criminal penalty or damages associated with court decisions. District Courts hear misdemeanor criminal cases and civil matters in which no more than $25,000 is at issue. They also conduct arraignments in felony cases that ultimately will be heard in Superior Court, along with civil cases in which more than $25,000 is at issue. The Massachusetts District Courts comprise Probate and Family Court, Land Court, Housing Court, Juvenile Court, Boston Municipal Court, and the District Court. Clinicians in Massachusetts are most likely to interact with the District Court and Boston Municipal Court in the civil commitment process and with the Probate and Family Courts in matters involving guardianships, conservatorships, end-of-life decisions, and treatment refusal. The federal system has trial courts, referred to as District Courts, for specific jurisdictions (e.g., the U.S. District Court for the Southern District of New York and the U.S. District Court for the Northern District of Illinois).

If a party is disappointed by the outcome of a trial, the decision can be appealed in a court at the next level: an appellate court. There are numerous grounds for appeal, such as errors made by the judge; misconduct on the part of opposing counsel, witnesses, or jurors; and withholding of evidence. Prosecutors cannot appeal a verdict of not guilty in a criminal case because of the constitutional prohibition against double jeopardy (i.e., being tried twice for the same offense) contained in the Fifth Amendment. However, prosecutors can file an appeal if a criminal case has been dismissed.[6]

Most jurisdictions have appellate courts at two levels: an intermediate appellate court and a supreme court. The federal system of appellate courts is divided into 13 judicial districts with a Circuit Court of Appeals for each. Decisions made by those courts can be appealed to the U.S. Supreme Court. State systems also have intermediate and higher appellate courts. Massachusetts, for example, has the Court of Appeal and the Supreme Judicial Court. Matters that reach the highest appellate level tend to be those that are of greatest importance for defining fundamental legal principles within that court's jurisdiction, including interpretations of the Constitution. The law evolves when appellate courts interpret case law and statutes. In doing so, the appellate courts consider novel fact patterns that may arise in a case, the evolution of the law on similar issues in other jurisdictions, and changes in society and technology. For example, when the Fourth Amendment prohibition against unreasonable search and seizure was passed by Congress in 1789, cell phones and computers had not been invented, and electronic eavesdropping did not exist. With those technological developments, appellate courts had to determine how 18th-century legal principles applied to modern technology.

Prior decisions by appellate courts, referred to as precedents, control judicial decisions in subsequent cases. This is known as the doctrine of stare decisis. There are three important points to keep in mind about precedents. First, only appellate-level decisions have value as precedents. Each new case that goes to trial is decided on its own merits, within the framework of legal rules established by appellate courts. Second, once established, precedents are said to be "controlling" and must be followed when similar cases arise in legal disputes. However, appellate courts can reverse themselves and change the law. Third, legal precedents apply only within a court's jurisdiction. Thus, the decision of the Massachusetts Supreme Judicial Court is not binding on the Supreme Court of New Hampshire. Reflecting the independence of the federal appellate process, the decision of one federal Circuit Court of Appeals is not binding on the other Circuit Courts. Conflicting decisions by two or more Circuit Courts are resolved when the U.S. Supreme Court agrees to hear a case addressing the issue in question and decides how the law should be interpreted and applied in the case at hand and going forward.

Appellate courts can overturn their own prior decisions when changes in fundamental societal beliefs reveal past decisions to be inconsistent with modern society. For example, a series of modern U.S. Supreme Court cases have reversed prior decisions that allowed for capital punishment of individuals with intellectual disabilities[7] and adolescents.[8] The new decision then serves as the precedent for subsequent cases in which the same legal issue arises, but cases in which the earlier precedent was applied stand as previously decided.

LAW, ETHICS, AND THE ADVERSARIAL SYSTEM

Types of Witnesses

There are two basic types of witnesses—fact witnesses and expert witnesses—and clinicians may be called to serve as either type. A fact witness is any person who has firsthand knowledge of a matter. There is no requirement of special expertise or training; the fact witness needs only to have personal knowledge related to the event (or events) involved in the legal dispute. Young children can be fact witnesses, as can individuals with intellectual disabilities, so long as they are deemed to have testimonial capacity (i.e., they had the ability to understand the event in question at the time it occurred, can make sense of the event and incorporate it into testimony, have adequate memory of the event, and can convey those recollections in a reasonably coherent fashion). In addition, the proposed fact witness must be able to appreciate both the requirement that he or she tell the truth and the significance of the oath to do so.[9] Fact witnesses can testify only on matters within their personal knowledge and cannot offer hearsay testimony to prove that an event occurred. Hearsay is information that the witness learned from someone else. For example, in a trial in which Defendant B is accused of having robbed a bank, Witness A can testify that he saw Defendant B rob the bank if he actually did see the defendant do so. However, if Witness A did not see the robbery but was told by someone else that the defendant robbed the bank, Witness A cannot offer that testimony, as it is hearsay.

Anyone with relevant knowledge can offer testimony as a fact witness. In order for expert testimony to be admissible, there must be a subject at issue that is beyond the knowledge of the trier of fact. The proposed expert testimony must be such that it will assist the trier of fact in making a decision. Once the trier of fact has determined that expert testimony is needed, the expert chosen must be qualified to offer that testimony. Some, but not all, states require that the judge determine whether the proposed expert is qualified to testify as an expert. That determination is based on the proposed expert's knowledge, education, skills, and experience.[10] The witness's qualification as an expert is explored in an examination referred to as a voir dire. In states that follow this practice, the judge will then decide whether or not to designate the witness as an expert. In jurisdictions where judges do not designate the witness as an expert, the expert's qualifications will be explored on direct examination by the party proposing him or her as an expert, and opposing counsel will have an opportunity to question the witness about his or her credentials.

Unlike fact witnesses, expert witnesses can use hearsay evidence subject to certain restrictions in some jurisdictions. Expert Witness A would generally be allowed to use information provided by bystanders to support his or her opinion that Defendant B was manic and not criminally responsible at the time of a crime.

An Overview of Ethics in the Legal Process

The core ethical principles of medicine are autonomy, beneficence or nonmaleficence, and justice. These principles are discussed in detail in chapter 15. Ethical principles, by nature, are agreed-on rules that are unenforceable unless one has previously agreed to be bound by them, such as by joining an organization that espouses a code of ethics. When it is determined that certain ethical principles are essential to the functioning of society, they become legal principles enforceable either by a governmental entity, if it is an offense against the state, or through the civil justice system by a private party who claims to have been injured by another party.

As noted previously, the law is a mechanism for governing society that allows people to understand the rules of behavior in advance and to resolve conflicts that arise in the course of human interactions. Experience and belief, especially in situations involving conflict, are inevitably subjective, as expressed by the axiom that there are at least two sides to every story, as well as the legal version of that axiom: legal disputes are like pancakes—they always have two sides. A more pointed expression of this phenomenon, often used in reference to divorce litigation, is that there are at least three sides to every story: his, hers, and the truth.

The purpose of the legal system is to resolve disputes, even while acknowledging that it cannot always determine the truth. It is often said that the law is not about truth but about justice. In an adversarial system, justice is a matter of making sure that both parties, usually through their legal counsel but sometimes by representing themselves (called proceeding pro se), can present witnesses and evidence and have their arguments heard by a neutral fact finder. That process, like any fair contest, is governed by rules for the proceedings, including rules governing the admissibility of evidence.

The success of this adversarial process—two parties in a dispute looking to a neutral fact finder to resolve the conflict—depends on certain underlying principles. First, the law—case law or common law, as well as legislatively enacted statutes—provides a set of rules by which individuals and groups can choose to govern their behavior. Second, the adversarial process is based on the notion of fairness: the decision maker must be neutral, the rules of law must be applied equally to all parties, and everyone must have access to the courts and the opportunity for legal representation. In short, the playing field should be level and the contestants equally matched as they present their versions of facts and argue about how the law should be applied to those facts.

Fairness is not always achieved, of course. Attorneys differ in quality, and access to high-quality legal representation is commonly determined by the client's financial resources. In addition, a number of societal and political factors may bias the ostensibly neutral juror or judge and the legal process at large. Clinicians often struggle with, and joke about, the idea of professional ethics for attorneys. Like physicians and other clinicians, attorneys have a code of ethics that is designed to preserve the fairness and integrity of the legal process and to hold attorneys to high professional standards of behavior. One of the attorney's most important professional obligations is "zealous representation of the client within the bounds of the law."

That obligation often strikes nonattorneys as odd. It implies, after all, that a criminal defense attorney will argue zealously and put all of his or her effort into defending a client, even in the face of overwhelming evidence of guilt. It further implies that the attorney representing the plaintiff or defendant in a civil action will work just as hard in the client's cause, even if there are potentially fatal weaknesses in the client's claim and evidence. Public reaction ranges from disdain to outrage at this apparent dishonesty and willingness to lie on behalf of the client.

Public outrage would be justified if this professional obligation were unfettered. An attorney violates his or her ethical principles and risks both disbarment and criminal penalties if he or she introduces testimony or evidence known to be false. A prime example of this is the defense attorney who allows the defendant to testify that he or she is innocent, even though the defendant has already confessed guilt to the attorney. This is referred to as "suborning perjury." Skeptics may ask: how does the criminal defense attorney zealously defend a client, ethically and legally, who has admitted guilt to the attorney?

We turn to the protections of rights provided by federal and state constitutions to answer that question. These constitutions, as interpreted by the U.S. Supreme Court and state appellate courts, balance the interests of the state against the rights of the defendant. The essence of a criminal case, after all, is an accusation by the state that the defendant has committed an offense against society that is punishable by a fine, imprisonment, or both. In some jurisdictions and in federal cases, the death penalty is also available. In short, the goal of the prosecution is to deprive the defendant of life, liberty, or property. The U.S. Constitution stipulates that the federal government and the states can do so only if the defendant has been provided with both procedural and substantive due process.

Procedural due process, as embodied in the Fifth Amendment to the U.S. Constitution, requires that the defendant be given notice of the charges, an opportunity to confront witnesses testifying against him or her, and a chance to defend himself or herself. The opportunity to defend oneself includes the right to an attorney at public expense if the defendant cannot afford one, as well as the right to a mental health expert at public expense if psychiatric issues are involved and the defendant cannot afford such assistance.

Substantive due process speaks to the underlying fairness of any efforts to deprive citizens or other residents of the United States of life, liberty, or property. One aspect of substantive due process is that in criminal cases, the burden is on the prosecution (i.e., the state) to prove the guilt of the defendant rather than on the defendant to prove his or her innocence. The rationale for this approach arises from the recognition that the government's financial, investigatory, and legal resources far outstrip those of the average criminal defendant. It would be fundamentally unfair to require that those accused of crimes not only prove their innocence but also do so as if their resources were equal to those of the state. An example of this effort to level the playing field is the requirement that the prosecution turn over all its evidence, including exculpatory evidence, to the defense. The defense, on the other hand, is not required to turn over all its evidence to the prosecution, even if it supports the prosecution's allegations. In short, our criminal justice system is set up in such a way that fairness, justice, and society's best interests are served by requiring the state to use its superior resources to prove the defendant's guilt beyond a reasonable doubt, with the defense using everything in its power to challenge the state to do so. In this way, we, as a society, can have some reasonable measure of confidence that the state is playing by the rules and that only the truly guilty are convicted. This is captured in Blackstone's ratio, attributed to the English jurist William Blackstone: "It is better that ten guilty persons escape than that one innocent suffer."[11] In spite of this ancient and grand pronouncement, cases of wrongful conviction occur, including in cases of capital punishment, for reasons ranging from inaccurate eyewitness and scientific evidence to misconduct by police and prosecutors.[12]

This sounds like a very one-sided process, yet these protections represent carefully considered provisions determined to be necessary in order to protect defendants from prosecutorial misconduct or bias and ensure that they are not crushed by the greater abilities and resources of the state. Keep in mind that this system, which seems to primarily serve the interests of criminal defendants, was actually designed to prevent all citizens, especially the innocent, from inappropriate use of the power of the state.

The system is not entirely one-sided, however. It balances the interests of the state in protecting society against the rights of the defendant. Defense counsel and prosecuting attorneys are bound by the same rules of zealous, but honest, advocacy. Indeed, prosecutors who offer false testimony or introduce evidence known to be false are at even greater risk than defense attorneys. The constitutional prohibition against unreasonable search and seizure, contained in the Fourth Amendment and applied to the states through the

Fourteenth Amendment, can lead to the exclusion of evidence of guilt if that evidence was obtained without a warrant or in the absence of probable cause.

Due Process and Its Special Relevance to Mental Health Practice

The concept of due process permeates much of mental health law. The due process clause of the U.S. Constitution (Fifth Amendment), applied to the states through the Fourteenth Amendment, states that no person shall be "deprived of life, liberty, or property, without due process of law." Life, liberty, and property have been held to include freedom from involuntary confinement, freedom to make one's own treatment decisions, and all the rights specified in the Bill of Rights. Any governmental action that would impinge on those liberty interests requires that the rights of the individuals affected be protected by due process. For example, the U.S. Supreme Court has held that confining a person to a hospital against his or her will constitutes a significant deprivation of liberty interests, requiring that the person who is confined be accorded due process protections.[13,14] Exactly how much process is due varies according to the liberty interest affected, the nature and extent of the deprivation, and the government's interests that are being furthered by the deprivation. Where fundamental liberty interests are involved, such as freedoms of speech, religion, association, and the right to due process itself, the government's action must further a compelling state interest that justifies the deprivation.

Conclusion

The law is a collection of principles, promulgated as constitutions, statutes, regulations, and case law that establish a framework for the functions of society and the behavior of its members. It provides a civilized mechanism for the resolution of conflicts between individuals, with extensive protections for individuals who are accused of crimes. The law is a living thing that has evolved over time and continues to evolve, while the general principles remain intact. The dynamic nature of the law can mean that there is less certainty and clarity than clinicians would like when trying to care for patients and discovering that those efforts are constrained by legal requirements. It is helpful to keep in mind that those legal requirements serve all people, including patients and clinicians, by protecting individual autonomy and legal rights.

FREQUENTLY ASKED QUESTIONS

Dr. A. and Dr. B. are discussing the care of Ms. M., who was just admitted to an inpatient psychiatric unit. Dr. B. wants to call Ms. M.'s family to tell them that she has been admitted and to get more information. Dr. A. says that "it is against the law" to do so. What does this mean?

The phrase "against the law" is generally used to mean that there is some legal prohibition against the action in question. This phrase should be used cautiously, as it suggests an absolute prohibition, whereas the legal requirements are often subject to interpretation in light of the facts, and exceptions may apply. There are exceptions to confidentiality that would allow Dr. B. to make that call. (For a detailed discussion of those exceptions, see chapter 9.) When a person states that something "is against the law," it is advisable to ascertain what that means and to seek the opinion of someone who has legal expertise with regard to the question.

A jury has awarded the plaintiff $250,000 in a malpractice case in which the defendant prescribed a medication that caused an allergic reaction. Subsequently, Dr. L. prescribes the same medication for Mr. K., who suffers a similar allergic reaction. Will Dr. L. be found to have committed malpractice, and will Mr. K. be awarded $250,000, because of the finding in the earlier case?

No. The malpractice case is a trial court case and does not establish a precedent that determines how subsequent cases, even those with similar facts, will be decided. There are numerous factual issues that will determine whether the general legal requirements for finding malpractice liability were present in Dr. L.'s treatment of Mr. K.

Attorney G. is representing Mr. Q., who is accused of robbing a grocery store. He tells her that he robbed the store because he needed money to feed his children. Attorney G. suggests that he plead not guilty. Is that ethical?

Yes. The state must prove that Mr. Q. is guilty, and the standard of proof is beyond a reasonable doubt. Attorney G.'s obligation, from both the legal and ethical standpoints, is to require the state to meet its burden of proof. So long as she does not put Mr. Q. on the witness stand to testify that he is innocent (which would leave her open to allegations of suborning perjury), she is meeting her obligations as an attorney.

REFERENCES

1. Fuller LL. *The Morality of Law*, revised edition. New Haven: Yale University Press; 1969.
2. Kelly JM. *A Short History of Western Legal Theory.* Oxford: Clarendon Press; 1992.
3. Friedman LM. *A History of American Law*, 3rd edition. New York: Simon & Schuster; 2005.
4. National Labor Relations Board. https://www.nlrb.gov/. Accessed July 26, 2016.
5. Boteless. In: Garner BA, ed. *Black's Law Dictionary*, 10th edition. St. Paul, MN; West Publishing; 2009.
6. *United States v. Scott,* 437 U.S. 82(U.S. Supreme Court 1978).
7. *Atkins v. Virginia,* 536 U.S. 304(U.S. Supreme Court 2002).
8. *Roper v. Simmons,* 543 U.S. 551(U.S. Supreme Court 2005).
9. Otto RK, Sadoff RL, Fannif AM. Testimonial capacity. In: Drogin EY, Dattilio FM, Sadoff RL, Gutheil TG, eds. *Handbook of Forensic Assessment: Psychological and Psychiatric Perspectives.* Hoboken, NJ: Wiley; 2011.
10. Brodsky SL. *Testifying in Court: Guidelines and Maxims for the Expert Witness.* Washington, DC: American Psychological Association; 2013.
11. Blackstone W. *Commentaries of Sir William Blackstone on the Laws and Constitution of England.* London: London; 1796.
12. Epps D. The consequences of error in criminal justice. *Harvard Law Review.* 2015;128(4):1065–1151.
13. *Humphrey v. Cady,* 405 U.S. 504, 509 (1972).
14. *Addington v. Texas,* 441 U.S. 418 (1979).

CIVIL COMMITMENT

RONALD SCHOUTEN AND PHILIP J. CANDILIS

Civil commitment is the process of involuntarily hospitalizing a person suffering from a mental illness or substance use disorder. It is one of the most common tasks undertaken by mental health professionals and one of the most challenging: the clinician is making a decision to confine a patient, often over his or her strenuous objection.

To clinicians, involuntary hospitalization is a clinical intervention intended to protect patients from the consequences of mental illness by providing treatment and a safe environment. To patients and patients' rights advocates, it is a deprivation of civil liberties and autonomy. As a result, a legal process for involuntary hospitalization exists that is designed to protect the rights of the patient during what the U.S. Supreme Court has described as a significant deprivation of liberty interests.[1,2]

THE BASICS OF CIVIL COMMITMENT

Civil commitment is generally a two-part process. First, a clinician decides that a person requires hospitalization for evaluation and treatment. As with any other illness, people with mental illness can choose to admit themselves to a hospital. In the ideal situation, the person in question accepts the clinician's recommendation and signs into the hospital voluntarily. If he or she refuses to do so, or lacks the capacity to make the decision, the next step is a short-term involuntary hospitalization. This requires that one or more authorized persons certify that the patient meets the jurisdiction's criteria for emergency hospitalization. Some jurisdictions (e.g., New York) require that two physicians or nonphysician clinicians examine the person and sign the authorization form. In other jurisdictions (e.g., Massachusetts), only one person—a physician, another designated mental health professional, or a police officer—needs to sign the form.

Temporary involuntary hospitalization typically lasts for up to 72 hours, although the length of confinement varies by jurisdiction. For example, Missouri applies a 96-hour limit.[3] New Mexico law provides that a person sent to an evaluation facility can request a hearing within 7 days,[4] and Connecticut allows a patient to be held for up to 10 days before a court must hold a commitment hearing.[5]

If the statutorily permitted time limit for temporary hospitalization is reached and the patient continues to refuse voluntary admission, the facility holding the patient must decide whether to pursue civil commitment through the legal process established in that jurisdiction. In some cases, it is clear that the patient meets the commitment criteria, and the treatment team is confident about the results of a commitment hearing. In many situations, however, the patient would benefit from a longer stay in the hospital but does not unequivocally meet the legal criteria for commitment. Responses to such situations vary. Some clinicians will file for commitment in order to keep the patient on the unit and allow time for further improvement while waiting for the hearing to be held. If improvement occurs, the petition for commitment is withdrawn. If no further improvement occurs, the facility must then decide whether to proceed with the hearing or discharge the patient.

If there is an evident need for further hospitalization but strict fulfillment of the commitment criteria is less clear, a better approach is to openly discuss the situation with the patient, any involved family members, and the patient's legal counsel and negotiate a solution. Having a patient agree to further inpatient treatment is much better for the treatment relationship and the prospects of adherence to treatment than an unnecessary adversarial process or threatening the patient with one.

Underlying Legal Principles

As discussed elsewhere in this book (chapters 1, 5, 6, and 8), all adults (including those with mental illness) are presumed to be competent in the eyes of the law, and all competent persons have the right to make their own health care decisions. These decisions include whether to accept or refuse hospitalization and treatment for mental illness. How, then, do we understand a system in which people can be taken off the street or from their homes, brought to a facility for an emergency evaluation, confined in a hospital, and treated against their will?

The civil commitment process, like other government actions in which individual rights are denied or limited, involves balancing the rights of the individual against the legitimate exercise of government control and pursuit of legitimate state interests. The principles of autonomy, personal liberty, and individual decision making are well established and have multiple protections. Balanced against them is the authority and responsibility of governments to intervene when an individual's exercise of rights threatens the rights, interests, and safety of others. Governments can also intervene to protect legitimate state interests, such as the prevention of suicide and protection of public health, safety, and welfare. This is known as police-power authority.

Mental illness is just one area in which a government can exercise its police powers to limit the rights of citizens. Infectious disease and public health are other well-known areas in which this authority can be exercised to protect individuals and society at large, with significant limitations on individual autonomy.[6,7] State and tribal governments have the right to order isolation and quarantine in order to prevent the spread of infectious diseases, and the federal government can detain and medically examine people entering the United States or traveling between states who are suspected of carrying communicable diseases. Those who do not comply with government-ordered isolation and quarantine can be punished criminally with fines and imprisonment.[8]

The authority of governments to impose isolation and quarantine, let alone criminal penalties for failure to comply, is rarely invoked. In contrast, there is a long history of governments exercising their authority to confine mentally ill persons. Indeed, mental illness is unique among clinical conditions in that involuntary commitment is available as a standard element of illness management. Yet, as noted above, the Supreme Court has declared repeatedly that involuntary commitment constitutes deprivation of a person's fundamental liberty interests, including the rights to freedom of movement and association. Consequently, a person can be deprived of those rights only after due process of law (see chapter 1) and for a compelling state interest.

The conditions and procedures for civil commitment vary among jurisdictions, but the Supreme Court has laid out the minimal policies and procedures that must be followed to protect the constitutional rights of those who are hospitalized against their will. The main goal of these procedures is the protection of the patient's liberty interests through adherence to due process requirements. Those requirements, found in the Fifth and Fourteenth Amendments, are met by giving notice of the proceedings, providing access to legal representation, holding a hearing before a neutral fact finder, upholding the patient's right to offer and confront witnesses, and adhering to established standards for commitment. At a minimum, the state must prove that the person meets the criteria for commitment on the basis of clear and convincing evidence.[2] As noted in chapter 1, that is a higher standard of proof than the minimal preponderance-of-the-evidence standard used in civil litigation, but it is lower than the beyond-a-reasonable-doubt standard applied in criminal cases. The Court's rationale has been that the deprivation of liberty in civil commitment is substantial enough to require a higher level of proof than the minimal legal standard of a preponderance of evidence but that the state's interest in public safety and the nonpunitive purpose of confinement allows for a lower standard of proof than the standard of beyond a reasonable doubt.

As noted in chapter 1, state statutes and case law can provide a higher level of protection of liberty interests than required by the U.S. Constitution but not a lower level. In Massachusetts and the District of Columbia, for example, judges presiding over commitment proceedings must be convinced beyond a reasonable doubt that the person subject to the commitment proceeding, commonly referred to as the respondent, meets the statutory commitment criteria.

Criteria for Commitment

Society's changing attitudes toward the mentally ill are reflected in the history of civil commitment and its evolving standards. The most recent stages of this evolution have been marked by a shift from a *parens patriae*, or need-for-treatment, model to a police-power, or dangerousness, model. The Latin term *parens patriae*, which means "parent of the country," reflects the legal concept that the state is acting as protector of those citizens who cannot care for themselves. Under this model, the state has the authority to confine and treat persons who are ill and not able (or are unwilling) to pursue treatment on their own.

As autonomy became a fundamental component of medical ethics and individual rights gained greater judicial protection, the need for treatment under the *parens patriae* doctrine was replaced largely by a dangerousness model in most jurisdictions. In these jurisdictions, the presence of an untreated mental illness is not sufficient for commitment unless there is also evidence of dangerousness to self or others. In Maryland and the District of Columbia, dangerousness to self or others is the sole criterion for commitment. The decision to focus on dangerousness alone as a basis for commitment was a disappointing development for clinicians and professional organizations, such as the American Psychiatric Association, which advocated the use of hospitals for treatment rather than confinement.[9]

While all jurisdictions in the United States now include dangerousness to self or others as a basis for commitment, commitment laws exhibit a great deal of variety. As a result, it is important for clinicians to know and understand the criteria in the jurisdiction in which they practice. The variation in these statutes largely results from differences in several key characteristics:

1. The definition of mental illness, which may include or exclude conditions that are primarily related to substance abuse, dementia, intellectual disabilities, and other "organic" conditions (e.g., those caused by a medical condition or physical trauma).

2. The definition of dangerousness, which includes dangerousness to property as well as persons in some jurisdictions (e.g., Delaware, Washington, and federal jurisdictions) but not others.

3. The extent to which need for treatment (*parens patriae*) is included as a criterion. For example, some statutes require a finding that the patient's condition will deteriorate and give rise to a risk of harm.

4. The criteria used for determining dangerousness. The majority of jurisdictions provide specific definitions of "dangerousness to self" and "dangerousness to others," while a smaller number of states give the court broader discretion in determining dangerousness.

5. Use or nonuse of the "gravely disabled" criterion. This criterion specifies that the person, by virtue of a mental illness, is unable to provide for his or her own protection in the community and that there is no less-restrictive alternative to civil commitment. In other words, the necessary resources cannot be provided through available home care, a nursing home, or another facility that is less restrictive than a locked hospital ward. This is another need-for-treatment (*parens patriae*) criterion. Oklahoma and the District of Columbia are unique among U.S. jurisdictions in not specifically providing gravely disabled criteria in their commitment statutes, leaving it to the court's discretion in determining overall dangerousness.

6. Use or nonuse of the criterion of lack of capacity to make treatment decisions, including the decision to be hospitalized. Basically, this standard means that the person is in need of treatment, is gravely disabled, or poses a risk to others and lacks the capacity to make a treatment decision.

7. Consideration of whether the person subject to commitment is likely to benefit from treatment. Indiana, Kentucky, South Dakota, and Utah include this criterion.

Just to add to the confusion, and to further underscore the need for clinicians to be familiar with their own jurisdiction's commitment criteria, each of the criteria can appear in various combinations among the state statutes.[10,11]

The requirements for temporary emergency evaluation are generally similar to those for civil commitment (e.g., the dangerousness criterion must be met for both). They differ in that temporary emergency evaluation occurs pursuant to the authority of one or more designated parties, such as clinicians or police officers, whereas civil commitment occurs on the authority of a judge after a court hearing. And of course, they differ by jurisdiction as well. In states that have different standards for emergency hospitalization than for civil commitment, the criteria are less stringent than those for civil commitment. The rationale for this is that emergency hospitalization is for a shorter period, usually 72 hours, and is intended for initial evaluation and treatment. Civil commitment, however, is for an extended period (e.g., 6 months), depriving the patient of liberty for a longer period of time.

HOW IT WORKS

While the need to civilly commit a patient is most commonly confronted by mental health professionals, practitioners in any clinical field may need to be involved in the process. Emergency medicine physicians are highly likely to confront these situations, as are family practitioners, internists, and pediatricians, as well as medical students on clinical rotations, interns, residents, and trainees in other clinical fields. In academic medical centers, or other settings where access to mental health services is readily available, these evaluations and decisions are generally made by mental health specialists. The following case vignette illustrates a common scenario and equally common challenges that can be encountered by practitioners in all specialties.

Vignette: Whether to Commit

Mr. L. is a 28-year-old man with a history of depression, one prior suicide attempt, and two prior psychiatric hospitalizations. Friends bring him to the emergency room because he has been drinking heavily for several days and talking about killing himself. They report that he has been having trouble with his boss and has made comments about "payback time." He has also made threatening comments to them, although they have not yet taken the comments seriously. They are uncertain whether he has access to weapons.

When examined by Dr. S., the Emergency Medicine resident on call, Mr. L. exhibits neurovegetative signs and symptoms of depression, including the feeling that life is not worth living. He denies any intent or plan to harm himself, yet expresses hopelessness about his job and the prospects for any improvement in his life. Asked about his feelings toward his boss, Mr. L. becomes agitated and accuses his boss of plotting to fire him. He denies any plan to harm his boss but comments that "someone will give the SOB what he deserves someday." Mr. L. also denies any intent to harm his friends, saying that he was "just messing" with them. He refuses to answer questions about access to weapons, saying it is none of Dr. S.'s business, and he lectures her about his right to bear arms under the Second Amendment. Dr. S. notes to herself that this is not an unusual attitude among people in the community. She is also vaguely aware that some states have passed laws restricting a physician's ability to ask patients routinely about the ownership of firearms and to include that information in the medical record,[12] and she wonders whether her own state has such a law.

Dr. S. concludes that, at the very least, Mr. L. would benefit from hospitalization for evaluation and treatment of his depression. His irritability and refusal to answer questions about weapons concern her, but she decides not to pursue the inquiry, given his comments about Second Amendment rights. Mr. L. declines her offer of voluntary hospitalization, noting that he will lose his job if he does not show up in the morning and will "never hear the end of it" if coworkers find out he has been hospitalized in a "psych ward." "Besides," he tells her, "I'm fine, and I promise I won't hurt myself or anyone else. Even if something happens, you don't have to worry about being sued. I don't have any family."

Now what? Dr. S. still believes that Mr. L. needs treatment and is concerned that he poses a risk of harm to his boss. Yet he raises arguments that are, on their face, reasonable: concerns about his job and about stigma and embarrassment. He denies any intent or plan to harm himself or anyone else and has promised that he will not harm himself. (A discussion of the "contract for safety" can be found in chapters 4 and 8.) Still, Mr. L. has classic symptoms of depression, appeared depressed and irritable on examination, and minimized his symptoms and statements. She also notes that he has made a prior suicide attempt and finds his comment that "if something happens" he has no family more provocative than reassuring. Convinced that Mr. L. needs to be in the hospital but uncertain whether she can override his refusal, Dr. S. calls in a psychiatric consultant for guidance. After considering the standards outlined below, they decide that an emergency 72-hour initial evaluation is appropriate. After ruling out the possibility that his symptoms are caused by another medical process or intoxication, Dr. S. and her psychiatric consultant complete the necessary legal and clinical paperwork and search for an inpatient bed.

Applying the Commitment Criteria

Since Mr. L. declines hospitalization, should Dr. S. hospitalize him against his will? As she notes, there are a number of reasons not to accept Mr. L.'s decision. But does he meet the criteria in their jurisdiction?

For the purposes of discussing Mr. L.'s case, we will assume that he is in Massachusetts and apply that state's standard. Please remember that the criteria and processes for emergency hospitalization and civil commitment, as well as the terminology, vary widely among the states. We apply the Massachusetts standard here to illustrate general principles and show how one state engages in this process. It is critical that every clinician learn the specifics of how the process works in his or her jurisdiction.

Massachusetts, like other jurisdictions, has a specific definition of mental illness for the purposes of both emergency involuntary hospitalization and civil commitment: "mental illness shall mean a substantial disorder of thought, mood, perception, orientation, or memory which grossly impairs judgment, behavior, capacity to recognize reality or ability to meet the ordinary demands of life, but shall not include alcoholism or substance abuse."[13] On the basis of statutory language and case law in Massachusetts, persons with other conditions, such as intellectual disabilities (previously referred to as mental retardation), or neurologically based behavioral disorders, such as dementia, do not fulfill the definition of mental illness. The form used for emergency hospitalization in Massachusetts defines mental illness as follows:

> For purposes of admission to an inpatient facility under Section 12, "Mental Illness" means a substantial disorder of thought, mood, perception, orientation, or memory which grossly impairs judgment, behavior, capacity to recognize reality or ability to meet the ordinary demands of life. Symptoms caused solely by alcohol or drug intake, organic brain damage or intellectual disability do not constitute a serious mental illness.

Persons with substance-related disorders, like Mr. L., are eligible for involuntary commitment to a mental health facility if the need for hospitalization is the result of a coexisting mental illness independent of or exacerbated by substance abuse or organic brain damage. The same is true for persons with intellectual disabilities.[14] In the absence of a coexisting mental illness, voluntary admission is available to these persons on their own request if they are at least 16 years old or, if they are minors (under age 18), on the request of their parents. In other words, parents have the authority to hospitalize their children who are less than 18 years of age, and anyone 16 years or older can voluntarily hospitalize him or herself.

States that exclude persons with primary substance use disorders or developmental disabilities from civil commitment provide alternative procedures for involuntary hospitalization. In Massachusetts, for example, a separate portion of the mental health statute allows for commitment of a person with a substance use disorder to a treatment facility for a period not to exceed 90 days, with periodic reviews, and up to 1 year of supervised outpatient treatment.[15] The commitment is based on findings that the person meets the statutory definition of an "alcoholic" or "substance abuser" and that there is a likelihood of serious harm as a result.

Mr. L. would meet the Massachusetts definition of mental illness for involuntary hospitalization by virtue of his symptoms of depression, including suicidal ideation. While there is evidence that alcohol abuse is a problem for him, it is not the primary basis on which he meets the commitment criteria, even though it would certainly be an appropriate issue for his hospitalization and treatment.

Once it has been determined that Mr. L. meets the state's definition of mental illness, the next step is to determine whether he meets the criteria for emergency hospitalization. Under the Massachusetts standards, Mr. L. must, in the opinion of the person certifying him for admission, fulfill one or more of the criteria for likelihood of serious harm, defined as follows:

(1) a substantial risk of physical harm to the person himself as manifested by evidence of, threats of, or attempts at suicide or serious bodily harm; (2) a substantial risk of physical harm to other persons as manifested by evidence of homicidal or other violent behavior or evidence that others are placed in reasonable fear of violent behavior and serious physical harm to them; or (3) a very substantial risk of physical impairment or injury to the person himself as manifested by evidence that such person's judgment is so affected that he is unable to protect himself in the community and that reasonable provision for his protection is not available in the community.[16]

Mr. L. would meet the first criterion, concerning danger to himself, by virtue of his statements to his friends and the information obtained on examination—this is all appropriate evidence. His expression of passive suicidal ideation would generally not be enough to trigger involuntary commitment. However, Dr. S. is correct in her judgment that Mr. L.'s symptoms of depression, previous suicide attempt, refusal to discuss his access to weapons, expressed hopelessness, substance abuse, job-related stresses, and lack of family support, combined with passive suicidal ideation, constitute evidence that he meets the criterion of self-harm. For a detailed discussion of suicide risk assessment, see chapter 4.

Would Mr. L. also meet the criterion of harm to others? No one has reported a specific threat, yet the assessment of risk to others, like the assessment of risk to self, cannot be made solely on the basis of whether the patient expresses a desire to harm himself for others. The risk of violence must be assessed in the larger context of the patient's mental status, history, and life circumstances, including interactions with possible victims and life stressors. Indeed, as research on targeted violence has shown, we need to be concerned about persons who pose a risk of violence, not just those who make a threat. Some persons who pose a risk of violence will also threaten violence, but many will never threaten their target directly. However, they will often reveal their hostility, intent, and plan to someone other than the intended victim.[17] Thus, the wise and cautious clinician will pursue multiple sources of information in the course of assessing the risk of violence, rather than rely solely on the patient's report. Violence risk assessment is discussed in detail in chapter 3.

In this case, Mr. L. expressed clear hostility toward his boss, in statements made to Dr. S and others, and talked about his boss getting "what he deserves someday." In addition, Mr. L. refused to answer the question about whether he had access to weapons, which is a legitimate basis for concern in this context. Dr. S.'s uncertainty about whether she could rightfully ask Mr. L. questions about weapons ownership was the result of her misunderstanding of information she had read in the news. Florida has, in fact, passed a statute that penalizes physicians if they ask about firearms in the patient's home or document such information in the medical record.[12] But those limitations do not apply if there is a good-faith belief that such information is relevant to the safety and welfare of the patient or others. The statute states, in part:

> A health care practitioner licensed under chapter 456 or a health care facility licensed under chapter 395 shall respect a patient's right to privacy and should refrain from making a written inquiry or asking questions concerning the ownership of a firearm or ammunition by the patient or by a family member of the patient, or the presence of a firearm in a private home or other domicile of the patient or a family member of the patient. *Notwithstanding this provision, a health care practitioner or health care facility that in good faith believes that this information is relevant to the patient's medical care or safety, or the safety of others, may make such a verbal or written inquiry.* [Emphasis added.][12]

The presence of firearms in the home or other access to weapons is always a relevant question and should be part of the assessment whenever there are concerns about potential suicidality or violence to others. Clinicians should be aware, however, that three other states—Missouri, Montana, and Minnesota—had passed measures similar to Florida's as of 2015.

Mr. L. could also have fulfilled the criterion of posing a danger to others if there had been evidence that his statements or behaviors had provided a reasonable basis for his friends to fear for their safety. Although his friends denied having such fears, if information was obtained indicating that his boss feared violence at Mr. L.'s hands, that criterion would be fulfilled.

In practice, the reasonable-fear-of-harm criterion is often overlooked, perhaps because it requires a judgment call in assessing what people are experiencing. In fact, trainees often ask, "How do we know whether the fear other people claim is reasonable? How do we know they are telling the truth?" The answer to the first question is that we do our best to assess the seriousness of the risk, regardless of whether an explicit threat has been made, and consider whether a reasonable person would be fearful under the circumstances. The second question tacitly acknowledges that mental health professionals have no inherent skill or expertise as lie detectors. Our task in these situations is to do our best to assess the concerns objectively, in context, and with the benefit of all the collateral information that is available. We are not obligated to be perfect, only to act carefully and in good faith.

The application of the third criterion, which we refer to as the gravely-disabled criterion, is more questionable in Mr. L.'s case. While he is having conflicts at work, he otherwise appears to be functioning normally, his overall health is good, and his judgment does not appear to be so impaired by his mental illness that he is unable to provide for his basic needs and protection in the community. This criterion applies to persons whose illness prevents them from attending to their most basic needs, such as a homeless person who refuses shelter during a winter storm because of paranoid delusions. In such situations, emergency commitment to a psychiatric facility would be appropriate only if no less-restrictive alternative were available. In the case of the homeless person, that would be a shelter the patient would accept.

Dr. S. wondered whether Mr. L. had the capacity to make an informed decision regarding voluntary hospitalization. The lack of capacity to make informed treatment decisions is a primary component of the civil commitment standard in a number of states and is an essential component in some others, but it plays no role in Massachusetts. In Utah, for example, the standard allows for civil commitment if the court finds "clear and convincing evidence" of the following circumstances:

(a) the proposed patient has a mental illness;

(b) because of the proposed patient's mental illness the proposed patient poses
     a substantial danger . . . to self or others, which may include the inability
     to provide the basic necessities of life such as food, clothing, and shelter, if
     allowed to remain at liberty;

(c) *the patient lacks the ability to engage in a rational decision-making process*
     regarding the acceptance of mental treatment as demonstrated by evidence of
     inability to weigh the possible risks of accepting or rejecting treatment . . . .
     [Emphasis added.]

(d) there is no appropriate less-restrictive alternative to a court order of
     commitment; and

(e) the local mental health authority can provide the individual with treatment
     that is adequate and appropriate to the individual's conditions and needs. In
     the absence of the required findings of the court after the hearing, the court
     shall forthwith dismiss the proceedings.[18]

Massachusetts does not include a specific finding of impaired decision-making capacity in its civil commitment criteria, but as in many other states, impaired decision-making capacity may be considered in determining whether hospitalization is necessary (e.g., by considering whether the patient's lack of insight into his or her illness is likely to result in deterioration of the patient's condition). Michigan's definition of a "person requiring treatment" and subject to civil commitment includes, as one subtype, a person "who has mental illness, whose judgment is so impaired that he or she is unable to understand his or her need for treatment and whose continued behavior as the result of this mental illness can reasonably be expected, on the basis of competent clinical opinion, to result in significant physical harm to himself, herself, or others."[19]

After Dr. S. and her psychiatric consultant decide that Mr. L. meets the criteria for emergency hospitalization, they begin the necessary paperwork while looking for a hospital that will accept him. The shortages of inpatient beds at public and private hospitals, combined with the strict criteria for hospitalization applied by managed care companies, have made the process of hospitalizing a patient almost as challenging as the evaluation itself. This is a particular problem with hospitalization of children and adolescents, for whom inpatient psychiatric beds are in very short supply and who must often be housed in emergency rooms until an inpatient bed becomes available. As a result, many institutions have specialists whose sole task is to find beds and negotiate with insurers and facilities.

The Massachusetts form that Dr. S. fills out is titled "Application for an Authorization of Temporary Involuntary Hospitalization." It includes the words "Application Pursuant to 12(a)" on one side and "Authorization Pursuant to Section 12(b)" on the other side. Sections 12a and 12b are sections of Chapter 123, the mental health statute in Massachusetts. In essence, the 12(a) section is a request to another facility to admit the patient, and the 12(b) section is the form signed by the physician who accepts the patient into a facility. This form is commonly referred to as a "pink paper," since it is usually printed on pink paper, and the process of being involuntarily admitted to a psychiatric facility is often referred to as being "pink-papered" or "Section 12'd." Other states have similar euphemisms for their processes—for example, in Florida, being committed is referred to as being "Baker Acted," after the eponymous state law.

In Massachusetts, the criteria for temporary hospitalization are the same as those applied if the process subsequently moves ahead to a full civil commitment under MGL Ch. 123 Sec. 7 & 8. Recall that some jurisdictions apply different standards to the initial temporary hospitalization and the longer-term commitment, as we discuss below.

Any licensed physician, licensed psychologist, certified psychiatric nurse clinical specialist, licensed independent clinical social worker, or police officer may file the

Sec. 12(a) Application for an Authorization of Temporary Involuntary Hospitalization. But only a designated physician (i.e., one with admitting privileges to the specific facility) can admit the patient under Sec. 12(b), and only after the physician certifies that he or she has examined the patient within 2 hours after admission (or notes that the examination was delayed because of an emergency at the hospital) and that the patient meets the emergency admission criteria. This is the law's way of ensuring that patients are assessed in a timely fashion and that a physician attests that the state's criteria for involuntary admission criteria are met.

CLINICAL CHALLENGES IN CIVIL COMMITMENT

The decision to hospitalize a patient is first and foremost a clinical matter, albeit one that is subject to specific legal guidelines. The patient has an illness, and the clinician must decide how best to treat it. In this case, Dr. S. believes that Mr. L. should be hospitalized for his benefit and for the benefit of others. As in other clinical situations, his consent to hospitalization and treatment, as well as active participation in his treatment, are the desired outcomes.

Few people relish the idea of being hospitalized, and that is especially true when it comes to psychiatric hospitalization. There are multiple reasons for this. Mr. L. cites the risk to his job and the stigma of a psychiatric hospitalization. Denial of the existence or seriousness of his symptoms ("I'm fine"), or an undisclosed desire to be free to carry out suicidal or violent impulses, may also play a role. In addition to resistance from the patient, family members or friends may oppose hospitalization, either denying the need for treatment or offering assurances that they can take care of the patient. The availability of family support is, in fact, a valid consideration in deciding whether to involuntarily hospitalize a patient, but it is just one of the risks and benefits to be weighed. Clinicians should expect to confront some or all of these issues when considering whether to hospitalize a patient.

It is often difficult to predict how patients will react to the news that they are going to be admitted to a hospital against their will. While some may accept this decision passively, or even welcome it, it is important to anticipate resistance or overt hostility and aggression. As with all treatment decisions, the decision to hospitalize the patient should be explained calmly and directly, with specific details about why the decision was made. A primary difference between this and other treatments is that the patient's informed consent to hospitalization (i.e., voluntary admission) is sought, but his or her informed refusal is not allowed.

When patients become aware that they are not being given a choice in the matter, it is not uncommon for them to become argumentative and agitated. The louder the patient's objections, the calmer the clinician should try to be. Most important, clinicians should take steps to protect themselves, the patient, and others. In a well-functioning emergency room, hospital security personnel who have training and experience in how to deescalate a situation in which a patient is becoming increasingly agitated can use redirection and shows of force to maintain safety. They should be the front line in managing physical outbursts.

Clinicians working in such settings should get to know the security personnel in their facilities and make every effort to build respectful professional relationships with them. Those relationships can make the difference between safety in the workplace and a potentially career-ending injury. Clinicians should also request training in anticipating and managing aggressive behavior. Programs such as MOAB (Management of Aggressive Behavior)[20] provide instruction on identifying behavioral cues for aggression, maintaining an adequate distance between yourself and a potentially angry patient or family member, deescalating conflict, and positioning yourself physically in order to leave a potentially dangerous setting. Some courses also provide basic self-defense training, for those situations in which deescalation is unsuccessful. For more on violence risk assessment and management of aggressive behavior, see chapter 3.

Let us return to the case vignette:

Mr. L. is quite upset at the prospect of hospitalization and attempts to leave the emergency room. Wisely, Dr. S. has apprised hospital security of the situation, and security personnel are on hand to prevent him from leaving and to manage any aggressive behavior. Their presence, as a show of force, is enough to convince Mr. L. to stay and listen to Dr. S.'s explanation. She tells him that he will be transported by ambulance to a nearby hospital with a psychiatric unit, where he will be evaluated by another physician, who will decide whether he should be admitted. Mr. L. is also told that he will have an opportunity to sign himself into the hospital voluntarily. Even so, Dr. S. makes it clear that she is not giving him a choice and that she will be sending him to the hospital. Mr. L. grudgingly agrees to go.

On his arrival at the accepting facility, Mr. L. is assessed by the designated physician, who completes the Authorization Pursuant to Section 12(b) form, indicating that Mr. L. was examined within 2 hours after his arrival, certifying that he requires hospitalization, and specifying the basis for that decision. In addition, the physician offers Mr. L. an Application for Care and Treatment on a Conditional Voluntary Basis, which Mr. L. refuses to sign.

The conditional voluntary, or CV, admission differs from a standard voluntary hospitalization in that the patient agrees to be hospitalized and treated but cannot leave the hospital at will. The patient may refuse to sign the form, or the physician may reject the application on the grounds of the patient's incapacity to make decisions, bringing the clinical assessment full circle. If the patient signs the form and the physician accepts the application, the patient's release is conditional on the facility superintendent's requirement, at his or her discretion, of 3 days' notice that the patient wants to leave. This is known as a "three-day paper." Once filed, it gives the facility up to 3 business days to decide whether to release the patient or to file for civil commitment. Other jurisdictions have similar processes but with different terminology.

Regardless of the terms used, a key component of voluntary admission is ensuring that the person who accepts admission has the capacity to make that decision. The importance of that step was made clear in the landmark Supreme Court case *Zinermon v. Burch*.[21] In that case, Mr. Burch was allowed to sign himself into Florida State Hospital when he was floridly psychotic and unaware of his surroundings. The Supreme Court held that those circumstances presented a sufficient basis for finding a violation of Mr. Burch's constitutional due-process rights under 42 U.S.C. Sec. 1983, which allows lawsuits for civil rights violations. The Court ruled that his due process rights had been violated by Florida's failure to put measures in place to prevent an incapacitated person from admitting himself to the hospital voluntarily and incompetently waiving his right to have his commitment reviewed by a judge. Unlike Massachusetts, Florida had no requirement for certifying the capacity to consent to voluntary admission, and hospital personnel had not taken it upon themselves to assess Mr. Burch's capacity to make that decision.

In addition to offering patients an opportunity for voluntary admission, psychiatric facilities in Massachusetts and other states must offer the opportunity to consult with legal counsel; consultation can be provided by a public agency if the patient cannot afford to hire an attorney. The temporary involuntary hospitalization is for a period of 72 hours. By the end of that period, if the patient refuses voluntary hospitalization, or is considered not to have the capacity to accept admission, the facility must decide whether to file for civil commitment.

The process of evaluating, admitting, and treating the patient elicits clinical information that may provide the basis for filing a petition for civil commitment or guardianship, but also raise privilege issues (see Chapter 9). States vary as to whether they regard that information as falling within the scope of the psychotherapist–patient privilege. Massachusetts law, for example, that:

> Except as hereinafter provided, in any court proceeding and in any proceeding preliminary thereto and in legislative and administrative proceedings, a patient shall have the privilege of refusing to disclose, and of preventing a witness from disclosing, any communication, wherever made, between said patient and a psychotherapist relative

to the diagnosis or treatment of the patient's mental or emotional condition. This privilege shall apply to patients engaged with a psychotherapist in marital therapy, family therapy, or consultation in contemplation of such therapy.[22]

That statutory provision was interpreted in *Commonwealth v. Lamb*.[23] In that case, the court held that the psychotherapist-patient privilege applied in a proceeding to determine whether Lamb would be committed as a sexually dangerous person. Massachusetts has the usual exceptions to the privilege, however, including waiver (i.e., if the patient is aware that the content of discussions with the therapist will not be confidential and directly or implicitly consents to have the therapist testify). In Massachusetts, the privilege is deemed to have been waived if the patient is first given what is now referred to as the Lamb warning. This consists of a statement that communications between the clinician and the patient will not be privileged and that the clinician may disclose treatment information in the event of any legal or administrative proceedings.

However, the privilege does not apply in Massachusetts if involuntary hospitalization or dangerousness is involved.

> The privilege granted hereunder shall not apply. . . [i]f a psychotherapist, in the course of his diagnosis or treatment of the patient, determines that the patient is in need of treatment in a hospital for mental or emotional illness or that there is a threat of imminently dangerous activity by the patient against himself or another person, and on the basis of such determination discloses such communication either for the purpose of placing or retaining the patient in such hospital, provided however that the provisions of this section shall continue in effect after the patient is in said hospital, or placing the patient under arrest or under the supervision of law enforcement authorities.

That exception did not apply in *Lamb* because Lamb was already in state custody and the hearing was being held to determine whether he should be committed indefinitely as a sexually dangerous person, so there was no imminent risk. Thus, although the privilege may not apply to emergency hospitalization, it resumes once the patient is hospitalized and the imminent risk has passed. The Massachusetts Supreme Judicial Court (the state's highest court) clarified the imminent-risk exception in 2015, holding that it applies when a clinician concludes that a patient poses an imminent risk of harm to self or others, and the clinician is offering testimony for the purpose of initial hospitalization or retention of the patient in the hospital if he or she is about to be discharged.[24]

Massachusetts is not alone in this approach. Connecticut also extends the psychotherapist–patient privilege to court-ordered psychiatric examinations and guardianship proceedings, and requires a warning of lack of confidentiality before the clinician's testimony can be admitted:

> Communications made to or records made by a psychiatrist in the course of a psychiatric examination ordered by a court or made in connection with the application for the appointment of a conservator [guardian] by the Probate Court for good cause shown may be disclosed at judicial or administrative proceedings in which the patient is a party, or in which the question of his incompetence because of mental illness is an issue, or in appropriate pretrial proceedings, provided the court finds that the patient has been informed before making the communications that any communications will not be confidential and provided the communications shall be admissible only on issues involving the patient's mental condition.[25]

Like Massachusetts, Connecticut has a number of exceptions to the psychotherapist–patient privilege, including imminent dangerousness. For example, the Connecticut statute states:

> Communications or records may be disclosed when the psychiatrist determines that there is substantial risk of imminent physical injury by the patient to himself or others or when a psychiatrist, in the course of diagnosis or treatment of the patient, finds it necessary to disclose the communications or records for the purpose of placing the patient in a mental health facility, by certification, commitment or otherwise, provided the provisions [for psychotherapist–patient privilege] shall continue in effect after the patient is in the facility.[25]

Florida provides the following two exceptions to the psychotherapist–patient privilege:

1. For communications relevant to an issue in proceedings to compel hospitalization of a patient for mental illness, if the psychotherapist in the course of diagnosis or treatment has reasonable cause to believe the patient is in need of hospitalization.
2. For communications made in the course of a court-ordered examination of the mental or emotional condition of the patient.[26]

In Georgia, however, the psychotherapist–patient privilege, as laid out in its statutes and applied to civil commitment, governs all communications involved in the evaluation or treatment of the patient by a psychiatrist, psychologist, or counselor, with no exceptions other than the patient's waiver of the privilege.[27] The privilege does not apply to information obtained in the course of court-ordered forensic evaluations.

As these examples show, the applicability of the psychotherapist–patient privilege in civil commitment and other mental health proceedings varies among the states. In some states, a clinician who fails to notify the patient of the lack of privilege and obtain a waiver may be barred from testifying about information a patient has divulged during the course of treatment. Failure to give the Lamb warning, however, may not be problematic if the jurisdiction has an imminent-risk exception and it is applicable, or if the patient accepts conditional voluntary admission and there is no need for a commitment proceeding. On the other hand, the privilege might be invoked in the absence of a waiver in hearings to authorize involuntary treatment (see chapter 7) and guardianship (see chapter 6), as long as there is no imminent danger. To avoid such situations, each clinician must understand the law in his or her own jurisdiction. In jurisdictions where the privilege is specifically extended to commitment situations, the clinicians should warn the patient about the lack of confidentiality and obtain a waiver, in anticipation of the privilege being raised at the hearing.

Let us turn back to the case vignette:

Mr. L. refuses to accept admission on a conditional voluntary basis and becomes increasingly agitated and aggressive on the unit, claiming that the hospital is imprisoning him at the behest of his boss and demanding to be released. He exhibits evidence of psychosis and is offered anti-psychotic medication, which he refuses. With the 72-hour period of temporary hospitalization drawing to a close, Mr. L.'s inpatient psychiatrist files a petition for civil commitment. The court schedules the hearing for 3 days after the filing.

Events in the commitment process must take place within a certain time frame, which varies among jurisdictions. In Massachusetts, for example, the hearing for the initial civil commitment must be held within 4 days after the filing. As a practical matter, patients can, and often do, request or accept a delay in order to obtain a specific attorney or for other scheduling reasons.

The location of commitment hearings, like other aspects of the commitment process, varies among jurisdictions. In many states, judges come to the hospital to hold commitment hearings. This arrangement has obvious advantages. Patients do not need to be transported to the courthouse, nor do they need to wait in the courthouse should the hearing be delayed, which happens often. In addition, hearings held in the hospital support patient safety by maintaining the clinical environment and presence of clinical staff. Some states, such as Missouri, have experimented with the use of video teleconferencing for civil commitment hearings. Arguably, this technology can provide for speedier hearings and avoid the burdens of travel for the patient, hospital staff, judge, and court officers. The 4th Circuit Court of Appeals upheld the constitutionality of teleconference commitment hearings in 1995,[28] although in some states the idea has met with resistance from patient advocates, who argue that it deprives the respondent of the right to confront witnesses and the full benefits of a public hearing.

Jurisdictions also differ with regard to the availability of a jury trial for civil commitment. All 50 states and the District of Columbia allow judges to make commitment decisions. However, 19 jurisdictions (including the District of Columbia) give respondents the right to request a jury trial for commitment. One of the 19, New Mexico, allows the respondent to request a jury trial after an initial 30-day commitment.

The length of the initial commitment is another factor that varies among jurisdictions. The initial commitment in Massachusetts is for 6 months, with subsequent commitments for 1 year, although the court can specify a shorter period if the circumstances warrant it. In fact, such extended commitments are rare except in forensic cases (e.g., if a person has been found not guilty by reason of insanity). Lengths of stay in psychiatric units of general hospitals are now usually measured in days, not months, reflecting the period of time required for medications and other treatment interventions to take effect, as well as the impact of managed care.

Not only did Mr. L. refuse voluntary admission, however; he also refused treatment with antipsychotic medication. In Massachusetts, as elsewhere, all adults are presumed to be competent in the eyes of the law and have a right to make their own treatment decisions. In nonemergency situations, a patient in Massachusetts cannot be forcibly treated with antipsychotic medications until a court, following a full adversarial hearing, has declared that the patient is incompetent to make treatment decisions, has determined that the patient would accept treatment if he or she were competent, and has approved the proposed treatment. These hearings, known as Rogers hearings, after the name of the lead plaintiff in the seminal 1983 case (*Rogers v. Commissioner, Department of Mental Health*), were originally held only in probate courts. The authority to adjudicate these issues was later extended to district courts in order to lessen the burden on probate courts and avoid delays. Thus, the issue of Mr. L.'s treatment refusal would be heard by the district court at the time of the commitment hearing.

A court may determine that a patient meets the criteria for civil commitment but retains the capacity to refuse treatment with antipsychotics. After all, one may remain competent for one purpose but not another. Although rare, this finding leads to a more focused decision-making assessment, as well as great consternation among insurers, since they must provide reimbursement for a hospital stay even though the patient is refusing treatment that would lead to an earlier discharge. Treatment refusal is discussed in detail in chapter 7.

OUTPATIENT COMMITMENT

Inpatient civil commitment has always been an imperfect process, at best. This is especially true in the current environment of cuts in public spending for inpatient facilities and managed care restrictions in private facilities. These pressures, which translate into demands to avoid hospitalization and reduce the length of stay, have raised barriers to admission to the point that patients must be at high risk and virtually unmanageable in the community. As a result, patients are now more ill at the time of both admission and discharge than ever before, which often concerns those clinicians responsible for making discharge decisions. On the other hand, advocates for shorter hospital stays point out that patients historically were often retained in the hospital when outpatient treatment would have been both safe and feasible. The current pressures on the inpatient system do seem to have had two positive effects: a more objective approach to risk assessment and the development of a broader array of transitional care services, such as partial hospital programs.

Failure to adhere to outpatient treatment is the leading cause of relapse among people with mental illness. This, in combination with the lack of treatment resources noted above and the increased protections afforded for the right to refuse treatment, has exacerbated a classic revolving-door problem. In order for patients to be involuntarily hospitalized, they must become sufficiently ill that they pose a danger to themselves or others, in some cases actually causing serious harm. They are then hospitalized and treated against their will; they recover, are discharged, stop their treatment, and then become ill again.

Involuntary outpatient commitment, also referred to as assisted outpatient treatment (AOT) or community treatment orders (CTO), was developed to address this problem. The goal of AOT is to ensure that people diagnosed with a serious chronic mental illness receive treatment and adhere to it. It is an effort to prevent deterioration of their condition to the point where they meet the dangerousness criteria for inpatient commitment. In essence, this is a process by which a person is ordered by a court to follow a treatment program, with failure to do so resulting in a return to the hospital, a court hearing, or admission to another treatment facility for evaluation and treatment. AOT is available in the majority of U.S. states and the District of Columbia, as well as in Canada, the United Kingdom, and Australia. As of this writing, only five states do not have AOT procedures: Connecticut, Maryland, Massachusetts, New Mexico, and Tennessee.

However, AOT is not without controversy. First and foremost, critics argue that it deprives a person of the right to make his or her own treatment decisions, often without a judicial determination that the person lacks the capacity to do so. A Cochrane review observed that there have been few studies of the efficacy of AOT, and those that have been performed had small numbers of participants.[29] The results of these studies provided little evidence for the efficacy of compulsory community treatment with respect to efficient use of health services, cost reduction, or improvements in patients' social functioning, mental state, quality of life, or satisfaction with care.

In contrast, the renowned violence researcher Jeffrey Swanson and his colleagues concluded that such programs can lead to a reduction in overall service costs but require an investment of substantial resources by the state and lead to increases in medication costs. Their study of AOT in New York City showed a 43% reduction in net costs in the first year and an additional 13% reduction in the second year.[30]

A detailed discussion of the pros and cons of AOT is beyond the scope of this chapter, but the programs have been popular with legislatures. Their popularity with patients, clinicians, and the courts, however, remains an open question. Indeed, as the Treatment Advocacy Center has pointed out, even in jurisdictions that have AOT programs, their effectiveness and use vary greatly.[31] As with other social and public health services, the success of AOT depends heavily on the community's commitment to making it work and willingness to provide the necessary resources.

CONCLUSION

Civil commitment is one of the few areas of health care in which the judgment of the clinician and the patient's wishes are commonly in stark contrast. Indeed, the civil commitment process itself means that the clinician and the patient could not reach an agreement about what treatment is necessary and best for the patient. State statutes give designated clinicians and some others the ability to exercise the power of the state in confining people against their will. As in other areas where the power and the authority of the state can be used to override the will and preferences of the individual, legal protections are in place to make sure that the intrusion into individual liberty represented by involuntary hospitalization is limited, justified, and subject to judicial review. Civil commitment processes vary among the states, and all clinicians should become familiar with the rules and procedures where they practice.

FREQUENTLY ASKED QUESTIONS

Can I be sued if I involuntarily hospitalize a patient who is released when he or she gets to the hospital?

In our litigious society, anyone can be sued for anything; the question is whether the suit survives a motion to dismiss or, if it proceeds, whether it is successful. The basis for any such lawsuit is generally false imprisonment or defamation. Such suits are rarely success-ful because state statutes provide a good-faith defense—that is, they protect the clinician from liability if he or she acts in good faith.

If a person makes threats to harm others but does not exhibit mental illness on exam-ination, can he or she be committed to a psychiatric facility on an emergency basis?

No. Civil commitment is intended for people whose dangerousness arises from a serious mental illness, not for preventive detention of potential criminals, so it would be inap-propriate to confine a person with no mental illness to a treatment facility. Antisocial personality disorder and other mental disorders characterized by repeated antisocial acts (e.g., pedophilia) are not the basis for involuntary hospitalization in nonforensic mental health facilities. However, threats to harm others might provide an appropriate basis for invoking the so-called Tarasoff duty to protect. (See chapters 3 and 9.) Maryland and the District of Columbia are unusual in having dangerousness as the sole criterion for civil commitment.

Can someone besides a clinician request that a patient be hospitalized involuntarily?

Yes. A parent can request involuntary hospitalization for a minor child. The ability of a person other than a clinician to make such a request for an adult depends on the juris-diction and the adult's legal status. Generally speaking, any interested person can file a petition to have another person civilly committed, at which point that person is afforded all the protections of due process; commitment is not automatic. If a court has found that the patient is incompetent and has appointed a guardian, the guardian may, in some states, have the authority to voluntarily admit the person under guardianship. In other states, however, the guardian has that authority only if it has been specifically granted by the court. Instruments such as a durable power of attorney for health care or health care proxy contain a so-called springing clause: when the person who has executed the docu-ment is found to have lost the capacity to make treatment decisions, the authority of the power of attorney or the agent appointed under the health care proxy "springs" into existence. In both cases, the person who now holds the power has the authority to make any and all decisions that the principal (the person who executes the document) could have made for himself or herself when competent. Depending on the jurisdiction, this may include decisions about providing consent to voluntary admission to a hospital and treatment with antipsychotic medications, or even electroconvulsive therapy (ECT). Some states specifically exclude such decisions from the durable power of attorney.

Can someone be involuntarily hospitalized or detained for examination without first being examined in person?

Yes. In most states, a person who is authorized to apply for temporary hospitalization and who has information leading him or her to believe in good faith that there is a basis for emergency hospitalization or evaluation can complete the legal form and indicate the basis for the application, with an explanation for the fact that no direct examination was conducted. In most jurisdictions, police can request an evaluation or temporary hospitalization if an authorized clinician is not available.

Under what circumstances is assisted outpatient treatment, or outpatient commitment, likely to be used?

Outpatient commitment may be appropriate if a patient does not require inpatient hospitalization but has demonstrated a pattern of nonadherence to treatment that results in a risk of danger to self or others. Outpatient commitment is used to ensure that the patient participates in treatment; a patient who fails to appear for treatment is brought to the hospital for treatment or admission, as needed.

REFERENCES

1. *Humphrey v. Cady,* 405 U.S. 504, 509 (1972).
2. *Addington v. Texas,* 441 U.S. 418 (1979).
3. Chapter 632, Missouri Revised Statutes, Comprehensive Psychiatric Services. §632.305.1 Detention for evaluation and treatment, who may request—procedure—duration—disposition after application. (2014).
4. Chapter 43: Commitment Procedures New Mexico Statutes Article 1: Mental Health and Developmental Disabilities. §43-1-10: Emergency mental health evaluation and care. (2011).
5. Orlando J. Involuntary civil commitment and patients' rights. *OLR Research Report* 2013; 2013-R-0041. Accessed January 9, 2016, 2016. https://www.cga.ct.gov/2013/rpt/2013-R-0041.htm.
6. Gostin LO. The resurgent tuberculosis epidemic in the era of AIDS: reflections on public health, law, and society. *MD Law Review.* 1995;54(1):1–131.
7. Ries NM. Public health law and ethics: lessons from SARS and quarantine. *Health Law Review.* 2004;13(1):3–6.
8. Title 42—The Public Health and Welfare Chapter 6A—Public Health Service Subchapter II—General Powers and Duties Part G—Quarantine and Inspection Unites States Code, §271 Penalties for Violation of Quarantine Laws (1953).
9. Stromberg CD, Stone AA. A model state-law on civil commitment of the mentally ill. *Harvard Journal on Legislation.* 1983;20(2):275–396.
10. Pinals DA, Mossman D. *Evaluation for Civil Commitment.* New York: Oxford University Press; 2012.
11. Treatment Advocacy Center. State-by-state standards for civil commitment (Involuntary Treatment). 2011. Accessed January 8, 2016. http://www.treatmentadvocacycenter.org/browse-by-state.
12. Chapter 790 Weapons and Firearms Florida Statute Title XLVI Crimes §790.338 (2014).

13. 104 Code of Massachusetts Regulations 27.00: Department of Mental Health Licensing and Operational Standards for Mental Health Facilities. Vol Subpart B 27.05: General Admission Procedures. Boston, Massachusetts; 2008.

14. *Commonwealth v. Frederick D. DelVerde*, 401 Mass. 447(Supreme Judicial Court 1988).

15. Massachusetts General Laws, Chapter 123 §35 Commitment of Alcoholics and Substance Abusers.

16. Massachusetts General Laws, §1 Definitions.

17. Fein RA, Vossekuil B. *Protective Intelligence and Threat Assessment Investigations: A Guide for State and Local Law Enforcement Officials.* Washington, DC: U.S. Dept. of Justice, Office of Justice Programs, National Institute of Justice; 2000.

18. Utah Human Services Code, §62A-15-631 Involuntary commitment under court order—examination—hearing—power of court—findings required—costs. (2013).

19. Michigan Mental Health Code (1974).

20. MOAB Training International I. 2015. Accessed September 26, 2015. https://www.moabtraining.com/courses/moab_courses.php.

21. *Zinermon v. Burch* 494 U.S. 113(U.S. Supreme Court 1990).

22. Title II Actions and Proceedings Therein, Massachusetts General Laws §Chapter 233 § 20B (a) Privileged communications; patients and psychotherapists; exceptions (2015).

23. *Commonwealth v. Lamb,* 365 Mass. 265(Supreme Judicial Court 1974).

24. *Walden Behavioral Care v. K.I.,* 471 Mass. 150(Supreme Judicial Court 2015).

25. General Statutes of Connecticut, §Sec. 52-146 c-f (2011).

26. Florida Statutes, Title VII Evidence §Section 90.503 Psychotherapist-patient privilege (2015).

27. *Wiles v. Wiles,* 264 Ga. 594(Supreme Court 1994).

28. *U.S. v. Baker,* 45 F. 3rd 837(U.S. Court of Appeals 4th Circuit 1995).

29. Kisely SR, Campbell LA, Preston NJ. Compulsory community and involuntary outpatient treatment for people with severe mental disorders. *Cochrane Database of Systematic Reviews* 2011, Issue 2. Art. No.: CD004408. 2011.

30. Swanson JW, Van Dorn RA, Swartz MS, Robbins PC, Steadman HJ, McGuire TG, Monahan J. The cost of assisted outpatient treatment: can it save the states money? *American Journal of Psychiatry.* 2013;170:10.

31. Stetlin B, Geller J, Ragosta K, Cohen K, Ghowrwal J. *Mental health commitment laws: A survey of the states.* Treatment Advocacy Center; 2014. http://tacreports.org/storage/documents/2014-state-survey-abridged.pdf.

/// 3 /// VIOLENCE RISK ASSESSMENT

JENNIFER L. PIEL AND RONALD SCHOUTEN

Psychiatrists and other mental health professionals are commonly called on to assess persons with mental illness who may be dangerous to others. Although the terms "dangerousness" and "violence" may be used to convey a person's risk of harm to self, these terms are used more frequently to indicate the risk of harm to another person. Accordingly, unless otherwise noted, we use these terms in this chapter to refer to the probability that a person will commit an act of violence directed at one or more other persons. Violence risk assessment refers to the process of evaluating the risk that a person will act violently toward others. A discussion of acts of violence committed to advance political causes or ideologies is beyond the scope of this chapter.

Assessment of the risk of violence has become a necessary part of mental health practice. Although most patients are not violent, a small percentage of people with actively symptomatic mental illness may be at increased risk for violence, and that risk is routinely assessed in a variety of mental health settings, including emergency rooms, hospital consultation services, and outpatient clinics. Assessing the risk of violence has become an essential part of the decision-making process regarding hospitalization, discharge, and outpatient management.

In addition to their obligations to their patients, mental health professionals have a responsibility to protect the public, which includes assessment and management of patients who have risk factors for violence. The landmark California case *Tarasoff v. Regents of the University of California*[1] confirmed that harm caused by a patient to third parties may result in legal liability for the patient's psychotherapist if he or she knew that the patient posed a risk of harm to an identified victim. *Tarasoff* is discussed in more detail in chapters 8 and 9.

Although this chapter focuses on clinical risk assessments, courts also call on mental health professionals to help them make important decisions when a person's risk of violence is at issue. These evaluations are often performed by forensic psychologists or psychiatrists, clinicians with formal training in addressing mental health issues related to the law. Forensic practitioners may be asked, for example, to offer opinions on the risk of violence in the context of a court hearing about the appropriate disposition for a criminal offender, treatment refusal by an incarcerated person, or conflict over child custody.

Regardless of the setting, violence risk assessment is widely considered a core skill of mental health clinicians. This chapter explores key topics related to violence and assessment of the risk for violence, including associations between mental illness and violence.

VIOLENCE AND ITS SUBTYPES

Violent behavior can be divided into two broad subtypes: affective and predatory violence.[2] Affective violence, also referred to as reactive or impulsive violence, occurs in response to some provocation, real or imagined. It is an unplanned violent response to an event in the perpetrator's environment, commonly occurs under the influence of substance abuse or illness, and is often ego dystonic (i.e., out of character for the perpetrator and leading to regret afterward). Affective violence can occur as the culmination of a prolonged conflict between persons who know each other or it can be spontaneous, such as an incident of road rage. It may also be preceded by threatening behavior, in large part because the violent act itself is the perpetrator's response to feeling that he or she is in danger from the victim.

Unlike affective violence, which is generally marked by an elevated state of emotional arousal, predatory violence is characterized by a relatively low level of arousal (although there may be an emotional display during the violent act itself). The violence is planned and often not preceded by a direct threat to the intended victim, since this would reduce the chance of a successful attack. Persons who have committed an act of predatory violence generally do not feel remorse or regret unless they were unsuccessful in carrying out the violent act or it has had consequences that adversely affect their lives (e.g., criminal charges).

Mental health practitioners most commonly find themselves assessing and managing incidents of affective violence associated with acute exacerbations of mental illness. Targeted violence, while less commonly encountered, poses a greater challenge, as the would-be perpetrator who happens to be a patient may be reluctant to disclose his or her plans. In fact, the true predator with a violent goal is likely to withhold that information, out of fear that the clinician will intervene. Nevertheless, patients may share their feelings of hostility toward another person, as well as their thoughts of causing harm, as happened in the *Tarasoff* case. That case and its progeny made clear that clinicians who fail to take steps to protect the intended victim might be held liable. While perpetrators of targeted violence usually do not directly threaten their intended victims, they do often make indirect threats by communicating their intent to third parties, including therapists. Allowing the patient to talk and taking the time to listen carefully—an increasing challenge in the age of managed care and the time constraints it imposes—will help clinicians accomplish the task of assessing the risk of violence.

PREDICTION OF VIOLENCE RISK

The ability to predict violent behavior has long been a topic of interest and concern in the mental health community. In 1983, the American Psychiatric Association (APA) filed an *amicus curiae* (friend of the court) brief in *Barefoot v. Estelle*.[3] The APA argued that psychiatrists have limited ability to predict future violence with any accuracy and that courts should not accept psychiatric expert testimony on the subject. The court rejected the APA's position.

The APA's argument was based on the fact that, until the early 1990s, research on, and clinical attention to, violence was focused primarily on clinicians' ability to predict dichotomously which persons would be violent and which persons would not. In addition, the APA pointed out the difficulty of predicting the occurrence of relatively infrequent events, such as homicide, and the high rate of false positive predictions that result.

Since that court decision, much has been learned about risk factors for violence from an epidemiologic perspective. The binary approach of risk prediction has given way to risk assessment. This approach aims to stratify dangerousness on the basis of risk factors that have been identified at the population level. Our understanding of violence is evolving, and there is increasing research on the base rates of certain acts of violence and the factors associated with them.[4] Clinicians are well advised to familiarize themselves with the growing literature about the risk factors associated with future dangerousness.

RISK FACTORS FOR VIOLENCE

Violence can be viewed as the result of interactions among three sets of risk factors: individual, environmental, and situational factors.[5] While we focus on factors that increase the risk of violence, it is important to keep in mind that there are also factors that confer protection against the risk of violence. Individual risk factors and protective factors are characteristics of a person that contribute to or decrease violence risk, respectively.

Individual protective factors include family and community ties, compliance with treatment, and a stable employment. Environmental risk factors are conditions in the person's environment that allow for violence. Access to weapons, association with violent persons, and easy availability of victims are examples. Situational risk factors, which are also referred to as triggers, are life events or health issues that can trigger a violent act on the part of someone who is already predisposed to violence; examples are financial problems, loss of a relationship, job loss, and acute illness affecting either the person of concern or a family member.[6,7] In assessing the risk of violence, mental health professionals look for factors that are statistically associated with an increased risk of violence and are known to precede the occurrence of violent acts. In general, violence risk factors—individual, environmental, and situational—are divided into two broad categories: static and dynamic.

Static risk factors, which are stable and not readily changeable, are typically demographic factors or circumstances in a patient's history. Examples are age, gender, and previous exposure to violence. Dynamic risk factors are those that can change over time, such as the severity of mental health symptoms and status with respect to substance use, compliance with treatment, and access to firearms.[8]

Static factors contribute to one's overall risk of future violence, but it is important for the clinician to recognize that they are rarely amenable to clinical intervention. In contrast, clinicians can work with patients to reduce the risk of violence by modifying dynamic risk factors—for example, by treating active mental illness or substance abuse.

It is important for mental health clinicians to directly ask patients who are new to them, as well as long-term patients, about risk factors for violence, such as any recent or current violent thoughts, fantasies, or acts. There is no evidence that the risk of violence will be increased by asking a patient about violent or homicidal ideas.[9] Of particular importance is whether the person has active thoughts of violence directed at a specific person or other target. The following paragraphs describe additional key risk factors that have the most empirical support.

Demographic and Historical Factors

The single best predictor of the risk of future violence is a history of violent behavior.[10] For people with a history of violence, the age at the time of the first violent act is also significant. Persons who commit violent acts starting at a young age, particularly before adolescence, are more likely to engage in future violent behavior than are those who start at an older age. Witnessing or experiencing abuse as a juvenile is another significant risk factor.[11]

Male sex is associated with an increased risk of violence in the general population. Men commit more violent crimes per capita than do women. In 2011, women accounted for approximately one-fifth of persons arrested for violent crimes.[12] Among persons with mental disorders, however, men and women have similar base rates of violent behavior. Robbins and colleagues[13] reported that the prevalence of violence in the year after discharge from a psychiatric hospital was similar for male and female patients who had committed violent acts (approximately 25% for women and 30% for men). Violent acts committed by women, as compared with those committed by men, were more likely to occur in the home, more likely to be directed at family members, and less likely to result in criminal arrest. In addition, female perpetrators of violence were less likely to cause serious injury to their victims.

Although women are often considered to be less violent than men, it is important for clinicians to recognize that women with mental illness are at greater risk for violence than the general population of women. Mental health and other clinicians must be careful not to underestimate the risk of violence on the part of women.[14]

Another risk factor for violence is young age, regardless of whether there is a history of violence. Persons with the greatest likelihood of violent behavior are those in their late teens to early 20s.[15]

Vignette 1: History of Violence

Mr. K. is a 50-year-old man who comes to see you for his first appointment. During the assessment, you learn that he has a criminal record. What do you want to know about Mr. K.'s history of violence and criminal behavior?

A history of violence is the factor that is most predictive of future violence. In light of that fact, it is important for clinicians to explore the details when the person being evaluated has a history of violence. The circumstances surrounding the violent act, including when it occurred, the type of violence, the persons involved, the presence of a weapon, and the severity of any injuries are all useful inquiries to aid the risk assessment. This information should be sought first from the person being evaluated, although in some situations collateral sources may need to be consulted and may provide information that differs from the patient's account. As discussed in chapter 9, the clinician must be mindful of both the duty to maintain patient confidentiality and the exceptions to that duty. It is also important to be aware that states place restrictions on access to official databases containing records of arrests and convictions.

Mental Illness

It is a common public perception that mental illness increases the risk of violence. This belief is bolstered by media portrayals of persons with mental illness as violent and attention to high-profile criminal cases in which mental illness is asserted as a defense or is believed to have played a role. In view of the widespread misperception about the link between mental illness and violence, it is important for mental health providers to be familiar with the empirical evidence on the relationship between mental illness and violence, as well as the risk associated with particular psychiatric conditions. Studies of violence commonly focus on persons with severe mental illness, such as schizophrenia, major depressive disorder, or bipolar disorder.

Contrary to the public perception, there is no clear link between mental illness and acts of violence that receive attention in the media, such as school shootings.[16] There is evidence that untreated, active symptoms of severe mental illness are associated with an increased risk of violence, but that risk is largely mediated by substance use.[17,18] What is clear is that people with severe mental illness are more likely to be victims of violence than perpetrators of violence.[19,20] They are more than twice as likely to be attacked, sexually assaulted, or mugged as persons in the general population who do not have mental disorders.[21]

In 1990, Swanson and colleagues published the first large-scale epidemiologic study on the relationship between mental illness and violence.[15] The authors surveyed community samples by asking about the occurrence of minor violence (e.g., hitting someone with a fist) and serious violence (e.g., using a weapon) to harm or threaten another person. They found a modest positive association between violence and mental illness. Swanson et al. found that the combination of substance use and serious mental illness had the strongest association with violence. Despite the modest overall association between mental illness and violence, the proportion of violent acts attributable to serious mental illness alone (population attributable risk) in 1 year was approximately 4%.

Since 1990, additional epidemiologic studies have informed our understanding of the relationship between mental illness and violence. One of these investigations, the MacArthur Violence Risk Assessment Study, found that the rates of violence among persons discharged from a psychiatric hospital were similar to the rates in a matched control group from the same neighborhoods.[22] However, substance use was positively associated with increased violence; comorbid substance abuse was found to be responsible for much of the violence in this population of patients discharged from psychiatric hospitals. A more recent study by Van Dorn and colleagues[23] confirmed these findings. In a 1-year period, the rates of violence were 0.8% among persons with no mental illness or substance abuse, 2.9% among those with serious mental illness, and 9.4% among those with both substance use disorders and serious mental illness.

A closer look at the empirical studies reveals some additional important findings. First, most persons with mental illness are not violent. Second, roughly 3% to 5% of violent incidents involving third parties are attributable to mental illness other than substance abuse.[15,24] Violence risk among persons with mental illness is commonly mediated by other risk factors that are stronger predictors. Elbogen and Johnson[25] concluded, "Severe mental illness alone does not significantly predict future violence; rather, historical, dispositional, and contextual factors are associated with future violence." Their study revealed that those factors included serious mental illness, concurrent substance abuse or a history of substance abuse, and a history of conduct disorder or antisocial personality disorder.

Third, the research suggests that a subset of mental health conditions, rather than the presence of serious mental illness per se, is associated with future dangerousness.[24] This subset includes disorders that are characterized by active symptoms of psychosis, particularly a first episode of psychosis.[26,27] Several theories have been advanced for the association between psychosis and violence. For instance, psychotic persons who believe that they are being threatened or persecuted may preemptively engage in violence as a means of self-defense. Persons experiencing command auditory hallucinations may be directly instructed to commit violent acts.[26] In addition, psychotic disorders are associated with impaired judgment and decision making, which may contribute to the risk of violent behavior when a person is under stress or experiencing conflict with others.

Additional mental health–related factors that are associated with future violence include involuntary commitment to a psychiatric hospital[28] and lower intellectual functioning.[29] Traumatic brain injury is also associated with aggression.[30] Despite variation in the severity of brain injuries and symptoms after injury, aggression is a common and challenging sequela. Symptoms may include verbal outbursts and physical violence toward property or persons.

Conduct disorder and antisocial personality disorder are the most common disorders associated with violent behavior. Recent studies have concluded that among persons with schizophrenia, concurrent conduct disorder or antisocial personality disorder is associated with violence.[25,31]

Certain personality traits increase the risk of future violence, even when full criteria for a personality disorder are not met. These include entitlement, impulsivity, and low tolerance of frustration. Persons with a sense of entitlement, or narcissistic traits, may make threats or commit acts of violence in order to get what they want because they feel entitled to do so. Impulsive people and those with low frustration tolerance may be unable to control feelings of distress or anger, resulting in violent behavior. Personality traits that constitute individual risk factors for violence in the workplace include a tendency to feel that one is being treated unfairly, trait anger (i.e., anger as a personality trait vs. anger as a transient emotional state), hostility, reactivity to stress, and externalization of blame.[7]

Substance Abuse

Substance abuse, including alcohol, marijuana, and other illicit-drug use, is correlated with violent behavior among persons with mental illness and those without mental illness. In addition to a history of violent behavior, a substance use disorder is one of the strongest risk factors for violence. The study by Swanson and colleagues[15] mentioned above showed that substance use disorders constituted the most prevalent diagnostic category among persons who were violent in their community sample. Persons with substance use disorders had roughly a 14-fold increase in threatening or assaultive behavior as compared with persons who did not have a substance use disorder.

Alcohol is the substance most commonly cited as being associated with aggression and violent behavior. A recent study, for example, showed dose-dependent effects of alcohol on criminal behavior and violence.[32] As with other mental disorders, however, the association between alcohol consumption (or use of other substances) and acts of violence is complex because there are often confounding variables. For example, alcohol consumption on the part of the victim as well as the offender can increase the risk of injury.

Social and Environmental Factors

Low socioeconomic status is positively correlated with the risk of violence, as is a history of exposure to violence in one's environment, which is related to low socioeconomic status. A study of persons with severe mental illness showed that a triad of substance use, history of victimization, and past exposure to violence in the environment was strongly correlated with serious violence during a 1-year period; however, there was almost no serious violence in the absence of those three factors.[33]

Stressful life events are also associated with an increased risk of violence. Of course, numerous life events can be stressful to individual persons. Some commonly identified stressors include financial strain, unemployment, difficulties in romantic relationships, other interpersonal conflict, and health concerns.

Access to potential victims and access to weapons (firearms or knives) are additional risk factors for violence. With respect to both self-directed violence and violence against others, easy access to weapons increases the odds that those weapons will be used when one is violent.

Vignette 2: Access to a Firearm

The police bring Ms. S. to the emergency room after responding to a call from her husband that he is worried about her. Ms. S. has schizophrenia. She also has a history of methamphetamine and hallucinogen use, but she successfully completed treatment for substance use years ago. Ms. S.'s husband is now wondering whether "she is on something." He reports that his wife has been acting increasingly suspicious in the past week. She accused him of poisoning her, and she has been irritable. In the past, she has heard voices instructing her not to trust him. He called the police after finding a loaded gun under their bed. The couple has never previously owned a firearm. He has never seen her act this way. At the emergency room, Ms. S. is agitated and paranoid. She responds minimally to the psychiatrist's questions. She tells the psychiatrist, however, that her husband has been plotting to harm her and that she has had to take measures for her protection. She says she knows that he has been poisoning her because "he wants to marry someone else." She acknowledges that she got the firearm from a friend a couple of days ago.

The psychiatrist has reason to be concerned that Ms. S. is at risk for violence against her husband. Although most persons with schizophrenia are not violent toward anyone, the psychiatrist in this case has identified some key risk factors associated with an increased risk of violence. Two facts are of particular concern: Ms. S. has a paranoid delusion, and she has recently obtained a firearm. Persons with psychotic beliefs are at increased risk for engaging in violence against a person they misperceive as a persecutor. Substance abuse is also strongly associated with dangerousness, and Ms. S. has a history of substance abuse, although it is not yet clear whether she has recently used methamphetamine or other substances. If so, this could further disinhibit her and contribute to her paranoia and aggression. It is unclear whether she has been taking her antipsychotic medication.

APPROACH TO VIOLENCE RISK ASSESSMENT

In typical evaluations for treatment purposes, clinicians appropriately tend to rely heavily on the clinical interview and direct observations of the patient. This is especially true of psychotherapy, in which the therapist is attempting to understand the patient's view of the world and his or her relationships. Evaluations of dangerousness are conducted by integrating information from a variety of sources: the person being evaluated, collateral sources, the mental status examination, relevant aspects of the physical examination, and appropriate testing. The weight afforded these sources of information is likely to depend on the context of the assessment.

Violence risk assessments, even when performed by treating clinicians, require an approach similar to that used in forensic settings, in which evaluators are more likely to rely on collateral information, such as criminal and court records, and reports from others, than on the patient's report. Clinicians should know the goals and circumstances of the assessment when evaluating dangerousness. What behavior prompted the assessment? How is it going to be used? When assessing a patient in the emergency room, for example, the mental health clinician should consider, in addition to the patient's potential for future violence, the appropriate disposition and treatment to reduce risk. In the forensic context, mental health professionals should ascertain the exact question at issue and the context in which it is being posed. For example, consultations involving stalking, potential threats of violence, continuation of civil commitment, and sexual dangerousness each require a somewhat different focus and expertise on the part of the evaluator.

Depending on the purpose of the evaluation, mental health professionals will need to familiarize themselves with relevant legal standards. This is true even in the clinical setting; clinicians should be familiar with local criteria for civil commitment and circumstances mandating a breach of patient confidentiality to warn or protect third parties, as discussed in chapters 2 and 9.

It is useful for the evaluator to consider factors used to quantify risk. These include the likelihood (probability) of harm, imminence of harm, and severity (magnitude) of the outcome.[34] In addition, the type of harm and identification of potential victims are important in assessing violence risk and in determining whether the clinician has a duty to warn or protect the likely victim.

METHODS OF ASSESSING RISK

There are three broad approaches to assessing the risk of violence: professional (clinical) judgment, use of actuarial data, and structured professional judgment. All three approaches make use of knowledge about risk factors. The professional judgment approach is commonly used in treatment settings, with clinicians exercising discretion in how they obtain information and using their professional judgment in weighing the information obtained and drawing conclusions about the risk of danger. Different clinicians can come to substantially different conclusions. A key criticism of this approach is that it lacks reproducibility.[35]

The actuarial approach calls for mental health professionals to elicit information about a set of predetermined variables associated with violence risk. This approach makes use of actuarial assessment tools, many of which have specific rules for weighting and scoring violence risk. The Violence Risk Appraisal Guide, a 12-item tool, is probably the most commonly used actuarial instrument.[36,37] Another commonly used tool is the Classification of Violence Risk (COVR), which was developed as part of the MacArthur Violence Risk Assessment Study to provide an estimation of violence risk among people with mental disorders.[38] These and other actuarial assessment tools are intended for specific populations. Before using these instruments, it is important to be familiar with them and to determine their applicability to the person being evaluated.

Assessments based on actuarial data limit the role of clinical judgment. On the one hand, they are more reliable than assessments based on professional judgment because different providers obtain the same information, which is then assessed within a standardized analytic framework that has been validated. On the other hand, this method excludes consideration of risk and protective factors that are specific to the person being evaluated but are not part of the actuarial tool,[35] and it does not allow for consideration of events that may increase or decrease the level of risk. For this reason, some mental health professionals use an adjusted actuarial approach known as structured professional judgment. This allows them to exercise discretion in using additional information and to adjust their assessments accordingly.

The structured professional judgment approach combines unstructured professional judgment with the use of a structured assessment tool. Research indicates that structured professional judgment is more accurate and reliable than professional judgment alone. With this approach, the clinician's interview is guided by a list of items associated with violence risk. Professional judgment is then used to make the final determination about dangerousness.

The most extensively studied tool used in structured professional judgment is the Historic, Clinical, Risk Management–20 (HCR-20), a 20-item tool that makes use of static and dynamic risk factors. The HCR-20 contains elements of both the clinical and actuarial approaches and provides an assessment of risk factors for interpersonal violence, the relevance of those risk factors to the risk of violence, and possible risk-management strategies.[39] It has been shown that use of the HCR-20 increases the accuracy of violence risk assessments made by psychiatric residents to a level comparable to that of assessments made by psychiatric attending physicians with more experience and training.[40]

Clinicians incorporate their knowledge of all the risk factors in their final assessment. Although it is easy to assume that a higher number of risk factors is correlated with increased dangerousness, a simple quantitative approach should be used with caution. As discussed with respect to actuarial tools, for any one person, there may be important risk factors that are not addressed by the assessment tool. Furthermore, all risk factors are not equal. The clinician should use reasonable judgment to determine which factors are most important for any specific examinee.

MANAGEMENT OF VIOLENCE RISK

In performing violence risk assessments in the clinical setting, clinicians also simultaneously consider risk-management options, such as disposition and treatment. Prudent clinicians match the level of violence risk with the level of management intervention. Risk-management interventions focus on reducing modifiable risk factors.

Involuntary Hospitalization

For patients with a high risk of imminent violence, the prudent mental health clinician will consider hospitalization after the initial evaluation. Although the criteria for involuntary civil commitment differ by jurisdiction, as discussed in chapter 2, the primary basis for civil commitment is that the patient is both mentally ill and dangerous to self or others. Many states have additional bases for commitment, such as grave disability (inability to care for oneself), but the focus here is on dangerousness. The constitutional protection of due process requires that courts oversee the involuntary commitment process and allow the patient an opportunity to be heard. The petitioner (the clinician seeking commitment) has the burden of sufficiently convincing the court that the respondent (the patient) has a mental illness and, because of that mental illness, is dangerous to self or others. Mental illness alone is an insufficient basis for involuntarily confining someone in a psychiatric hospital.[41]

Voluntary psychiatric hospitalization is an option for acutely ill patients who are competent to consent to hospitalization. In *Zinermon v. Burch*,[42] the U.S. Supreme Court ruled that patients with mental illness must be competent to consent to voluntary psychiatric hospitalization. The Court held that allowing Mr. Burch to sign himself into a psychiatric hospital when he did not have the capacity to make that decision constituted a deprivation of his due process rights. This case is discussed in more detail in chapter 2.

States may differ as to what constitutes a mental disorder for the purposes of civil commitment, and the legal definition may differ from the definition in the *Diagnostic and Statistical Manual of Mental Disorders*. Many states provide a statutory definition of mental disorder, but some do not.[43] For example, some states specify that the mental illness must be "serious," some consider developmental disabilities or neurocognitive conditions separately from mental disorders, some exclude certain personality disorders, and some distinguish between substance use disorders and mental disorders. The court ultimately determines what conditions meet the legal standard. Some persons who are assessed as being dangerous may not meet the criteria for involuntary commitment on the basis of their mental health condition. More detailed information about these criteria can be found in chapter 2.

For the purpose of involuntary commitment, establishing the likelihood of dangerousness according to the requisite jurisdictional criteria can also be challenging. Most states require a likelihood of imminent dangerousness. Some jurisdictions require recent violent behavior or explicit threats to harm someone.[44] Even with several risk factors, including easy access to weapons and escalating agitation, the criteria for involuntary hospitalization may not be met, depending on the jurisdiction. It is important for clinicians to have an understanding of local legal standards for civil commitment.

Other Interventions

Management interventions are aimed at affecting modifiable risk factors. For persons with psychiatric symptoms who pose a risk of violence, monitoring the status of symptoms is an appropriate measure for ongoing assessment of violence risk. In addition to monitoring performed by the clinician, it can be helpful for the patient and family members to monitor symptoms and make note of any circumstances associated with worsening symptoms. Take, for example, a patient with schizophrenia. If the patient's past acts of violence have been associated with worsening psychotic symptoms, interventions are aimed at monitoring psychosis and compliance with antipsychotic medications. Such a patient may be a good candidate for a long-acting, injectable antipsychotic medication if medication compliance is an issue.

Similarly, if a patient becomes aggressive when consuming alcohol, interventions should be aimed at reducing alcohol use. For example, treatment approaches may include medications designed to reduce cravings or otherwise minimize the likelihood of alcohol consumption, measures to reduce access to alcohol, regular urine toxicology screening to monitor alcohol intake and encourage accountability, and support services, such as Alcoholics Anonymous. Psychotherapeutic modalities, such as therapy aimed at tolerance of stress, are appropriate for some patients. If marital conflict is an issue, couples counseling may be helpful.

Clinicians should pay careful attention to a patient's access to or movement of weapons. Knowing the patient's military and work history is helpful, since people trained in the use of firearms or other weapons are more likely to feel comfortable owning and handling them. If the patient suddenly purchases a weapon or already has one and moves it from one location to another (e.g., from a locked closet to the drawer of a bedside table), this should be explored in detail. For patients at elevated risk, one should consider attempting to remove the weapon from the patient's possession, perhaps by relocating it with a relative or friend. It is useful to educate patients about firearm safety, such as removing and keeping ammunition separate from the firearm and using a gun lock, gun safe, or other safety devices.

AN EXAMPLE OF VIOLENCE RISK ASSESSMENT

The following case is an example of the complicated clinical issues and management challenges encountered in the course of violence risk assessment.

Vignette 3: Risk of Violence

Mr. G. is a 30-year-old man with schizophrenia. He receives treatment at a community mental health center, where he has regular appointments with a psychiatrist, and is also involved in a symptom-management group. He has appointments at the mental health center on a weekly basis. Mr. G. presents for a scheduled outpatient appointment with his psychiatrist and reports that he is very upset with his neighbor. He lives in an apartment with his mother. He states that for the past several days, his neighbor has been making a lot of loud banging sounds from his apartment. Mr. G. complains that he cannot concentrate or watch television because of the disruption and that it interferes with his sleep. He claims that the neighbor's noise is intentional and that he'd "like to do something to shut him up," referring to the neighbor. The psychiatrist is concerned about Mr. G.'s risk of violence toward the neighbor.

What should the psychiatrist do? The first step is to assess Mr. G.'s risk factors for violence. One approach would be to use structured professional judgment. Assessment tools such as the HCR-20, discussed above, that can be used in this context as a memory aid, prompting the psychiatrist to inquire about key risk factors during the assessment. In the HCR-20, risk factors are coded as absent, possibly present, or actively present. The HCR-20 may be scored, but scores are not classified into categories of risk; instead, the psychiatrist will use the tool as one source of information in rendering a clinical judgment.

Vignette 3, Continued

Mr. G. tells his psychiatrist that he always takes his antipsychotic medication. However, the psychiatrist knows that Mr. G. has a history of inconsistent compliance with his medication. Without it, he develops paranoid beliefs that others "want to mess" with him. In the past, he delusionally believed that his neighbor was stealing his rent checks so that he would be evicted. When off his medication previously, Mr. G. stopped attending his mental health appointments.

When asked, Mr. G. acknowledges that he has never liked his neighbor. He denies any specific plans of harming his neighbor currently. He has had verbal conflicts with the neighbor in the past, prompting the apartment manager to call the police on more than one occasion. Mr. G. has never had any criminal charges against him. Although he was in some fights as a juvenile, he reports no recent physical altercations, no history of serious violence, and no history of using a weapon during a violent act.

With Mr. G.'s consent, the psychiatrist calls his mother for collateral information. She confirms that their neighbor has been making a lot of noise lately and explains that he is remodeling his apartment. She states that there have been no conflicts between her son and the neighbor in the previous year and confirms that her son has been taking his psychiatric medication as prescribed. Although frustrated with the noise, she says, he has been coping with it by using earplugs when in the apartment; he has also been spending more time outside the apartment, engaged in activities that he enjoys. The psychiatrist learns that Mr. G. has a meeting planned with the neighbor and the apartment manager to establish some quiet times until the project is complete.

Given what the psychiatrist knows about Mr. G. and the collateral information from his mother, the psychiatrist concludes that Mr. G.'s risk of violence remains relatively low. Although he has some risk factors for violence, he has been taking his medications, and he denies any plans to harm the neighbor, has been using strategies to cope with the stressor (e.g., earplugs), and has a plan to address his concerns in a nonviolent manner by talking with the neighbor and the apartment manager. In this scenario, it is probably reasonable to continue his regular outpatient mental health management and reinforce use of his coping skills. Mr. G. will return to the clinic for his group meetings and other appointments, with ongoing assessment and consideration of any need for changes in his treatment program.

Consider a different scenario: Mr. G.'s mother reveals that her son has not been taking his medication as prescribed because he thinks that his neighbor may have poisoned it. Mr. G. has told his mother that their neighbor is intentionally making noise in order to drive him out of the apartment complex. She has seen her son pace around the apartment, and he has seemed more irritable lately. His sleep pattern has been disturbed.

Mr. G.'s risk of violence is higher in this second scenario. He has not been taking his medication, has exhibited paranoia, and has a history of escalating verbal confrontation in the setting of paranoid beliefs. Yet his mother remains a source of social support, and he has been keeping his appointments. Although continued outpatient management may remain a reasonable management strategy, efforts to improve medication adherence should be considered. This patient may be an appropriate candidate for longer-acting, injectable antipsychotic medication, as an alternative to oral medication that must be taken daily. Another strategy might be to minimize opportunities for interaction with the neighbor until Mr. G.'s paranoia subsides. Treatment planning could include, for example, arranging for Mr. G. to participate in a day hospital program or to receive additional support at the mental health center. In many jurisdictions, he would probably not meet the criteria for involuntary hospitalization on the basis of legal interpretations of the dangerousness criterion for commitment. Mr. G. has not had any recent altercations with the neighbor and denies current plans to harm him or anyone else. Voluntary hospitalization for his worsening symptoms might be an option in some jurisdictions.

COMMON ERRORS IN ASSESSING VIOLENCE RISK

Mental health professionals vary in their level of training for violence risk assessment as well as in their level of comfort in making such assessments. Identified here are several common errors that clinicians make in evaluating patients for the risk of violence.

Assessment Based Only on an Inquiry about Thoughts of Harming Others

In various clinical settings, potentially dangerous patients are often asked only whether they have thoughts of harming others. If the patient says "No," the assessment may end there. Although it is important to ask patients specifically about such thoughts or plans, this question should not be the sole inquiry in a violence risk assessment.

A prudent clinician will take into account the context of the evaluation. Has the patient been brought in by the police? Does the patient display signs of agitation on mental status examination? Like the assessment of suicide risk (which also requires more than just asking the patient about current suicidal thoughts), an assessment of the risk of violence must take into consideration the basis for the evaluation and risk factors (discussed above) that are relevant to the patient and the situation.

Underestimation of Violence Risk for Women

Mental health clinicians tend to underestimate the risk of violent behavior on the part of women. As stated above, it is true that rates of violence are lower for women than for men in general community samples. This is not true, however, for persons with mental illness. In this population, women's rates of committing violent acts are similar to the rates for men.

Overreliance on Diagnosis

It is critical for mental health clinicians to recognize that no single diagnosis indicates that a patient is currently dangerous. A common error is for clinicians to conclude that a patient is at high risk for future violence because of a previous diagnosis of antisocial personality disorder, for example. A psychiatric diagnosis alone is not a good predictor of future violence; studies have shown that it is the presence of active symptoms, rather than the presence of a diagnosis, that is associated with an elevated risk.[25] As discussed in the section on risk factors for violence, certain symptoms or conditions are associated with an increased risk of violence, but it is the combination of risk factors that supports an assessment of dangerousness.

One-Time Assessment

Clinicians should not think of violence risk assessment as a one-time evaluation but rather as an evaluation that is ongoing, with monitoring required for any changes in the patient's risk factors and circumstances. A person's risk of violence is dynamic—many risk factors can change over time, and new risk factors may emerge. Most people who are considered to be at high risk for violence at a certain point in time do not remain at elevated risk over time. Prudent clinicians perform and document violence risk assessments at critical junctures in patient care, such as at the time of hospital admission and again at discharge. This is true, too, in outpatient settings, where mental health clinicians work with patients over time. Thinking of risk assessment as an ongoing process, rather than a one-time event, is a helpful approach.

Reliance on the Presence or Absence of a Specific Threat

In determining whether an individual patient poses a risk of violence, clinicians often focus on whether the patient has made an actual, specific threat. While specific threats must be taken seriously, as we know from the study of targeted violence in the field of law enforcement, the analysis should focus on whether the person poses a threat of violence, not on whether he or she has made a specific threat.[45] Although some persons who commit acts of physical violence against others make threats beforehand, many do not.

LIABILITY

In assessing the risk of violence, mental health clinicians have legal responsibilities to protect the public as well as clinical responsibilities to provide appropriate treatment for their patients. If a patient injures or kills another person, the mental health clinician may face claims of malpractice or other liability. When it comes to violence, claims of malpractice tend to focus on the clinician's failure to adequately perform one or more of the following tasks: assessment of the risk of violence, identification of the potential targets of the patient's violence, and establishment of a risk-management plan in accordance with the level of violence risk.

A patient who has engaged in violent behavior may sue his or her mental health clinician, alleging that the clinician did not meet the standard of care in assessing and treating the patient. The patient is seeking damages from the clinician for any harm (financial or otherwise) that the patient has incurred. As with other areas of potential malpractice liability, the law does not require that mental health providers be perfect in their assessment and treatment. A bad outcome, such as a patient harming another person, does not necessarily mean that the clinician's performance fell below the standard of care. Rather, as discussed in chapter 8, the law dictates that mental health clinicians must provide the level of care that would be provided by a reasonably prudent clinician in similar circumstances.

Whenever a mental health clinician assesses a patient's risk of violence, it is critical to document that assessment, including the process of weighing risk factors and making decisions about management. Having a record of risk factors and the rationale for management considerations helps the clinician monitor the patient's level of risk over time. Such documentation is also useful in communicating risk factors to other clinicians who may come into contact with the patient. If there is a liability claim, documentation is vital in demonstrating to the court the clinician's reasonable assessment and use of professional judgment in making management decisions.

Third parties may also sue psychiatrists or other mental health providers when patients injure someone. Victims of violence or their representatives (in the event of the victim's death) may file civil legal suits against clinicians. As noted in the introduction to this chapter, the landmark *Tarasoff* case[1] created a legal duty for psychotherapists in California to take measures in some circumstances to protect third parties from potentially violent patients: "When a therapist determines, or pursuant to the standards of his profession should determine, that his patient presents a serious danger of violence to another, he incurs an obligation to use reasonable care to protect the intended victim against such danger." *Tarasoff* is discussed in more detail in chapter 9, on confidentiality.

In the decades since the *Tarasoff* decision, nearly all states have defined psychotherapists' responsibilities toward third persons. However, there is marked variation in the *Tarasoff*-type requirements from one jurisdiction to another. Some jurisdictions mandate that clinicians protect third parties; other jurisdictions permit clinicians to breach confidentiality in order to protect third parties but do not mandate that clinicians do so. Common means for clinicians to discharge their duty to protect third parties include warning the intended victim, notifying the police, changing medication or increasing visit frequency, and seeking hospitalization for the patient.

One of the more common examples of liability to third parties involves claims of negligent or premature discharge from a psychiatric hospital. The widely cited case of *Naidu v. Laird*[46] is illustrative. In this case, Ms. Laird brought suit against Dr. Naidu, alleging that the psychiatrist was negligent in releasing a patient from the psychiatric hospital. The patient had a history of noncompliance with his medications. During his hospitalization, he refused medication at times, became uncooperative, and asked to leave against medical advice. More than 5 months after his discharge from the hospital, while the patient was off his psychiatric medication and in a psychotic state, he killed Ms. Laird's husband in a motor vehicle accident. A jury awarded a verdict against Dr. Naidu. On appeal, the court upheld the verdict. This case is informative because it raises the concept of foreseeability. Although the case has been cited as an extreme example of holding a clinician accountable for his patient's acts for a long period after hospital discharge, the court held that the foreseeability of harm due to the patient's potential violence, rather than the passage of a certain amount of time, is an issue for the trier of fact (the jury, in this case) to consider. Here, it was not unforeseeable that the patient would stop taking his medication and become dangerous to others.

Although the focus of the *Naidu* case was foreseeability, the case also underscores the importance of adequate assessment and documentation of the risk of violence before the decision is made to discharge the patient from the hospital. There was evidence that Dr. Naidu did not properly review the patient's records and history before releasing him. Prudent clinicians should recognize that, depending on the context, the standard of care for assessment of violence risk may require one or more clinical interviews with the patient, a review of medical records, consideration of information from collateral sources, and collaboration with other members of the treatment team.

Mental health clinicians should be familiar with their local laws. Failure to adhere to local requirements may make a clinician liable for the harm that a patient inflicts on a third party.

CONCLUSION

The assessment of violence risk has become a core responsibility for mental health clinicians. Practicing clinicians should familiarize themselves with risk factors for violence. Although research has increased our understanding of the factors associated with violence, assessment of the risk of violence is not an exact science. The clinician is tasked with making estimates of the likelihood of future violence that are based on reasonable assessments of violence risk. It is important to recognize that an individual patient's level of risk is dynamic, changing over time as risk factors change or new ones emerge. As new information becomes available to clinicians, they should incorporate that information into their risk assessments and management plans. The management plans should be matched to the level of risk posed by the patient. Failure to reasonably assess violence risk and execute proper plans for managing it can lead to liability on the clinician's part.

FREQUENTLY ASKED QUESTIONS

If my patient assaults another person, can I be held liable?

That depends on the law regarding duty to third parties (the Tarasoff duty) in the jurisdiction where you work. In most jurisdictions, there can be liability if the clinician knows or should have known that the patient poses a risk of serious harm to an identifiable person.

People I meet equate mental illness with violence. What can I say to them?

People with serious mental illness are responsible for a small percentage of violent crimes. Serious mental illness is associated with a small, but statistically significant, increased risk of violence. However, most of that risk is accounted for by coexisting conditions (e.g., substance abuse or a diagnosis of conduct disorder or antisocial personality disorder) and a history of violence or exposure to violence.

Is ownership of a firearm a primary risk factor for violence?

Firearm ownership, in and of itself, is not a risk factor for violence. However, if the person in question is otherwise at high risk for harm to self or others, easy access to a firearm constitutes a major risk factor for violence.

Is there an easy way to remember the risk factors for violence?

There are numerous risk factors—too many to fit into an easy mnemonic. It is helpful to consider that violence is the result of the interaction of three categories of risk factors (individual, environmental, and situational) and then to learn the factors within each category.

My patient becomes very angry with his parents when his psychosis is exacerbated. He has never threatened to harm them or others, however, so I have not worried about him hurting anyone. Is that reasonable?

You should respond if a patient makes threats, but you also need to consider whether he or she poses a threat even in the absence of any threatening statements.

REFERENCES

1. *Tarasoff v. Regents of the University of California,* 17 Cal. App. 3rd 425(California Supreme Court 1976).
2. Siegel A, Victoroff J. Understanding human aggression: insights from neuroscience. *International Journal of Law and Psychiatry.* 2009;32:209–215.

3. *Barefoot v. Estelle,* 463 U.S. 880 (1983).

4. Norko MA, Baranoski MV. The state of contemporary risk assessment research. *Canadian Journal of Psychiatry-Revue Canadienne De Psychiatrie.* 2005;50(1):18–26.

5. Fein RA, Vossekuil B, Holden GA. *Threat Assessment: An Approach to Prevent Targeted Violence.* Washington, DC: U.S. Department of Justice, National Institute of Justice; Sept, Report No. NCJ 155000; 1995.

6. Schouten R. Workplace violence: an overview for practicing clinicians. *Psychiatric Annals.* 2006;36(11):790–797.

7. Schouten R. Workplace violence and the clinician. In: Simon RI, Tardiff K, eds. *Textbook of Violence Assessment and Management.* Washington, DC: American Psychiatric Press; 2008:501–520.

8. Douglas KS SJ. Violence risk assessment—getting specific about being dynamic. *Psychology Public Policy and Law.* 2005;11(3):347–383.

9. American Psychiatric Association. Guideline IV: Assessment of risk for aggressive behaviors. In: *American Psychiatric Association's Practice Guidelines for the Psychiatric Evaluation of Adults,* 3rd edition. Washington, DC: American Psychiatric Press; 2015. http://psychiatryonline.org/doi/10.1176/appi.books.9780890426760.pe02.

10. Klassen D, O'Connor WA. A prospective study of precipitants of violence in adult male mental health admission. *Law and Human Behavior.* 1988;12:143–158.

11. Klassen D, O'Connor W. Demographic and case history variables in risk assessment. In: Monahan J, Steadman HJ, eds. *Violence and Mental Disorder: Developments in Risk Assessment.* Chicago: University of Chicago Press; 1994:229–258.

12. Federal Bureau of Investigation. *FBI Uniform Crime Report: Crime in the United States, 2011.* Washington, DC: United States Department of Justice, Federal Bureau of Investigation, Criminal Justice Information Services Division; 2011.

13. Robbins PC, Monahan J, Silver E. Mental disorder, violence, and gender. *Law and Human Behavior.* 2003;27(6):561–571.

14. Taylor PJ, Bragado-Jimenez MD. Women, psychosis and violence. *International Journal of Law and Psychiatry.* 2009;32:58–64.

15. Swanson JW, Holzer CEI, Ganju VK, Jono RT. Violence and psychiatric disorders in the community: evidence from the Epidemiologic Catchment Area Surveys. *Hospital and Community Psychiatry.* 1990;41(7):761–770.

16. Barry CL, McGinty EE, Vernick JS, Webster DW. After Newtown—public opinion on gun policy and mental illness. *New England Journal of Medicine.* 2013;368(12):1077–1081.

17. Hodgins S. Violent behaviour among people with schizophrenia: a framework for investigations of causes, and effective treatment, and prevention. *Philosophical Transactions of the Royal Society B: Biological Sciences.* 2008;363:2505–2518.

18. Fazel S, Gulati G, Linsell L, Geddes JR, Grann M. Schizophrenia and violence: systematic review and meta-analysis. *Plos Medicine.* 2009;6(8):e1000120.

19. Appleby L, Mortensen PB, Dunn G, Hiroeh U. Death by homicide, suicide, and other unnatural causes in people with mental illness: a population-based study. *Lancet.* 2001;358:2010–2012.

20. Teasdale B. Mental disorder and violent victimization. *Criminal Justice and Behavior.* 2009;36:513–535.

21. Hiday VA, Swartz MS, Swanson JW, Borum R, Wagner HR. Criminal victimization of persons with severe mental illness. *Psychiatric Services.* 1999;50:62–68.

22. Steadman HJ, Mulvey EP, Monahan J, et al. Violence by people discharged from acute psychiatric inpatient facilities and by others in the same neighborhoods. *Archives of General Psychiatry.* 1998;55(5):393–401.

23. Van Dorn R, Volavka J, Johnson N. Mental disorder and violence: is there a relationship beyond substance use? *Social Psychiatry and Psychiatric Epidemiology.* 2012;47(3):487–503.

24. Swanson JW, McGinty EE, Fazel S, Mays VM. Mental illness and reduction of gun violence and suicide: bringing epidemiologic research to policy. *Annals of Epidemiology.* 2015;24(5):366–376.

25. Elbogen EB, Johnson SC. The intricate link between violence and mental disorder. *Archives of General Psychiatry.* 2009;66(2):152–161.

26. Douglas KS, Guy LS, Hart DS. Psychosis is a risk factor for violence to others: a meta-analysis. *Psychological Bulletin.* 2009;135(5):679–706.

27. Large M, Mullin K. Risk assessment and screening for violence. *Eur Psychiatry.* 2011;26(2):132–132.

28. Choe JY, Teplin LA, Abram KM. Perpetration of violence, violent victimization, and serve mental illness: balancing public health concerns. *Psychiatric Services.* 2008;59(2):153–164.

29. Hodgins S. Mental disorder, intellectual deficiency, and crime: evidence from a birth cohort. *Archives of General Psychiatry.* 1992;49(6):476–483.

30. Rao V, Rosenberg P, Bertrand M, et al. Aggression after traumatic brain injury: prevalence and correlates. *Journal of Neuropsychiatry & Clinical Neuroscience.* 2009;21:420–429.

31. Hodgins S, Tihonen J, Ross O. The consequences of conduct disorder for males who develop schizophrenia: associations with criminality, aggressive behavior, substance use, and psychiatric services. *Schizophrenia Research.* 2005;78:323–335.

32. Popovici I, Homer JF, Fang H, French MT. Alcohol use and crime: findings from a longitudinal sample of U.S. adolescents and young adults. *Alcoholism: Clinical and Experimental Research.* 2012;36:532–543.

33. Swanson JW, Swartz MS, Essock SM, et al. The social-environmental context of violent behavior in persons treated for severe mental illness. *American Journal of Public Health.* 2002;92:1523–1531.

34. Dvoskin JA, Heilbrun K. Risk assessment and release decision-making: toward resolving the great debate. *Journal of the American Academy of Psychiatry and the Law.* 2001;29(1):6–10.

35. Otto RK. Assessing and managing violence risk in outpatient settings. *Journal of Clinical Psychology.* 2000;56:1239–1262.

36. Rice ME, Harris GT, Hilton NZ. The violence risk appraisal guide and sex offender risk appraisal guide for violence risk and the Ontario domestic assault risk assessment and domestic violence risk appraisal guide for wife assault risk assessment. In: Otto RK, Douglas KS, eds. *Handbook of Violence Risk Assessment.* New York: Routledge; 2010:99–119.

37. Harris GT, Rice ME, Quinsey VL. Violent recidivism of mentally disordered offenders: the development of a statistical prediction instrument. *Criminal Justice and Behavior.* 1993;20:315–335.

38. Monahan J. The classification of violence risk. In: Otto RK, Douglas KS, eds. *Handbook of Violence Risk Assessment.* New York: Routledge; 2010:187–198.

39. Douglas KS, Reeves KA. Historical-Clinical-Risk Management (HCR-20) violence risk assessment scheme. In: Otto RK, Douglas KS, eds. *Handbook of Violence Risk Assessment.* New York: Routledge; 2010:147–185.

40. Teo AR, Holley SR, Leary M, McNiel DE. The relationship between level of training and accuracy of violence risk assessment. *Psychiatric Services.* 2012;63(11):1089–1094.

41. *O'Connor v. Donaldson,* 422 U.S. 563(U.S. Supreme Court 1975).

42. *Zinermon v. Burch,* 494 U.S. 113(U.S. Supreme Court 1990).

43. Weinstock R, Piel J, Leong GB. DSM-5 and civil competencies. In: Scott C, ed. *DSM-5 and the Law: Changes and Challenges.* New York: Oxford University Press; 2015:152–176.

44. N.H. Rev. Stat. Ann(1998).

45. Fein RA, Vossekuil B. *Protective Intelligence and Threat Assessment Investigations: A Guide for State and Local Law Enforcement Officials.* Washington, DC: U.S. Dept. of Justice, Office of Justice Programs, National Institute of Justice; 2000.

46. *Naidu v. Laird,* 539 A.2d 1064(Supreme Court of Delaware 1988).

///4/// PRACTICE AND MALPRACTICE IN THE EVALUATION OF SUICIDAL PATIENTS

GARY JACOBSON

Suicide is final, the last word. One cannot answer back. Often, the drama of suicide is the intended message. "Now you know how I feel. Now you know what you have done to me." From talking with patients who survived serious suicide attempts, we know that some have the fantasy that they will be able to look down from heaven and see the torment of those they feel have wronged them. For others, the urge to die is a desire to end intolerable pain, either psychic or physical. It is the end of coping: "Stop the world, I want to get off." Still others attempt to end their lives during a psychotic episode or overdose on drugs when they meant only to obtund their pain or induce euphoria.

It is never easy to hear a patient threaten suicide, whether the threat is overt or implied. The natural empathy that most clinicians bring to their work is essential in dealing with a patient who is considering suicide, but it is strained by the urgent neediness of the acutely suicidal patient, worn down by the ongoing threat of loss with the chronically suicidal patient, and challenged by the rejection implicit in the patient's contemplation of self-induced death. When a clinician actually loses a patient by suicide, both the distress and the stress persist for a long time. Malpractice worries compound the matter. Records are reviewed and re-reviewed by risk managers. The clinician is questioned by others and engages in self-questioning about what could have been done differently. That is the mark of a conscientious clinician. Even in this difficult circumstance, it is reassuring to be able to conclude that with the facts that were available at the time, the clinician did all that he or she could have done.

Most mental health clinicians, at some time in their careers, are called on either to evaluate or to treat suicidal patients. Each year in the United States, over 500,000 people visit a hospital because of injuries due to a suicide attempt. Suicide is the 10th leading cause of death in the United States. About 35,000 to 40,000 people in the United States die from suicide each year, or about 12 persons per 100,000 population. Men are more likely than women to die by suicide, and the incidence is increased in the military and among the middle-aged and the elderly. Guns account for more deaths from suicide than drug overdoses. About 1,800 people commit suicide in hospitals each year. A suicide attempt in the hospital constitutes one of the Joint Commission's leading "sentinel events," which are unanticipated events leading to death or serious injury.[1–3]

Much of what we know about suicide risk is based on population studies. Although it is important to be familiar with these general risk factors, clinicians are called on to treat individual patients, not populations. In practice, therefore, we need to understand each patient's history and presenting symptoms, as well as the life issues—the contextual variables—that affect the patient.

Too often, a physician whose patient has attempted or completed suicide will claim that he or she was "only the med doctor," whose sole responsibility was to prescribe effectively and do "monthly med checks." In fact, the prescribing physician has entered into a doctor–patient relationship that is not limited to writing prescriptions and performing periodic medication checks. Even if the patient understands that this is the doctor's main function, the patient and the family have the right to assume that the physician will not abrogate his or her duties to take reasonable steps to protect the patient's life and safety. Similarly, the cognitive-behavioral therapist who has embarked on a 6-week course of treatment with a patient cannot defer the assessment of suicide risk to the prescribing physician. All treating clinicians must directly evaluate suicide risk in an ongoing fashion, work closely enough with the patient's other clinicians to properly evaluate the risk, or ideally, both.

A comprehensive evaluation of a patient for suicide risk is the contemporary standard of care. Failing to conduct such an evaluation of a patient who subsequently makes a suicide attempt may be seen as negligence because failing to look is foreseeably connected to failure to find.

The best way to avoid malpractice liability arising from suicide is to perform a comprehensive evaluation of suicide risk, to act responsibly on the basis of the results of that evaluation, and to document the risks and benefits of that action. Documenting a comprehensive evaluation not only provides essential clinical information but also serves as evidence that a thorough evaluation was indeed performed. This chapter describes how to perform a comprehensive assessment of suicide risk and, through case vignettes, what can happen when the assessment is not comprehensive or is not performed properly.

EVALUATION OF SUICIDE RISK

What constitutes a comprehensive evaluation? Many professional organizations have published guidelines for the assessment of suicide risk, including the American Psychiatric Association, the Joint Commission, the American Association of Suicidology, and several agencies of the federal government.[1-7] Expert witnesses in malpractice cases may use these guidelines to support their arguments.[8] Alternatively, testifying experts may go directly to the medical literature, which is the basis for the guidelines in the first place, or they may make the case that their own clinical observations reflect the views of a large enough number of experts to be considered a standard of care. While these three sources of support for standards of care in evaluating suicide risk—organizational guidelines, medical literature, and commonly agreed on clinical observation—may emphasize different aspects of suicide risk, they all include these key categories that must be addressed for a comprehensive evaluation: suicidal ideation, history of suicide attempts or family history of suicide, diagnoses and symptoms correlated with an increased risk of suicide, and stressors. A fifth category, protective factors, is included in many guidelines as well.

Suicidal Ideation

Failure to ask about suicidal ideation is rare because it is usually the first factor clinicians are taught to consider. An overdependence on this factor and the failure to inquire broadly enough are common errors in suicide risk assessment. Asking a patient, "Have you had thoughts about hurting or killing yourself?" and "Have you had such thoughts in the past month or so?" will capture more relevant information about risk than simply asking, "Do you have suicidal thoughts?" Frequent thoughts about suicide even if there is no plan, frequent thoughts about dying or being killed in the absence of serious medical illness or other potentially life-threatening circumstances and which the patient welcomes rather than fears, and an obsessive search for suicide methods on the Internet are all forms of suicidal ideation.

Asking about plans is routine, and in the context of suicidal thoughts, the purchase of a handgun, the accumulation of pills, or rehearsing a plan for suicide is especially worrisome. Rehearsing suicide, such as standing on the bridge with the idea of jumping, sitting in a car with the garage door closed and briefly turning on the engine, or visualizing the suicide act, is considered a prelude to an actual attempt and therefore constitutes a psychiatric emergency.[9] The absence of a plan on the part of a patient with suicidal ideation, however, is not reassuring, since many patients impulsively decide on a method as the opportunity presents itself or in response to a situational trigger. Such impulsive decisions are especially likely as the frequency, intrusiveness, and intensity of suicidal ideation increase.

Some health screens ask specific questions about suicidal ideation. The depression module of the Patient Health Questionnaire, a self-report scale included in the Mental Health Research Network's primary care electronic medical record, includes this question: "Over the last two weeks, how often have you been bothered by thoughts that you would be better off dead or of hurting yourself in some way?" Patients reporting frequent thoughts of death or self-harm were six times as likely to make a suicide attempt and five times as likely to die of suicide over the course of the next year as those not reporting such thoughts. This is a promising public health approach to screening for suicidal risk and an indication of the need to provide more intensive reviews of at-risk patients over a protracted period of time. However, the absence of such reports cannot be taken as an assurance of safety. In a study of over 1.2 million outpatients using the Patient Health Questionnaire, 39% of attempts at suicide and 36% of actual suicide deaths occurred in patients who answered "Not at all" to the question of whether they had thoughts of death or self-harm.[10]

Inquiring about homicidal ideation is a standard part of the assessment for suicidal ideation. Approximately 2% of suicides are preceded by homicide, often of a relative or other person known to the perpetrator.[11,12] Mental health professionals should also be alert to the phenomenon of "suicide by cop," which involves intentionally harming or killing a police officer in order to be killed by police in return.[13] More broadly, mass murderers often end their lives either through a direct exchange with police or by directing their weapons against themselves. There are suggestive reports that over half of such mass murderers have had major psychiatric symptoms, such as acute paranoia, delusions, and depression.[14] In contrast, suicides by people driven by religious or political impulses, such as suicide bombers or people who engage in mass shootings until they are killed by police, are rarely related to mental illness.[15] Overall, when it comes to the joining of homicide and suicide, we have a lot to learn about the interaction of identity, emotionality, vulnerability, social pressure, belief systems, and the acting out of violence.

At one time, it was common to see the following note as the total documentation of suicide risk: "No SI/HI." While brevity can be a virtue, inquiring about suicidal ideation (SI) and homicidal ideation (HI) is only the beginning of a comprehensive assessment of suicide risk. To end the assessment there would be to miss signs of potentially lethal risk in many patients. While some patients may feel relieved at being able to tell a potentially helpful person about their suicidal thoughts, other people, even if acutely suicidal, will flatly deny such thoughts.

Using the patient's yes-or-no response to a brief question about suicidal ideation, posed in an interview or during a nursing shift, as the definitive criterion for determining the patient's safety can provide a false sense of security and does not meet the level of care that a reasonable clinician would exercise. One study dramatically demonstrated the problem: of 76 patients who killed themselves in the hospital or immediately after discharge, almost 4 out of 5 (78%) had denied suicidal ideation in the last communication documented in the medical chart.[16]

Other people who know the patient may have information that the patient chooses not to divulge or that is missed in answers to yes-or-no questions. If family members or reliable significant others are available, it is the standard of care to collect data from them to the extent permitted by patient privacy protections. Furthermore, under state law and the Health Insurance Portability and Accountability Act (HIPAA), those rights can be overridden in a life-threatening emergency. In such a situation, the confidentiality of the therapist–patient dyad, which is designed to foster long-term trust, yields to the immediate need of preserving life. If the clinician decides that confidentiality must be overridden, the patient will learn its limits and may lose trust in the clinician. However, if the clinician explains this decision as an exercise of duty on behalf of the patient's life and safety, long-term trust is usually enhanced, not diminished. A detailed discussion of confidentiality can be found in chapter 9.

The rules of confidentiality limit what information clinicians may disclose, but under most circumstances, they do not prevent clinicians from receiving information about the patient. If family members already know that the patient is in outpatient treatment or in a hospital, talking to them and listening to what they have to say does not violate confidentiality per se. Even though the clinical staff may not be able to divulge information about the patient without his or her permission (except in the case of a life-threatening emergency), the staff can certainly ask for and receive information from the family and, indeed, may have a duty to do so.

Vignette 1: Rules of Confidentiality

A 57-year-old man was brought to the hospital by his wife after an overdose and was admitted. He claimed that the overdose was accidental and signed a request to be released. He told his wife by phone that he was successful in fooling his doctors and actually had plans to kill himself as soon as he could get out. He told her that he did not hold her responsible for his drinking and depression, which he was tired of fighting, and that she would be better off without him. His wife immediately called the unit and told a nurse not to trust her husband's improvement and not to discharge him. The nurse replied that, unfortunately, neither she nor the doctor could talk with her, since the patient had steadfastly refused permission to do so. An hour after he was discharged, the patient killed himself.

This case illustrates both a common misunderstanding of the rules of confidentiality, which kept critical information from being reported to the clinical team, and the hazards of relying solely on a patient's denial of suicidal intent. Evaluations that consist of checklists and turn primarily on whether the box for "SI" is checked yes or no run the risk of missing the true picture. The conclusion and subsequent checking off of "no SI" may be based on a 2-minute period of routine clinical rounds during which the patient did not volunteer suicidal ideation either because it was transiently absent or because the patient's alliance with the clinician was insufficient to allow for disclosure of intimate feelings.

For some patients, the social embarrassment and loss of self-esteem that the prospect of psychiatric hospitalization holds may seem more daunting than struggling to stay alive. To avoid hospitalization, such patients may disavow suicidal intent, making statements such as, "I think about it, but I would never do it." Patients who are already hospitalized are usually aware that to admit to suicidal ideation will mean delayed discharge or at least reduced privileges, and many will therefore be tempted to lie about suicidal ideation. The interviewer needs to anticipate this possibility by considering all the patient's answers in the context of the entire assessment and the interviewer–patient relationship. Thus, the interviewer should not immediately dismiss or accept the patient's denial of suicidal ideation on the basis of those statements alone.

Some patients will not allow themselves to be vulnerable with an interviewer they mistrust or with whom they are angry. This is a particular challenge in working with adolescents. Age-appropriate adolescent development may result in initial difficulty with trusting adults. When asked if she had suicidal thoughts, one adolescent girl answered, "Why should I tell you? I don't even know you." With adolescents and even adults, the refusal to answer the question about self-destructive ideation should be taken as a probable "yes" until further exploration allows a more confident conclusion that the answer is "no."

The trust and candor that are fostered by a therapeutic alliance are critical in treating suicidal patients, helping them endure fear, loneliness, or self-disparagement. Making it clear to patients—even those who are psychotic—that you understand their distress and will try to help, inquiring about symptoms and explaining side effects, and attending to physical ailments, as well as simple gestures such as making sure that a hospitalized patient has enough food, can be life-saving and stabilizing.

Maintaining a therapeutic relationship with patients who have borderline personality disorder or narcissistic personality disorder may require more empathy and support and less interpretation, at least at the beginning. At the same time, the therapist must explicitly and repeatedly reject the idea of suicide as a solution. The therapist's steadfast rejection of suicide as a solution, together with a willingness to help the patient seek other solutions and initiate those solutions, is often experienced as supportive. It can reassure the emotionally depleted patient that someone actually cares and, beyond that, has skills and techniques that may make a difference.

With borderline personality disorder, the greatest risk is posed by ever-present, ego-syntonic thoughts of suicide as a justifiable alternative to an unsatisfying world, along with a tendency to see the therapist's efforts to help as futile or inadequate. The patient's endorsement of suicidal ideation or its opposite, the denial of such ideation, may feel manipulative to the therapist. In addition, many patients with borderline personality disorder have a history of self-harm, such as repeatedly cutting themselves or abusing drugs or alcohol, but without any wish to die and without any prior serious injury. While the patient may have a history of such behavior stopping short of actual suicide, it is unwise to assume that at worst the patient will continue a nonlethal pattern of acting out. The rate of suicide is increased among patients with borderline personality disorder, and each clinical crisis should be evaluated separately with respect to suicide risk.

Another reason why inquiring about suicidal ideation as a stand-alone risk factor violates the standard of care for evaluating risk is that the urge for suicide is often discontinuous during a high-risk episode. In the presence of a sympathetic doctor or nurse, or while distracted by a visitor or even an event as mundane as a baseball game on television, the patient may not have a conscious suicidal impulse. However, hours later, when the patient is alone or the distraction has ended, emptiness may come flooding back, along with a strong wish to die.

History of Suicide Attempts

The single most predictive historical risk factor for another attempt or a completed suicide is a history of suicide attempts. The greater the number of attempts, the greater the risk of future attempts. Furthermore, the increased risk of suicide after one or more potentially lethal attempts lasts a lifetime, and the more lethal the method used in the attempt, the greater the risk of eventual death by suicide.[17,18]

Aside from a personal history of suicide attempts, the suicide of a first-degree relative is a risk factor. The most likely explanation for this risk factor is twofold: certain genetic traits appear to be correlated with an increased risk, and the suicide of a family member seems to break a taboo, introducing the idea of a path for another family member to take in response to intolerable stress.[19]

The past cannot be modified, but it can be used as an opening into the patient's feelings at present and a precaution for the future. Therefore, it is important not just to note prior attempts but also to investigate the patterns and circumstances of those attempts. Detailed knowledge of past attempts provides guidance for treatment planning. The patient who makes attempts only when intoxicated requires monitoring of alcohol use in addition to other interventions that will facilitate abstinence. Patients who are rejection-sensitive (seen in association with personality disorders and in people who have had attachment issues in childhood) and make attempts after abandonment need to have this correlation made explicit, with treatment aimed at increasing resilience and establishing safety plans for addressing such events when they occur. Finally, patients with significant genetic loading for depression or a pattern of recurrent depression and suicide attempts, despite intervening periods of improvement, need early-warning systems and close monitoring for long periods of their lives. As an example, the onset of sleep disturbance in a patient with bipolar disorder is a frequent prelude to a frank manic episode. Rather than wait to see if the sleep disturbance goes away after several nights, as one might with other patients, the clinician can warn the patient that poor sleep is an early indication that more trouble lies ahead without intervention, and ask the patient to report sleep disturbance as soon as it occurs. In the clinical vignette below, the patient's history suggests that the return of significant anxiety along with sleep problems was an early warning that her depression would worsen dramatically. An agreement not to "wait and see" but to establish these symptoms as an early-warning sign to be reported might have allowed earlier intervention.

Vignette 2: Warning Signs

A 34-year-old woman with postpartum depression made two suicide attempts after the birth of her first child. The first attempt, 6 weeks after giving birth, was by overdose, and the second, a month later, was by asphyxiation with a plastic sheet over her head in a remote wooded area. She was discovered and hospitalized each time and treated with antidepressants augmented by a second-generation antipsychotic medication used to quell anxiety, improve sleep, and improve mood. The medications were helpful, and she and her husband, who had a supportive relationship, received couple's counseling on coping with her illness. However, her bleak mood persisted after each attempt, and her suicidal ideation, fearfulness, sense of inadequacy, and insomnia recurred, requiring hospitalization. Each time she was hospitalized, her symptoms substantially improved, and she was discharged to her home, with arrangements made for assistance with childcare. Approximately 12 weeks postpartum, she was discharged for the last time. She was given the same medications that appeared to have resulted in improvement in the hospital. Upon discharge, she was given an emergency number to call, and an outpatient appointment with a psychiatrist was made for a month later. One week later, she died of an overdose of her medications. She left a note saying that she loved her husband and her new baby and knew they loved her, but she could not shake her profound depression.

Both the biological and the psychological changes in postpartum depression can be profound and long-lasting.[20] The pressures on the patient from her own wishes and those of her family to show the expected joys of having a new child can lead both the patient and caregivers to experience relief and hope when symptoms improve, but to deny signs of a relapse.

In this case, a follow-up outpatient visit was scheduled for a month after discharge, which was much too long an interval, given the patient's repeated and potentially lethal prior attempts. Giving her an emergency number to call for assistance was part of the discharge plan for the patient's safety and is a part of many such plans. This is useful if the patient wants to live and can reach out for help. It is also helpful to family members, who may witness deterioration even before the patient does. An emergency number to call is clearly not useful, however, when a patient has shown that she wants to avoid being found during a suicide attempt, as this patient did. If it is not possible to schedule an in-person follow-up evaluation shortly after discharge, scheduling a telephone or telemedicine interview is preferable to depending on an ambivalent patient to initiate a call for help, especially to an anonymous or unfamiliar resource.

Associated Diagnoses or Symptoms

While formal diagnoses are commonly used in research on the prevalence of suicide and attempted suicide, symptoms rather than formal diagnoses are often the common denominators of increased risk. For example, the symptoms of depressed mood with hopelessness, intolerable psychic anxiety, and severe insomnia,[21] all of which are major correlates of an increase in suicide risk, occur in depression, anxiety, psychosis, substance abuse, personality disorders, and brain injury.

Depression

Both unipolar depression and bipolar depression are associated with a risk of suicide. Studies in the mid-20th century attempted to make sense of suicide by conducting so-called psychological autopsies.[22] Those studies showed that about 90% of the patients were suffering from mental illness, usually a form of depression. Depression, often combined with secondary substance abuse or other diagnoses, remains the most prevalent symptom associated with the risk of suicide. For this reason, an assessment of suicide risk is the standard of care for all depressed patients.

Anxiety

Anxiety in its several forms is the most common mental disorder among adults in the United States. About 18% of U.S. adults report having had an anxiety disorder, including panic attacks, within the previous 12 months. The symptoms are judged to be severe in 23% of adults with anxiety disorder, or 4% of all U.S. adults. Severe symptoms of anxiety, in turn, are correlated with an increased suicide risk.[23]

Psychosis

The schizophrenia-spectrum illnesses and bipolar illness with psychosis influence suicide risk on many dimensions. Patients with hallucinations urging them to harm or kill others may act on those hallucinations and in remorse kill themselves.[24] Some patients may believe that the only way to avoid the psychotic imperative to harm others is to kill themselves instead.

The deterioration of cognitive function that accompanies schizophrenia does not blot out the patient's perception of failing to make progress. The young patient with schizophrenia can observe that while his or her peers go to college, date, find jobs, and get married, the patient's own social life is limited to home, hospitals, and support groups. These observations may all lead to depression. Moreover, depression may be part of the patient's biological loading, which is the case, for example, with patients who have schizoaffective psychosis.

Psychosis itself and the frequent symptom of paranoia significantly interfere with accurate social perception and interaction so that guidance or offers of a therapeutic alliance from professionals may not be accepted or may be misinterpreted. In addition, patients with schizophrenia and bipolar disorder often stop taking medications, resulting in mental turmoil and suicide attempts. Clinical planning needs to attend to both of these risks.

Substance Abuse

Alcohol and drug use disorders are associated with a risk of attempted suicide that is more than six times the risk for persons without such disorders. Among veterans, the risk of actual death by suicide among substance abusers is two or three times the risk for those without these disorders. Along with post-traumatic stress disorder (PTSD) and traumatic brain injury, which themselves increase suicide risk, substance use disorders are prevalent among veterans.[25]

Personality Disorders

Patients with borderline or narcissistic personality disorder tend to have frequent egosyntonic thoughts of suicide and to discount the therapist's efforts to help. When control of one's life seems out of reach, suicide may be seen as a way to have ultimate control and as a justifiable alternative to an unsatisfying world.

When a patient with borderline personality disorder is asked about suicidal ideation, the response, whether affirmative or negative, may not be stable and therefore cannot be taken at face value when the patient is in turmoil. Either response may seem manipulative and therefore hard to assess. In addition, many borderline patients have a history of nonlethal self-harm, such as cutting or substance abuse. The therapist cannot assume that because the patient has a history of repeated cutting rather than a history of suicide attempts, he or she will turn to cutting and not to suicide. Patients with borderline personality disorder are at increased risk for suicide apart from their history, and each crisis should be assessed carefully for lethal potential.[26]

Brain Damage

Patients with chronic traumatic encephalopathy, such as professional athletes who have suffered repeated head injuries or soldiers with traumatic brain injury, have increased rates of depression, suicidal ideation, and suicide.[27,28] Severe depression that is chronic or recurrent may cause damage to the brain, specifically to the hippocampus, suggesting that the memory issues seen in depression may also have a structural basis.[29]

Stressors

The stressful circumstances under which patients become suicidal are often overlooked or evaluated superficially. Yet understanding the precipitating circumstances and ameliorating them or helping the patient cope with them are critical for an effective treatment plan. Failure to address these stressors can be judged as a departure from the standard of care. Without such assessment and intervention, patients who improve in the supportive but artificial environment of a hospital unit and who are then discharged to an environment where the same stressors are present are at high risk for relapse.

Factors precipitating suicidal ideation often involve loss, trauma, loss of self-esteem, and intolerable pain, both physical and psychic. Commonly, a given set of circumstances precipitates more than one factor. Divorce, or loss of employment or income, may involve both trauma and a drop in self-esteem. Other common circumstances are confusion about or a change in gender identity; pending criminal or civil litigation with attendant shame, guilt, or fear; sexual or emotional abuse; psychological and physical trauma in wartime, an inexorable decline in bodily functions, which occurs in many neurological syndromes; and the experience of "crashing" after an episode of substance abuse or mania. In psychotic depression, the stressors may not be real-world factors but instead may be delusional.

Suicidal wishes are sometimes a response to loss of self-esteem. The suicidality comes from both a wish to avoid facing what seems to be an intractable dilemma and the need for self-punishment. The ancient Japanese practice of hara-kiri or seppuku, ritualized suicide by sword in response to disgrace, was meant to restore honor through a demonstration of atonement and courage. While ritualized suicide in a nonpsychotic person is extremely rare, an understanding of the connection between suicidality and the wish to restore honor is helpful in attempting to intervene with patients who are experiencing a loss of self-esteem and considering suicide.

Loss of self-esteem and a shift in identity may lead to distorted perceptions of one's circumstances. For example, the vignette below concerns a man whose wealth most people would consider more than adequate for survival. He did not—with tragic consequences.

Vignette 3: Distorted Perceptions

During the last economic downturn, a well-to-do executive was laid off and had to give up his country club membership. He did not tell his wife. Instead, he came home early and wrote a note stating that having grown up poor, he could not face a return to poverty, nor could he imagine his child having to grow up in poverty. After his wife left the house, he drank heavily and then killed his young daughter and himself. He left an estate of several million dollars.

This man was clearly not poor. However, the loss of his job and his country club membership triggered an overwhelming decline in self-esteem. He could no longer maintain his identity as a successful person who had managed to climb out of poverty and who could look down on his former "lower-class" self. The shame he felt prevented him from finding comfort in his family.

Both the stressful circumstances and the patient's psychological responses to them can usually be revealed in a clinical interview, and an exploration of these issues can be key in developing an effective treatment plan and preventing a relapse. Effective clinical planning for a patient who has made a prior suicide attempt requires a full understanding of the stressful circumstances in which the attempt took place, as well as an ongoing assessment of those circumstances—whether they have improved, remain unchanged, or have worsened—and the consequent changes in the patient's psychological outlook.

The hope is that treatment will improve the patient's capacity to cope with the remaining stressors, as well as those that might arise in the future. In addition to the support that the therapeutic alliance provides, interventions that can help the patient cope with stressors include medications that stabilize affect, cognitive approaches, and provision of social supports. Documentation should go beyond notes about changes in symptoms (e.g., reductions in suicidal ideation and depressed affect) to include assessments of stressors and interventions aimed at improving the patient's ability to cope with them.

Protective Factors

Two main factors are thought to inhibit suicidal impulses—having children in the home and belonging to a religion that forbids suicide—although their inhibitory effect is often weak. Deeply depressed patients with a negative cognitive shift may believe that their children will be better off without them. Many people contemplating suicide discount their religious affiliation or are angry with God for making them suffer.

However, protective factors can be very useful in treatment. Directly discussing with the patient the long-term impact of a parent's suicide on children can challenge the patient's tendency to minimize the repercussions. For patients who have a positive association with religion or simply may be open to it, pastoral counseling may bring comfort, reduce guilt and anxiety, and offer a new perspective and hope.

SPECIFIC POPULATIONS

Even though suicidal behavior has self-harm as a unifying characteristic, the statistics, risk factors, and presentation can differ across different populations.

YOUTH

According to the Centers for Disease Control and Prevention (CDC), suicide is the second leading cause of death among adolescents and young adults 15 to 24 years of age and the third leading cause of death among children 10 to 14 years old.[30] In a study of over

26,000 college students, more than half reported that they had thought about suicide at least once in their lives; 15% had thought about making an attempt, and 5% had actually made an attempt at some point in their lives.[31]

Young persons are particularly susceptible to a range of experiences that are associated with an increased risk of suicide, including fights, alcohol and drug use, victimization (e.g., being bullied), and forced sexual experiences. Depression and physical impairments are also associated with an increased risk of suicide in this age group.[32]

Clusters of suicides have occurred among young people, suggesting that one person's suicidal behavior may have a contagious quality for that person's peers. A study that analyzed the impact of extensive newspaper coverage on the spread of suicide attempts among 13- to 19-year-olds showed that the more sensational the coverage (as indicated, for example, by headlines and numbers of stories), the greater the chances of subsequent suicide clusters.[33] Since then, with the ubiquity of social media and the expansion of 24-hour television news outlets, the potential for contagion has grown.

As clinicians, we have a duty to be aware of the risk factors for suicide in youth, as well as the contagious potential of suicide in this age group and the new capacities of social media to target and victimize vulnerable youth. Verbal bullying by peers through social media or the distribution of sexually revealing or unflattering photographs to embarrass classmates can be devastating, leading to suicide as a way to escape the pain of humiliation and betrayal by friends and peers.

The Elderly

Contrary to common assumptions, the suicide rate for the elderly is consistently higher than the suicide rate in young people. According to the CDC, suicide rates level off for women after the age of 60 years but continue to rise for men. Women more easily form affiliation groups earlier in their lives than men and draw from those social supports should they become widowed or disabled. Strikingly, suicide attempts by persons who are 85 years of age or older are more lethal than attempts by younger persons. The CDC estimates that there are about 25 suicide attempts for each suicide death among young persons. The ratio is closer to 4 to 1 among elderly persons. The elderly are more likely to be dealing with isolation, disability, chronic pain, cognitive loss, financial threats, and dependency, all of which are risk factors for depression and suicide.[34] What is sometimes overlooked, however, is the fact that older patients, however frail, may retain the dynamics of their younger selves, including romantic attachments, jealousies, and guilt, and suicide remains an option for those who see no other way to escape what they consider intolerable pain in their lives.

Vignette 4: Evaluating Risk in Elderly Patients

After undergoing surgery to correct an abdominal hemorrhage, an 82-year-old woman refused to allow her husband to come into her hospital room and asked the nurses to keep him out, insisting that he was not her husband. Concerned that the previously competent patient was suffering a brain insult from her recent anesthesia or had become psychotic, the attending physician treated her with very small doses of haloperidol. Her refusal to see her husband persisted. With her first semisolid meal, she asked for a butter knife. Since there was neither bread nor butter on her tray, she was asked why she needed the knife. "To kill myself" was her answer. The consulting psychiatrist determined that she was fully oriented and knew clearly that the man waiting at the door to see her was her husband. "I have been married to him for over 25 years," she said. "He is my second husband." She knew that a butter knife would not kill her. However, she believed that should she actually die, she would meet her first husband, and he would know that she had remarried. The suicide idea was to gain his sympathy, ward off his anger, and help relieve her guilt, just in case he might know about her second marriage.

In evaluating suicide risk in the elderly, the same factors that must be addressed in younger persons—ideation, history, symptoms, and stressors—are relevant. The stressors in late life often go beyond physical impairment and pain, encompassing end-of-life issues that are revealed only by careful inquiry. Patients are often appreciative when the clinician addresses these issues directly, and some patients may welcome a referral for pastoral counseling.

Middle-Aged Persons

While the suicide rates for both younger and older Americans have remained stable over the past decade, the rate for those in middle age (35 to 64 years old) rose by 28% from 1999 to 2010. The suicide rate for whites in middle age jumped by 40% during the same period.[35] Proposed reasons for these dramatic increases in suicide in the middle-aged white population have ranged from the impact of the economy and job loss to the prescription drug and opiate epidemic to the general experience of displacement in a culture that tends to place more value on young adulthood than on old age.

The Military

Rates of suicide attempts and deaths by suicide have increased by almost 60% among active-duty military personnel in the past decade.[36] Furthermore, the increase in risk persists beyond active duty, with veterans at higher risk for suicide than nonveteran civilians.[37] In this population, clinicians need to pay special attention to symptoms of PTSD, as well as to difficulties in adjusting to civilian life.

EMERGING FIELDS OF KNOWLEDGE

Current knowledge about suicidal behavior has been informed and advanced by developments in genetics and neuroimaging.

Genetic Factors

Suicidality is a complex set of behavioral phenotypes. Much of the early genetic research has been directed at studies of families with a high incidence of suicide, suggesting a possible genetic trait. Most of these studies have shown higher rates of suicide and attempted suicide among relatives of those who have made an attempt or have died by suicide than among relatives of nonsuicidal controls.[38] All large-scale population studies show increased rates of suicide among the offspring of suicidal parents as compared with the offspring of nonsuicidal parents.[39] In addition, suicide rates among persons who lost a parent to suicide are higher than the rates among persons who lost a parent to homicide or an accident, again suggesting a genetic trait. These studies are the basis for considering suicide in a family member as a separate risk factor.

With the development of techniques to isolate genes, two genes related to the serotonergic system have been proposed as risk factors: one conferring a susceptibility to suicidal behavior in general, and the other conferring a specific susceptibility to repeated lethal attempts to kill oneself. Suggestions that at least some suicidal behaviors are related to the serotonergic system have been largely sustained. These studies have shown increased serotonin-receptor subtypes and decreased serotonin metabolites in platelets, lymphocytes, cerebrospinal fluid, and brain tissue obtained from suicide victims at autopsy.[40]

A long list of other biological systems and genetic groupings that appear to be dysregulated in suicide involve the hypothalamic–pituitary–adrenal axis and neurotrophins and neurotrophin receptors. These result in abnormalities of neuroimmune functions, brain-derived neurotrophic factor, dopamine receptor D2, catechol-O-methyltransferase, and monoamine oxidase type A.[41] Even this list is not all-inclusive, nor does it reflect the complexity of genetic factors. Genes do not act alone but interact with each other, epigenetic changes may occur, and genetic influences operate differently under different biological, environmental, social, and psychological circumstances.[42]

Brain Imaging

There are many modalities for imaging the brain, including magnetic resonance imaging (MRI) and functional MRI, diffusion tensor imaging, positron-emission tomography, and magnetoencephalography. However, imaging research is expensive, and suicide studies using imaging usually involve small samples. In an effort to address this problem, a number of imaging centers have adopted a uniform research protocol for imaging studies, resulting in the acquisition of data from a collective series of 4,000 patients. These findings may be useful for identifying distinctive findings in patients who have made previous suicide attempts or who have other risk factors for suicide in the future. In addition, efforts are underway to trace the brain functions in a few persons multiple times as a way of understanding and predicting temporal changes in brain organization. The results are preliminary and cannot yet be correlated with suicidal behavior. However, there are promising findings from imaging studies that have correlated changes in brain systems with suicide and attempted suicide. Changes have been identified in the frontal neural systems and in the serotonergic system in adolescents as well as adults, confirming the genetic findings.[43]

Clinical Implications

What are the clinical implications of studies that correlate suicidal behavior with brain changes and genetic traits? The genetic studies highlight the importance of obtaining a detailed family history with respect to suicidal behavior. In the case of a positive family history, especially if it is characterized by violent attempts or persistently strong ideation, consider the possibility that brain structural and genetic factors play a part in the patient's suicidality, and take into account in your treatment planning that the patient may need closer and longer-term monitoring than patients without such a family history. If plans for treatment include antidepressant medication, consider using genetic testing, if available, to determine which antidepressants may be most effective. If genetic tests for diagnosing schizophrenia and other disorders in their prodromal state become available for clinical use, the test results will provide clinicians with important information about risk factors. Look for developing research confirming multiple studies of the relevance of one or a few genetic factors. Look for brain-scan syntheses that aggregate results from several studies or that target specific subpopulations such as adolescents.

No brain imaging studies or genetic tests have yet become a specific standard of care for assessing suicidal patients. Although the prospects that these areas will contribute clinically to the assessment of risk factors is not yet in sight, research and technology are headed in that direction.[44]

DUTIES TO ACT ON THE RESULTS OF THE EVALUATION

After performing a comprehensive evaluation of a patient's suicide risk (i.e., considering the various risk factors, protective factors, impressions from the interview, knowledge of the field, and information from others), you must make decisions on behalf of the patient. With a suicidal patient, these decisions must constitute reasonable steps to protect the patient's life.

When there are no explicit guidelines to inform your decision making, ask this question for the protection of the patient: "How are my actions protecting this patient's life against the risks that I have evaluated?" With regard to limiting your liability for a potential malpractice suit, ask yourself this question: "How have I documented the risks that I have found and also the benefits of the steps I am taking to mitigate the risks and protect the patient?"

The first major decision that must be made in managing the risk posed by a potentially suicidal patient is whether to hospitalize the patient or provide outpatient care.[45] If the decision is made to hospitalize the patient, additional decisions must be made about precautions, including safety observations, that should be ordered in the hospital, the timing of discharge, and appropriate discharge planning.

Hospitalization or Outpatient Care

Some clinicians depend on suicide risk scales in deciding whether to hospitalize a patient or provide outpatient treatment. These scales, which rate a patient's risk of suicide as high, moderate, or low, tend to be static checklists that are not comprehensive and do not consider the ways in which the listed items interact with each other. They are therefore best used as a guide to remind the evaluator of the range of factors to be considered.

The SAD PERSONS scale, which is widely used in emergency rooms to rate suicide risk, has come under specific criticism. This scale assesses the following factors: **S**ex, **A**ge, **D**epression, **P**revious suicide attempts, **E**thanol use, **R**ational thinking, **S**ocial supports, **O**rganized plan, **N**o spouse, and **S**ickness. A numerical value is assigned to each of the risk factors, with higher scores associated with male sex, age under 19 years or over 45 years, depression, previous attempts, ethanol use, loss of rational thinking, lack of social supports, having an organized plan for suicide, no spouse, and sickness (physical illness). A study of patients who were evaluated with the use of SAD PERSONS and then followed for 6 months revealed that the scale failed to identify the majority of those who required either psychiatric admission or community-based psychiatric aftercare and that it did not predict repetition of self-harm.[46]

The Columbia-Suicide Severity Scale[47] covers the ages of occurrence of suicidal ideation and its lifetime pattern. It probes key aspects of suicidal behavior and ideation multiple times using different and overlapping questions. It has been widely tested for both adults and adolescents and for military personnel as well as civilian populations. As such, it is among the most detailed and widely used suicide assessment tools.

Even with detailed instruments, however, rating scales are a supplement and not a replacement for clinical judgment. Ideation, history, symptoms, and stressful circumstances are not static items that can easily be assigned a numerical value. Rather, they are dynamic, interrelated factors. Certain factors, when appearing together, seem to suggest a specific short-term risk. A rapid rise in the intensity of suicidal intent over a few hours or days, social or personal alienation, hopelessness, insomnia with nightmares, and marked agitation or irritability constitute an "acute suicidal affective disturbance" that is claimed to be present in 15% to 20% of patients who subsequently commit suicide.[48]

Moreover, with the exception of a person's history and genetic traits, risk factors can and do change over time. Some factors change rapidly. For example, the return of a spouse to "give the marriage another chance" or the dropping of criminal charges may dramatically alter the conditions under which the patient became suicidal. In addition, a patient who is able, with the therapist's help, to express previously suppressed emotions may experience relief from both physiological and psychological pressures that previously seemed intractable. It is important to examine the stability of such improvement. It may represent a breakthrough, with ongoing relief of symptoms, or the symptoms may recur as soon as the clinician leaves the room.

Some change takes time. We know that depression may take weeks to resolve and that a resolution of depression that is sufficient to ensure the patient's safety may have several phases, with some symptoms resolving earlier than others. For example, patients whose motor retardation has improved with medication may still feel severely depressed and be at the same or even greater risk for a suicide attempt. With pressure from the insurance plan or hospital to discharge such a patient, it is up to the clinician to perform a comprehensive clinical evaluation and to establish treatment and discharge plans that are based on the full clinical findings.

The lack of a short-term response in patients with suicidal impulses increases the risk. The psychotic or paranoid patient who can receive no comfort from a conscientious clinician, the patient who remains devastated despite prospective changes in his or her circumstances, the deeply depressed patient whose fixed mood is unlikely to yield and who has given up the wish to get better, and certainly the patient who has made a suicide attempt and regrets having survived are all candidates for safety precautions.

An interview device known as a "contract for safety" or "no harm contract" asks the patient to agree or "contract" not to hurt himself or herself, or to call or warn the clinician if the patient feels the urge for self-harm. Sometimes this question is put in writing and the patient is asked to sign the "contract." Asking a patient to contract for his or her safety is not always useless. The patient can say "no," and this will help clarify an otherwise uncertain assessment. The clinician with a solid therapeutic alliance with the patient may use the request to ask the patient to notify the clinician of increased desperation with the reliability of response being a function both of the strength of the alliance and the patient's mental status. Other than that, the use of a "contract for safety" is both meaningless legally and misleading clinically. [49]

Patients at high risk for suicide require ongoing 24-hour care or, at a minimum, a further emergency evaluation while kept in a safe environment. The greatest barriers to referring a high-risk patient for 24-hour protective care are the patient's resistance and the clinician's wish not to disrupt the patient's life. The decision not to hospitalize a suicidal patient requires the establishment of an alternative mechanism for close monitoring, such as family vigilance and partial hospitalization.

The benefits of the alternative to hospitalization need to be persuasive, given the risk that the alternative approach may fail to protect the patient. From both a clinical and a risk-management perspective, it is essential to discuss this risk–benefit analysis with the patient (and, ideally, with his or her family) and obtain informed consent to the plan. The risk–benefit analysis, the discussion of this analysis with the patient, the family's involvement in the discussion, and the patient's consent should be documented in the medical record.

Clinicians usually have little trouble determining that a patient is at low or high risk for suicide. But what does it mean to be at moderate risk? For any other medical condition, a moderate risk of dying constitutes an urgent situation, requiring initiation of treatment, close monitoring of the patient, and an assessment of whether the treatment is effective. In the case of suicidality, moderate risk may mean that there is uncertainty (i.e., not enough evidence to establish a high risk or a low risk) or that a risk is clearly present but the risk is not imminent. Documenting the reasons for designating the patient as having a moderate risk will help point the way to follow-up.

Safety Precautions during Hospitalization

Hospitalization does not guarantee safety. The admitting and attending physicians are responsible for making independent judgments about treatment, including deciding on the frequency of safety checks. Unfortunately, many hospitals consider it adequate to check high-risk patients who are on "suicide precautions" every 15 minutes. In the hospital unit, 15-minute checks do not ensure the safety of a patient who is seriously suicidal.[50]

The most common means of suicide in a psychiatric unit is asphyxiation by hanging with a sheet or clothing. A high protuberance is not necessary for asphyxiation. Patients who are determined to kill themselves can use a low object, such as a bed frame, to hold a ligature and lean against it until they become unconscious. It takes 3 to 5 minutes to cause major brain damage or death, which is well within the 15-minute interval that is often used for checking high-risk patients.

In addition, there are many other means that can be used to harm oneself or end one's life. Patients have swallowed watches or socks, and choked. They have used small pencils to jab their eyes and blind themselves, they have received contraband from visitors, saved it until no one was watching, and then used it for self-harm. Fifteen-minute checks for patients at high risk of suicide violate the first standard of care: taking reasonable steps to protect the patient's life. The default approach to precautions for patients judged to be at high risk of suicide in the hospital is constant observation[51] or, in rare cases, 5-minute checks.

Readiness for Discharge and Discharge Planning

Managed care decisions about readiness for discharge in the case of a patient who has been hospitalized because of suicide risk are legitimate opinions but are not a substitute for the independent judgment of the attending clinician. Readiness for discharge to outpatient care should be documented by the absence of or a substantial reduction in suicidal ideation and by improvement in the symptoms associated with suicide risk. In addition, there should be improvement in the relevant stressful circumstances or in the patient's capacity to cope with them. It is essential, from a risk-management standpoint, to document the pros and cons of discharge and the analysis leading to the discharge decision. Discharge of patients with intermittent suicidal ideation requires explicit attention and documentation.

Vignette 5: Discharge

A 36-year-old woman was hospitalized after a drug overdose precipitated by a marital argument. She now states that she is feeling better and has decided to seek a divorce. Her objective symptom of insomnia and flat affect and her reported depressed mood have improved. However, she does not state that she is free of suicidal thoughts. Rather she says, "I felt urges to hurt or kill myself almost all the time before I took the Tylenol overdose. I still think about it but not as much, and I don't feel the need to act on those thoughts. I would like to go home. I miss my family. I am OK to be discharged." The patient agreed to stay in the hospital for several more days. This permitted time for further planning for support after her intended separation and a slight increase in her medication. Her suicidal thoughts continued to diminish in their intensity and frequency and then resolved.

After an acute episode of intense suicidal ideation or a suicide attempt, some patients continue to have suicidal thoughts as a correlate of their depression or psychosis or because the conditions they face are still overwhelming, but they are otherwise not chronically suicidal. For such patients, the goal of treatment is the complete resolution of suicidal ideation, as it is for the patient described in this vignette. For other patients, full resolution is probably not possible because the ideation is a baseline or chronic condition.

When patients have some residue of suicidal ideation or other significant risk factors but are not deemed to require continued hospitalization, the clinician's obligation is to plan for close follow-up after discharge, through partial hospitalization or intensive outpatient care initiated within a day or so after discharge, in order to ensure the patient's continued improvement. Family members, with the patient's consent, are often made a part of the discharge planning. They can be educated about the nature of the patient's illness and can learn to recognize early signs of a return of symptoms. With adolescent patients or even with adults who are forgetful, family members can be asked to give the patient his or her medication. They must be informed about possible side effects and what to do should the patient refuse the medication.

The clinician needs to make an assessment of the capacity of the family to understand and follow through on safety matters. However, family members are not part of the professional treatment team and should not be relied on as if they were. Professional oversight for the patient and for support provided by the family is the responsibility of the clinician in charge of the patient's aftercare.

If the patient was hospitalized after a suicide attempt, the clinician may want to see greater improvement before discharge than for patients who were hospitalized for other reasons. Many patients are still vulnerable at the time of discharge. For the first week after discharge, the risk of suicide is three times as high as the risk in the general population.[52] It is not unusual for patients admitted for suicide to want to be discharged before their clinical team has concluded that they are ready to do so. The law in many states allows a patient to petition for discharge—even against medical advice—and the clinician must then decide whether to release the patient even with a less than ideal disposition, or to apply for court commitment to ensure continued hospital care.

We know that patients with a history of suicidal risk who sign themselves out of the hospital while still symptomatic actually do have higher rates of suicide, especially if they then do not engage in intensive outpatient follow-up.[51]

As an alternative to court commitment, a careful and empathic explanation to the patient and the family that a few more days in the hospital might resolve the agitation, mood lability, or other symptoms of concern and allow a safer discharge can be persuasive and achieve the desired outcome of an agreed-on discharge date and aftercare arrangements.[51] It is important to explain to the patient and to concerned family members what would be gained by a few more days in the hospital. The ability to determine that the improvement in symptoms and reduction in suicidal ideation are stable is a powerful argument, as is the need to make safe transfer-of-care plans, especially if the patient has a history of volatility and if the attempt was potentially lethal.

Fortunately, most state laws require that a voluntarily admitted patient give advance written notice, generally addressed to the hospital's executive, if he or she wants to leave the hospital before the clinician believes that discharge is warranted. The purpose of the notice is to allow the hospital to determine whether commitment of the patient is now indicated and, if so, to take legal action in order to initiate that commitment. If commitment is pursued, state laws may require the clinician to warn the patient that the results of examinations and the content of clinical interviews may be disclosed to the court. These topics are discussed in more detail in the chapters on civil commitment (chapter 2) and confidentiality and privilege (chapter 9).

The few days before actual commitment can be critical. If the clinician approaches the patient with candor and explicit concern for the patient's welfare, the patient may respond surprisingly well to the move for commitment, interpreting it as evidence of the hospital's concern rather than as an adversarial act. A positive response is an opportunity to ask the patient to withdraw the advance notice for discharge. The clinician, in turn, can withdraw the hospital's petition for commitment and agree to work hard to reach mutually agreeable terms for discharge. However, the period during which discharge readiness is disputed can also be dangerous. The patient may interpret a move to file for commitment as a sign that he or she will never be discharged and, as a result, may make a suicide attempt or become assaultive. The following vignette provides an example.

Vignette 6: Refusing Commitment

A 27-year-old man with a history of suicide attempts, mood instability, alcohol and opiate abuse, and violence was admitted to the hospital. He had served a prison term for breaking and entering and robbery. Shortly after admission, he requested opiate pain medication. On being told by a nurse that his request had been denied, he hit the nurse. He apologized and several days later filed a notice that he wished to leave the hospital. His attending psychiatrist told him that he was still concerned about the patient's labile mood and would file for commitment. The patient climbed over the psychiatrist's desk and punched the psychiatrist in the face.

Some patients make it clear that they have no current wish for self-harm, but if a specific event occurs or perhaps fails to occur, they are equally clear that they will kill themselves. This is referred to as contingent suicidality[52] and is illustrated in the following vignette.

Vignette 7: Contingent Suicidality

A mother who completed an inpatient alcohol detoxification program had two children in the custody of the Department of Children and Families. Anticipating an upcoming custody hearing, she said, "If the state takes my kids away, I have nothing to live for. I'll know in 10 days. I promise you I won't do anything until then. After that, no promises."

Some patients remain chronically and intermittently suicidal as their baseline level of functioning. The causes are various but include chronic depression with pessimism and a sense that the option of ending their lives is one way to preserve some measure of control.

With chronically suicidal patients, it is important to identify and document the factors that appear to increase the short-term risk, such as loss of supportive relationships, substance abuse, or noncompliance with medication or outpatient treatment. Plans for care after discharge can then be designed to provide protection against these factors or at least to give an early warning to outpatient treatment providers.

In each of the cases in which some elements of increased risk are still present at discharge, continued hospital care may be problematic, since suicidal behavior does not appear to be imminent. With some patients, further hospital care may not have benefits or may even be regressive. Under these circumstances, a second-opinion review of the discharge plan can be clinically useful and may be protective of the discharging clinician. When that second opinion also includes an interview with the patient, it often has a positive effect on a patient whose self-esteem has been depleted, making the patient feel more cared about as a valuable person. Also, the patient may relate differently to a second clinician and divulge more information.

Vignette 8: Concealing Information

A 45-year-old, recently divorced man was admitted for depression with suicidal ideation. As part of his initial examination, he was asked if he had a gun at home. He said no. Just before discharge, he was withdrawn and sullen, giving clipped answers to his attending doctor and the nursing staff, but denied the return of suicidal ideation. He was again asked if he had a gun at home, and the question was broadened to ask about access to firearms. Again, he said no, but unconvincingly. He appeared to be more anxious. A second opinion was sought from a senior hospital clinician on readiness for discharge and the plan for outpatient therapy at a clinic near the patient's home. A few minutes into the second-opinion interview, the patient complained about the arrogant attitude of his attending physician and said, "I wouldn't talk to him if he paid me." He then went on to admit that he had a gun in the glove compartment of his car, which was parked in the hospital parking lot, and never intended to live long enough to go home. The perception of his attending physician as arrogant was a surprise not only to the attending physician but also to the nurses on the unit, who perceived him as a humble and careful doctor.

As this case illustrates, transference is in the mind of the beholder and not always apparent in an inpatient setting, where interviews, which are often held while the clinician is standing, consist of a stark sentence or two, or last for five minutes or less. The attending physician's clinical sense that the patient was hiding something and the request for a second opinion may have saved the patient's life. Results of a second opinion are usually not this dramatic, but they do often lead to recommendations for additional safety measures on discharge. At a minimum, if the second opinion is independent of the first and is comprehensive, the issue of possible negligence is significantly diluted.

TRANSFER OF CARE

Whenever the care of a patient who has been at risk for suicide is being transferred from one caretaker to another, the governing principles are similar to those for discharge. Communication to the receiving caretaker should include the reason for the transfer, relevant history, success or failure of treatments provided, and current clinical status of the patient. In addition, a period of transfer between caretakers that is appropriate for the patient's condition should be specified, with plans for ensuring the patient's safety during the transfer period, until the patient is under the care of the new therapist or facility.

Let us look at some common pitfalls. When a potentially suicidal patient is transferred from an emergency room at a general hospital to a separate psychiatric hospital, the transfer is usually made by ambulance, which is a secure method of transportation. However, when the patient is transferred to a psychiatric unit within the first hospital, "sitters" are sometimes assigned to watch the patient in the emergency department before and during the transfer. There have been cases in which an untrained sitter permitted the patient to go to the bathroom or make a phone call near an open door and the patient simply walked out of the hospital. In one case, the patient deliberately walked into street traffic, with lethal results. Emergency departments are obligated to educate those acting as patient sitters on their role with suicidal patients.

Knowing that certain terminology is accepted by managed care and sometimes by state law as an acceptable "passport" to inpatient services, the referring clinician may routinely check the box that says "dangerous to self or others," regardless of whether the danger is life-threatening or is considered to be imminent. It may not even be the main reason for referral.

If the patient appeared to be at risk for suicide before hospitalization but the receiving clinician does not believe that the patient is currently at risk in the hospital, this judgment, along with the reasons for it, should be stated explicitly in the medical record. Failing to comment on "dangerous to self or others" as the reason for admission will be hard to defend if the admitting clinician provides no safeguards and the patient does harm himself or herself in the hospital. If the clinician becomes a defendant in a malpractice suit to recover damages, the likelihood is that this check-marked statement of dangerousness will be blown up and projected for the doctor and jury to see.

When a clinician stops practicing or the clinician or patient moves while the patient is in active treatment, the transferring clinician has a duty not to abandon the patient but to make recommendations for continued treatment if needed. Because suicidality may be a relapsing condition, it is best not to leave the task of finding a new clinician to the patient alone but instead to help select a new therapist. Otherwise, the patient may conclude, despite advice to the contrary, that treatment is not actually needed and may refrain from seeking help. It can be hard for a layperson to select a new therapist without guidance, and the frustration itself may result in hopelessness.

Warnings that the patient should not discontinue his or her medicine except under clinical supervision should be repeated and recorded. To the extent that family members can be usefully involved, they too should be warned, with the major side effects of discontinuation specified. These include a lowering of the seizure threshold when an anticonvulsant is discontinued, a return of depression or development of the serotonin withdrawal syndrome when a selective serotonin-reuptake inhibitor (SSRI) is stopped abruptly, and a return of hallucinations when an antipsychotic agent is stopped.

Unsupervised discontinuation of these medications can be directly linked to the return of suicidal impulses, and this too should be specified.

In some cases, it is the patient who abandons the therapist. For example, the patient may not show up for appointments or may violate the terms of the treatment by becoming intoxicated and not being cogent enough to call the therapist. The patient may threaten the therapist out of paranoia or may demand inappropriate prescription medications. The patient may also just "quit." Even in these circumstances, the clinician has a duty to assess the short-term risk and to advise the patient how to obtain alternative treatment. This is best done in person and in writing or in a telephone call documented in the medical record. If the risk of suicide is judged to be significant, the family and/or the police will need to be notified.

Most hospitals have a policy that requires a post-discharge appointment within a specified period, usually within 7 days. Long waits for follow-up are an invitation to relapse. With patients who were admitted to the hospital because of suicide risk, an outpatient appointment is often made for the day of or following discharge. It is the standard of care to discuss a safety plan with the patient for the interim period, including a discussion of where to turn for help at night or on the weekend. A discharge note should include a review of the patient's risk factors at discharge, how the patient's symptoms have improved, in what ways the patient's stressors have improved and/or how the patient's coping capacity is more robust, and the plan for addressing the return of suicidal pressures. [53]

CONCLUSION

The threat of suicide without actual completion is common enough that clinicians can become inured to the risk, especially with short hospital stays and pressure on clinicians to tolerate risk. Suicide and brain damage from a serious attempt remain major preventable causes of death and injury, respectively, according to the Joint Commission. They are the causes of action in psychiatric malpractice cases that bring the highest judgments for damages and that result in major trauma for the survivors of the suicide or attempted suicide, including the treating clinicians.

The best defense against malpractice is to safeguard the patient. To do so with a potentially suicidal patient, the clinician must evaluate the patient comprehensively, base interventions on that evaluation, and document the benefits of protective treatment decisions given the assessed risk. Not all lives can be saved, but the diligent effort to save a patient's life is among the highest callings for physicians and other health care professionals.

FREQUENTLY ASKED QUESTIONS

A 38-year-old, recently divorced man tells an emergency room psychiatrist that he is depressed and has frequent thoughts that life is not worth living. When asked whether he has fantasies about how he might die or has plans to hurt or kill himself, he denies both. However, he states that he is attracted to the idea of being in a place where he doesn't feel rejected and can imagine wanting to end his life in the future "if things don't start looking up." He recently bought a gun "for self-protection," since he had to move out of his home into a "tough neighborhood."

What risk factors are present? What else should the psychiatrist ask about?

Key risk factors for suicide in this patient's presentation are his depression, thoughts of death, recent divorce, and purchase of a gun. The fact that he does not have a specific plan for hurting or killing himself should not reassure the clinician that the risk of suicide is low. The patient should be asked about any thoughts he might have of hurting or killing others.

What are the appropriate next steps with this patient?

The next steps are a matter of clinical judgment that should be based on a detailed examination of factors that increase the risk and those that may be protective. If the patient has no family supports, has suffered additional losses, such as loss of a job, and is using drugs or alcohol, consideration of inpatient hospitalization is warranted. If he has family or other social supports, is gainfully employed, and has no history of substance abuse, he may be a good candidate for outpatient treatment. That treatment should start immediately, with prescription of an antidepressant, and a follow-up visit soon after the emergency room evaluation should be scheduled.

A 34-year-old woman who is 7 months' postpartum goes to see her therapist. She reports increasing melancholy, frequent episodes of uncontrollable crying, and feelings of shame that she cannot care for her baby and is a burden to her husband, who "deserves better." She describes persistent suicidal ideation, insomnia, and agitation during the day, with intermittent fantasies that her baby has died and been replaced by another infant. She was treated for depression in her mid-20s, at which time she made a suicide attempt. Her sister died by suicide 3 years ago. The patient assures the therapist that she would never act on her suicidal thoughts because it would cause too much pain. She does not want her husband to know how bad she is feeling and prohibits the therapist from speaking to him about her. She agrees to come back the next business day to see the therapist.

What steps would meet the standard of care in this case?

This case presents a compelling argument for hospitalization. Anything short of hospitalization poses a significant risk to the patient (and a risk to the therapist of a malpractice suit, should the patient harm herself). Nevertheless, continued outpatient treatment is still a possible option, but only after the relative risks and benefits of inpatient versus outpatient care have been carefully weighed. If outpatient treatment is chosen, the treating psychiatrist or other medication prescriber, as well as the patient's husband, should be informed and made part of the decision-making process. The risk of a suicide attempt, the importance of safety measures (e.g., securing any weapons in the home and restricting access to medications), and emergency resources should be discussed frankly and openly with the patient and her husband as well as any other family members helping to care for her. Whatever the decision, the therapist should document the decision-making process and the basis for the decision.

An 18-year-old high school senior is brought to the emergency room by his parents because he seemed "strange" after smoking marijuana. He started smoking marijuana daily a month earlier, after a classmate committed suicide. The patient did not know the classmate well but was upset by this event. He told his parents that he wondered what death was like and that he had looked at "how to do it" suicide websites on the Internet. He has been doing well in school except for the past month, is a member of the school basketball team, and plans to go to the senior prom. A serum toxic screen is positive for marijuana metabolites and amphetamines.

Given this presentation, what steps should the evaluating clinician take to meet the standard of care? Should the patient be asked to contract for safety?

The evaluating clinician should explore this patient's drug use more extensively and conduct a comprehensive suicide evaluation, including a discussion of the classmate's death. The behavior of looking at suicide websites is significant and needs to be carefully assessed. "Contracts for safety" are of limited value as they provide little information and cannot be relied on to prevent self-destructive behavior. If, after a comprehensive assessment, the patient is considered to be safe to go home, referrals for treatment and substance abuse evaluation are in order. The patient is an adult in the eyes of the law, so his parents are not automatically entitled to receive clinical information about him. The evaluating clinician must seek the patient's permission to discuss the findings with his parents but can receive information from them.

REFERENCES

1. Centers for Disease Control and Prevention. National Hospital Ambulatory Medical Care Survey: 2008 emergency department. Updated January 6, 2012. http://www.cdc.gov./nchs/data/ahcd/nhamcs_emergency/nhamsed2008.pdf. Accessed March 1, 2016.

2. Joint Commission. Sentinel Event Alert, Issue 46: A follow-up report on preventing suicide. November 17, 2010.

3. Knoll, JL. Inpatient suicide: identifying vulnerability in the hospital setting. *Psychiatric Times.* May 22, 2012. http://www.psychiatrictimes.com/suicide/inpatient-suicide-identifying-vulnerability-hospital-setting. Accessed March 1, 2016.

4. Jacobs, D, Brewer M. APA practice guidelines. *Psychiatric Annals.* 2004;34(5):373–380.

5. Joint Commission. Resources for Maintaining Behavioral Health Accreditation. February 24, 2014. http://www.jointcommission.org/accreditation/bhc_currently_accredited.aspx. Accessed December 26, 2015.

6. Know the warning signs of suicide. American Association of Suicidology. 2015. http://www.suicidology.org/resources/warning-signs. Accessed October 20, 2015.

7. Publications about suicide prevention. National Institute of Mental Health. 2015. http://www.nimh.nih.gov/health/publications/suicide-prevention-listing.shtml. Accessed December 26, 2015.

8. Recupero PR. Clinical practice guidelines as learned treatises: understanding their use as evidence in the courtroom. *Journal of the American Academy of Psychiatry and the Law.* 2008;36(3):290–301.

9. Simon R. Suicide rehearsals: a high risk psychiatric emergency. *Current Psychiatry.* 2012;11(7):29–32.

10. Simon GE, Coleman KJ, Rossom RC, et al. Risk of suicide attempt and suicide death following the completion of the Patient Health Questionnaire Depression Module in community practice. *Journal of Clinical Psychiatry.* 2016;77(2):221–227.

11. Large M, Smith G, Nielssen O. The epidemiology of homicide followed by suicide: a systematic and quantitative review. *Suicide and Life-Threatening Behavior.* 2009;39(3):294–306.

12. Logan J, Hill HA, Black ML, Crosby AE, Karch DL, Barnes JD, Lubell KM. Characteristics of perpetrators in homicide-followed-by-suicide incidents: National Violent Death Reporting System—17 US states, 2003–2005. *American Journal of Epidemiology.* 2008;168:1056–1064.

13. Suicide by cop. Suicide.org. 2014. http://www.suicide.org/suicide-by-cop.html. Accessed May 20, 2015.

14. Metzi J, MacLeish K. Mental illness, mass shootings, and the politics of American firearms. *American Journal of Public Health.* 2015;105(2):240–249.

15. Weatherston D, Moran J. Terrorism and mental illness: is there a relationship? *International Journal of Offender Therapy and Comparative Criminology.* 2003;47(6):698–713.

16. Busch KA, Fawcett J, Jacobs DG. Clinical correlates of inpatient suicide. *Journal of Clinical Psychiatry.* 2003;64(1):14–19.

17. Runeson B, et al. Method of attempted suicide as predictor of subsequent successful suicide: national long term cohort study. *British Medical Journal.* 2010;340:c3222.

18. Glenn CR, Nock MK. Improving the short-term prediction of suicidal behavior. *American Journal of Preventive Medicine.* 2014;47(3S2):S176–S180.

19. Baldessarini RJ, Hennen J. Genetics of suicide: an overview. *Harvard Review of Psychiatry.* 2004;12:1–13.

20. Fitelson E, Kim S, Baker AS, Leigh K. Treatment of postpartum depression: clinical, psychological and pharmacological options. *International Journal of Womens Health.* 2011;3:1–14.

21. McCall WV. Insomnia is a risk factor for suicide—what are the next steps? Sleep. 2011;34:1149–1150.

22. Weisman, AD. The psychological autopsy. *Suicide and Life-Threatening Behavior.* 1981;11(4):325–340.

23. Anxiety disorders among adults. National Institute of Mental Health. 2007. Updated May 2015. http://www.nimh.nih.gov/health/statistics/prevalence/any-anxiety-disorder-among-adults.shtml. Accessed October 13, 2015.

24. Wong Z, Öngür D, Cohen B, Ravichandran C, Noam G, Murphy B. Command hallucinations and clinical characteristics of suicidality in patients with psychotic spectrum disorders. *Comprehensive Psychiatry.* 2013;54(6):611–617.

25. Ilgen M, Kleinberg F. Substance use disorder, suicide, trauma, and violence. *Psychiatric Times.* January 20, 2011. http://www.psychiatrictimes.com/substance-use-disorder/link-between-substance-abuse-violence-and-suicide#sthash.YkyB9WxJ.dpuf. Accessed October 1, 2015.

26. Linehan M, Korslund K, Harned M, et al. Dialectical behavior therapy for high suicide risk in individuals with borderline personality disorder. *Journal of the American Medical Association Psychiatry.* 2015;72(5):475–482.

27. Reger MA, Smolenski D, Skopp NA, et al. Risk of suicide among US military service members following Operation Enduring Freedom or Operation Iraqi Freedom deployment and separation from the US military. *Journal of the American Medical Association Psychiatry.* 2015;72(6):561–569.

28. Iverson GL. Suicide and chronic traumatic encephalopathy. *Journal of Neuropsychiatry and Clinical Neuroscience.* 2015. http://dx.doi.org/10.1176/appi.neuropsych.15070172.

29. Pedersen T. Recurrent depression linked to smaller hippocampus. *PsychCentral.com.* Retrieved December 27, 2015, from http://psychcentral.com/news/2015/07/06/recurrent-depression-linked-to-smaller-hippocampus/86512.html.

30. Sullivan EM, Annest JL, et al. Suicide trends among persons aged 10–24 Years, United States, 1994–2012. *Morbidity and Mortality Weekly Report.* 2015;64(8):201–205.

31. Drum DJ, Brownson C, Denmark AB, Smith SE. New data on the nature of suicidal crises in college students: shifting the paradigm. *Professional Psychology Research and Practice.* 2009;40(3):213–222.

32. Epstein JA, Spirito A. Risk factors for suicidality among a nationally representative sample of high school students. *Suicide and Life Threatening Behav.* 2009;39(3):241–251.

33. Gould MS, Kleinman MH, Lake AM, Forman J, Basset Midle, J. Responding to suicide clusters on college campuses. *Lancet Psychiatry.* 2014;1(1):34–43.

34. Centers for Disease Control and Prevention. Fatal injury data. July 13, 2015. http://www.cdc.gov/injury/wisqars/fatal.html. Accessed October 13, 2015.

35. CDC. Suicide among adults aged 35–64 years—United States, 1999–2010. *Morbidity and Mortality Weekly Report.* 2013;62(17):321–325.

36. Denning LA, Meisnere M, Warner KE, eds. *Preventing Psychological Disorders in Service Members and Their Families.* Washington, DC: National Academies Press; 2014.

37. US Dept of Veterans Affairs. *Report of the Blue Ribbon Group on Suicide Prevention in the Veteran Population.* Washington, DC: U.S. Government Printing Office; 2008.

38. Zai CC, de Luca V, Strauss J, Tong RP, Sakinofsky I, Kennedy JL. Genetic factors and suicidal behavior. In: Dwivedi Y, ed. *The Neurobiological Basis of Suicide.* Boca Raton, FL: CRC Press/Taylor & Francis; 2012.

39. Runeson B, Asberg M. Family history of suicide among suicide victims. *American Journal of Psychiatry.* 2003;160(8):1525–1526.

40. Bondy R, Buettner A., Zill P. Genetics of suicide. *Molecular Psychiatry.* 2006;11:336–351.

41. Pandey GN. Biological basis of suicide and suicidal behavior. *Bipolar Disorder.* 2013;15(5):524–541.

42. Guintivano J, Brown T, Newcomer A, et al. Identification and replication of a combined epigenetic and genetic biomarker predicting suicide and suicidal behaviors. *American Journal of Psychiatry.* 2014;171(12):1287–1296.

43. Cox Lippard ET, Johnston JA, Blumberg HP. Neurobiological risk factors for suicide: insights from brain imaging. *American Journal of Preventive Medicine.* 2014;47(3 Suppl 2):S152–162.

44. Zai CC, Manchia M, De Luca V, et al. The brain-derived neurotrophic factor gene in suicidal behaviour: a meta-analysis. *International Journal of Neuropsychopharmacology.* 2012;15(8):1037–1042.

45. Hirschfeld RM. When to hospitalize patients at risk for suicide. *Annals of the New York Academy of Sciences.* 2001;932:188–196; discussion 196–199.

46. Saunders K, Band E, Lascelles K, Hawton K. The sad truth about the SADPERSONS scale: an evaluation of its clinical utility in self-harm patients. *Emergency Medicine Journal.* 2014;10:796–798.

47. Posner K, Brown GK, Stanley B, et al. The Columbia-Suicide Severity scale: initial validity and internal consistency findings from three multisite studies with adolescents and adults. *American Journal of Psychiatry.* 2011;168(12):1266–1277.

48. Janin B. Acute suicidal affective disturbance. Clinical Psychiatry News Digital Network. May 28, 2015. http://www.clinicalpsychiatrynews.com/specialty-focus/depression/single-article-page/aas-acute-suicidal-affective-disturbance-proposed-as-new-diagnosis/ba11f5f413d60d417460cb19cc799413.html. Accessed December 27, 2015.

49. Simon RI. The suicide prevention contract: clinical, legal, and risk management issues. *Journal of the American Academy of Psychiatry and the Law.* 1999;27(3): 445–450.

50. Jayaram G. *Practicing Patient Safety in Psychiatry,* 1st edition. New York: Oxford University Press; 2015.

51. Joint Commission. Sentinel report 56. February 4, 2016. http://www.jointcommission.org/assets/1/18/SEA_56_Suicide.pdf. Accessed March 1, 2016.

52. Gutheil TG, Schetky D. A date with death: management of time-based and contingent suicidal intent. *American Journal of Psychiatry.* 1998;155(11):1502–1507.

53. Hunt IM, Kapur N, Webb R, et al. Suicide in recently discharged psychiatric patients: a case controlled study. *Psychological Med.* 2009;39(3):443–449.

INFORMED CONSENT

RONALD SCHOUTEN AND
KIMBERLY D. KUMER

Informed consent refers to a patient's right to make his or her own decisions about treatment, free from coercion, after receiving sufficient medical information from the clinician, and to have those preferences honored by the health care system. In other words, informed consent is a legal doctrine that codifies society's respect for and protection of a patient' s autonomy regarding treatment decisions. The ethical and clinical concepts of consent have existed for centuries, but legal enforcement of the evolving doctrine of informed consent did not begin until the mid-20th century, when notions of individual autonomy began to receive wider acceptance.

Since the introduction of the legal concept of informed consent, it has become an essential element of clinical practice and a possible basis for malpractice litigation, as discussed in chapter 8. In its early years, informed consent was met with resistance by many physicians and other clinicians. It was commonly viewed more as a legal burden than as an ethical obligation or an important component of clinical care. For some, the imposition of informed consent as a requirement impugned the physician's role as a learned benefactor who always knew and did what was best for the patient. Others saw it as yet another unnecessary burden on their time.[1]

The view that informed consent was primarily a legal requirement led many clinicians to believe that it could be satisfied simply by having the patient sign a consent form. But asking a patient to sign a form is not the same as obtaining informed consent; the consent form is merely evidence that the clinician and patient engaged in the informed-consent process. Informed consent is the substantive, interactive process in which the clinician and the patient exchange information through questions and answers and the patient makes a decision regarding the proposed treatment, seeking as much (or little) input from family members, friends, and the treating clinician as he or she chooses.[2] A signed form in the absence of the substantive process does not satisfy the requirement of informed consent.

The essential purpose of informed consent is to allow patients to make their own treatment decisions or, at the very least, to have their preferences honored if they can no longer actively participate in decision making.[3] Deference is given to the patient's exercise of free will and autonomy even if it conflicts with what the majority of other people might think best. Individual autonomy is not absolute. When patients' choices adversely affect the welfare or the rights of others, or are in conflict with other legitimate government interests, the state can exercise its police-power authority. In addition, society's interest in providing care to those who cannot care for themselves allows the state to intervene and provide that care under what is known as the government's *parens patriae* authority. These concepts are reviewed extensively in chapters 6, 7, and 15.

In this chapter, we describe the evolution of the doctrine of informed consent, its essential elements, its application in clinical practice, and some approaches to complicated clinical situations. Before doing so, we set the stage with a case vignette, which we refer to throughout the chapter.

VIGNETTE 1: ASSESSING CAPACITY TO MAKE TREATMENT DECISIONS

Mr. J. is a 21-year-old man with schizophrenia whose symptoms of self-deprecatory hallucinations and paranoia regarding the government are under variable levels of control. One evening, he comes to the emergency room because of abdominal pain. The surgeon on call, Dr. S., diagnoses probable appendicitis; the white blood cell count, vital signs, and physical examination indicate that the patient's condition is still stable, but Dr. S. recommends surgery. She discusses the relative risks and benefits of appendectomy with Mr. J. He refuses the surgery, explaining to Dr. S. that he does not have appendicitis, that his abdominal pain is a recurrent problem caused by a computer chip the federal government implanted in his abdomen. The government did so, he tells her, to monitor his whereabouts, after he refused efforts to recruit him as a spy. Dr. S. asks the psychiatry resident on call, Dr. A., to assess Mr. J.'s capacity to make treatment decisions. Dr. A. recognizes Mr. J. as a frequent visitor to the psychiatry emergency service and an occasional patient on the psychiatric inpatient unit. He greets Mr. J. and asks why he is there. Mr. J. replies that the government has once again been stimulating the computer chip in his abdomen, causing him pain. He acknowledges that Dr. S. thinks he probably has appendicitis and wants him to have surgery but argues that this will not alleviate the problem and will place him at unnecessary risk from the surgery and anesthesia. Mr. J. urges Dr. A. to read his chart, where he will see that Mr. J. has had similar pains in the past, which resolved when he was admitted to the inpatient unit. He explains that the government is unable to activate the computer chip on the inpatient unit because of the structure of the building. Dr. A. reviews the record and finds exactly what Mr. J. said he would find: multiple visits to the emergency room because of abdominal pain, with no discernible abdominal disorder, and resolution of the pain after admission to the inpatient psychiatric unit. No one diagnosed possible appendicitis on those previous visits. He also learns that Mr. J. has not been taking the antipsychotic medication prescribed by his outpatient psychiatrist. Dr. S. states that while this is not a surgical emergency, she is convinced that Mr. J. most likely has appendicitis, is at risk for peritonitis if his condition progresses, and should have an appendectomy. She again asks for a formal capacity evaluation. Dr. A. performs the evaluation and concludes that Mr. J. lacks the capacity to make an informed decision to refuse the surgery.

Before discussing Mr. J.'s situation, we provide the historical context for understanding the modern concept of informed consent.

THE HISTORY OF INFORMED CONSENT

Informed consent has a long history, with its origins traceable to ancient times. Historical sources reveal discussions of consent by philosophers and physicians in the era of Alexander the Great and later on in Byzantine times, with physicians asking for consent before performing difficult operations. Hippocrates advocated seeking the patient's cooperation in combating disease. Plato connected consent with the status of being a free person. The motivation for seeking consent in those ancient times may have included respect for patient autonomy but it could also have been an early form of defensive medicine, fueled by fear of the consequences of treatment failure.[4]

Leaping forward several hundred years, we note that respect for individual choice was a theme of Enlightenment philosophers, such as John Locke, John Stuart Mill, and Immanuel Kant. Locke, an Oxford academic, medical researcher, and political theorist, recognized that an individual's free choice was the foundation of a common representative government.[2] Mill, a Scottish moralist, economist, and political theorist, denied the right of the government or of individuals to infringe on the liberty of citizens without their consent, even for the citizens' own benefit, unless the rights of others were at stake. Quotations from Mill's *On Liberty* appear routinely in discussions of autonomy and medical ethics, particularly in cases involving decision making by the mentally ill.[5] Mill eloquently articulated the view that an individual's autonomy interest is paramount:

> The sole end for which mankind are warranted, individually or collectively, in interfering with the liberty of action of any of their number, is self-protection. That the

only purpose for which power can be rightfully exercised over any member of a civilized community, against his will, is to prevent harm to others. His own good, either physical or moral, is not a sufficient warrant. . . . The only part of conduct of any one, for which he is amenable to society, is that which concerns others. In the part which merely concerns himself, his independence is, of right, absolute. Over himself, over his own body and mind, the individual is sovereign.[6]

Mill went on to write, "Each is the proper guardian of his own health, whether bodily, or mentally, or spiritual. Mankind are greater gainers by suffering each other to live as seems good to themselves, than by compelling each to live as seems good to the rest."[6]

While these passages from Mill are often quoted in arguments for unfettered patient autonomy, Mill's libertarian views were not without limits. He did not believe that women, children, non-Caucasians, or the mentally ill had the right to autonomy. He also argued that the ultimate goal of autonomy did not relieve society of its obligation to help the individual make the "right choice."[5] Mill wrote:

It would be a great misunderstanding of this doctrine to suppose that it is one of selfish indifference, which pretends that human beings have no business with each other's conduct in life and that they should not concern themselves with the well-doing or well-being of one another, unless their own interest is involved. Human beings owe to each other help to distinguish the better from the worse, and encouragement to choose the former.[6]

Informed consent found a legal champion in the English common law courts in the area of tort law. (See chapters 1 and 6.) The courts had recognized the right of people to be left alone, and the touching of another person without his or her consent or justification was referred to as a trespass; it is now called battery.

The first documented account of the tort of battery in a clinical setting was in 1767 England, in the case of *Slater v. Baker and Stapleton*.[2] In that case, the defendants were successfully sued for negligence for failure to obtain consent. The plaintiff had broken his leg, which the defendants set, but he suffered a malunion. The defendants determined that the only hope for straightening the leg was to rebreak and reset it. They did, in fact, rebreak and reset the leg, using an experimental iron device, but without getting Mr. Slater's express consent to do so. The court found negligence, as the standard of practice at the time was to obtain consent before administering such a treatment. The court took special exception to such a painful and violent laying on of hands when the patient had not been given the opportunity to prepare himself. The rule described by the court in *Slater* was one of simple consent: the treater needed to get the patient's consent for treatment, but there was no requirement that the patient be provided with detailed information.

The law of consent remained largely unchanged until the early 1900s, when the number of cases raising questions about the authority of physicians to render treatment as they saw fit, without meaningful input from the patient, began to increase. One of the most famous judicial pronouncements regarding the fundamental right to make one's own medical decisions was by the New York Court of Appeals in *Schloendorff v. Society of New York Hospital.*[7] In that case, Schloendorff had agreed to be examined under anesthesia to determine whether a uterine tumor was malignant but had indicated that no surgery was to be performed, whether or not the tumor was malignant. The surgeon determined that the tumor was, in fact, malignant and removed it. Schloendorff sued the hospital for medical battery. Writing for the court, Justice Cardozo stated, "Every human being of adult years and sound mind has a right to determine what shall be done with his own body; and a surgeon who performs an operation without his patient's consent commits an assault for which he is liable in damages. This is true except in cases of emergency where the patient is unconscious and where it is necessary to operate before consent can be obtained." Justice Cardozo's lofty words and principles did not mean victory for Schloendorff, however. She lost her suit because she had sued the hospital, not the surgeon. The court, invoking a concept known as charitable immunity, ruled that a charitable institution could not be sued.

The growing importance of autonomy and individual choice reflected in *Schloendorff* was counterbalanced by societal deference to physicians as learned persons whose goal was to relieve suffering and cure illness. By the middle of the 20th century, physicians had come to be viewed as respected authority figures, and medical paternalism was the rule,[8] as was the adequacy of bare-bones, or simple, consent. Physicians were given deference not only in clinical matters but also in the pursuit of medical knowledge through experimentation on human subjects, which was often done without their consent. Physician researchers in Nazi Germany represented the lowest point in experimentation on human subjects with their horrific "research" on concentration-camp prisoners during the World War II era. After the war, Nazi war crimes were prosecuted at the Nuremberg Trials. These trials led to the establishment of the Nuremberg Code, which articulated basic ethical, moral, and legal principles that must be observed in medical experimentation with human beings.[2] An essential aspect of the code was consent.

The shift from simple to informed consent occurred in the mid-20th century in the United States. This shift was fueled by a number of societal forces, not the least of which were the civil rights movement, the increasing emphasis on individual liberties, and distrust of authority figures (including physicians).

It was in 1957 that the court in *Salgo v. Leland Stanford Jr. University Board of Trustees*[9] gave birth to the legal concept of informed consent. Salgo suffered paralysis of his lower extremities after undergoing transthoracic aortography—a rare but known complication of the procedure. He brought suit against the hospital and physician, alleging, among other things, lack of adequate consent. Salgo had consented to the procedure but had not been informed of the potential complications. The court held, "A physician violates his duty to his patient and subjects himself to liability if he withholds any facts which are necessary to form the basis of an intelligent consent by the patient to the proposed treatment. Likewise the physician may not minimize the known dangers of a procedure or operation in order to induce his patient's consent." With that, the court imposed on physicians an affirmative duty to disclose information in order to enable the patient to provide informed consent. It should be noted, however, that the *Salgo* court was not prepared to withdraw all deference to the judgment of physicians. The court held that "the physician has . . . discretion [to withhold alarming information from the patient] consistent, of course, with the full disclosure of the facts necessary to an informed consent." Withholding of information to avoid worsening a patient's physical or mental condition, known as therapeutic privilege, survives as an exception to informed consent even today, as we discuss below.

In 1960, two additional courts held that physicians breached the standard of care by failing to disclose the risks of treatments. In *Mitchell v. Robinson*,[10] the Missouri Supreme Court held that the plaintiff should have been informed about the risks inherent in insulin shock therapy. In *Natanson v. Kline*, the Kansas Supreme Court described the physician's duty as requiring "a reasonable disclosure . . . of the nature and probable consequences of the suggested or recommended . . . treatment, and . . . a reasonable disclosure of the dangers within his knowledge which were incident to, or possible in, the treatment he proposed to administer."[11] The amount and nature of the information to be shared were to be determined on the basis of what other physicians in the same specialty and locale would disclose under the circumstances. This became known as the professional standard of disclosure.

As the doctrine of informed consent spread, states adopted different standards for determining how much information was to be disclosed. Some commentators and courts were concerned that physicians were not disclosing information that was sufficient to enable patients to make meaningful choices in their care. A further concern was that the professional standard was defined by what practitioners usually did and focused on the content of the disclosure rather than on the patient's understanding of the information.[3] The result was the development of the materiality standard of disclosure: rather than rely on the medical profession to set the standard through the testimony of expert witnesses, the courts would consider the information that was objectively necessary for the average or reasonable person (see chapter 6) to be able to make a decision under the circumstances. A 1972 case, *Canterbury v. Spence*,[12] is commonly cited as the source of the more patient-oriented objective materiality standard.

In subsequent decisions, other courts further refined the materiality standard and provided for greater autonomy of the individual patient by applying a subjective standard of disclosure. This standard requires disclosure of information that the patient in question would find material to the decision. Still other courts chose to combine the standards of disclosure. Under this hybrid standard, the court looks at the standard of practice in the community, objective or subjective materiality, and the requirements under the circumstances.

As of 2007, just over half the states used the materiality standard (objective or subjective), with a minority of states using the professional standard. A still smaller group of states use a combined standard. The various standards are summarized in Table 5.1. As always, you should check the standard that applies in the jurisdiction in which you are practicing.

Massachusetts uses the subjective standard for informed consent but can be counted as one of those jurisdictions that apply a combined model. In *Precourt v. Frederick*,[13] the state's highest court held that determining how much information must be provided for full informed consent requires a balancing of and an accommodation among the patient's right to know and society's interest that medicine be practiced "without unrealistic and unnecessary burdens on practitioners." The court applied that standard in holding that a physician need not warn the patient of every possible rare side effect of a treatment (in this case, aseptic necrosis of the femoral heads after treatment with steroids to decrease inflammation in order to allow possibly sight-saving surgery). Furthermore, the court held that in order to prove malpractice based on lack of informed consent, the plaintiff

TABLE 5.1. Legal Standards for the Information That Must Be Provided as Part of the Informed-Consent Process

Standard	Required Information
Objective materiality	Information that a reasonable patient would find material in making a decision
Subjective materiality	Information that the patient in question would find material in making a decision
Professional	Information that reasonable practitioners would provide under the circumstances
Combined	Professional standard plus objective or subjective materiality plus reasonableness of the burden on clinicians

must prove that he or she would have rejected the treatment had the additional information been provided.

Whether information is or is not material is not always obvious. Information contained in the "black box warning" required by the Food and Drug Administration (FDA) for certain medications is considered material to a patient's decision making. Disclosure of the existence of the warning and discussion of its contents are consistent with the standard of care. However, use of an FDA-approved medication for an off-label purpose is not necessarily considered to be material information. That said, it is beneficial, from both clinical and risk-management perspectives, to tell a patient that a medication is not approved by the FDA for the purpose for which it is being prescribed and to explain why it is being used in this way, as part of the general informed-consent discussion.

As the concept of informed consent has evolved, so have views about which patients are entitled to its benefits. Mill, Justice Cardozo, and the vast number of other judges and commentators believed that autonomy and the exercise of individual preferences belonged only to those who had the capacity to exercise choice. The mentally ill, for example, were assumed to lack the ability to make informed decisions on their own, and this task was taken on by family members or treating clinicians. This was true even after the seminal informed-consent cases of the 1960s.

For example, in the early days of informed consent, Mr. J. in our vignette would have had little say in his treatment. He would probably have been presumed to be incompetent because of his mental illness. As a result, little thought would have been given to seeking Mr. J.'s informed consent, and the surgery might well have been performed in the absence of informed consent. Instead, the treatment team would have sought the consent of Mr. J.'s family members. Had Mr. J. agreed to the surgery, the surgeon might have proceeded, under the assumption that if Mr. J. was agreeing with the recommended treatment, he must be competent. Had he refused the treatment, the surgeon would have found someone else to give consent, unless one of the exceptions to informed consent, discussed below, applied.

While vestiges of that approach survive today, evolving notions of autonomy and the growth of patient advocacy led to radical changes in many jurisdictions regarding the rights of the mentally ill to make their own treatment decisions.[14] This was particularly true when it came to decisions about treatment with antipsychotic medication, a topic covered in detail in chapter 7.

More than 50 years after the development of the legal doctrine of informed consent, the law is clear that all adults, including those with mental illness, those with physical disabilities, and the elderly, are presumed to be able to make their own treatment decisions. Incapacity must be established before a person can be deprived of the opportunity to make his or her own decisions, and only a judge can declare someone legally incompetent.

THE ELEMENTS OF INFORMED CONSENT

Informed consent has three elements: information, voluntariness, and capacity. We explore each of these in turn.

Information

How much information must be provided to the patient in order for consent to be truly informed? From both clinical and risk-management perspectives, it is generally the case that the more information provided, the better. Full disclosure of every possible risk is obviously unrealistic and prohibitive for the physician and is generally unnecessary from the patient's perspective, as the Massachusetts Supreme Judicial Court acknowledged in *Precourt v. Frederick*.[13] As noted above, jurisdictions differ as to whether they apply the professional standard, an objective or subjective materiality standard, or a combination of standards.

How much information needs to be provided to Mr. J. in our vignette, under each of the standards? Under the professional standard, the amount of information to be provided is determined by the amount that other clinicians in the same circumstances would generally provide. Thus, in the case of Mr. J., the information that should be provided is the information that the average surgeon in the community would provide under similar circumstances if he or she were treating Mr. J.

In jurisdictions that use the objective materiality standard, the challenge is to understand the mind of the mythical "reasonable person." Even if Mr. J. has particular life experiences and preferences that might shape his decision, the obligation is to provide the information that a reasonable person would find material in deciding whether or not to have surgery. Such factors include the risks of infection, hemorrhage, prolonged disability, and death. The subjective materiality standard does not make it much easier, as the clinician must attempt to discern what information, above and beyond that which a reasonable person would want to know, would be material to Mr. J. However, Dr. S. can at least explore with Mr. J. what is important to him as they go through the informed-consent process. Whether the objective or subjective materiality standard applies, the likelihood of fully informed consent is increased when the clinician knows the patient and they have worked together before.

Determining how much information to provide can be confusing, largely because these are legal requirements. We suggest that you look at the legal standard as the minimum standard and instead focus on the elements of good clinical care, which include building a relationship through the sharing of information that will help the patient understand and participate in the decision-making process. The court in *Harnish v. Children's Hospital Medical Center*[15] listed six items of information to be covered by clinicians in Massachusetts. Coverage of these points during the informed-consent process should serve all clinicians well, regardless of the formal standard applied in the local jurisdiction. Indeed, if this information is provided in the course of the informed-consent discussion, the risk of ever falling short of the legal requirement is minimal. These are the six items:

1. The diagnosis and nature of the condition being treated;
2. The benefits that the patient can reasonably expect from the proposed treatment;
3. The nature and probability of the material risks involved in the treatment;
4. The inability to predict the results of the treatment;
5. The potential irreversibility of the procedure;
6. The likely results, risks, and benefits of alternative treatments and no treatment.

Dr. S., the surgeon in the vignette, might convey this information to Mr. J. as follows:

1. I believe you have appendicitis, an inflammation of your appendix, which is part of your intestine. If it gets worse, which it is likely to do, it could rupture, causing a much worse infection, called peritonitis, in the lining of your abdomen. Peritonitis could be fatal.
2. If we do the surgery, which we will try to do using small incisions with an instrument called a laparoscope, your abdominal pain should get better. We will also give you antibiotics to treat the infection. The surgery is important because the infection is in the appendix, and it is difficult to stop the infection just with medicine.
3. The risks of the procedure are relatively small, but they include bleeding, infection, and the risks of anesthesia, which the anesthesiologist will discuss with you. Depending on what we see when we go in with the laparoscope, we may need to make a larger incision, which will require more time to heal. The risk of death is extremely low in a procedure like this, but it does exist.
4. Very few things are certain in medicine. I believe that this surgery will clear up your abdominal pain and prevent you from having a much more serious infection. There is some chance that once we do the operation we will find that your appendix was not infected. The appendix does not perform an important function in

your body, so losing it will not harm you, apart from the discomfort of the surgery, and it will prevent you from having appendicitis in the future.

5. Once your appendix is out, we can't put it back, even if it is healthy.

6. Alternative treatments include giving you a course of antibiotics and watching to see whether the infection clears up. If it does, we might be able to avoid surgery. The problem is that the antibiotics may suppress the infection for a time, but the infection could then come back full force, once again putting you at risk for a very serious abdominal infection. The other possibility is to do nothing, but if we do nothing, there is a risk of peritonitis, and possibly death, as we discussed.

As noted above, informed consent is not a one-way street; it is a process of communicating information. The information provided by the treater is just the starting point and must be shaped in response to the patient's (or other decision maker's) questions. It is a dialogue, not a soliloquy. So for each of these six elements of information, Dr. S. should inquire whether Mr. J. has any questions, respond to them, and then document those questions and how they were answered.

Information other than that related to the diagnosis and proposed treatment is considered material to the patient's decision-making process.[16] In *Johnson v. Kokemoor*,[17] the Supreme Court of Wisconsin held that a physician must disclose his or her inexperience with respect to the procedure or treatment being offered, as information that can affect morbidity and mortality is material to the patient's decision-making process.

A clinician's actual or potential financial interests arising from a procedure have also been considered material information in obtaining a patient's consent. In *Moore v. Regents of the University of California*,[18] the Supreme Court of California held that, "A physician must disclose personal interests unrelated to the patient's health, whether research or economic, that may influence the physician's professional judgment and that a physician's failure to disclose such interests may give rise to a cause of action for performing medical procedures without informed consent or breach of fiduciary duty." In that case, a physician at UCLA Medical Center was treating Moore for hairy-cell leukemia. Over a number of years of treatment, Moore underwent a splenectomy and had multiple tissue samples collected. He eventually learned that his physician, in concert with the Regents of the University of California and two pharmaceutical companies, had patented and were profiting from a cell line developed from his tissue. While the court held that Moore was not entitled to profits from anything done with his discarded tissue, it also held that he should have been informed that the physician's interests in collecting tissue samples from him were financial, as well as clinical. Even though the disclosure of research and economic interests might dissuade the patient from choosing the best treatment, California law does not allow the physician discretion in deciding what to disclose: "It is the prerogative of the patient, not the physician, to determine for himself the direction in which he believes his interests lie."[18]

Voluntariness

The second element of informed consent is the voluntary nature of the patient's decision regarding treatment. In other words, the patient must not be coerced or unduly influenced by the clinician proposing the treatment. The line between overt coercion and more subtle persuasive influences of an everyday nature is the subject of much debate. There is a noteworthy difference between coercion and persuasion, however. With coercion, the aim is to use pressure or threats to compel the patient to make a desired decision. With persuasion, the aim is to use the patient's reasoning to arrive at a desired decision.[19] Although it is ethically and legally acceptable for treatment providers to attempt to persuade a patient to accept a recommended treatment option, it is unacceptable to coerce the patient to accept a treatment through threats of retaliation or abandonment.[3] For example, it would be coercion if Dr. S. told Mr. J. that he could never be treated in that hospital again if he refused the surgery. On the other hand, a lengthy discussion in which Dr. S. tried to convince Mr. J. that the surgery was in his best interests would be persuasion, even though it delayed Mr. J.'s departure from the emergency room.

This raises the question of whether a patient who refuses care deemed necessary by the treatment team can be kept from leaving the hospital. If the patient retains decision-making capacity, discussed below, he or she must be allowed to sign out against medical advice, even in an emergency. If the patient does not retain capacity but has previously stated that he or she would not want a specific treatment, the clinician may still be required to honor that preference, even in the case of a life-threatening emergency.[20]

It is also important to differentiate between coercion by treatment providers and coercion by family members or other important figures in patients' lives. These coercive efforts on the part of parties outside the treatment relationship are weighed differently in terms of evaluating the voluntary component of the informed-consent process. Family members have the right to make demands as conditions for continuing relations, and patients may make decisions based on these demands. Unless the treatment team has evidence of the patient's incapacity and also has evidence that those who are exercising a coercive influence have objectives that are contrary to the best interests of the patient, the patient's consent under such coercive influence usually meets both legal and ethical standards for valid consent.[2]

Capacity

While adequate information and voluntariness are essential for valid consent, capacity is truly the threshold issue. No matter how detailed the information provided or how willingly the patient agrees to the recommended treatment, the consent is not valid if the person giving it lacks the capacity to make an informed decision. That means that the patient must have the cognitive capacity to use the information that has been disclosed, be able to comprehend how it relates to his or her situation, and be able to process the potential ramifications of his or her decisions in a rational manner, free of delusion or a mistaken understanding of the facts caused by cognitive or other impairment.[3]

Psychiatrists and psychologists are frequently asked to evaluate a patient's ability to make treatment decisions. More often than not, this request is triggered by a patient's refusal to accept offered treatment; a patient's acceptance of recommended treatment is much less likely to stimulate a request for an evaluation of the patient's ability to make decisions. As noted earlier, this probably reflects a tendency on the part of clinicians to view a patient who accepts our recommendations as rational and one who rejects them as irrational. Over the past 25 years, however, there has been a gradual increase in the proportion of competency evaluations that are requested to assess a patient's capacity to consent to (as opposed to refuse) treatment.

The request for evaluation of a patient's decision-making capacity (ability to make treatment decisions) is frequently referred to as a request for a "competency evaluation." It is important to note the difference between the terms "capacity" and "competence" and how the use of these terms is changing.

Competence is a legal term that refers to a person's ability to exercise the rights and responsibilities of an adult.[3] All adults are presumed to be competent, whereas minors (as defined by age, which varies from one jurisdiction to another) are presumed to be incompetent. The issue of the competence of minors is addressed in detail in chapters 11 (on children) and 6 (on guardianship), as is the question of what happens when a person is found to be legally incompetent.

Capacity, on the other hand, is the ability to engage in specific or general categories of activities, such as making decisions about treatment. A capacity assessment made by health care professionals is a clinical evaluation of a person's ability to perform a task or execute a set of functions.[21] The clinical judgment that a patient lacks decision-making capacity, although it may lead to judicial proceedings for a competence determination and may be used to assist the court in making this determination, is not synonymous with and does not alter the patient's legal status.[5]

Only a judge can declare someone incompetent, and that occurs only if there is strong evidence to refute the presumption of competence.[5] If the judge declares a person globally incompetent, that person loses his or her status as a legal person and cannot engage in activities that are part of living a normal life and functioning in society (e.g., making treatment decisions or undertaking financial obligations). For that reason, judges tend to be more circumspect in declaring someone incompetent, instead considering specific competencies.

There is a trend for the courts to refer to a person as possessing or lacking certain abilities or capacities, instead of using the term "competence." Despite such changes in terminology, it remains important for clinicians to keep in mind that a clinical determination that a patient has cognitive or other deficits rendering him or her unable to make decisions does not alter that person's legal status; it merely signals that an alternative decision-making mechanism needs to be initiated. This process is described in more detail in chapter 6, on guardianship.

ASSESSING DECISION-MAKING CAPACITY

There are different models for assessing decision-making capacity, but the one developed by Appelbaum and Grisso is extremely useful and widely accepted.[3,22] Their model has four essential components that Dr. A. would use in his assessment of Mr. J.'s capacity. First, does the patient express a choice or preference? Mr. J. has clearly expressed a choice by declining the surgery. If he had been unwilling or unable to communicate a preference, there would have been a presumption of incapacity. Likewise, if he had vacillated in his choice, agreeing one hour and refusing the next, Dr. A. could have concluded that capacity was lacking. The ability to express a preference is not sufficient to establish capacity, but the inability to do so is a threshold criterion that is sufficient to establish the lack of capacity.[5]

Second, does the patient have a layperson's factual understanding of the basic and relevant information concerning his or her medical condition; the treatment options proposed; cause-and-effect relationships; the probabilities of risks, benefits, and prognoses; and his or her role as a decision maker? In essence, this component examines the patient's understanding of the basic facts concerning his or her medical situation. In Mr. J.'s case, that would mean determining whether he understood the information provided to him, as described above: "You have appendicitis. It is likely to get worse unless we do surgery, and if it gets worse and your appendix ruptures, you could become very sick and possibly die. Dr. S. wants to do a surgical procedure to remove the appendix with an instrument that requires only small incisions, but it may be necessary to make a larger incision."

In deciding whether Mr. J. has this level of understanding, Dr. A. would consider whether he has detected difficulties in Mr. J.'s cognitive functioning that affect his ability to comprehend the information disclosed by the physician. This could include marked intellectual disability or cognitive disorganization due to psychosis, delirium, or dementia. The ability to remember what one has been told is an essential feature of comprehension, and it is important to determine whether the patient is able to recall relevant information at the time the treatment decision is made.[5]

Third, does the patient appreciate and acknowledge the personal significance of the information presented, including the seriousness of his or her situation and the potential consequences of treatment decisions? This component, appreciation, is sometimes viewed as an understanding that goes beyond a factual grasp of consequences to a sense of what the consequences would really involve. An assessment that the patient fails to appreciate the significance of the information presented must be based on evidence that the patient's belief system is irrational, unrealistic, or a considerable distortion of reality, as a consequence of impaired cognition or affect.[3] Disagreement with the clinician is not a basis for concluding that the patient does not appreciate the significance of the information presented. It is not the patient's ultimate choice that is questioned but rather the underlying belief system on which that choice is based.

In determining whether Mr. J. appreciates the significance of the information that has been presented to him, Dr. A. would determine whether he had any potentially false beliefs as a result of denial, distortion, or delusions that might lead him to believe that what he has been told about his diagnosis and the proposed treatment is not true for him.[3] His belief that the government planted a computer chip in his abdomen is certainly a delusion, and his conclusion that his abdominal pain is the result of this device is obviously mistaken, even if he is correct and Dr. S. is wrong about the appendicitis. His belief that the government-inserted computer chip is the cause of his pain leads him to deny that he could have appendicitis, thus preventing him from appreciating the implications of his decision to refuse the treatment.

Finally, can the patient rationally manipulate the information in a meaningful and logical way to arrive at a decision? Rational people are entitled to make choices that many of us would consider irrational. This is the essence of individual autonomy.[3] This element of the capacity assessment looks at how the person makes the decision in question. It focuses on the process of decision making, not on the decision itself.

The reasoning process by which Mr. J. decides to refuse surgery is, arguably, rational. He has a deeply held belief that his pain is due to an implanted computer chip and that the pain will go away if he can be in a place where the chip cannot be stimulated by the federal government. In support of this belief, he offers evidence that he has had abdominal pain in the past and that it resolved when he was admitted to the inpatient psychiatric unit. In this case, the patient's underlying delusional beliefs undermine his rationality and make him unable to consider that he may have a true medical condition.

The most common causes of incapacity in the general hospital setting are delirium, dementia, and psychosis.[14,23] Contrary to common assumptions, depression is not a major contributor to decision-making incapacity.[24,25] Among cancer patients in an outpatient setting, impaired capacity has been found to be associated with older age, a relatively low level of education, and cognitive impairment. The evaluator should be mindful that the condition leading to incapacity may be treatable or remediable through education and that incapacity may therefore be temporary.

Religious beliefs pose a particular challenge in assessing the rational basis of decision making. Such beliefs are based on faith rather than logic or empirical proof. Religious beliefs are, by definition, neither rational nor irrational.[3] Until the mid-20th century, when autonomy became what Professor Alan Stone of Harvard Law School has referred to as medicine's "ethical trump card," society gave great deference to religious beliefs, placing them beyond the purview of the courts and other administrative bodies.[3] Persons who refuse treatment on the basis of religious belief (e.g., a Jehovah's Witness who refuses blood products or a Christian Scientist who eschews conventional medicine in favor of treatment provided by a Christian Science practitioner) are not considered irrational on that basis alone. Unless minors are involved and there is concern about their well-being, the religious convictions of competent adults are normally respected by the courts. In these situations, it is necessary to assess the genuineness of the religious beliefs, which should predate the medical decision at hand, be held by others, and be reflective of and consistent with the patient's actions in the past.[3] It is also important to ensure that the religious beliefs are related to the current medical problem. When a decision based on religious belief withstands clinical scrutiny, it should be respected, however eccentric it might seem.[3]

Just how much capacity does a person need to have in order to make treatment decisions and give consent? Ethically and legally, we do not require the same level of decision-making capacity for all decisions. Most persons who lack capacity in one area retain their abilities and capacity in other areas. A person whom a judge has found incompetent to stand trial is still presumed to be competent to make medical decisions, and a person who lacks the capacity to make one type of treatment decision may have the capacity to make other treatment decisions. For example, Mr. J. may lack the capacity to refuse an appendectomy but retain the capacity to make decisions about taking psychotropic medication.[19]

How much capacity is required depends on the nature of the condition and the risks of the proposed treatment.[26] Therefore, an assessment of capacity should take into

TABLE 5.2. Requisite Level of Capacity for Informed Consent to Treatment

Patient's Decision Regarding Treatment	Requisite Level of Capacity for Informed Consent	
	Treatment with Low Risk and High Benefit	Treatment with High Risk and Low or Questionable Benefit
Consent	Low	High
Refusal	High	Low

Source: Adapted from Roth et al.[27]

consideration the risk:benefit ratio of the proposed intervention and its possible outcomes.[5] As summarized in Table 5.2, which is adapted from Roth and colleagues,[27] less capacity is required for consent to low-risk, high-benefit treatments and refusal of high-risk, low-benefit treatments. Conversely, more capacity is required for consent to high-risk, low-benefit treatments and refusal of low-risk, high-benefit treatments.[5]

When should a patient's decision-making capacity be assessed? At face value, this question would seem to have a rather obvious answer. However, in reality, the clinical world offers many complex scenarios that make the answer to this question anything but apparent. From their research on decision-making functioning, Grisso and Appelbaum[3] identified several factors that should prompt clinical concern about the possibility of impaired capacity: an abrupt change in the patient's mental state, refusal of a low-risk treatment that is likely to be beneficial, consent to an especially invasive or high-risk treatment with a low likelihood of being beneficial, and the presence of one or more of the following risk factors for impaired decision making: specific diagnoses that can interfere with decision-making ability, old age, suggestive clinical symptoms, and situational factors that are of concern.

With the use of the Appelbaum–Grisso model, Dr. A.'s evaluation of Mr. J.'s decision-making capacity would include a clinical interview, a thorough assessment of the four elements of capacity, and a comprehensive mental status examination. In assessing capacity, it is important to listen to the patient in order to have a clear sense of his or her understanding of the clinical information that has been provided. Inadequate information can result in treatment refusal, triggering the request for a capacity evaluation. The consultant conducting the evaluation may find that the capacity issue resolves, often with the patient agreeing to the previously rejected treatment, once the patient has received additional information about the condition and the proposed treatment.

As noted above, Dr. A. found that Mr. J. expressed a preference and understood the basic facts about his condition and the proposed procedure. However, the examination revealed that he lacked an appreciation of the potential risks involved in his situation.

Moreover, Dr. A. concluded that Mr. J.'s decision making was not rational because it was based on his delusion that a device was implanted in his abdomen. This delusion led him to believe that his abdominal pain was caused not by an infection but by a signal that triggered the implanted device and to conclude that protection from the signal would alleviate his pain.

Structured instruments may be helpful in assessing capacity. A number of such tools are available for capacity assessments, although most of them are limited in their usefulness because they are intended for specific purposes or patient populations. The MacArthur Competence Assessment Tool (MacCAT-T), which was developed to address the limitations of these earlier tools, is a relatively short, structured interview that clinicians can use to obtain critical information about all four elements of the capacity to consent to treatment.[3] Despite the MacCAT-T's flexibility and ease of use, it has some limitations. For instance, it cannot be used with nonverbal patients (patients on respirators and those who are mute or catatonic, delirious, or profoundly mentally retarded). A more extensive overview of the MacCAT-T and other assessment tools can be found in Grisso and Appelbaum's *Assessing Competency to Consent to Treatment*[3] and Grisso's *Evaluating Competencies*.[21]

EXCEPTIONS TO INFORMED CONSENT

There are a few situations in which treatment can be provided in the absence of informed consent. These exceptions to the requirement of informed consent include emergencies, waivers, incompetence, and therapeutic privilege.

Emergencies

Emergencies are circumstances in which treatment without consent is justified because failure to intervene would likely result in serious, imminent harm to the patient. When the emergency exception is invoked, treatment can be provided to prevent serious and irreversible deterioration of the patient's condition. Once the patient's condition has been stabilized, informed consent must be obtained for the treatment to be continued. Had Mr. J. presented to the emergency room with an acute abdomen and fever, it would have been reasonable to invoke an emergency exception and provide treatment over his objection.

If the patient has an advance directive (see chapter 6) or has previously expressed clear preferences regarding treatment, these predetermined choices cannot be ignored or overridden, even in an emergency.[20,28] At a minimum, the clinician proposing the treatment should ask those who know the patient best whether these are still, or would be, the patient's preferences in the current situation.

Waiver

Patients have the right to waive informed consent and defer to the physician's judgment. Such waivers can be explicit or implied. With an express waiver, the patient explicitly declines information or participation in the decision-making process and instead defers to the treater or another decision maker. It is important for the clinician to determine and document that the patient knows that he or she is entitled to make the decision and that the patient has the capacity to waive this right. A waiver can also be implied by a patient's ongoing acceptance of a treatment, even if express consent was not obtained.

Incompetence

Incompetence is another exception to the legal requirement of informed consent. Although the issue of incompetence is closely related to the emergency exception, there are many cases of incompetence that are not emergencies.[2] Who should make the determination of incompetence and how it should be determined are topics of ongoing debates between medicine and the judicial system. These topics are explored in chapters 6 (on guardianship) and 7 (on treatment refusal).

Therapeutic Privilege

Therapeutic privilege is a challenging concept that is infrequently invoked as an exception to the requirement of informed consent. As embodied in statutes in some jurisdictions (e.g., New York), therapeutic privilege allows the treater to withhold information if its disclosure would be physically or emotionally harmful to the patient.[29,30] The purpose of this exception to the informed-consent requirement is to protect an otherwise competent patient from the worsening of a mental or physical condition as a direct result of the consent process itself. This exception is susceptible to being used as a manufactured excuse to avoid providing full information to the patient or as a defense against the claim that informed consent was not obtained.[19] Therapeutic privilege cannot be invoked simply because the information provided might lead the patient to refuse the recommended treatment.[5] In Mr. J.'s case, Dr. S. would not be justified in withholding information about the risks of surgical complications because it would add to Mr. J.'s reasons to refuse the surgery.

NEXT STEPS AFTER A DETERMINATION OF INCAPACITY

What happens after Dr. A. concludes that Mr. J. lacks decision-making capacity? There are several options, which vary according to the jurisdiction and are influenced by factors such as the expected duration of incapacity and the nature of the proposed treatment.[28]

In the case of a low-risk, high-benefit treatment that is routine, it is generally permissible to proceed with consent from family members. If the proposed treatment is more aggressive, invasive, or risky, there is a greater need to seek a formal alternative decision maker through the courts.[5]

A patient who is deemed to lack capacity but has not been through legal proceedings is referred to as *de facto* incompetent.[2] A patient who is adjudicated as incompetent (i.e., ruled to be incompetent by a judge) is referred to as *de jure* incompetent. The court will appoint a surrogate decision maker if there are specific decisions to be made and incapacity is expected to be limited in duration. The surrogate is often, but not always, a family member. When there are broader issues of incapacity, the court will declare the person incompetent and appoint a guardian. The incapacitated person is designated as the ward. The guardian's role is to protect the ward's interests, make decisions on the ward's behalf, and be accountable to the court.

Advance directives provide an alternative to the guardianship process in a situation in which a person becomes incapacitated. Guardianships and the development and use of advance directives, including health care proxies, are discussed in chapter 6.

If the patient has an advance directive, it ideally designates a substitute decision maker. Health care proxies and durable powers of attorney specifically designate the person who will make decisions in the event the principal (the person who executes the document) becomes incapacitated. Living wills express the principal's preferences with the intention of guiding unspecified decision makers in the event that the principal is incapable of making his or her own decisions.

Health care proxies and durable powers of attorney are legally binding documents that transfer decision-making authority to an agent through a "springing clause": the agent's authority springs into existence on a determination that the principal lacks capacity to make treatment or other specified decisions.[28] These instruments can be used for end-of-life treatment decisions and instructions, as well as for specific preferences with respect to other types of treatment.[5]

Advance directives are not without problems: there may be a question of competence at the time that the patient signed the advance directive, the patient can cancel an advance directive at any time, the patient must complete the legal paperwork before the document is needed, the directive may be difficult to apply given changes in the patient's medical condition or in the field of clinical medicine, and the capacity of the appointed decision maker may be called into question.[5]

When no advance directive exists, the family is usually approached to take over the decision-making process. Family conflicts sometimes arise in which the court is the last resort for judicial review and the appointment of a decision maker or public guardian.[3] Jurisdictions vary as to whether the substitute decision maker uses a best-interest or substituted-judgment standard for decisions made on behalf of the incapacitated person. These issues are discussed in detail in chapter 6.

Another possible outcome following the capacity evaluation is that Dr. S. could thank Dr. A. for his consultation and then ignore his conclusion and proceed with the treatment. This would be more likely to happen if Mr. J. agreed to surgery and Dr. A. concluded that he lacked capacity. In both cases, by ignoring Dr. A.'s conclusion, Dr. S. opens herself to criticism from both ethical and legal standpoints.

MALPRACTICE AND INFORMED CONSENT

Failure on the part of treaters to obtain consent has provided a basis for personal injury claims for hundreds of years. As noted above, in the mid-20th century, the formal legal doctrine of informed consent became an essential element of the standard of care and a basis for malpractice claims against physicians and other health care professionals. It is rare for a malpractice claim to be based solely on failure to obtain informed consent, as proof of the claim would require that the plaintiff establish that he or she would have forgone the procedure had the full information been provided.[19] In the absence of an actual injury caused by alleged negligence, a malpractice claim based solely on inadequate consent is unlikely to be successful. However, inadequate consent can lead to other complaints about the treatment, increasing the risk of malpractice litigation.[31,32]

The converse is also true: adequate informed consent can play an important role in reducing liability. Through the sharing of information and joint decision making, the informed-consent process strengthens the clinician–patient relationship, reducing the risk that an adverse outcome will lead to litigation.[33–35]

Documentation of the informed-consent process is important. If the consent was verbal, the clinician should write a note in the record stating the information that was provided, the questions the patient asked, the answers to those questions, and the patient's response. While informed-consent forms are required by many institutions, they often contain generic information and do not speak to the specific concerns of the patient. For that reason, we advise an additional note in the record to provide more substance for the documentation of consent.

CONCLUSION

One of the greatest changes in medicine and all of health care over the centuries has been the change in the relationship between those who provide treatment and those who receive it. The once paternalistic relationship, in which all knowledge and authority rested with the provider, has yielded to a relationship in which the patient's decision-making authority is honored and protected on the basis of ethical, clinical, and legal principles. Clinicians best serve their patients, and themselves, by treating informed consent as a process that protects the patient's right to make treatment decisions and reduces liability risk rather than as a burden imposed by the legal system. Completing a checklist of the three elements of legal informed consent—information, voluntariness, and capacity—will fulfill the technical requirements for obtaining informed consent. But true informed consent calls for a dialogue between the clinician and the patient that respects the patient's autonomy and enhances clinical care.

FREQUENTLY ASKED QUESTIONS

What is informed consent?

Informed consent is a process in which the clinician shares information about the diagnosis and the proposed and alternative treatments, the patient has an opportunity to ask questions, and the patient either gives or withholds consent. The signing of a consent form, without further discussion, does not meet the requirements of informed consent. A signed consent form is merely a piece of evidence that the informed-consent discussion occurred.

For what treatments do I have to obtain informed consent?

All of them. Informed consent must be obtained any time a clinician is offering to provide treatment to a patient.

Are consent forms always required?

No. From a legal standpoint, consent can be verbal in many situations. For treatments that are invasive or that pose a moderate or high risk, such as surgical procedures and anesthesia, informed-consent forms are generally required. Individual practices and institutions have their own rules about which procedures require consent forms.

Is there a difference in the standards for capacity for informed consent and capacity for informed refusal?

No. The same functional capacities are required for both. These include the abilities to make a choice and state a preference, understand the basic facts, appreciate the importance of the situation and the consequences of one's decision, and reach a decision through a rational process.

REFERENCES

1. Schouten R. Informed consent—resistance and reappraisal. *Critical Care Medicine.* 1989;17(12): 1359–1361.
2. Appelbaum P, Lidz C, Meisel A. *Informed Consent Legal Theory and Clinical Practice.* New York: Oxford University Press; 1987.
3. Grisso T, Appelbaum P. *Assessing Competence to Consent to Treatment.* New York: Oxford University Press; 1988.
4. Dalla-Vorgia P, Lascaratos J, Skiadas P, Garanis-Papadatos T. Is consent in medicine a concept only of modern times? *Journal of Medical Ethics.* 2001;27(1):59–61.
5. Schouten R, Edersheim JG, Hidalgo JA. Legal and ethical issues in psychiatry I: Informed consent, competency, treatment refusal, and civil commitment. In: Stern TA, Fava M, Wilens TE, Rosenbaum JF, eds. *Massachusetts General Hospital Comprehensive Clinical Psychiatry,* 2nd edition. New York: Elsevier; 2015:912–920.
6. Mill JS. On Liberty; of the limits to authority of society over the individual. In: *The Basic Writings of John Stuart Mill: On Liberty; The Subjection of Women; Utilitarianism.* New York: Random House; 2002.
7. *Schloendorff v. Society of New York Hospital,* 211 N.Y. 125, 105 N.E. 92 1914.
8. Starr P. *The Social Transformation of American Medicine.* New York: Basic Books; 1982.
9. *Salgo v. Leland Stanford, Jr. University Board of Trustees,* et al. 154 560 Cal.App.2d 560(California Court of Appeals 1957).
10. *Mitchell v. Robinson,* 334 S.W.2d 11(Supreme Court of Missouri 1960).
11. *Natanson v. Kline,* 354 P.2d 670(Supreme Court of Kansas 1960).
12. *Canterbury v. Spence,* 464 F.2d 772(U.S. Court of Appeals, D.C. Circuit 1972).
13. *Precourt v. Frederick,* 481 N.E.2d 1144(Massachusetts Supreme Judicial Court 1985).
14. Schouten R, Brendel RW. Legal aspects of consultation. In: Stern TA, Fricchione GL, Cassem EH, Jellinek MS, Rosenbaum JF, eds. *The Massachusetts General Hospital Handbook of General Hospital Psychiatry,* 6th edition. Philadelphia: Saunders Elsevier; 2010:349–364.
15. *Harnish v. Children's Hospital Medical Center,* 439 N.E.2d 240(Supreme Judicial Court of Massachusetts 1982).
16. Iheukwumere EO. Doctor: are you experienced? The relevance of disclosure of physician experience to a valid informed consent. *Journal of Contemporary Health Law Policy.* 2002;18:373–419.
17. *Johnson v. Kokemoor,* 545 N.W.2d 495(1996).
18. *Moore v. Regents of The University of California,* 51 Cal. 3d 120; 271 Cal. Rptr. 146; 793 P.2d 479(Supreme Court of California 1990).

19. Simon R. *American Psychiatric Press Review of Clinical Psychiatry and the Law,* Volume 3. Washington, DC: American Psychiatric Press; 1992.

20. *Shine v. Vega,* 429 Mass. 456(Supreme Judicial Court of Massachusetts 1999).

21. Grisso T. *Evaluating Competencies,* 2nd edition. New York: Kluwer Academic/Plenum; 2003.

22. Appelbaum PS. Assessment of patients' competence to consent to treatment. *New England Journal of Medicine.* 2007;357(18):1834–1840.

23. Mujic F, Von Heising M, Stewart RJ, Prince MJ. Mental capacity assessments among general hospital inpatients referred to a specialist liaison psychiatry service for older people. *International Psychogeriatrics.* 2009;21(4):729–737.

24. Ganzini L, Lee MA, Heintz RT, et al. The effect of depression on elderly patients' preferences for life sustaining treatment. *American Journal of Psychiatry.* 1994;151:1631–1636.

25. Vollmann J, Bauer A, Danker-Hopfe H, Helmchen H. Competence of mentally ill patients: a comparative empirical study. *Psychological Medicine.* 2003;33(8):1463–1471.

26. Schouten R. Informed consent, competency, treatment refusal, and civil commitment. In: Stern TA, ed. *Massachusetts General Hospital Psychiatry Update and Board Preparation.* Boston: MGH Psychiatry Academy; 2012:430–434.

27. Roth LH, Meisel A, Lidz CW. Tests of competency to consent to treatment. *Am J Psychiatry.* 1977;134(3):279–284.

28. Brendel RW, Schouten R. Legal concerns in psychosomatic medicine. *Psychiatric Clinics of North America.* 2007;30(4):663–.

29. Dickerson DA. A doctor's duty to disclose life expectancy information to terminally ill patients. *Cleveland State Law Review.* 1995;43:319–350.

30. Hodkinson K. The need to know—therapeutic privilege: a way forward. *Health Care Analysis.* 2013;21(2):105–129.

31. Krause HR, Bremerich A, Rustemeyer J. Reasons for patients' discontent and litigation. *Journal of Cranio-Maxillofacial Surgery.* 2001;29(3):181–183.

32. Gogos AJ, Clark RB, Bismark MM, Gruen RL, Studdert DM. When informed consent goes poorly: a descriptive study of medical negligence claims and patient complaints. *Medical Journal of Australia.* 2011;195(6):340–344.

33. Gutheil TG, Bursztajn H, Brodsky A. Malpractice prevention through the sharing of uncertainty—informed consent and the therapeutic alliance. *New England Journal of Medicine.* 1984;311(1):49–51.

34. McIlwain JC. Clinical risk management: principles of consent and patient information. *Clinical Otolaryngology.* 1999;24(4):255–261.

35. Collier A. The management of risk. Part 2: Good consent and communication. *Dental Update.* 2014;41(3):236–241.

///6/// GUARDIANSHIPS, CONSERVATORSHIPS, AND ALTERNATIVE FORMS OF SUBSTITUTE DECISION MAKING

RONALD SCHOUTEN AND REBECCA W. BRENDEL

"Every human being of adult years and sound mind has a right to determine what shall be done with his own body."[1] These words, written by Justice Benjamin Cardozo in 1914, are part of the foundation of the modern doctrine of informed consent, discussed at length in chapter 5. But what happens when the person of adult years is not of sound mind? How do decisions about medical care, let alone routine decisions about finances, housing, or other aspects of daily life, get made on that person's behalf? What steps can people take, while they are still of sound mind, to make sure that their preferences are honored, should they become incapacitated and unable to express their preferences and make their own decisions? This chapter addresses those questions by discussing the legal concepts of guardianship and conservatorship, the specific functional incapacities underlying them, and the processes used to establish them, which differ among jurisdictions. This chapter also discusses the use of advance directives and other alternative forms of substitute decision making as a means for individuals to ensure that their preferences regarding life decisions, including finances, are honored when they have lost the capacity to express their choices. Guardianships of children are discussed in chapter 11.

GUARDIANSHIPS AND CONSERVATORSHIPS

In the Anglo-American legal system, decision making on behalf of those unable to make decisions for themselves has traditionally been addressed through guardianships and conservatorships. These are formal legal processes in which a court declares the person in question to lack the capacity for making life decisions or managing his or her affairs and appoints someone else to act on behalf of the incapacitated person. Guardianships and conservatorships are a mixed blessing for those subject to them. On the one hand, the objective of the proceedings is to protect the incapacitated person from exploitation and neglect. On the other hand, the appointment of a guardian or conservator deprives the incapacitated person of the ability and freedom that other adults enjoy in the normal course of their lives, including the right to make decisions about what medical treatments to receive, where to live, and whether to marry or to enter into other contracts.

The roots of the modern concept of guardianship can be traced back to ancient Rome, where it was an established legal concept, and it subsequently influenced early English law. Following enactment of *De Prerogativa Regis* (The Prerogative of the King) in England in 1324, the property of "lunatics" (those who once had reason but lost it) and "idiots" (those without reason from birth) was put in the custody of the king, who would manage the assets and use them to provide for the incapacitated person. This protected the incapacitated person from exploitation and reimbursed the Crown for the costs of support.[2]

Terms and Definitions

The terms used for guardianship and conservatorship proceedings differ somewhat among jurisdictions. In the majority of states in the United States, conservatorships and guardianships of the estate are proceedings to protect the property of a person who lacks the capacity to manage his or her own financial affairs. Guardianships of the person are proceedings that provide for the protection of a person who lacks the capacity to make one or more nonfinancial life decisions, such as decisions about health care and living arrangements.

Some states use the term "guardianship" for both protection of the person and protection of the estate, while others use the term "conservatorship" for both purposes. For example, California's civil commitment statute[3] provides for a temporary conservatorship for persons judged to be gravely disabled. The conservator's job is to make decisions about health care, finances, housing, food, and other aspects of daily living on behalf of the incapacitated person. In Massachusetts, a guardianship is established to address decisions about daily living, including those related to most health care matters, with the guardian making decisions on behalf of the incapacitated person. If the person is also unable to manage his or her finances, then a conservatorship is established. In Connecticut, financial matters are assigned to a guardian of the estate, and personal matters are assigned to a guardian of the person. As always, it is important to know the terms used in the jurisdiction in which you practice, as well as the nuances of the rules that apply.

Regardless of the jurisdictional differences in terms and definitions, the processes are quite similar: a person is declared to lack decision making capacity, and someone else is appointed to make decisions on that person's behalf. In conservatorships, the person appointed to make decisions is the conservator; the person who is the subject of the proceeding has been traditionally referred to as the conservatee. In guardianships, the person appointed to make decisions is the guardian, and the person subject to the guardianship has historically been referred to as the ward. The modern, preferred practice under the Uniform Probate Code is to use the term "incapacitated" rather than "incompetent" and to refer to the conservatee or ward as the incapacitated person.

For simplicity, this chapter follows the majority approach in applying the terms "guardianship" and "guardian" to those situations in which a person has been declared incapacitated with regard to making decisions about matters other than finances (i.e., guardianship of the person). We use the terms "conservatorship" and "conservator" for situations in which a person has been declared incapacitated with regard to managing his or her finances (i.e., conservatorship of the estate).

Standards for Decision Making

Guardians and conservators are charged with making decisions on behalf of the incapacitated person according to one of two basic standards, or a combination of them. The first, and more traditional, is the best-interest standard: what would be in the best interest of the incapacitated person? The second is the substituted-judgment standard: what would the incapacitated person have chosen before becoming incapacitated? As of 2012, of 52 U.S. jurisdictions surveyed (50 states plus the District of Columbia and U.S. Virgin Islands) 28 had statutes that did not specify the standard (or standards) to be used. Six others specified that a best-interest standard is to be applied by guardians and conservators. Eighteen jurisdictions had statutes that included some type of substituted-judgment standard, but 14 of them also directed the decision maker to apply a best-interest standard.[4] Once again, it is important to understand the standard that applies where you practice.

A detailed analysis of the guardianship and conservatorship standards in every jurisdiction is beyond the scope of this chapter. Instead, we highlight the major approaches, one of which should apply in the state in which you practice

CAPACITY

The threshold for appointment of a guardian or conservator is the determination that the person in question has lost the capacity to engage in specific activities. The term "capacity" appears to have been used as early as 1485 in England to describe "mental receiving power, ability to take in impressions, ideas, and knowledge," and an "active power of mind, talent" and had been used 5 years earlier in a legal setting to indicate "legal qualification," just as it is used today.[5] Capacities are assessed on a sliding scale, as discussed in chapter 5 on informed consent. A person engaged in complicated estate planning, business dealings, or investments will be expected to have a higher level of capacity than someone who is making a decision about hiring someone to mow the lawn.

The determination that someone has become incapacitated is often divided into two parts: impairment in decision-making ability and impairment in the ability to take care of oneself and/or to manage one's affairs. As discussed in chapter 5, all adults are presumed to be competent in the eyes of the law. In other words, they are viewed as being legal persons with full authority to manage their lives and relationships, personal as well as business, and to incur and discharge obligations. Only a judge can declare someone legally incompetent or incapacitated, thereby stripping the person of his or her status as a legally recognized agent. When possible, courts avoid declaring a person to be globally incapacitated so as not to deprive that person of full legal status. Rather, courts try to limit declarations of incapacity to the loss of circumscribed functional capacities, such as testamentary capacity (the capacity to make a will), testimonial capacity (the capacity to testify in court), financial capacity (the capacity to manage one's financial affairs), and the capacity to make medical decisions.

It is common for clinicians to be asked to opine about a given patient's "competence," usually in relation to medical decision making. That evaluation is a clinical assessment of whether the patient possesses or lacks certain functional capacities. The clinician's opinion with respect to the patient's capacity, or lack thereof, does not alter that person's legal status. Instead, the clinical assessment provides a basis for the next steps to be taken for alternative decision making, where needed. In most jurisdictions, a determination of incapacity can mean that a family member or friend assumes the role of decision maker for routine matters. When formal legal obligations are involved, such as business transactions or serious medical decisions, or when a patient has no suitable person to serve in the role of decision maker, guardianship or conservatorship may be legally required, in which case the court will use the clinician's assessment of incapacity as evidence to be considered in the proceedings.

Some important changes in the nomenclature and the process of protective proceedings have occurred over recent years, many of which are reflected in the Uniform Adult Guardianship and Protective Proceedings Act (UAGPPA).[6] The UAGPPA is a model statute for adult guardianships and other protective proceedings, written with the hope of establishing uniform protective proceedings in all states. As of 2016 it had been adopted by 44 states, as well as the District of Columbia and Puerto Rico.

The UAGPPA reflects the trend in the law of talking about "capacity" rather than "competency" and focusing on the specific functional capacities that have been lost or retained. This approach promotes the tailoring of a guardianship or conservatorship to the person's needs and preferences, allowing him or her to retain as much independence and freedom as possible. It defines an "incapacitated person" as "an individual who, for reasons other than being a minor, is unable to receive and evaluate information or make or communicate decisions to such an extent that the individual lacks the ability to meet essential requirements for physical health, safety, or self-care, even with appropriate technological assistance." The Massachusetts capacity evaluation form, shown in Appendix 1, lays out the capacities the court considers in determining whether a person requires a guardian or conservator. Guardianships and conservatorships are not permanent; they can be removed if the person under protection regains his or her capacity. The Massachusetts form that is used when a person under protection seeks to remove a guardianship or conservatorship is shown in Appendix 2.

Evaluating Capacity

The evaluation of capacity requires an assessment of the functional abilities the patient lacks and retains, which the court will consider in determining whether to authorize a guardianship or conservatorship and, if so, establishing its terms. Moye[7] describes six factors to be assessed as part of the evaluation:

1. *The underlying medical condition that is causing functional disability.* In addition to identifying the cause, which can include a wide range of disorders affecting every system of the body, it is important to specify whether the condition is permanent or whether it is temporary (i.e., has a reversible cause). Thus, incapacity due to

dementia from Alzheimer's disease should be distinguished from dementia due to delirium. The prognosis and prospects for improvement should be included in the evaluation, as well as the effects of medications and psychosocial stressors.

2. *The level of cognitive functioning.* As defined by the UAGPPA, cognitive impairment causing incapacity is present when a person "is unable to receive and evaluate information or make or communicate decisions." The assessment should note the presence and impact of disorganized thinking, hallucinations, delusions, anxiety symptoms, mania, depression, lack of insight, impulsivity, or noncompliance with recommended treatment.[8]

3. *The person's ability to function on a daily basis, including self-care and medical decision making.* This assessment should include consideration of the person's ability to perform activities of daily living, such as eating, toileting, and dressing, as well as instrumental activities of daily living, such as making health care decisions, managing finances, and carrying out transactions in the community.

4. *Preferences of the individual in question.* This information is important both for preserving the individual's autonomy and for guiding future decision making by a guardian or conservator.

5. *The risk of harm and need for supervision.* The assessment should include the risks that the individual faces if guardianship or conservatorship is not established. Factors that mitigate risk, such as social or family support, should be included. This information is important, in part, because it helps the judge determine the appropriate relative levels of restriction and freedom.

6. *Means to enhance capacity.* The goal of these proceedings is to protect and optimize the incapacitated person's health and well-being. The assessment should consider any measures that will contribute to those goals, such as evaluation for a hearing aid or improved eyeglasses, visiting health services, and clinical treatments of various types.

The assessment of capacity requires knowledge of the applicable criteria, skills in assessing cognition and functional abilities, and a framework to guide the assessment. In a separate article, Moye and colleagues[9] recommend an approach for consultant psychologists to use when asked to conduct capacity evaluations. With some slight modifications, this approach can also be used by treating clinicians to evaluate the capacities of their own patients.

This approach is framed by three questions. First, what specific capacity (or capacities) must be assessed? Is the focus of the assessment the ability to make decisions about treatment, the ability to live alone, or one of the other specific capacities discussed below?

Second, what are the criteria for determining the presence or absence of these capacities? Finally, how will the assessment be conducted? The clinician must not only know the criteria to be used for the assessment of capacity but also decide how to obtain the information required to apply those criteria. Depending on the capacity in question, the possible approaches include some combination of the following: a basic clinical interview, including a mental-status examination and cognitive assessment; a neuropsychological assessment; a medical workup; a review of records; administration of a structured instrument or testing; interviews with collateral sources of information; and an occupational-therapy evaluation.[10] The evaluating clinician should consider carefully whether he or she is actually qualified to conduct the assessment. For example, treating clinicians are often asked to offer an opinion regarding a patient's capacity to drive. The treating clinician's interactions with the patient are limited to periodic office visits or perhaps observation on an inpatient unit, not driving in a car with them. The clinician might legitimately comment on the possible impact of the patient's mental or physical condition on his or her driving ability. Indeed, in some cases, the answer to the question is obvious. If the level of capacity or incapacity is less clear, however, determination of the patient's actual driving ability should be left to a specialized examination, such as that conducted by the state police or department of motor vehicles.

Once the assessment has been conducted, the data must be synthesized and the findings communicated. It is at this point that all the information that has been obtained is examined as a whole. A thorough analysis includes consideration of the information that is known, any gaps in the data that would otherwise inform or alter the findings, and alternative explanations or theories regarding actual or apparent incapacity and its causes.

Treating clinicians who assess their patients' capacities should take advantage of opportunities for reassessment as circumstances change. Changes in medical conditions, family events, or living conditions can influence the nature and extent of any deficits or abilities.

Although guardianships and conservatorships are important legal proceedings intended to protect incapacitated individuals, they come at the price of infringing on individual rights and freedoms. Thus, a governing principle of these proceedings is to use them as a last resort when there is no less intrusive means to protect the patient. Alternatives to guardianships and conservatorships, discussed below, include advance directives and decision-making laws that do not require formal court involvement. If these less intrusive approaches are not feasible, respect for the person and his or her retained capacities can be maximized with a limited guardianship, in which the guardian is granted only the powers that are required for the safety and protection of the incapacitated person, who retains as many abilities and powers of self-determination as possible.

TYPES OF CAPACITY

Vignette: Testamentary Capacity

Ms. P. is a 67-year-old woman with a history of bipolar disorder and numerous psychiatric hospitalizations over the course of her life. When acutely manic, she has responded well to a combination of electroconvulsive therapy (ECT) and antipsychotic medications. In her manic state, however, she typically refuses those treatments, and her physicians and family members take various steps to override her refusal. Once she recovers, she expresses gratitude for her treatment and apologizes for causing trouble, blaming her treatment refusal on her illness. Ms. P. has demonstrated her appreciation for the care she has received by making a provision in several versions of her will to leave $1 million to the hospital where she has been treated. She has arranged to leave the remainder of her estate to her children and grandchildren.

After a long period of stability, Ms. P. has a prolonged manic episode during which she travels impulsively, buys a vacation timeshare, makes down payments on two expensive automobiles although she rarely drives, and marries a man she has met on her travels. While she is a woman of some wealth, with total assets worth just under $2 million, the purchases exceed even her budget and are out of keeping with her usual thrifty ways. Ms. P. also instructs her lawyer to draft a new will, in which she cancels her prior bequest to the hospital and instead leaves $500,000 to her new husband's children to start a cat shelter, $1 million to her new husband, and the remainder to her family members. Two weeks after changing her will, she is hospitalized through the efforts of her children and outpatient psychiatrist.

On admission, Ms. P. refuses ECT and antipsychotic medication, insisting that she feels fine, that the purchases and the marriage made perfect sense, and that there is "lots more money where that came from." The hospital gets authorization to provide treatment over her objections, and Ms. P. recovers. She and her daughter ask the attending psychiatrist, Dr. H., whether he can assist the family in putting some measures in place that would eliminate any delays caused by Ms. P.'s refusal of treatment, should she again become manic. They also ask whether the marriage can be annulled and whether, in the event of another manic episode, something can be done to protect Ms. P.'s assets if she goes on a shopping spree. Dr. H. refers them to Ms. P.'s attorney, but before she can meet with her attorney, Ms. P. has a stroke that leaves her with expressive aphasia and right hemiparesis.

Testamentary Capacity

Testamentary capacity refers to a person's legal ability to determine how his or her assets, or estate, will be distributed after death. The standard instrument that directs the division of assets is a will, formally referred to as a last will and testament. The individual who has executed a will is referred to as the testator. Trusts can be used to manage assets during a person's lifetime, control how the estate will ultimately be distributed, and minimize tax consequences. Logically, this area of the law is known as trusts and estates.

A person who dies without having made a will is said to have died *intestate*. Rules about how the estate is divided up when a person dies intestate, including the portions that go to a surviving spouse, children and other descendants, and other relatives, vary from one state to another. State laws also offer some basic protections for individuals whom it would be unjust to disinherit. Most notably, even when there is a will, a surviving spouse may be entitled to claim an *elective share*, which provides a legally determined minimum inheritance if the surviving spouse is disinherited or dissatisfied with what the decedent has provided for the spouse in the will.

This is a complex area of the law, with rules that address every possible contingency. For example, there are rules governing what portion of the estate will go to a surviving spouse of a second marriage when there are children from the first marriage and the decedent did not make a new will after that marriage. The essential document, however, is the will: a statement by the decedent of how he or she wanted property and possessions distributed after death. Rooted in ancient notions of property rights, laws governing trusts and estates protect a person's control over the disposition of assets he or she has acquired over a lifetime, whether they were earned or inherited.

The extent to which the law favors honoring the decedent's final choices regarding his or her assets can be seen in two aspects of trusts and estates law: the presumption of capacity to make or change a will and the low threshold for a determination of testamentary capacity. Anyone who wishes to challenge the validity of a will on the basis that the testator lacked testamentary capacity will have to overcome the presumption of testamentary capacity. The law favors private disposition of assets and generally discourages interventions by courts after the testator's death to revisit wills. In addition, in order to prevent challenges to a will, many wills include a forfeiture clause, also called a no-contest clause, which revokes the bequest to any person already named in the will who challenges it unsuccessfully. This clause prevents those who inherit less than they had hoped from challenging the will and, should the challenge fail, keeping their original share, even after the estate has incurred the legal expenses of fighting the challenge.

The threshold for testamentary capacity is quite low in recognition of the law's preference for private action to dispense of assets. The general legal standard for testamentary capacity includes four elements. First, the testator must have a general understanding of the nature and extent of his or her assets. This does not require a perfect memory of bank records or property holdings, but rather knowledge of the categories of assets and the approximate value in each category. In Ms. P.'s case, grandiosity associated with her mania appears to have led her to believe that she had much more money than she really did, as evidenced by her statements, her large bequests to the animal shelter and her new husband, and relatively little left to her family members, who previously were to receive 50% of her estate.

Second, the testator must be aware of the persons who would normally be his or her heirs, referred to as "the natural objects of his/her bounty." When leaving little or nothing to a family member who would be expected to get a substantial share, the testator will often include a bequest of $1.00 to that person. By doing so, the testator acknowledges that the person would normally inherit a share of the estate but that the testator has chosen to leave the person only a token amount. Ms. P. leaves something to her children, thus indicating that she is still aware of them. However, she has eliminated the bequest to the hospital, a charity with which she had a long-standing relationship, and instead leaves a sizable amount to the offspring of her new husband to establish a cat shelter. The questionable validity of her marriage, as well as possible undue influence, both discussed below, may also provide a basis for challenging her testamentary capacity.

Third, the testator must have an understanding that the document he or she is signing or executing is a will and must understand its purpose and its effects. This does not seem to have been a problem in Ms. P.'s case, except that she does not appear to have been aware that she was substantially reducing her children's and grandchildren's inheritance when she modified her will.

Fourth, the testator must be free of what is referred to somewhat archaically as "insane delusion." This means that the testator's decision about how to divide up the estate was not made on the basis of a false belief arising from an illness or infirmity. For example, a testator who leaves nothing to his children because he falsely believes they have formed a conspiracy against him most likely lacks testamentary capacity (unless, of course, the existence of such a conspiracy or a reasonable basis for belief in a conspiracy can be established). While a delusion may invalidate a will, testators are entitled to express their own preferences and annoyances, and even idiosyncratic beliefs. For example, if this same person wrote his children out of the will because they have not visited him as often as he would like, this would not indicate lack of capacity. In Ms. P.'s case, her mania and the associated impulsivity and grandiosity arguably influenced her decision making, indicating that she was under the influence of an "insane delusion." An irrational belief may also be the basis for finding an insane delusion. For example, if Ms. P., free of mania, decided to leave her grandchildren out of her will because she believed they no longer cared for her, with no evidence that that was true, her decision might be considered to reflect an irrational belief. On the other hand, changes in affection do happen and are not necessarily irrational or dispositive on the issue of capacity.

Even if a testator meets the criteria for testamentary capacity, a will or trust may be invalidated if the testator was subject to undue influence. Deathbed wills are particularly suspect in this regard.[11] Undue influence is deemed to have occurred if the testator did not act autonomously and was under pressure from or under the overwhelming influence of another individual. Since the standard for testamentary capacity is so low, persons who have serious mental or physical disorders may be deemed to possess testamentary capacity despite having problems that make them susceptible to undue influence. A wide variety of physical and mental disorders can make people susceptible to undue influence, even in the absence of an acute illness. For example, a caregiver may gain the trust and affection of a physically dependent elderly person in order to get some portion of his or her assets. However, courts are unlikely to find undue influence unless there is compelling evidence that the testator was reliant or dependent on the influencing individual in substantial ways and was subordinated to that person's influence.

Treating clinicians are drawn into trust and estate issues with their patients in several ways. Medical students and residents, in particular, may be asked to witness the signing (called the execution) of a will. This usually occurs in an inpatient setting, when the prospect of death motivates a patient to execute a first will or modify an existing will or trust. Witnesses to the signing indicate, by their signature, that they believe the testator was of sound mind and body at the time of the signing. Caution is advised here. The fact that a person executing a will is hospitalized indicates that he or she is ill or injured, and implies that they are not of sound mind or body. By virtue of a clinician's training, his or her signature on a statement that a patient is of sound mind and body carries with it a presumption of authority and knowledge. It implies that the clinician has exercised professional judgment and determined that the testator's physical or mental state is sufficient to execute the document (i.e., that the person has testamentary capacity). Signing as a witness without doing an assessment of testamentary capacity may lead to embarrassing and unpleasant moments on the witness stand, should the will be contested.

In addition, while situations do arise when a will must be executed at the bedside, the circumstances may later be portrayed as suspicious and provide a basis for a challenge to the will.[11] Wills generally must be notarized, although there are a few exceptions. For example, holographic (handwritten) wills may not need to be notarized or otherwise witnessed.

Challenges to wills most commonly occur after the testator has died, requiring a postmortem assessment of the decedent's mental status at the time the document was executed or changed. In order to avoid such challenges and the need for postmortem assessment, it is wise for attorneys and their clients to seek an evaluation of testamentary capacity at the time the document is to be executed. Treating clinicians may be asked to conduct such an evaluation. As discussed later in this chapter and elsewhere in this book, it is better for all concerned if the treating clinician contributes only clinical information and leaves such an assessment to an independent, objective evaluator.

The decedent's medical records will be reviewed in the event of a contested will. Regardless of any active questions of testamentary capacity, the treating clinician should anticipate such a review, especially in the case of elderly patients. The patient's care is best served by an actual description of his or her cognitive ability, rather than abbreviations, which provide little information about a patient's mental state. Shorthand phrases such as "Alert and oriented x 3" do not provide useful clinical information under the best of circumstances and say very little about testamentary capacity. In the event of a challenge to a will, the author of such a notation may be asked to explain why it does, or does not, indicate cognitive ability sufficient to execute a will.

Contractual Capacity

The capacity to enter into a contract encompasses the ability to understand the nature of the agreement, the effect of the contract (i.e., what obligations are imposed), and the subject matter of the contract. As noted above, the more complicated the agreement, the greater the capacity required. Ms. P. made down payments on two expensive automobiles. Arguably, her mania and the associated impulsivity and grandiosity prevented her from understanding the nature of the contracts and what she was agreeing to do (i.e., make ongoing payments on two luxury automobiles even though she rarely drove). In light of this, the contracts might be voidable, and she would then be free of the obligations.[12,13] However, courts must make difficult decisions regarding contractual capacity. For example, if Ms. P. seemed to be behaving normally at the time of the transactions or if there was insufficient evidence of incapacity for an average salesperson to be concerned, there could be a presumption of capacity that would allow the transaction to stand in the interest of fair practice. In addition, the extent to which a seller must inquire about whether a buyer has a conservator may vary depending on the transaction in question, evidence of obvious incapacity, and/or jurisdictional requirements.

Financial Capacity

Financial capacity refers to an individual's ability to manage his or her own finances. This includes the ability to perform everyday financial transactions, such as writing checks, making purchases with cash, making rational purchasing decisions, and being reasonably free from financial exploitation. Financial capacity overlaps considerably with contractual capacity. As such, an individual's knowledge of financial matters, skills in carrying out transactions that can range from simple handling of cash to complex investment decisions, and judgment on financial matters should be considered.[12,13] Ms. P.'s down payments on the automobiles are evidence of both poor financial judgment and lack of knowledge of the obligations she was undertaking by making those payments.

Capacity to Marry and Divorce

Marriage is a specific type of contract, and the capacity to marry and divorce incorporates elements of contractual and financial capacities. In English common law, and in U.S. jurisdictions with outdated statutes, "idiots and lunatics" were prohibited from marrying. The movement toward promoting and protecting the rights of people with disabilities has led to substantial changes in this regard, with a greater willingness to acknowledge that individuals who have limited capacity in some areas may retain capacities in other areas. Thus, states are more willing to consider whether individuals with disabilities have the capacity to marry. However, the criteria for that capacity are not always carefully defined. In general, courts consider whether the individual has the ability to understand the nature of the marriage contract, as well as his or her financial responsibilities as a consequence of entering into that union.[14] Ms. P.'s decision to marry someone she had just met during a period of impulsive travel, while she was under the influence of mania, is open to question with regard to her judgment, her vulnerability to someone who might take advantage of her, and her awareness of the obligations associated with marriage.

With the growth of the geriatric population in the United States, questions regarding the capacity of elderly patients to marry or divorce are increasing. We have evaluated cases in which a 90-year-old woman decided to divorce her husband of 65 years and a 77-year-old wealthy divorced man suddenly married a younger woman whose motives for entering into the union were questioned. The capacity to make such decisions is presumed; it is certainly possible for people of advanced years to decide to get out of difficult relationships that they have tolerated for a long time, to find love, or to decide that a long-term companion deserves the protections that come with marriage. On evaluation, both of these individuals were found to have significant dementia, with impaired capacity in terms of memory, judgment, and appreciation of the consequences of their decisions. On the other hand, we have evaluated other individuals with some cognitive deficits who clearly recognized the commitments they were making by marrying and expressed rational reasons for doing so at a late stage of life.

Testimonial Capacity

Testimonial capacity refers to an individual's ability to offer sworn testimony in legal proceedings. Assessments of testimonial capacity are more challenging than one might expect, as they require determinations regarding the individual's ability to understand an event at the time it occurred and his or her current ability to make sense of the event and incorporate it into testimony. The person's memory for the event in question must be assessed, and he or she must have the capacity to convey those recollections in a reasonably coherent fashion. Finally, the person must be able to appreciate both the requirement that he or she tell the truth and the significance of the oath to do so.[15] Because of the complexity of these evaluations, and the impact that a witness's testimony may have on the well-being of others, this is another capacity assessment that should not be undertaken casually, and perhaps not at all, by the patient's treating clinician. On the other hand, notes excusing a patient from jury duty have less potential for negative impact and are routinely, and appropriately, provided by treating clinicians (These notes are discussed in more detail in chapter 16).

ADVANCE DIRECTIVES

Guardianships and conservatorships are a time-honored, but imperfect, means of protecting incapacitated individuals. As noted above, there is uncertainty about the best way for guardians and conservators to make decisions on behalf of those they are charged with protecting. The latter half of the 20th century saw an increased emphasis on autonomy and civil liberties in all aspects of society. This was especially true with regard to decisions about medical treatment and end-of-life care. Developing case law, followed by statutory changes, such as the Patient Self Determination Act of 1990, reflected the belief that each of us should have our preferences honored not only while we have the ability to express them but even after we have lost the capacity to do so. The Patient Self Determination Act specifies that patients must be asked whether they have an advance directive and, if not, must be offered an opportunity to execute one when they are admitted to a health care facility, join a health maintenance organization, or enter hospice care.

Durable Power of Attorney

A variety of approaches, some old and some new, allow individuals to direct the choices made on their behalf during a period of incapacity. These advance directives allow a person to specify choices and preferences regarding a wide range of events before those decisions need to be made. The oldest of the advance directives is the durable power of attorney (DPA). A power of attorney (POA) is a document that allows one person (the principal) to grant to another person the authority to make legally binding decisions on his or her behalf. Traditionally, that authority lapsed when the principal became incapacitated. The solution to that problem is the DPA, which contains a springing clause: the authority under the DPA becomes effective (springs into effect) only when and if the principal becomes incapacitated. Some states, such as Florida, have merged the POA and DPA so that the POA survives the incapacity of the agent. The essence of a DPA is the appointment of an alternative decision maker when the principal becomes incapacitated and most needs someone to represent his or her interests and preferences. The principal may also choose to include specific instructions in the document that tell the agent what to do in certain circumstances (e.g., withholding life-saving treatment when a medical condition is deemed to be terminal). Some states allow for separate instructional advance directives, often referred to as living wills (discussed below), others allow only for advance directives that appoint an agent, and some allow for a hybrid of the two types.

In some states, the DPA can be used in any situation, including health care. Assuming Ms. P. lived in one of these states, if she had executed a DPA, appointing her daughter as her agent, a finding by her treating clinician that she lacked the capacity to make decisions about treatment would have triggered her daughter's authority to do so. At that point, Ms. P.'s daughter could have authorized treatment, including ECT and antipsychotic medications. In addition, she would have had the authority to manage all her mother's financial affairs. Other states set limits on the use of DPAs for health care decision making, excluding treatments such as ECT, antipsychotic medication, abortion, sterilization, and admission to psychiatric facilities. Some states restrict medical decision making to DPAs specifically designated for health care.

Living Will

As described above, the living will is an advance directive that was developed in response to increasing concerns about end-of-life decision making. It is essentially a document that provides instructions about what is to be done in end-of-life situations. Living wills usually suffer from instructions that lack specificity (e.g., "no heroic measures"), leaving them open to interpretation. These documents are legally binding in some states but not in others. Even where they have no legal authority, living wills can be useful as part of a substituted-judgment analysis, providing evidence of the choices the incapacitated person would have made before becoming incapacitated.

Health Care Proxy

Health care proxies (HCPs) are a specific type of advance directive that allow the person executing the document (the principal) to appoint a decision maker (the agent) whose authority is contingent on a springing clause. In this way, it functions just like the DPA. The proxy is the legal instrument itself, but the term is commonly, and inaccurately, used to refer to the agent. The model statute establishing HCPs provides that the agent has the authority to make any and all decisions that the principal could have made before he or she became incapacitated. Even in jurisdictions that take a strict rights-driven approach to treatment refusal regarding antipsychotic medication, ECT, or hospitalization (see chapter 7), the agent may have the authority to consent to all these treatments—just as the principal could have done before becoming incapacitated.

Two features of HCPs provide a greater level of protection for patient autonomy than the more traditional DPA. First, from a legal standpoint, everyone is presumed to have the capacity to both execute and revoke an HCP. Therefore, execution and revocation can take place even when the principal is apparently incapacitated. This can lead to a situation in which the principal is incapacitated and the agent approves treatment for the condition that is causing the incapacity, but the principal refuses the treatment and revokes the authority of the agent. If this occurs, the HCP can be used as evidence of what the principal would have chosen when he or she had the capacity to make the choice.

Second, the HCP can include detailed instructions about what decisions should and should not be made by the agent on the principal's behalf. Those instructions can include exclusion of treatments that would be likely to be used for the condition (or conditions) causing the incapacity. For example, if Ms. P. had executed an HCP and instructed that she was never to receive ECT or antipsychotic medication, those instructions would have to be honored until such time as a judge deemed that they should be overridden. Such a decision might require evidence that would override the presumption of capacity at the time the HCP was executed.

Treating clinicians are on the front lines of efforts to increase the use of advance directives. As such, they have an opportunity to confirm, or refute, a patient's capacity to execute an advance directive, such as an HCP. Considerations include the patient's understanding of the document and its implications, awareness of the choices available, and appreciation of the various risks and benefits in light of the medical situation and interpersonal relationships.[16] Patients may have the clinical capacity to execute an HCP even if they do not have the capacity to make a medical decision. Moye et al. have proposed a set of criteria for determination of the capacity to execute an HCP, which include an understanding of the implications of appointing an agent, the ability to identify an appropriate agent, consistency with regard to the choice of an agent, and consideration of the risks and benefits of choosing the particular agent, (i.e., does the proposed agent have a history of not fulfilling responsibilities).[16] In general, the threshold for determining that a person has the capacity to execute an HCP is low because the document can be revoked at any time. In addition, when a patient disagrees with the agent, the disagreement invalidates the authority of the agent appointed by the HCP.

Much has been written about the potential value of HCPs and other advance directives for people with chronic and severe mental illness. Proponents argue that use of these documents will reduce coercion in treatment and result in earlier interventions, better outcomes, and preservation of individual autonomy.[17,18] It is not clear that these potential benefits can, or will, be realized, in part because the limited use of advance directives has constrained the research on the subject.[19]

OTHER SUBSTITUTE DECISION MAKERS

Advance directives, of any type, are underused. In their absence, the traditional approach has been to ask the next of kin to make medical decisions on behalf of an incapacitated person, although some states do not legally recognize this authority even though it is used in the medical context. Over the past 20 years, there has been a trend toward the establishment of statutory provisions that specify who is to take on the role of alternative decision maker. Illinois, for example, gives the highest priority to the patient's guardian, followed in descending order by the patient's spouse, adult child, parent, and more distant blood relatives, and ending with a close friend or the guardian of the estate.[20] As of this writing, more than 40 states have established provisions for specifying substitute decision makers.

The appointment of a substitute decision maker is governed by case law in those states that do not have statutes that speak to the question. The determination often turns on the relative risks and benefits of the treatment. Decisions about treatments that are relatively low risk, minimally intrusive, and likely to yield benefits are generally left to family members. As the risk and intrusiveness increase, and the probability of benefits decreases, the law is more likely to require formal appointment of a decision maker and provide guidelines for how the decisions are to be made (i.e., specifying a best-interest or substituted-judgment analysis).[20]

Some states either limit or require additional court oversight for decisions about specific invasive treatments or the irrevocable effects of a decision to withhold treatment. For example, specific provisions and oversight may be imposed in the case of do-not-resuscitate/do-not-intubate orders.

THE TREATING CLINICIAN'S ROLE IN EVALUATING CAPACITIES

In addition to the assessment of a patient's capacity to make medical treatment decisions, described in chapter 5, clinicians may be asked to render an opinion regarding a number of other capacities. That opinion may become the basis for a medical certificate for a guardianship or conservatorship or may trigger the springing clause in an HCP or DPA. As discussed in multiple chapters throughout this volume, evaluations of this type are essentially forensic. That is, they do not have a clinical goal, but instead put the evaluating clinician in the position of rendering a decision that has a primarily legal purpose. Forensic evaluations should generally be conducted by clinicians who have no treatment relationship with the patient, in part because the clinician is ethically obligated to be an advocate for the patient.

In the typical case involving a forensic consultation, such as a personal injury case or question of fitness for duty, "advocacy" on the part of the treating clinician generally means doing what the patient wants. In some cases, a patient who is aware of failing abilities will agree to a guardianship, and an opinion by the treating clinician that the patient is incapacitated does not give rise to a conflict. More commonly, however, the patient is reluctant to accept evidence of incapacity, and the treating clinician's opinion, and potential testimony, to the contrary can be a potentially fatal blow to the therapeutic relationship. In addition, the bias that naturally arises from the clinician–patient relationship may interfere with the clinician's objectivity in assessing capacity. To complicate matters further, rendering an opinion about a patient's capacity may put the treating clinician in conflict with one or more of the patient's family members.

For these reasons, it is generally recommended that treating clinicians not conduct capacity evaluations that have a primarily forensic purpose. Can or should a treating clinician conduct an assessment of capacity for other purposes? As mentioned elsewhere in this book, the answer depends on where the particular evaluation lies along a continuum that extends from a note excusing a patient from work or school because of illness (of course) to expert testimony on behalf of the patient in a criminal or civil case (virtually never). Treating clinicians routinely and appropriately provide notes that support absence from and return to work or school and are obligated to complete forms documenting treatment and progress for disability insurers. At the other end of the continuum, where an assessment of capacity is needed in a court case to address questions of liability, damages, or criminal responsibility, it is ill advised for the treating clinician to take on that task. There are, of course, points between the extremes. As discussed in chapter 16, a clinician can, with the patient's consent, testify as a "treating expert," offering expert testimony while disclosing the limits of his or her information and acknowledging the treatment relationship. A common example is a treating clinician on an inpatient psychiatric service who testifies in support of the patient's civil commitment. (This situation is discussed in detail in chapter 2.)

Where do certificates of incapacity in guardianships and conservatorships stand in all of this? The treating clinician has an ongoing obligation to provide good care and to be honest and as accurate as possible in establishing a diagnosis. The prospect of having to testify about that diagnosis, and the prognosis, in a proceeding that will potentially limit a patient's freedom may have a chilling effect on the clinician's willingness to be accurate and complete. In most cases, the proceeding is aimed at protecting the best interests of the patient. If the patient is agreeable, and there are no family conflicts, the treating clinician's role is often limited to completion of the medical certificate (see Appendix 1). In cases with the potential for more conflict because of the patient's opposition to the proceedings or family turmoil, the treating clinician is advised to restrict his or her role to that of a fact witness, as described in chapters 1 and 16. This may include providing medical records, as authorized by the patient, the patient's representative, or the court. The treating clinician can request that an independent evaluator complete the medical certificate, allowing the clinician to remain in the role of treater and advocate.

CONCLUSION

One of the most challenging events in life is the loss of capacity to engage in activities that were previously a routine part of life. All adults are presumed to have the ability to make their own decisions about health care and finances, to agree to marriage and other contracts, and to testify in court and execute a will. One or more of those capacities may be lost, temporarily or permanently, at some point in life. Society has long had processes for determining the presence or absence of an individual's capacities to make personal or financial decisions and for appointing an alternative decision maker if capacity is lacking. Clinicians play a number of important roles in these processes. The clinician may be the first to notice signs of incapacity in one or more areas and is best suited to identify reversible causes of any decline in abilities. Clinicians may be asked to complete medical certificates for use in formal guardianship or conservatorship proceedings, although in contested cases or those in which the clinician has no knowledge of the patient's abilities to engage in a particular activity, this task is best left to an independent evaluator. Of all the roles that clinicians may play in the determination of capacity, the most important are preparing patients for the possibility of incapacity by encouraging them to execute a health care proxy or other advance directive and counseling patients and their family members if incapacity occurs.

FREQUENTLY ASKED QUESTIONS

I've been asked to perform a competency evaluation of a patient. If I conclude that the patient is incompetent, what rights will that patient lose?

A clinician's conclusion that a patient is "incompetent" does not deprive the patient of any legal rights. Only a judge can declare a person to be legally incompetent or, in more modern language, incapacitated. Clinicians assess a patient's capacity to engage in certain activities, usually treatment decision making. Those clinical opinions are relied on by judges but they are not dispositive of the issue. A clinician's opinion that the patient lacks the capacity to engage in a specific activity is a signal to the treatment team that the patient may not be able to provide valid consent to or refusal of treatment, in which case an alternative means of decision making, such as use of an existing health care proxy, should be considered.

Following a stroke, Mr. J. is unable to do calculations, pay his bills, and manage his finances. He is alert and clearly articulates his preferences regarding his medical treatment. Should a substitute decision maker be appointed to make decisions on his behalf?

Individuals who lose certain capacities may still retain others. Even if an assessment reveals that Mr. J. is no longer capable of managing his finances, it may show that he is otherwise cognitively intact and able to make other decisions. If that is the case, then it might be appropriate for a conservator (guardian of the estate) to be appointed, while Mr. J. retains full authority over his other life decisions.

Mr. S. has been hospitalized for 2 weeks with pneumonia. He is 89 years old and is having difficulty clearing secretions. Mr. S. agreed to DNR status during his previous hospitalization. His family has asked his nurse and the second-year medical resident to witness the new will that Mr. S. is going to execute. One of his sons, who is an attorney, assures the resident and nurse that this is a simple matter and that their signatures are merely formalities. What should the nurse and resident know before they agree to serve as witnesses?

The first thing they should know is that their medical skills and training imply that they have expertise regarding Mr. S.'s mental state and his testamentary capacity. Thus, their signatures on the document indicating that Mr. S. is of sound mind and body will carry greater weight than signatures by lay witnesses. They should not sign unless they understand the criteria for determining testamentary capacity, have examined Mr. S. with regard to those criteria, and find that he meets them. They also should not sign unless they are prepared for the possibility that at some point they may be asked to testify in court that Mr. S. possessed testamentary capacity.

What are health care proxies and how do they work?

A health care proxy is a legal document executed by one person (the principal) who grants authority to another person (the agent) to make any and all decisions on his or her behalf in the event he or she becomes incapacitated. The principal's treating clinician is responsible for certifying incapacity. Everyone is presumed to have the capacity to execute, and revoke, a health care proxy.

REFERENCES

1. *Schloendorff v. Society of New York Hospital,* 211 N.Y. 125, 105 N.E. 92 1914.
2. McGlynn M. Idiots, lunatics and the Royal Prerogative in early Tudor England. *Journal of Legal History.* 2005;26(1):1–24.
3. Lanterman-Petris-Short Act, Cal. Welf & Inst. Code, §Sec. 5000 et seq.
4. Frolik LA, Whitton LS. Symposium: The uniform probate code: remaking American succession law: article: the UPC substituted judgment/best interest standard for guardian decisions: a proposal for reform *University of Michigan Journal of Law Reform.* 2012;45(Summer):739–760.
5. Moye J, Marson DC, Edelstein B. Assessment of capacity in an aging society. *American Psychologist.* 2013;68(3):158–171.
6. National Conference of Commissioners on Uniform State Laws. Uniform Adult Guardianship and Protective Proceedings Act. In: Commission UL, ed. *Uniform Law.* Chicago, IL: Uniform Law Commission 2007.
7. Moye J. A conceptual model and assessment template for capacity evaluation in adult guardianship. *Gerontologist.* 2007;47(5):591–603.
8. Grisso T, Appelbaum PA. The MacArthur Treatment Competency Study III: abilities of patients to consent to psychiatric and medical treatment. *Law and Human Behavior.* 1995;19:149–174.
9. Moye J, Armesto JC, Karel MJ. Evaluating capacity of older adults in rehabilitation settings: conceptual models and clinical challenges. *Rehabilitation Psychology.* 2005;50(3):207–214.
10. Grisso T. *Evaluating Competencies,* 2nd edition. New York: Kluwer Academic/Plenum; 2003.
11. Peisah C, Luxenberg J, Liptzin B, et al. Deathbed wills: assessing testamentary capacity in the dying patient. *International Psychogeriatrics.* 2014;26(2):209–216.
12. ABA/APA Assessment of Capacity in Older Adults Project Working Group. *Assessment of Older Adults with Diminished Capacity: A Handbook for Lawyers.* Washington, DC: American Bar Association Commission on Law and Aging; American Psychological Association; 2005.
13. ABA/APA Assessment of Capacity in Older Adults Project Working Group. *Assessment of Older Adults with Diminished Capacity: A Handbook for Psychologists.* Washington, DC: American Bar Association Commission on Law and Aging; American Psychological Association; 2008.
14. Matloff J. Comment: idiocy, lunacy, and matrimony: exploring constitutional challenges to state restrictions on marriages of persons with mental disabilities. *American University Journal of Gender, Social Policy and the Law.* 2009;17:497–520.
15. Otto RK, Sadoff RL, Fannif AM. Testimonial capacity. In: Drogin EY, Dattilio FM, Sadoff RL, Gutheil TG, eds. *Handbook of Forensic Assessment: Psychological and Psychiatric Perspectives.* Hoboken, NJ: John Wiley & Sons; 2011.

16. Moye J, Sabatino CP, Brendel RW. Evaluation of the capacity to appoint a healthcare proxy. *American Journal of Geriatric Psychiatry.* 2013;21(4):326–336.

17. Swanson J, Swartz M, Ferron J, Elbogen E, Van Dorn R. Psychiatric advance directives among public mental health consumers in five US cities: prevalence, demand, and correlates. *Journal of the American Academy of Psychiatry and the Law.* 2006;34(1):43–57.

18. Schouten R. Commentary: psychiatric advance directives as tools for enhancing treatment of the mentally ill. *Journal of the American Academy of Psychiatry and the Law.* 2006;34(1):58–60.

19. Campbell LA, Kisely SR. Advance treatment directives for people with severe mental illness. *Cochrane Database of Systematic Reviews.* 2009(1).

20. Brendel RW, Schouten R. Legal concerns in psychosomatic medicine. *Psychiatric Clinics of North America.* 2007;30(4):663–676.

MEDICAL CERTIFICATE FOR GUARDIANSHIP OR CONSERVATORSHIP

MEDICAL CERTIFICATE GUARDIANSHIP OR CONSERVATORSHIP	Docket No.	**Commonwealth of Massachusetts The Trial Court Probate and Family Court**
INSTRUCTIONS FOR COMPLETION This document will be used by the Probate and Family Court in the process of determining whether to appoint a guardian and/or conservator to assume responsibility for this individual in some or all areas of decision-making and functioning. If, however, a guardianship or conservatorship is being sought for an intellectually disabled person, do not use this document. A separate Clinical Team Report is required.		_____ ▼ Division

To the registered physician, licensed psychologist, certified psychiatric nurse clinical specialist or a nurse practitioner completing this document:

You must complete this document. If there is any information about which you do not have direct knowledge, you are encouraged to make inquiry of such other persons as may be necessary to complete the entire form. These persons might include other healthcare professionals and/or others acquainted with the individual (*e.g.*, family members or social service professionals). If you receive information from others, the names of those individuals must be listed in the Certification Section and attribution identified.

If you are completing this form on the computer and additional space is required for any narrative section, the section will expand to permit additional information. <u>Do not use medical terminology and/or abbreviations without explaining them in terms that a lay person can understand.</u>

ALL OF THE ATTACHED PAGES AND SECTIONS CONTAINED THEREIN MUST BE COMPLETED.

To the Honorable Justices of the Probate and Family Court:

The undersigned hereby certifies under the penalties of perjury that I am:

- ☐ a registered physician specializing in the area of: _____.
- ☐ a licensed psychologist.
- ☐ a certified psychiatric nurse clinical specialist.
- ☐ a nurse practitioner with experience in the area of: _____.

I am prepared to present a statement of my qualification to the Court by written affidavit or personal appearance if directed to do so.

I personally
examined: _____ _____ _____ _____
                   First Name   Middle Name   Last Name   (age)

who resides at _____ _____ _____ _____ _____
              (Address Line 1) (Apt, Unit, No., etc.) (City/Town) (State) (Zip)

on _____

                         Date(s) of Examination(s)

Prior to examination, I informed the patient that communications would not be confidential.

- ☐ Yes.
- ☐ No, Explain:

1. CLINICALLY DIAGNOSED CONDITION(S) THAT RESULT IN INCAPACITY

   A. Description of mental and physical condition

      Describe the individual's mental and physical conditions necessitating the appointment of a guardian and/or conservator, including the date of onset and disease course.

   B. Stability of mental and physical condition and living setting

      I. In the past 90 days, has the individual's mental and/or physical condition changed?

         ☐ Yes   ☐ No   ☐ Uncertain

         If yes, please explain:

      II. In the past 90 days, has the individual's living setting (i.e., community, hospital, nursing facility) changed?

          ☐ Yes   ☐ No   ☐ Uncertain

          If yes, please explain:

   C. Prognosis for Improvement

      With reasonable medical certainty, within the next 90 days, is the individual's mental and/or physical condition likely to change substantially?

      ☐ Yes   ☐ No   ☐ Uncertain

      If yes, explain whether the condition is likely to worsen or improve, as well as if there are any aggravating factors that could make the individual appear confused but could improve with time or treatment (*e.g.*, delirium, acute medical illness, the interaction of multiple medications, hearing loss, vision loss, bereavement, etc.):

If improvement is possible, the individual should be re-evaluated in _____ weeks.

D. List all Medications (or attach list):

Name	Dosage/Schedule	If an anti-psychotic medication indicate with a checkmark.
		☐
		☐
		☐
		☐

Could any of these medications impair mental functioning: ☐ Yes   ☐ No   ☐ Uncertain

If yes, explain:

2. INABILITY TO RECEIVE AND EVALUATE INFORMATION OR TO MAKE OR COMMUNICATE DECISIONS

A. Alertness/Level of Consciousness

Overall

Impairment: ☐ None   ☐ Mild   ☐ Moderate   ☐ Severe   ☐ Non-Responsive

B. Memory and Cognitive Functioning (e.g., memory, comprehension, reasoning, judgment, planning, insight)

Overall

Impairment: ☐ None   ☐ Mild   ☐ Moderate   ☐ Severe

C. Emotional and Psychiatric Functioning (e.g., mood, anxiety, psychotic, substance use and other disorder)

Overall

Impairment: ☐ None   ☐ Mild   ☐ Moderate   ☐ Severe

Describe how impairments in A, B, and/or C cause the individual to have an inability to receive and evaluate information or make or communicate decisions:

3.1 GUARDIANSHIP: INABILITY TO MEET ESSENTIAL REQUIREMENTS FOR PHYSICAL HEALTH, SAFETY, AND SELF-CARE

If seeking guardianship of the person, complete section 3.1. If seeking only a conservatorship, do not complete this section. Limited Guardianship is preferred by the Court; describe how the guardianship may be limited. Describe how the assessment was performed and give specific examples.

    A. Areas in which the individual <u>is able</u> to meet the essential requirements for physical health, safety, and self-care:

        Describe the individual's retained abilities and adaptive behavior for physical health, safety, self-care for which the guardianship may be limited (*e.g.,* ability to manage ADL's and IADL's such as health, hygiene, home, communication, driving, leisure, social; functioning in the community; ability to express treatment choices and make medical decisions; ability to complete any or some legal transactions).

    B. Areas in which the individual <u>is unable</u> to meet essential requirements for physical health, safety, or self-care: Describe the impairments in physical health, safety, and self-care for which the individual requires a guardian.

    C. If individual is unable to make any decisions for him or herself or is unable to meet any essential requirements for physical health, safety, and self-care (*i.e.,* requires a full guardianship), describe why:

3.2 CONSERVATORSHIP: INABILITY TO MANAGE PROPERTY OR BUSINESS AFFAIRS EFFECTIVELY

If seeking conservatorship of the estate and affairs, complete section 3.2. If seeking only a guardianship of the person, do not complete this section. Limited Conservatorship is preferred by the court; describe how the conservatorship may be limited. Describe how the assessment was performed and give specific examples.

A. Areas in which the individual <u>is able</u> to manage property or business affairs effectively:

Describe the individual's retained abilities and adaptive behavior for management of property and estate for which the conservatorship may be limited (*e.g.*, ability to manage allowance, bills, donations, investments, real estate, protect assets, resist fraud).

B. Areas in which the individual <u>is unable</u> to manage property or business affairs effectively:

Describe the impairments in the management of property and business affairs for which the individual requires a conservator. Describe how the person has property that will be wasted or dissipated unless management is provided and/or how protection is necessary to provide money for the support, care and welfare of the person or those entitled to the person's support.

C. If the individual is unable to make any decisions about, and is unable to manage, any property or business affairs effectively (*i.e.*, requires a full conservatorship), describe why:

4. VALUES AND PREFERENCES

Describe the individual's values, preferences, and patterns, including previously described preferences (*e.g.*, under durable power of attorney, advance directive, health care proxy, or living will documents), whether the individual accepts or opposes the guardianship/conservatorship, where the individual prefers to live, what makes life meaningful for the individual, and religious or cultural considerations.

5. SOCIAL NETWORKS AND RISK OF HARM TO SELF OR OTHERS

    A.   Social Network Relationships

        Social Support (Check one)

        ☐ Very good supportive network   ☐ Some support from family and friends   ☐ Limited or nonexistent support

        Social Skills (Check one)

        ☐ Very good social skills   ☐ Good social skills   ☐ Poor social skills

    B.   Nature of Risks

        Describe the significant risks facing this individual and specify whether these risks are due to this individual's condition and/or due to another person harming or exploiting him or her:

    C.   The individual's risk of harm to self or others is: ☐ Mild   ☐ Moderate   ☐ Severe

    D.   The likelihood of harm is: ☐ Almost Certain   ☐ Probable   ☐ Possible   ☐ Unlikely

6. RECOMMENDATIONS FOR LEVEL OF CARE/SUPERVISION NEEDED, INCLUDING HOUSING

    A.   An institutional placement being pursued at the following:

        ☐ Nursing home/ Rehabilitation   ☐ Psychiatric facility   ☐ Other facility   ☐ None   ☐ Uncertain

        If none, skip to section 7; if yes, answer:

    B.   The individual requires the following level of supervision:

        ☐ Locked facility   ☐ 24 hr. supervision   ☐ Some   ☐ None

        Less restrictive placement options have been pursued:

        ☐ Yes   ☐ No   ☐ Uncertain

        The placement is anticipated to be:

        ☐ Long-term   ☐ Short-term   ☐ Uncertain

Describe the specific reasons for placement and efforts made to preserve the person's social support system (*e.g.*, placement in community of residence or near family):

7. RECOMMENDATIONS FOR APPROPRIATE TREATMENT AND HABILITA-TION: The individual may benefit from:

Educational potential, training, or rehabilitation	☐ Yes	☐ No	☐ Uncertain
Technological assistance or accommodations	☐ Yes	☐ No	☐ Uncertain
Mental health treatment	☐ Yes	☐ No	☐ Uncertain
Occupational, physical, or other therapy	☐ Yes	☐ No	☐ Uncertain
Home and/or social services	☐ Yes	☐ No	☐ Uncertain
Medical treatment, operation or procedure	☐ Yes	☐ No	☐ Uncertain

Other: _____

Describe any specific recommendations:

8. ATTENDANCE AT HEARING
   ☐ It would be clinically harmful for the individual to attend the hearing. Describe why:

   ☐ The individual is able to attend the court hearing
   What accommodations, if any, would enable the individual to attend the hearing:

9. CERTIFICATIONS

This form was completed based on an in-person clinical evaluation of the individual: who ☐ is ☐ is not a patient under my continuing care and treatment.

In addition to a clinical examination, other sources of information for this examination:

☐ Review of medical record.

☐ Discussion with health care professionals involved in the individual's care.

☐ Discussion with family or friends.

☐ Other _____

Names and titles/relationships of those individuals who assisted in preparation of this report:

Name	Title/Relationship

List any tests which bear upon the issues of incapacity and date of tests:

Test	Date

This document must be signed and dated by the person completing it. It does not need to be notarized.

I hereby certify that the evaluation of diagnosis, cognition, and function is within the scope of my professional competence based upon my education, training, and experience. I further certify that this report is complete and accurate to the best of my information and belief.

Signed under the penalties of perjury:

_____   Date _____
      SIGNATURE OF CLINICIAN

_____   _____
      (Print name)   License type, number, and date

Office
Address: _____ _____   _____ _____ _____
      (Address) (Apt, Unit, No., etc.) (City/Town) (State) (Zip)

Office
Phone: _____

MEDICAL CERTIFICATE FOR TERMINATION OF GUARDIANSHIP AND/OR CONSERVATORSHIP

MEDICAL CERTIFICATE FOR TERMINATION OF ☐ GUARDIANSHIP AND/OR ☐ CONSERVATORSHIP	Docket No.	Commonwealth of Massachusetts The Trial Court Probate and Family Court
INSTRUCTIONS FOR COMPLETION This document is to be used by the Probate and Family Court in the process of determining that a person under guardianship or conservatorship no longer meets the standard for establishing said guardianship or conservatorship. If, however, the termination is being sought for any other reason, do <u>not</u> use this document. Instead, the Medical Certificate Guardianship or Conservatorship form is required.		▼ _____ **Division** _____ _____ _____ _____ _____

To the Honorable Justices of the Probate and Family Court:

The undersigned hereby certifies under the penalties of perjury that I am:

- ☐ a registered physician specializing in the area of _____.
- ☐ a licensed psychologist.
- ☐ a certified psychiatric nurse clinical specialist.
- ☐ a nurse practitioner with experience in the area of: _____.

I am prepared to present a statement of my qualifications to the Court by written affidavit or personal appearance if directed to do so.

I personally
examined _____ _____ _____

                 First Name   Middle Name   Last Name

             (print name of incapacitated person or protected person)

who resides at _____ _____ _____ _____ _____

           (Address)   (Apt, Unit, No., etc.) (City/Town)   (State) (Zip)

on _____

       Date

☐ Who is under guardianship and no longer has a clinically diagnosed condition that results in an inability to receive and evaluate information or make or communicate decisions to such an extent that the individual lacks the ability to meet essential requirements for physical health, safety, or self-care.

☐ Who is under a conservatorship and

    ☐ No longer has a clinically diagnosed impairment in the ability to receive and evaluate information or make or communicate decisions, and property will no longer be wasted or dissipated unless management is provided.

    ☐ No longer has a clinically diagnosed impairment in the ability to receive and evaluate information or make or communicate decisions and protection is no longer necessary or desirable to obtain money for the support, care, and welfare of the person or those entitled to the person's support.

Prior to the examination, I informed the patient that communications with me would not be privileged:

    ☐ Yes.

    ☐ No, Explain:

DESCRIBE IN DETAIL THE CLINICAL AND FUNCTIONAL FINDINGS SUPPORTING THE DISCHARGE OF THE GUARDIANSHIP AND/OR CONSERVATORSHIP:

CERTIFICATIONS

This form was completed based on an in-person clinical evaluation of the individual who □ is   □ is not a patient under my continuing care and treatment.

In addition to a clinical examination, other sources of information for this examination:

- □ Review of medical record;
- □ Discussion with health care professionals involved in the individual's care;
- □ Discussion with family or friends;
- □ Other.

Names and titles/relationships of those individuals who assisted in preparation of this report:

Name	Title/Relationships

List any tests which bear upon the issue of incapacity and date of tests:

Test	Date

This document must be signed and dated by the person completing it. It does not need to be notarized.

I hereby certify that the evaluation of diagnosis, cognition, and function is within the scope of my professional competence based upon my education, training, and experience. I further certify that this report is complete and accurate to the best of my information and belief.

Signed under the penalties of perjury:

Date _____   _____

Signature of Clinician

_____

Print Name

_____   _____

(Office Address)   (Apt, Unit, No., etc.)

_____   _____   _____

(City/Town)   (State)   (Zip)

Office Phone #: _____

_____

License type, number, and date

///7/// TREATMENT REFUSAL

ARIANA NESBIT, STEVEN K. HOGE, AND DEBRA A. PINALS

Approximately 10% of psychiatric inpatients refuse antipsychotic medications at some point during their hospitalization.[1-4] These situations are often difficult for treating psychiatrists, as well as for other staff involved in patient care, and can lead to frustration, helplessness, and anger. However, if managed well, treatment refusal serves as an opportunity to gain a better understanding of the patient's concerns, values, and wishes, which in turn can lead to a stronger therapeutic alliance (defined as a cooperative working relationship between client and therapist and considered by many to be an essential aspect of successful therapy[5]).

VIGNETTE 1: INVOLUNTARILY HOSPITALIZED PATIENT

Mr. V., a 22-year-old man, is brought to the hospital by emergency medical services after threatening his father with a kitchen knife. According to his father, over the past 3 weeks, Mr. V. has become increasingly disorganized and withdrawn, and he has been talking loudly to himself in his room. In the emergency department, Mr. V. is malodorous, is responding to auditory hallucinations, and states that he has been hearing the voice of the Devil telling him that he must kill his father. He refuses to sign himself into the hospital, stating that he is not ill. He is admitted involuntarily on the grounds of risk of harm to others due to mental illness. Once in the hospital, Mr. V. refuses to take prescribed antipsychotic medications because he is convinced that the staff members are working with the Devil and are trying to poison him. As the period of emergency commitment expires, the inpatient psychiatrist files for civil commitment, and a judge orders a continuation of the involuntary inpatient commitment, agreeing that Mr. V. poses an imminent risk of harm to his father.

RIGHT TO REFUSE TREATMENT

History

As discussed in chapter 5, all adult patients are presumed to be competent to make decisions about their care on the basis of the doctrine of informed consent and the related concept of informed refusal. In principle, patients voluntarily admitted to psychiatric institutions have the right to refuse treatment, as their voluntary status allows them to choose to leave the hospital.[6] Historically, however, patients involuntarily committed to psychiatric hospitals have had significantly more limited rights than voluntarily hospitalized patients and those in outpatient settings.[2] For much of the 20th century, patients were committed to psychiatric hospitals on the basis of their need for treatment. Involuntary civil commitment was understood to be based on paternalism, with the state exercising its *parens patriae* power to provide care for those with mental disorders. In that context, it was clear that the purpose of civil commitment was treatment, and persons who were in need of treatment for mental illness but refused it could be hospitalized against their will. As a result of reforms in the 1960s and 1970s, however, civil commitment came to be justified by the state's police powers, with the criteria for commitment based on dangerousness.[2,6-8] Since the justification for commitment was no longer the need for treatment, it was possible to question whether the state had the authority to involuntarily treat a patient who had been committed. (*Parens patriae*, police powers, and civil commitment are described in detail in chapters 1 and 2.) In Vignette 1, Mr. V. is committed to the hospital on the grounds that he poses a danger to others because of mental illness, which in most states is not a sufficient basis for treating him against his will.

Legal Criteria

Currently, every jurisdiction recognizes that all patients who have not otherwise been found to be incompetent (or for whom court-ordered treatment is not required for other specific reasons) have the right to refuse treatment. How these rights are defined and managed depends on the jurisdiction, the type of facility, and the patient's legal status.[2,9] There are two legal models for dealing with treatment refusal: the rights-driven model and the treatment-driven model (see Table 7.1).[10]

TABLE 7.1. Procedures for Adjudication of Treatment Refusal, According to State

Procedure for Adjudication	State
Involuntary medication is permitted at the time of admission to a state hospital (often with the requirement of approval by an MD or clinical committee)	GA, MD, MI, MO, NJ, NC, PA, SC, TN, WV
An administrative hearing (not through the court system) is required for involuntary medication	ME, NE, NV, NH
Involuntary medication is allowed upon judicial commitment	AL, AR, AZ, DE, DC, KS, ID, IN, LA, MI, MT, WI, WY, UT
Involuntary medication is allowed upon judicial commitment provided that evidence of the need for medication is presented	MN, FL, IA, OK, RI, WA
Involuntary medication requires a separate judicial hearing, which often occurs at the time of commitment	AK, IL, TX
Involuntary medication requires a separate judicial hearing, which occurs after commitment	CA, CO, HI, KY, MA, NY, ND, OH, OR, SD, VT, VA
Involuntary medication requires a separate judicial order for a guardian	CT, NM

Source: The information presented in the table is from Beinner, 2007.[10]

The treatment-driven model emphasizes protection of the patient's right to adequate treatment during involuntary hospitalization. A patient, under this model, has a limited right to refuse care if it is determined to be inappropriate. Because the standard is based on the appropriateness of treatment, determinations are generally left in the hands of psychiatrists or multidisciplinary panels. Formal judicial review is uncommon. As long as the treatment is deemed appropriate by the reviewer, it will be allowed to proceed. Federal courts tend to favor the treatment-driven model, because in several cases, the U.S. Supreme Court has found that determinations of appropriateness based on professional judgment sufficiently protect patients' rights as defined by the Constitution.[11] Constitutional rights that were considered in these federal court rulings include rights to free speech, freedom from cruel and unusual punishment, equal protection, and due process, along with consideration of issues related to the right to privacy, which some courts have found to arise from several other constitutional rights.[2,6,12]

Many states recognize more extensive rights than those established by the U.S. Constitution and federal courts and have thus adopted rights-driven models of adjudication. These models are based on state statutory law, state constitutions, or common law rights.[2,6,13] The rights-driven approach emphasizes individual autonomy and attempts to minimize differences in the right to refuse treatment between voluntarily and involuntarily hospitalized patients. As discussed in chapter 6, in general, only patients who lack treatment-specific decision-making capacity can be treated against their will, except in the case of an emergency. Advocates of the rights-driven model argue that committed patients should have the same protection. Therefore, in contrast to the treatment-driven model, in which committed patients are allowed to refuse only inappropriate treatment, the rights-driven model stipulates that treatment refusal, in the absence of an emergency, can be overridden only if the patient is deemed incompetent. Since a determination of competence requires a legal judgment, the adjudication of the question is assigned to the court system.[2,6] Patients are entitled to legal representation and have the full panoply of rights associated with legal due process: the right to legal representation, the right to timely notice, the rights to call witnesses and to cross-examine the hospital's witnesses, and the right to an expert to assist the patient's attorney. When attempting to override a patient's treatment refusal, a psychiatrist practicing in a state with a rights-driven model should be prepared to testify regarding the patient's lack of decision-making capacity and need for treatment. For example, in our case vignette, the psychiatrist treating Mr. V. would explain in court that Mr. V. lacks insight into his mental illness, that he is unable to appreciate his need for treatment or make rational decisions about it, and that the treatment is medically appropriate.

States with rights-driven models differ with regard to how treatment decisions are made following an adjudication of incompetence. In some jurisdictions, a guardian is appointed to make treatment decisions on behalf of an incompetent patient, as would occur for an incompetent medical or surgical patient. In other jurisdictions, appellate courts have expressed concern that family members, who usually act as guardians, might not adequately represent the interests of incompetent psychiatric patients. Courts in those jurisdictions have ruled that only judges are sufficiently neutral and objective to make treatment decisions, particularly for decisions about the use of ECT or antipsychotic medications.

There are competing formulations regarding how decisions about treatment for incompetent patients should be made. The treatment decisions may be based on the patient's "best interests." Using this standard of surrogate decision-making, the court or guardian would make treatment decisions based on what a reasonable person would choose as being in the patient's best interests. Alternatively, when a court is the decision-maker, the court may make more individualized and subjective treatment decisions based on what the patient would want if he or she were competent. This "substituted judgment" approach has evolved through case law to require consideration of evidence such as family and religious beliefs that may influence the patient's treatment decisions, the patient's stated preferences when competent, the prognosis with and without treatment, and possible side effects of the treatment.[6,14] Guardianship and the standards for surrogate decision making are discussed in detail in chapter 6.

In accordance with the doctrine of informed consent, competent patients must be provided with information that allows them to make their own decisions about medical care. The patient can then consent to or refuse the proposed treatment, with the potential for the refusal to be overridden if the patient is deemed to lack the capacity to make an informed decision about treatment. There are a few exceptions that allow the physician to bypass the full process of obtaining informed consent, whether the patient is agreeing to or refusing treatment, and for which formal adjudication of treatment refusal is not required. For example, physicians are allowed to provide treatment as necessary without obtaining full informed consent in emergency situations.

In the case vignette, if Mr. V. attacked his father or anyone else in the hospital, it would be appropriate to administer medications involuntarily on an emergency basis because of concerns about imminent danger (in which case, the physician would be likely to administer intramuscular or sublingual medication). To consider a situation an emergency, some courts require either the threat or the actual occurrence of significant bodily injury to the patient or another party. Other courts use a broader definition of emergency, including severe pain and the likelihood of rapid clinical deterioration as emergency situations.[6] As discussed in chapter 5, the emergency exception extends only to treatment that is necessary to stabilize the patient's clinical condition; it does not apply to treatment that is ongoing once the emergency has passed. Not infrequently, however, emergency treatment will lead to sufficient resolution of the symptoms that the patient regains capacity and can consent to, or explicitly refuse, the treatment.

There are variations in the approaches to treatment refusal in different forensic settings. (In this context, "forensic settings" refers to correctional settings, including jails, prisons, and forensic facilities for the detention of psychiatric patients before adjudication of guilt or after a finding of not guilty by reason of insanity in the criminal justice system.) For example, rulings in cases such as *Washington v. Harper* and *U.S. v. Loughner* have determined when treatment refusal on the part of prisoners and pretrial detainees, respectively, can be overridden through various provisions and procedures.[15,16] In *Washington v. Harper* (1990), the Supreme Court addressed the question of whether a man with a mental disorder could be involuntarily treated with antipsychotic medications. The Court ruled that prisoners who were found to present as "dangerous" to the institution and for whom medication was medically appropriate could be involuntarily treated. In the *Loughner* case, the U.S. Ninth Circuit Court of Appeals found that pretrial detainees could be involuntarily medicated under the same circumstances.[15-17]

In recent years, the U.S. Supreme Court has ruled that in limited circumstances a criminal defendant can be involuntarily medicated for the purpose of restoration of competence to stand trial.[18] A particularly controversial and ethically complicated situation arises when a prisoner refuses treatment that could restore competence to be executed.[19]

PREVALENCE AND OUTCOME OF TREATMENT REFUSAL

Across psychiatric treatment settings, rates of refusal of psychotropic medication range from 2% to 44%. When forensic settings are excluded, approximately 10% of psychiatric inpatients refuse antipsychotic medications at some point during the hospital course.[1-4] Patients who refuse recommended medication generally lack insight, have more negative attitudes toward treatment, and are more severely psychotic than patients who provide consent to such treatment. Inconsistently reported risk factors for treatment refusal include higher socioeconomic status, lack of insurance, higher prescribed doses of antipsychotic medications, lack of prescribed anti-parkinsonian agents, and a greater number of past psychiatric hospitalizations.[1,4]

Patients may refuse treatment for a variety of reasons (see Box 7.1). Some reasons are rational, such as those based on side effects or religious beliefs. Others are irrational and result from delusional or other disordered thinking.

Although many patients will refuse treatment at some point during their hospitalization, most episodes of treatment refusal are short and self-limited. About 50% to 90% of refusals in civil settings last for less than 1 week.[20] In one prospective study, researchers interviewed psychiatric inpatients who voluntarily accepted treatment after initially refusing it. Of these 38 patients, 15 accepted treatment because, with encouragement from staff and/or family, they became convinced that the medication would be beneficial to them. Twelve patients decided to take the medication because they believed that it would help them to obtain a desired objective, such as discharge from the hospital. The remaining patients offered a variety of other explanations for acceptance of treatment.[1]

In the less common case of persistent refusal, even in states with rights-driven models, where refusals generally last longer than in states with treatment-driven systems (13.0 days vs. 2.8 days), the refusal is overturned in more than 90% of cases.[1,2,4,21]

In the vignette, if Mr. V. is in a jurisdiction with a rights-driven model of adjudication, at either his commitment hearing or a separate court proceeding, the judge may determine whether Mr. V. can be treated against his will. If Mr. V. is in a jurisdiction with

---

BOX 7.1
Common Reasons for Treatment Refusal

REASON

Side effects

Prior adverse reaction to medication

Lack of insight into illness and/or need for medication

Delusions about the medication itself

Distrust of provider

Attempt to exert autonomy

Transference issues

Stereotypic response to distress

---

a treatment-driven model, he is likely to receive treatment earlier because a judicial determination of incompetence is not required. Studies have shown that rights-driven models of review can result in delayed treatment, which lead to prolonged hospitalization, as well as to considerable costs for the time devoted to each case by judges, lawyers, paralegals, psychiatrists, and independent psychiatric evaluators.[1,22,23] In addition to the economic costs, other costs include the potential for prolonged suffering related to untreated illness; the risk of an increased number of assaults, requiring use of restraints and seclusion; and damage to the therapeutic relationship caused by "adversarialization" of the process.[3,22] Proponents of treatment-driven models argue that these costs can be diminished with more efficient and informal procedures without any significant change in the clinical outcome because, as discussed above, the vast majority of refusals are overturned regardless of the system of review and decision making. Furthermore, it has been argued that clinicians could spend more time actually working with patients if they did not have to dedicate so many hours to paperwork required by the court.[22]

However, it has also been argued that rights-driven models provide incentives for psychiatrists to more thoroughly discuss medication decisions with their patients.[22] Moreover, proponents of rights-driven judicial mechanisms point out that these systems can help patients feel that they have a voice in a clinician-dominated process.[11] In one rights-driven setting, by the end of the study period, most patients decided to take medications voluntarily after discussion with their psychiatrists.[1] In this study, only 18% of treatment refusers were brought before a court, where their refusal was consistently over-ridden. A significant number of patients, 23%, were discharged from the hospital without treatment.

Patients who require court-ordered medication in the hospital are at increased risk for nonadherence after discharge, as well as for treatment-resistant illness.[20] It is important to keep in mind that a patient's perception of coercion can be reduced by providing information about medications and the process of adjudication.[9]

ASSESSMENT AND MANAGEMENT OF TREATMENT REFUSAL

When a patient refuses recommended treatment, the clinician must first assess the reasons for refusal (see Box 7.1). The appropriateness of the treatment should be considered, particularly if the need for a specific treatment is not clear-cut and the risk–benefit ratio is narrow. A thorough review of the records, including the patient's history, diagnosis, and response to previous medication trials, should be performed. Current and previous side effects should be explored, including the use of appropriate laboratory tests and instruments such as the Abnormal Involuntary Movement Scale.

Throughout the assessment of the refusal and the care that follows, the psychiatrist should engage the patient. Clinicians often make the mistake of shifting too quickly into an adversarial role and viewing the refusal as a legal problem to be overcome as quickly as possible. Instead, the treating clinician should consider the refusal as a potential opportunity to better understand the patient's values and concerns, which in turn may help to strengthen the therapeutic alliance. Legal or administrative proceedings should not be instituted unless absolutely necessary; even if an adversarial mechanism is required, it is important to continue to engage the patient and to try to maintain a working alliance. Throughout all stages of management, communications relevant to the patient's refusal and the facts pertinent to the clinician's decisions should be documented, including indications for treatment, response to prior treatment, reasons that the refusal is due to the illness, and any legal proceedings.[6] When a patient declines the medications that have been prescribed, the psychiatrist should first engage the patient in a dialogue about treatment with the goal of helping the patient to accept the proposed treatment or a reasonable alternative.[24] These discussions may provide opportunities for the psychiatrist to address bothersome side effects and clarify misconceptions about medication. They may also provide an opening for the patient to express frustration and voice unmet needs that may underlie the treatment refusal.[6]

Shared decision-making and self-directed care can be helpful techniques to use in such discussions.[24] It can also be helpful to figure out what the patient's specific goals are—for example, to be able to go back to work—and to focus discussions on how the proposed treatment can help him or her achieve these goals. Negotiations may be more successful if other staff and family members are involved in helping the patient recognize the potential benefits of treatment.[6] Throughout, the psychiatrist should be clear that he or she is acting in the best interest of the patient.

Clinicians should assess their patients' side effects from medications. As noted, patients may refuse medications because of side effects or other very real and practical concerns about their medications (see Table 7.1).[3] Because there are numerous ways to ameliorate side effects, such as changing the type of medication, overall dose, or dosing schedule or adding adjunctive medications, it is important to address the concerns about side effects that patients raise. Concerns about side effects should rarely be the reason for serious mental illness to go without long-term treatment in the absence of further justification for avoiding medication.

Patients may have had negative experiences with medications in the past and may presume, sometimes correctly, that they will have similar effects from the medication currently being prescribed. It is important to realize that seemingly minor and benign effects, such as constipation or dry mouth, may be cause for distress, depending on the patient's specific concerns. For example, a clinician may assume that a patient of normal weight would see that the benefits from an antipsychotic that would allow the patient to live independently in the community clearly outweigh the risk of minor weight gain; however, the patient may find this side effect unacceptable.[6] Similarly, if a patient places a high value on activities such as reading or watching television, blurring of vision related to the anticholinergic properties of some antipsychotics may be intolerable. Of note, patients tend to find side effects more disturbing if they are not prepared to expect them. Patients may also experience adverse effects in idiosyncratic ways and develop delusional beliefs about the effects.[3,6] For example, if not warned about the potential side effect of postural hypotension, a patient with paranoia who experiences dizziness may view it as a sign that he or she is being poisoned and may therefore refuse treatment.

Extrapyramidal side effects, particularly akathisia and dystonias and dyskinesias that affect the muscles of the eyes, mouth, and throat, are often the most disturbing adverse reactions to antipsychotic medications. Some patients may also experience a dysphoric response to antipsychotics, which has specifically been associated with poor compliance and a poor prognosis.[25] Prescribing clinicians should always ask patients about impotence, decreased libido, and retrograde ejaculation in relation to medication because they may be embarrassed to mention these particular effects [6] and simply stop taking the medication because of them.

There are also several common illness-related reasons that patients refuse medication. Patients who do not believe that they have an illness are unlikely to accept treatment. Not surprisingly, poor insight is a major risk factor for medication refusal.[1,19,26-28] Similarly, patients with mania may feel wonderful and therefore see no reason why they should take medications that will make them feel less euphoric. As mentioned above, patients may also refuse treatment on the basis of delusional beliefs; for example, they may think that the prescribing physician is attempting to poison them.[6]

Treatment refusal can also originate from issues related to the doctor–patient relationship. A poor therapeutic alliance is consistently associated with poor adherence to treatment.[27-29] Specific issues may involve transference (defined as the displacement or projection onto the therapist of unconscious feelings and wishes originally directed toward important persons, such as parents, in the patient's childhood[5]) or a breakdown in trust—if, for example, the psychiatrist breaches confidentiality or does not meet with the patient when promised. A patient who has little control over other areas of his or her life may refuse medication as a way to exert autonomy. Refusal may also be a way for the patient to communicate frustration or obtain more attention from staff.[6]

The context of the refusal may suggest the reasons for it. Patients on inpatient units are most likely to refuse medications shortly after admission, often because they do not believe that they need to be hospitalized.[1] Reasons that patients may start refusing medications later in the course of hospitalization include increasing distrust of staff and development of negative transference or other interpersonal difficulties as discussed above; in less verbal patients, refusal may be a stereotypic response to distress.[6,14] In forensic settings, prisoners may refuse medications with the hope of being transferred to a hospital or in order to remain incompetent to stand trial.

Persistent Refusal

If negotiations regarding treatment refusal are unsuccessful, two options exist: discharge the patient against medical advice or use formal mechanisms in an attempt to resolve the issue. If the treatment facility is in a jurisdiction where an override of refusal requires a determination of incompetence, and the patient seems to have the capacity to refuse the treatment, as described in chapter 6, the clinician may be forced to discharge the patient against medical advice or to continue to work with the patient in an unmedicated or suboptimally medicated state. There are also situations in which it may be preferable to respect the wishes of the patient. For example, when the risk of harm without treatment is low, discharge may be preferable to putting the patient through an adversarial process that could exacerbate any distrust of the psychiatric system, increase the chance that the patient will avoid seeking help when needed in the future, and reinforce the patient's opposition to medication should the judge find the patient competent or concur with the patient's refusal. Even if the decision is to discharge the patient, the discharge should not constitute an abandonment of the patient; follow-up care should still be provided.[6]

Formal mechanisms to adjudicate treatment refusal should be used if negotiations fail, if discharge is not a safe option, if the patient continues to meet criteria for commitment, and if the patient does not appear to be competent to make treatment decisions. Even during this adversarial process, the clinician should attempt to preserve the therapeutic alliance, candidly informing the patient of the decision to try to override his or her refusal and the reasons for that decision. The clinician should describe the formal procedures to the patient, including the fact that conversations and clinical information will not be kept confidential, since this information will be necessary for adjudication by the consultants or the judge. The patient should be encouraged to participate in the adjudication process, which can be less coercive and more therapeutic if the patient has a way to express his or her thoughts and wishes during the process.[30] Throughout the process of adjudication, it is important to continue the dialogue and negotiation with the patient, not only to maintain the therapeutic alliance but also because, as discussed above, many patients will eventually decide to take medications voluntarily.

When formally adjudicated, treatment refusal is overridden in the vast majority of cases. Once the court or other decision-making body decides to override the refusal, the judgment should be explained to the patient. The treating psychiatrist must then make provisions to offer and ultimately administer the medications in accordance with the authorized plan. At this point, even when the proposed medication is available only in oral form, most patients will accept it and eventually come to acknowledge the need for treatment.[31] Although it is not legally required, the prescribing clinician should continue to engage the patient in a discussion of decisions about treatment and to respect his or her wishes about treatment whenever possible in order to maintain or repair the alliance and increase the likelihood of long-term adherence to treatment.

If the patient does voluntarily accept treatment, it is important to re-explore reasons for the initial refusal in order to facilitate longer-term treatment planning. Elucidating and documenting these reasons can be particularly helpful in the case of relapse and future hospitalizations, both for negotiating treatment and for use in legal proceedings, particularly in jurisdictions where substituted-judgment standards are used.[6] Psychiatric advance directives and joint crisis plans can also be helpful in planning for future refusals. These forms allow patients to document their treatment preferences should they be deemed incompetent to make treatment decisions in the future.[32,33]

Refusal of Antipsychotic Medications in Outpatient Settings

The mental health community has debated the concept and practice of outpatient commitment for several decades. This type of mandated treatment is designed to prevent recurrent hospitalization by addressing the issue of treatment refusal in outpatient settings.[34,35] Currently, all states except for Connecticut, Maryland, Massachusetts, New Mexico, and Tennessee have some form of civil outpatient commitment; however, specific statutes vary substantially, and only a minority of states actually implement such laws.[36,37] These court orders often require patients to adhere to prescribed treatment in order to maintain outpatient status; however, the requirements are difficult to enforce because there are no provisions for involuntary medication administration. Outcomes of this intervention continue to be debated, especially given that in the few studies that compared mandated with voluntary treatment, success was seemingly dependent on effective implementation and availability of intensive community-based services. The results of these studies are difficult to generalize to other jurisdictions with different statutes, funding, and locally available services.[38] Additional discussion of outpatient commitment can be found in chapter 2.

Refusal of Antipsychotic Medications in Nursing Homes

Antipsychotic medication use in nursing homes has gained attention in recent decades. Antipsychotics are frequently used to address the behavioral and psychological symptoms of dementia, despite evidence suggesting a limited benefit of these medications in patients with dementia.[39] Antipsychotic use in the elderly is particularly problematic because this population is at increased risk for such adverse effects as orthostatic hypotension, sedation, cardiovascular events, and falls. Moreover, the Food and Drug Administration has issued a black-box warning concerning the risk of death associated with the use of atypical antipsychotics in elderly patients with dementia.[40,41]

Before the Omnibus Budget Reconciliation Act of 1987 (OBRA '87), antipsychotics were used freely in nursing homes as a form of "chemical restraint," often without an appropriate diagnosis and sometimes for the convenience of staff. OBRA '87 laid out revisions to the statutory Medicare and Medicaid requirements for nursing homes, including limitations on the use of antipsychotic medications. This act was intended to protect nursing home residents from inappropriate or excessive use of antipsychotics.[40] As in other settings, treatment refusal in nursing homes can occur. In most jurisdictions, legal remedies are available to address treatment refusal in a nursing home, allowing the consulting psychiatrist to obtain authorization of treatment over the patient's objection.

Federal laws also assert that nursing home residents or their legal health care decision makers must provide informed consent before they are given any medication, including an antipsychotic.[42] Federal legislation allows individual states to decide the process by which a patient is deemed incompetent. Some states have specific regulations regarding use of antipsychotics in incompetent nursing home patients. For example, in Massachusetts, where antipsychotics are considered "extraordinary treatment," administration of an antipsychotic medication over the objection of the patient or health care proxy or in a person who is thought to lack the ability to make treatment decisions requires a specific probate court hearing, during which the judge must make a determination of incompetence and then authorize a medication treatment plan. In Massachusetts, the substituted-judgment paradigm is used to make the decision about the treatment plan, which means that the judge hears testimony and determines what treatment the incompetent person would want if he or she were competent.[43]

Refusal of Electroconvulsive Therapy

Electroconvulsive therapy (ECT) is an effective therapy for many psychiatric disorders and is considered a first-line treatment for catatonia, psychosis in a patient with neuroleptic malignant syndrome, and mania during pregnancy.[44] Despite the proven efficacy of ECT, many states heavily regulate its use. The reasons for government involvement in and regulation of ECT parallel the reasons for regulation of antipsychotic use in a patient who refuses such treatment, including advocacy by patients' rights groups and prior misuse of the treatment. However, in contrast to involuntary antipsychotic treatment, which all the states address in administrative codes and/or legislation, 33 jurisdictions in the United States do not specifically comment on involuntary ECT.[45] In these jurisdictions, providers should follow the American Psychiatric Association guidelines and requirements by the Joint Commission on Accreditation of Health Care Organizations, which include evaluation of and agreement on the appropriateness of ECT by a psychiatrist with ECT privileges.[44-46]

In the absence of specific legislation or regulatory provisions, involuntary treatment with ECT should proceed by the same mechanism as involuntary treatment with any other medical therapy or procedure in that jurisdiction. The state statutes that do address ECT vary widely. For example, in some states, patients who are involuntarily committed to a hospital are not eligible to receive ECT, whereas other states allow involuntary ECT if a court finds clear and convincing evidence that the patient is incompetent to make treatment decisions and that the treatment is appropriate on the basis of substituted judgment.[45]

CONCLUSION

The right to refuse treatment with antipsychotic medications has only recently been recognized. When a patient refuses recommended treatment, psychiatrists and other treating clinicians should explore the reasons for refusal and attempt to negotiate treatment with the patient. If such negotiations are unsuccessful, the treatment team may either discharge the patient or attempt to override the treatment refusal through formal mechanisms. There are two models of mechanisms for adjudication of treatment refusal: the rights-driven model and the treatment-driven model. The mechanism used varies depending on the jurisdiction and treatment setting, and treating clinicians must be aware of local practices, which are driven generally by case law, policy, and/or statutory requirements. Regardless of the outcome, treating clinicians should attempt to maintain a positive therapeutic alliance, use shared-decision making to reach an agreement, engage patients even in adversarial processes, and when appropriate, plan for future treatment refusals as part of working with patients over the long-term. Refusal of ECT and refusal of antipsychotic medications in outpatient settings and nursing homes are handled in a variety of ways, depending on the location of practice, and readers should be familiar with the laws in their jurisdiction.

FREQUENTLY ASKED QUESTIONS

Is a patient who is involuntarily committed to a hospital still able to refuse antipsychotic medication?

The procedure for treating a patient involuntarily with antipsychotic medications varies according to the location and type of hospital the patient is committed to, and readers should be familiar with the legal or administrative mechanisms relevant to their jurisdiction (see Table 7.1). In some states, involuntary treatment can begin after an administrative hearing within the hospital, which does not involve the legal system. In other states, involuntary treatment requires a judicial hearing, which may occur only after commitment to the hospital.

Why are the procedures for involuntary psychiatric treatment, particularly with antipsychotics, different from the procedures for involuntary treatment with other medical therapies and surgical procedures?

Historically, mental health patients have had very limited rights to refuse treatment. Over the past century, however, many jurisdictions have started to offer greater protections for mentally ill patients who refuse treatment, on the basis of concerns about the quality of care delivered in psychiatric institutions, the risk of tardive dyskinesia, distrust of the motives of family members authorizing treatment, and the view of some courts that antipsychotic treatment is especially intrusive, affecting thought. These jurisdictions use competence as the criterion for decisions about treatment refusal. In other jurisdictions, treatment refusal by a psychiatric patient who is competent may be overturned if it is deemed appropriate to do so, and the patient may be treated involuntarily on the determination of a single doctor or a panel. These less stringent protections are justified on the grounds that the person has already been committed, that commitment is intended for treatment, and that the state has an interest in providing that treatment. The patient who is refusing treatment has an interest in receiving appropriate treatment but not in refusing treatment altogether.

Can you treat a patient with electroconvulsive therapy against his or her will?

Many states address involuntary ECT in specific statutes, and these statutes vary widely: some states do not allow any involuntarily committed patients to receive ECT, whereas others allow involuntary ECT for patients who are deemed to be incompetent and for whom treatment is believed to be appropriate on the basis of a substituted-judgment decision-making process.

Is there any way to force a patient to continue taking prescribed antipsychotics as an outpatient?

Almost all states have some form of mandated outpatient treatment, usually referred to as "outpatient commitment." However, there is no form of mandated outpatient treatment that provides for forced administration of medications. Outpatient commitment statutes, which vary widely, are difficult to enforce, and few are actually implemented.

Are there things that a clinician can do to try to make the relationship with a treatment-refusing patient less adversarial?

Yes. Before seeking formal adjudication of the treatment refusal, the clinician should carefully assess the reasons for the refusal, engage the patient in discussions about his or her treatment, negotiate treatment, and try to use the refusal as an opportunity to learn more about the patient's values and concerns, which may help strengthen the therapeutic alliance. Even if a legal or administrative proceeding is ultimately required, it is important to continue to engage the patient and try to maintain the therapeutic alliance throughout the process.

REFERENCES

1. Hoge SK, Appelbaum PS, Lawlor T, et al. A prospective, multicenter study of patients' refusal of antipsychotic medication. *Archives of General Psychiatry.* 1990;47(10):949–956.

2. Appelbaum PS. *Almost a Revolution: Mental Health Law and the Limits of Change.* New York: Oxford University Press; 1994.

3. Owiti JA, Bowers L. A narrative review of studies of refusal of psychotropic medication in acute inpatient psychiatric care. *Journal of Psychiatric and Mental Health Nursing.* 2011;18(7):637–647.

4. Kasper JA, Hoge SK, Feucht-Haviar T, Cortina J, Cohen B. Prospective study of patients' refusal of antipsychotic medication under a physician discretion review procedure. *American Journal of Psychiatry.* 1997;154(4):483–489.

5. VanderBos G, ed. *APA Dictionary of Psychology,* 1st edition. Washington, DC: American Psychological Association; 2007.

6. Appelbaum PS, Gutheil TG. *Clinical Handbook of Psychiatry and the Law.* 4th ed. Philadelphia: Lippincott Williams & Wilkins; 2007.

7. Hoge SK, Appelbaum PS, Geller JG. Involuntary treatment. In: Tasman A, Hales RE, Frances A, eds. *American Psychiatric Press Review of Psychiatry,* Vol. 8. Washington, DC: American Psychiatric Press; 1989:432–450.

8. Large MM, Ryan CJ, Nielssen OB, Hayes RA. The danger of dangerousness: why we must remove the dangerousness criterion from our mental health acts. *Journal of Medical Ethics.* 2008;34(12):877–881.

9. Pinals DA, Mossman D. *Evaluation for Civil Commitment.* New York: Oxford University Press; 2012.

10. Beinner, W. *Non-emergent involuntary medication state-by-state report, 2007.* http://mentalhealth.vermont.gov/sites/dmh/files/report/DMH-State_by_State_Involuntary_Medication.pdf. Accessed June 24, 2015.

11. Monahan J, Hoge SK, Lidz C, et al. Coercion and commitment: understanding involuntary mental hospital admission. *International Journal of Law and Psychiatry.* 1995;18(3):249–263.

12. *Youngberg v. Romeo,* 457 U.S. 307(1982).

13. Perlin ML. Decoding right to refuse treatment law. *International Journal of Law and Psychiatry.* 1993;16(1–2):151–177.

14. Wettstein RM. The right to refuse psychiatric treatment. *Psychiatric Clinics of North America.* 1999;22(1):173–182, viii.

15. *Washington v. Harper,* 494 U.S. 210 (U.S. Supreme Court 1990).

16. *U.S. v. Loughner,* **672 F.3d 731** (9th Cir. 2012).

17. Levine HS, Gage BC. Commentary: involuntary antipsychotics in prison—extending Harper, contracting care? *Journal of the American Academy of Psychiatry and the Law.* 2015;43(2):165–170.

18. *Sell v. U.S.,* 539 U.S. 166 (U.S. 2003).

19. Leong GB, Silva JA, Weinstock R, Ganzini L. Survey of forensic psychiatrists on evaluation and treatment of prisoners on death row. *Journal of the American Academy of Psychiatry and the Law.* 2000;28(4):427–432.

20. Russ MJ, John M. Outcomes associated with court-ordered treatment over objection in an acute psychiatric hospital. *Journal of the American Academy of Psychiatry and the Law.* 2013;41(2):236–244.

21. Appelbaum PS, Hoge SK. The right to refuse treatment: what the research reveals. *Behavioral Sciences and the Law.* 1986;4:279–292.

22. Schouten R, Gutheil TG. Aftermath of the Rogers decision: assessing the costs. *American Journal of Psychiatry.* 1990;147(10):1348–1352.

23. Veliz J, James WS. Medicine court: Rogers in practice. *American Journal of Psychiatry.* 1987;144(1):62–67.

24. Patel SR, Bakken S, Ruland C. Recent advances in shared decision making for mental health. *Current Opinion in Psychiatry.* 2008;21(6):606–612.

25. Lambert M, Schimmelmann BG, Karow A, Naber D. Subjective well-being and initial dysphoric reaction under antipsychotic drugs—concepts, measurement and clinical relevance. *Pharmacopsychiatry.* 2003;36 (Suppl 3):S181–190.

26. Droulout T, Liraud F, Verdoux H. [Relationships between insight and medication adherence in subjects with psychosis]. *Encephale.* 2003;29(5):430–437.

27. Fenton WS, Blyler CR, Heinssen RK. Determinants of medication compliance in schizophrenia: empirical and clinical findings. *Schizophrenia Bulletin.* 1997;23(4):637–651.

28. Lacro JP, Dunn LB, Dolder CR, Leckband SG, Jeste DV. Prevalence of and risk factors for medication nonadherence in patients with schizophrenia: a comprehensive review of recent literature. *Journal of Clinical Psychiatry.* 2002;63(10):892–909.

29. McCann TV, Boardman G, Clark E, Lu S. Risk profiles for non-adherence to antipsychotic medications. *Journal of Psychiatric and Mental Health Nursing.* 2008;15(8):622–629.

30. Winick B. *The Right to Refuse Mental Health Treatment.* Washington, DC: American Psychological Association; 1997.

31. Schwartz HI, Vingiano W, Perez CB. Autonomy and the right to refuse treatment: patients' attitudes after involuntary medication. *Hospital and Community Psychiatry.* 1988;39(10):1049–1054.

32. Campbell LA, Kisely SR. Advance treatment directives for people with severe mental illness. *Cochrane Database Systematic Reviews.* 2009(1):CD005963.

33. Khazaal Y, Manghi R, Delahaye M, Machado A, Penzenstadler L, Molodynski A. Psychiatric advance directives, a possible way to overcome coercion and promote empowerment. *Frontiers in Public Health.* 2014;2:37.

34. Miller RD. Coerced treatment in the community. *Psychiatric Clinics of North America.* 1999;22:183–196.

35. Rowe M. Alternatives to outpatient commitment. *Journal of the American Academy of Psychiatry and the Law.* 2013;41(3):332–336.

36. Treatment Advocacy Center. *Assisted outpatient treatment laws.* 2011. http://treatmentadvocacycenter.org/solution/assisted-outpatient-treatment-laws/. Accessed September 5, 2015.

37. Appelbaum PS. Assessing Kendra's Law: five years of outpatient commitment in New York. *Psychiatric Services.* 2005;56(7):791–792.

38. Swanson JW, Swartz MS. Why the evidence for outpatient commitment is good enough. *Psychiatric Services.* 2014;65(6):808–811.

39. Maher AR, Maglione M, Bagley S, et al. Efficacy and comparative effectiveness of atypical antipsychotic medications for off-label uses in adults: a systematic review and meta-analysis. *Journal of the American Medical Association.* 2011;306(12):1359–1369.

40. Epstein-Lubow G, Rosenzweig A. The use of antipsychotic medication in long-term care. *Medicine and Health, Rhode Island.* 2010;93(12):372, 377–378.

41. Schneider LS, Dagerman KS, Insel P. Risk of death with atypical antipsychotic drug treatment for dementia: meta-analysis of randomized placebo-controlled trials. *Journal of the American Medical Association.* 2005;294(15):1934–1943.

42. Braun J, Frolik L. Legal aspects of chemical restraint use in nursing homes. *Marquette Elder's Advisor.* 2000;2(2):21–31.

43. *Rogers v. Commissioner of the Mental Health Department,* 390 490(1983).

44. American Psychiatric Association. *The Practice of Electroconvulsive Therapy: Recommendations for Treatment, Training, and Privileging.* 2nd edition. Washington, DC: American Psychiatric Association; 2001.

45. Harris V. Electroconvulsive therapy: administrative codes, legislation, and professional recommendations. *Journal of the American Academy of Psychiatry and the Law.* 2006;34(3):406–411.

46. Joint Commission on Accreditation of Healthcare Organizations (JCAHO). *Comprehensive Accreditation Manual for Hospitals: The Official Handbook (CAMH).* Oak Brook Terrace, IL: JCAHO; 2002.

/// 8 /// MALPRACTICE

JENNIFER L. PIEL AND PHILLIP J. RESNICK

Even the most skillful clinician cannot prevent all injuries to patients. Although some injuries in health care can occur even when the highest standards of practice are followed, others are the result of substandard care on the part of the clinician. Mental health clinicians may be subject to civil liability for negligent or intentional acts that deviate from the standard of care of their profession and cause their patient harm. As described in chapter 1, the accused health care provider in a malpractice action is the defendant. The person (or a representative of the person) bringing the action for alleged harm is the plaintiff.

Civil legal suits brought by patients against physicians, including psychiatrists, are typically referred to as medical malpractice actions. Suits brought by patients against nonphysician mental health providers (i.e., psychologists, social workers, or counselors) are most commonly referred to as professional liability claims. Despite the difference in terminology, the general principles of liability are similar across these professional disciplines. The term "malpractice" is used in this chapter to refer to professional liability claims, regardless of the mental health discipline.

Physicians and other health care providers often criticize medical malpractice laws for the high costs of adverse judgments and medical malpractice insurance and for driving practitioners to engage in defensive medicine in an effort to limit liability risk. Society, however, has long recognized that substandard care may result in injury and has taken the position that those injured by the negligent acts of others, including health care providers, should be compensated for the harm they suffer. Malpractice law exists to provide that compensation and to maintain high standards of care for health care disciplines.

HISTORY OF MALPRACTICE LAW

Medical malpractice laws in the United States have their origins in English common law. Common law refers to laws that develop through court decisions (i.e., it is judge-made law). Medical malpractice suits in the United States are usually filed in state courts. Although the general framework is similar among the states, malpractice laws are state-specific. The malpractice standards in each state are developed through court cases and statutes passed by state legislatures.

Since the 1960s, the frequency of medical malpractice suits has increased, and in recent decades, lawsuits filed by plaintiffs alleging malpractice have become relatively common in the United States.[1] Physicians are sued more than other types of health care providers, but professionals in any health care discipline may have a professional liability suit filed against them. One study showed that, for the period from 1991 through 2005, 7.4% of all physicians had a malpractice claim against them, with 1.6% of the claims leading to a payment.[2] The incidence of malpractice claims varied across specialties, with psychiatry at the low end of claims. In each year of the study period, 2.6% of psychiatrists were sued.

Although mental health professionals are sued for malpractice less frequently than clinicians in other medical specialties, the incidence of suits against psychiatrists and other mental health practitioners has increased over the past four decades. In 2005, Professional Risk Management Services,[3] a liability insurance carrier for psychiatrists, reported psychiatric claims in the following categories for cause of action: incorrect treatment (31%); suicide or attempted suicide (15%); drug reaction (9%); incorrect diagnosis (9%); improper supervision (6%); unnecessary commitment (6%); undue familiarity, meaning sexual misconduct (4%); breach of confidentiality (2%); and other causes (18%). Although claimants often allege more than one cause of action against professionals in malpractice suits, the percentages provided here are for the primary complaint. These complaints represent the major categories of liability against mental health providers.

In addition to medical malpractice lawsuits, psychiatrists and other mental health clinicians may face disciplinary actions or sanctions from other bodies. The Health Care Quality Improvement Act of 1986,[4] a federal law, established the National Practitioner Data Bank and requires health care entities to report actions of malpractice and other disciplinary measures against physicians. A goal of the legislation was to encourage reporting of actions against physicians who, before the act was passed, could relocate across state lines and thereby avoid disclosure of past discipline or malpractice claims to state licensing boards. Mental health clinicians also may face discipline from state licensing boards and professional organizations on the basis of allegations of malpractice or misconduct. In contrast to practitioners in other medical specialties, psychiatrists are more likely to be disciplined by state medical licensing boards.[5]

FUNDAMENTALS OF MALPRACTICE LIABILITY

Tort law, also called personal injury law, governs suits by patients or their representatives against health care professionals. Torts are civil wrongs, as opposed to criminal wrongs; the penalty typically consists of monetary damages paid to the victim rather than a fine paid to the state or imprisonment. Medical malpractice actions are a category of tort relating to professional liability. Most malpractice claims are based on the theory of negligence, but malpractice may also be used to refer to some intentional torts that arise in the context of clinical practice. Negligence, as a legal concept, is based on the principle that in specific situations, people owe a duty of reasonable care in their conduct toward others. Negligence may occur when a person unintentionally causes harm to another as a result of failure to exercise due care. An intentional tort occurs when the person performs a deliberate act that causes harm to another person, such as battery (physical contact without consent or justification) or false imprisonment (willful detention without consent or justification). For example, a patient who is restrained in the emergency room could file a claim for the intentional torts of battery and false imprisonment. The defenses to both allegations would be that there was justification for the touching and confinement without consent (e.g., the patient posed a risk of harm to himself or others unless restrained).

In rare cases, psychiatrists and other mental health practitioners face criminal charges for their conduct. Criminal charges require a more serious deviation from the standard of care. This may occur, for example, when a patient accuses a clinician of sexual assault, or in circumstances suggesting that a provider acted with reckless disregard for her patient, resulting in harm to the patient. A recent example is that of Dr. Conrad Murray, who worked as a personal physician for singer Michael Jackson. Dr. Murray was charged with involuntary manslaughter for the death of Mr. Jackson after administering an intoxicating combination of medications, including a powerful anesthetic, to the singer at home.[6]

When a medical malpractice suit is based on negligence, the plaintiff must establish each of the four elements of the tort of negligence: duty of reasonable care, dereliction of the duty, direct causation, and damages. These four elements, commonly referred to as the 4 D's of negligence, are discussed in more detail in this chapter. To prevail in the lawsuit, the plaintiff must prove to the trier of fact each of the four elements to a preponderance-of-evidence standard (more likely than not), which is typical of civil legal suits for monetary compensation. In a jury trial, the jury is the trier of fact and determines liability. In a bench trial, the judge rules on the issue of liability. For more details on the civil legal system, see chapter 1. In contrast to actions based on negligence, in which the plaintiff needs to establish the four elements of negligence, in actions based on intentional torts, the plaintiff needs to prove only that the defendant's actions caused harm.

Duty of Reasonable Care

The first element of negligence is the duty of care. People owe a general duty to others to exercise a reasonable degree of care in carrying out their activities. People are not expected to prevent all injuries to everyone, but they are expected to conduct themselves in a manner that avoids careless injury to those with whom they come into contact or with whom they have a special relationship. For example, when driving a car, one owes a duty to exercise the degree of care that a reasonable driver would exercise under similar circumstances.

In medical malpractice, the duty of reasonable care arises from the provider–patient relationship, typically referred to as the doctor–patient relationship. In the absence of a doctor–patient relationship, a physician (or other mental health provider) owes no duty of care to a patient and will therefore not be subject to malpractice liability for claims from that patient. Accordingly, in lawsuits for alleged medical malpractice, the court will determine whether a doctor–patient relationship existed between the plaintiff and the defendant provider. States vary in their precise definitions and nuances in determining whether a doctor–patient relationship has been established. Ordinarily, it is clear whether the plaintiff and defendant provider have established a treatment relationship. This occurs when both parties knowingly and voluntarily interact in a treatment role. Evidence of a treatment relationship includes such affirmative acts on the part of the physician as examining the patient, making a diagnosis, ordering tests or treatments, making entries in the patient's medical record, or otherwise agreeing to be the patient's provider.[7]

Can a doctor–patient relationship be established in the absence of face-to-face communication? Yes, in-person assessments are not necessary as the basis for a doctor–patient relationship; such relationships may be formed via telephone communications or online consultations, for example. The nature and scope of the communication will determine whether a doctor–patient relationship is established. On-call or covering physicians may establish a doctor–patient relationship if they take (or, based on the facts of the case, should have taken) affirmative steps in the care of a colleague's patient.

In some cases, a duty of care may arise from the supervisory relationship of a provider to trainees or other members of the treatment team. Most of this chapter focuses on liability incurred by one person as a result of personal negligence. In certain circumstances, however, a person may be liable for the negligence of another person. The concept of vicarious liability and the doctrine of *respondeat superior* (Latin for "let the master respond") apply to situations in which an employee commits a tort within the scope of employment and the employer is held responsible for the employee's conduct. In health care, *respondeat superior* may be applied to clinical supervisors and trainees, physicians and physician extenders in their practice, and other team leaders and their staff. In such cases, the supervisor (or employer) may incur liability in the absence of any personal wrongdoing toward the claimant. Liability is established when it is determined that the supervisor's status conferred sufficient control over the negligent supervisee's conduct and the negligent conduct occurred in the scope of employment. In cases of vicarious liability, both the supervisor and supervisee may be held liable.

The standard of care, like the duty of care, is based on clinical practice but determined by the law. In medical malpractice cases, health care providers are expected to exercise the degree of care that a reasonably prudent provider would exercise in similar circumstances. Psychiatrists and other mental health providers are required to adhere not to "best practices" but rather to reasonable and prudent practices. Similarly, prudent care does not mandate that the patient's treatment be successful in curing disease or alleviating symptoms. In a malpractice case against a psychiatrist after a patient's suicide, the Massachusetts Supreme Judicial Court stated, "The [defendant] psychiatrist owed a legal duty to treat the decedent in accordance with the standard of care and skill of an average member of the medical profession practicing psychiatry."[8] If a provider has used a treatment that is not mainstream, he or she may nevertheless avoid liability by demonstrating that the treatment used represents the care provided by a respectable minority of practitioners and can therefore be considered a reasonable standard of care.

The standard of care is influenced by the provider's circumstances and discipline. Thus, the standard of care for a psychiatrist may be different from the standard of care for a psychologist. In fact, even within the discipline of psychiatry, the standard of care can vary by subspecialization; a psychopharmacologist, for example, may be held to a different standard than a psychoanalyst. Expert witnesses retained in malpractice cases are usually of the same discipline as the defendant—and this is sometimes required by law in the jurisdiction—in order to speak to the relevant standard of care.

Within a discipline, most jurisdictions use a national standard of care. In this way, a psychiatrist in California, for example, is held to the same standard of care as a psychiatrist in Florida. Moreover, an expert psychiatric witness from California could testify regarding the standard of care for a psychiatrist in Florida. A minority of jurisdictions adhere to a local standard rather than a national standard. In these jurisdictions, the relevant standard focuses on customary practice in the local jurisdiction. Some states categorize expert witness testimony as the practice of medicine and will allow only physicians licensed to practice in that jurisdiction to testify as experts in malpractice cases. Other states require that expert witnesses spend some set portion of their professional time treating patients instead of devoting all their time to being an expert witness.

Even a national standard may be nuanced, however, by local customs, resources, or the nature of the particular provider's job responsibilities. Depending on the jurisdiction and the unique facts of the malpractice case, a psychiatrist working in an inpatient setting may be held to a different standard of care than a psychiatrist consulting in a primary care clinic, for example. A specialist may be held to a higher level of care than a generalist. By illustration, a psychiatrist with specialty certification in geriatric psychiatry may be held to a different standard of care than a general psychiatrist in treating the same elderly patient. Professionals holding themselves out as having advanced expertise may be held to the standard of specialists.

Dereliction of Duty

The second element of malpractice—dereliction of the duty of care—requires proof that the provider departed from the relevant standard of care. In most cases of alleged medical malpractice, the standard of care is outside the experience of laypersons, requiring the use of expert witnesses. The judge is responsible for determining the admissibility of expert testimony. Rule 702 of the Federal Rules of Evidence (which has been adopted by many state courts) permits scientific, technical, or other specialized knowledge to be admitted if it will assist the trier of fact in understanding the evidence in the case.

In rare cases, the alleged claims of malpractice are within the understanding of laypersons, and expert witnesses are not required. If members of the jury can be expected to understand the alleged negligent conduct from their own experience, no expert testimony is necessary. Take, for example, a patient who trips on the stairs of a physician's office and is injured. The members of the jury, from their own knowledge and experience, may determine whether the physician was negligent in maintaining the stairs in the absence of an expert opinion on the topic. The situation is within the scope of the jury's personal experiences. In these cases, if dereliction of duty is established, the case proceeds to the issue of damages. Expert testimony may still be required on the issue of damages, the causal relationship between the dereliction of duty and the alleged damages, or the applicability of the legal principles in question to the circumstances.

In some additional cases, the medical malpractice is so obvious that medical expert testimony is not needed for the jury to understand the circumstances. This occurs, for example, when the legal concept of *res ipsa loquitor* (Latin for "the thing speaks for itself") applies. Under this doctrine, the occurrence of the act itself implies that negligence occurred because the cause of the injury was under the sole control of the defendant, the plaintiff did not contribute to the injury, and the injury is of a type that would not have occurred if there had been no negligence. A common medical example of this concept is the retention of a foreign object, such as a clamp or sponge, in a patient who has undergone surgery. In psychiatry, a claim may be based on *res ipsa loquitor* if a psychiatrist fails to adhere to a strict hospital policy, such as reviewing appropriateness for continued use of restraints at the required interval. In the majority of medical malpractices cases, expert opinion testimony is used to educate the jury about the relevant standard of care and whether the defendant clinician met the standard of care in the case at issue. In determining the standard of care, experts base their opinions on their training, knowledge, skills, and experience. Additional sources of information about the standard of care include practice guidelines, policies of relevant professional organizations, professional codes of ethics, scholarly literature, hospital or agency policies, and local laws.

Practice guidelines alone should not be used as the standard of care because the standard evolves over time and practice guidelines may be outdated.[9] The American Psychiatric Association's Practice Guidelines for the Assessment and Treatment of Patients with Suicidal Behavior,[10] for example, explicitly cautions that the practice guidelines are not equivalent to the standard of care. Practice guidelines advance practice habits that may or may not apply to the specific pattern of facts in the malpractice case at issue.[11] Such guidelines may put forth best practices rather than the standard of care, or they may advance a standard that has yet to find its way into clinical practice. In a Mississippi malpractice case, by way of illustration, the appellate court held that practice guidelines were suggestions of the standard of care; furthermore, on the basis of the specific facts of the case, the defendant was justified in departing from the guidelines to provide care for the patient.[12]

The standard of care may be defined, or influenced by, state case law or statutes. *Tarasoff v. Regents of the University of California*[13] is a case in point. In this famous 1976 case, the California Supreme Court's decision created a legal duty for therapists to protect identifiable third parties from their patients' reasonably foreseeable violent acts when certain conditions are met. Following *Tarasoff*, the majority of other states, either by case law or by statute, have imposed *Tarasoff*-type duties. Many states have enacted statutes that limit such duties— for example by requiring an explicit threat from the victim or clearly identifying the means for a clinician to discharge his or her responsibilities. (For a detailed discussion of *Tarasoff*, see chapter 9.) Expert testimony nevertheless plays an important role in determining whether the defendant deviated from the standard of care as defined by state statutes or case law.

Deviation from the standard of care should not be confused with outcome. The law is cognizant that medical care has inherent risks for patients and that injury or an adverse outcome may occur even if best practices are followed. A patient may have an unintended side effect from a medication or other treatment, for example. Even when injury has occurred, if the standard of care has been met, the mental health provider is unlikely to be held liable for malpractice.

Similarly, courts recognize a difference between care that deviates from the professional standard and errors in professional judgment. A patient may commit suicide even when the standard of care has been met. In *Siebert v. Fink* (2001),[14] a New York court stated that suicide itself does not establish negligence: "Should a psychiatrist fail to predict that a patient will harm himself or herself if released, the psychiatrist cannot be held liable for a mere error in professional judgment" when the judgment is based on appropriate assessment. Hence, mental health providers are not liable simply for errors of judgment.

Direct Causation

Medical malpractice requires a causal connection between the substandard care and the injury to the plaintiff. In malpractice actions, it is not uncommon for the plaintiff to claim (and even establish) that the defendant provider deviated from the standard of care. The issue then becomes whether the provider's deviation from the standard of care gave rise to the alleged harm. In other instances, there may be several causes that collectively gave rise to the plaintiff's injury; in these cases, the trier of fact must determine whether the health care professional's substandard conduct was a sufficient cause of the injury as defined by law. In still other cases, an intervening event may have caused the injury. For example, take a patient who has been psychiatrically hospitalized for depression and suicidal thinking. The patient's condition improves during the hospital course, and plans are made for his discharge, including an outpatient appointment for mental health services scheduled for 3 days after discharge. The day before his outpatient appointment, the patient's wife unexpectedly files for divorce. The patient attempts suicide by overdosing on his prescription pain medications. Here, the wife's action is an intervening event. If it was not reasonably foreseeable by the inpatient psychiatrist, the intervening event may suspend a claim of negligence (e.g., premature discharge) on the part of the psychiatrist. Regardless of the specific circumstances, the defendant should not be held liable if the injury would have occurred regardless of the substandard care. See Vignette 2, below, for another example of an intervening event.

To establish malpractice, the causal relationship between the alleged negligent act and the injury to the defendant must meet the criterion of causation. There are two concepts of causation: cause in fact and proximate causation (sometimes called legal causation). The concept of cause in fact requires that the defendant's act (or failure to act when there is a responsibility to do so) contributed to the plaintiff's injury. Cause in fact is established if the plaintiff would not have been injured "but for" the defendant's negligent conduct—in this case, the deviation from the standard of care. Suppose, for example, that a psychiatrist (the defendant) prescribed a psychotropic medication to a patient (the plaintiff) at a dose markedly outside the standard prescribing guidelines and the patient had a significant drop in blood pressure (a known effect of the medication), leading to lightheadedness, a fall, and a head injury from the fall. The question is this: but for the psychiatrist's prescription, would the plaintiff have sustained this injury?

What if, in addition to the psychiatrist's prescription, the patient took an extra dose of his regularly prescribed blood pressure medication before he fell? The law does not require the defendant's conduct to be the sole cause of the plaintiff's injury. It could be argued that although the psychiatrist's prescription was not the sole cause of the injury, it was a but-for cause that, when combined with the patient's error, led to the injury. In some cases, particularly in cases of multiple causation, the court may alternatively use a "substantial factor" test for cause in fact. In this example, the psychiatrist's prescription would be a substantial factor in the plaintiff's injury.

The second concept of causation is proximate causation, which limits liability to those harms that are reasonably foreseeable if an act of negligence occurs. In other words, was the plaintiff's injury a reasonably foreseeable consequence of the defendant's conduct? In the example above, was the patient's fall a reasonably foreseeable consequence of the psychiatrist's prescription? In a North Carolina case, *Williamson v. Liptzin*,[15] a patient sued his former psychiatrist, Dr. Liptzin, for failure to prevent the patient's violent actions after he had left treatment with Dr. Liptzin. The patient did not follow Dr. Liptzin's recommendations and, 8 months after termination of the treatment, shot and killed several people. The North Carolina Court of Appeals ruled that the defendant's alleged negligence was not the proximate cause of the patient's shootings because the events were not reasonably foreseeable by Dr. Liptzin.

Damages

The final element of medical malpractice claims is damages. Legal liability requires the plaintiff to prove that injury of some type occurred. If the mental health provider deviated from the standard of care but the plaintiff was not injured by that deviation, there is no malpractice. Expert testimony is commonly required to establish that an injury (or injuries) occurred and also to determine the fair compensation for the injury.

In medical malpractice cases, the court awards monetary damages to successful plaintiffs. Awards are meant to compensate the plaintiff for the injury and to "make the plaintiff whole" (i.e., restore the plaintiff as closely as possible to his or her state prior to the act of negligence). Compensatory damages include medical and related expenses, lost value of earnings, lost value of household services, and pain and suffering. Medical damages are calculated by reviewing medical and billing records and estimating future medical expenses. Earnings damages are income earnings lost as a result of the injury; these may include lost past and future earnings, as well as the value of employment benefits and bonuses that would have been received. Depending on the nature of any lost employment, these damages are calculated on the basis of the plaintiff's earning records before the injury, the duration of leave from work, and/or the type of work the plaintiff would be doing if not injured. Expert testimony by an economist is required in such cases. Lost value of household services, also the basis for economic testimony, is based on what it will cost to hire someone to perform work in the household that the plaintiff can no longer do. Pain and suffering damages may cover a range of experiences, including physical pain from the injury itself, physical pain from medical procedures performed to remedy the injury, and mental and emotional pain associated with the injury. Damages for pain and suffering are typically more difficult to calculate than other damages, and the trier of fact may be asked to identify a reasonable award for them. Many states put caps on awards for pain and suffering.

Punitive damages are awarded to the plaintiff in certain cases if the defendant is found to have acted so recklessly, maliciously, or deceitfully that the defendant should be punished or made a public example with the goal of deterring others from such behavior. Punitive damages are rare in medical malpractice cases. Examples of such cases in which punitive damages might be awarded include sexual misconduct with a patient, intentional alteration of medical records, and intentional violation of civil rights. Some states do not authorize punitive damages in malpractice cases, and others place limits on the amount of punitive damages that can be awarded.

Vignette 1: Standard of Care

Dr. F., a psychiatrist in private practice, prescribes an antidepressant medication to his patient, Ms. J. The medication is associated with lowering the threshold for seizures. After starting the medication, Ms. J. has a seizure at work and falls and injures herself. She sues Dr. F. for medical malpractice on the basis of negligence. Dr. F. wants to establish that he exercised the appropriate care in prescribing the medication. How is the standard of care determined?

Both parties—Dr. F. and Ms. J.—will put forth evidence on the reasonable standard of care required in these or similar circumstances. Expert testimony is needed in this case to offer evidence regarding the standard of care because psychiatric practice is outside the scope of the trier of fact (jury or judge). Ms. J., as the plaintiff, has the burden of proving all the elements of malpractice, including the standard of care. If she cannot offer an expert to establish the standard of care and to testify that Dr. F. breached it, she will fail in her malpractice claim. Dr. F.'s expert will rebut the testimony of Ms. J.'s expert by offering a different opinion of the standard of care. The specific facts of the case are important. A finding that Dr. F. deviated from the standard of care is likely if Ms. J. had a history of seizures and Dr. F. failed to inquire about this before prescribing the medication. Deviation from the standard of care is less likely to be found, however, if Ms. J. had no history of seizures and Dr. F. warned her of the risk of seizures during the informed-consent process. The experts would opine as to whether Dr. F. acted reasonably under the specific circumstances of the case. On the basis of the expert opinions, the trier of fact would determine whether Dr. F. failed to meet the appropriate standard of care, whether the patient suffered a harm, and whether there was a causal relationship between Dr. F.'s conduct and the injury.

SELECTED ISSUES IN MALPRACTICE

What follow are descriptions of several specific malpractice issues that are relevant to mental health professionals. This list is not comprehensive but rather illustrates key categories of claims put forth by plaintiffs against mental health clinicians.

Suicide

Although suicide is a rare event, mental health clinicians generally have a duty to assess the risk for suicide. The assessment of suicide risk is one of the most important and complex tasks performed by mental health providers. Despite the fact that the patient acts as the causal agent in suicide or attempted suicide, clinicians may nevertheless face malpractice actions on the theory that the clinician should have acted in a way to prevent the suicidal behavior. Malpractice claims by relatives in the aftermath of a patient's suicide constitute one of the largest categories of malpractice claims against mental health clinicians. Successful malpractice claims after patient suicide or attempted suicide result in the highest damages among psychiatric claims. A comprehensive review of suicide is provided in chapter 4.

Although suicide is a tragic event and hindsight bias may color the assessment of the provider's conduct, suicide in itself does not establish negligence on the part of the clinician. Rather, the plaintiff must prove that the psychiatrist or other mental health professional deviated from the standard of care in assessing or managing the patient's suicide risk. In the *Siebert* case, discussed above, the court acknowledged the role of professional judgment in cases of suicide, stating that a psychiatrist cannot be held liable for a patient's suicide on the basis of a mere error of professional judgment that occurs during treatment that meets the standard of care.

Types of malpractice actions after a patient's suicide may include allegations of inadequate assessment of risk, failure to reasonably identify the appropriate level of care (treatment setting), inadequate supervision (hospital or day-hospital setting), and premature discharge from psychiatric hospitalization. A lawsuit following a patient's suicide is more likely to be successful if the suicide occurred in a hospital setting (in contrast to an outpatient setting) because clinicians have more control over hospitalized patients.

Assessment and management of suicide risk call for the provider to make judgments about the degree of risk. It is important to note that foreseeability of suicide potential is not the same as predictability.[16] There is no standard of care for predicting rare events. Attempts to predict such rarely occurring events produce many false positive and false negative results. Rather, the standard of care requires the professional to adequately assess the patient's risk by ascertaining and weighing relevant risk factors and protective factors. Providers may rate the patient's acute risk as low to high and make management decisions on the basis of the assessed risk. For persons at elevated risk of suicide, particularly high risk, the provider is expected to take reasonable precautions to mitigate the risk and implement a reasonable treatment plan in proportion to the assessed level of risk. In a malpractice action, the trier of fact will review the steps taken by the clinician to assess the patient and the clinician's decisions based on the information that was available to the provider.

One strategy that mental health professionals sometimes use in an effort to reduce suicide risk is the establishment of a no-suicide "contract" with the patient. A no-suicide contract is a safety agreement with the patient aimed at preventing suicide. Although these agreements may have some clinical utility, they have no legal weight.[17] They do not protect a clinician in a malpractice action or in defense against a complaint to a professional licensing board. In some cases, these agreements may increase the risk of liability, if a clinician relies on such a contract to the exclusion of a formal risk assessment. Additional risk may be incurred by calling for the patient to enter into the contract when he or she lacks the capacity to do so.[18] No-suicide contracts should not be used as a substitute for an appropriate risk assessment.

Vignette 2: Suicide

Dr. P., a psychiatrist, has been treating Ms. L. for depression for the past 6 months. With steady improvement in her symptoms, Dr. P. lengthens the interval between his appointments with Ms. L. After his last appointment with her, and unbeknownst to Dr. P., Ms. L. stops taking her antidepressant medication. A couple of weeks later, after being fired from her job, Ms. L. overdoses on her husband's cardiac medications and dies. Ms. L.'s husband sues Dr. P. for medical malpractice related to the suicide. Is Dr. P. liable for the suicide?

Suits brought after a patient's suicide are based on the concept of medical negligence. Although a tragic event, suicide itself should not be regarded as prima facie evidence of medical malpractice. In such cases, both parties will obtain experts to give their opinions about what a reasonable clinician would do in similar circumstances. The plaintiff's expert might opine that Dr. P. failed to reasonably assess Ms. L.'s suicide risk or that the increased time between appointments was not appropriate in light of her risk for suicide, as well as that one of these failures was the proximate cause of Ms. L.'s suicide. In contrast, the defense expert is likely to say that Dr. P.'s actions were not the proximate cause of Ms. L.'s injuries under one of two theories in law: an intervening event or lack of foreseeability.[19] As noted above, in law, an intervening event is one that occurs after the allegedly negligent act and breaks the chain of causation. Here, Ms. L.'s nonadherence to recommended treatment and her abrupt loss of employment may be intervening events, breaking the chain of causation from Dr. P. Alternatively, the defense expert could say that, since Dr. P. was not aware that Ms. L. had stopped taking her medications, her suicide was not foreseeable and Dr. P. acted reasonably under the circumstances. Dr. P.'s defense would be served even better by documentation that Ms. L. had been warned about the hazards of discontinuing the medication on her own.

Breach of Confidentiality

Confidentiality is a tenet of the doctor–patient relationship that extends to mental health providers. The duty to maintain the patient's confidences encompasses communications made within the treatment relationship. It is the clinician's obligation to keep sensitive material private from persons outside the treatment relationship in the absence of the patient's consent to disclose such information. Confidentiality extends to communications made in the setting of group therapy, as established in the 1984 case of *State v. Andring*.[20] Preserving confidentiality is vital in fostering the patient's communication with the treating clinician. Breaching a patient's confidentiality may be the basis for a malpractice action or for a disciplinary action in response to a violation of professional ethics.

In certain instances, however, breaching confidentiality is required by law and does not require the patient's consent. For example, state laws may require reporting of certain communicable diseases or gunshot injuries. Of particular relevance to mental health, clinicians are mandated reporters for suspected child abuse or neglect. Similarly, in many states, they are required to report suspected abuse or neglect of the elderly or people with certain disabilities. In some states, there is also a requirement to report domestic violence.[21]

Psychiatrists and mental health providers may breach confidentiality to protect a patient from self-harm, such as when communication is needed to initiate involuntary treatment for a patient with suicidal intent. The landmark *Tarasoff* case, discussed above, created a duty for providers in California to take reasonable steps to protect a third party from the violent act of the provider's patient if the provider determines, or should reasonably determine on the basis of professional standards, that the patient poses a danger to an identifiable third party. The *Tarasoff* case, and subsequently established law in the majority of states, permits or requires providers to breach confidentiality when needed to warn or protect the endangered third party. The exact requirements of this principle are specific to the local jurisdiction.[22] For example, some jurisdictions permit disclosures to protect third parties, whereas other jurisdictions mandate such disclosures. Some jurisdictions require that the provider warn the intended victim; other jurisdictions call for the provider to take measures to protect the victim, which could include such measures as seeking hospitalization for the patient. Still other jurisdictions have declared that mental health professionals have no duty to third parties. In light of this variation across jurisdictions, clinicians should be familiar with the law that applies where they practice. (A detailed discussion of confidentiality and privilege can be found in chapter 9.)

Misdiagnosis

In medical malpractice cases, a plaintiff may be awarded damages for negligent misdiagnosis if the provider fails to make a timely diagnosis and the plaintiff can prove that harm occurred as a result of the failure. The specific allegation may be an inaccurate diagnosis or a delayed diagnosis. In the mental health fields, misdiagnosis claims may also include failure to adequately assess certain symptoms, such as suicidal thinking or neurologic symptoms. Harm in the form of illness progression, lost opportunity to treat a condition before it becomes irreversible, or violence to self or others, may occur when the diagnostic error results in no treatment, incorrect treatment, or delayed treatment.

Misdiagnosis by itself does not constitute negligence. Even when a provider adheres to the standard of care in evaluating a patient, a diagnosis may be inaccurate or delayed. This notion is central to the concept of differential diagnosis, which is used by health care providers to arrive at diagnoses. The standard of care requires that the provider perform a reasonable evaluation in arriving at the diagnosis, recognizing that the diagnosis may be clarified over time as new information is obtained. If a psychiatrist, for example, reasonably interviews a patient and obtains appropriate laboratory or other diagnostic tests in accordance with the standard of care, a misdiagnosis based on reasonable judgment is not malpractice. To establish medical malpractice, the plaintiff must establish that a reasonable provider, in the same or similar circumstances as those of the case in question, would not have erred in the diagnosis.

It is not uncommon in the field of psychiatry for diagnoses to be changed over time. A patient with prior episodes of depression, but no history of mania, is properly diagnosed with a depressive illness. If that same patient later has a manic episode, the diagnosis appropriately changes to a bipolar-spectrum illness, depending on the specific symptoms. The fact that the mental health professional initially diagnosed depression, based on these facts, would not constitute malpractice. On the other hand, if the patient has a family history of bipolar disorder and the psychiatrist prescribes an antidepressant without informing the patient of the possibility of triggering a manic episode and the warning signs that this may be occurring, the psychiatrist may be at risk for malpractice liability should the patient take the medication and have a manic episode.

Along these lines, psychiatric diagnoses are heavily influenced by patients' reports of their symptoms. When a patient provides inaccurate historical information—intentionally or not—it is likely to influence the provider's assessment and decision-making process in arriving at a diagnosis. Take, for example, a patient who describes a past episode of sustained elevated mood with changes in behavior. If the patient reports that he had not been using illicit substances at the time, when in fact he had, the psychiatrist may exclude a substance-induced disorder, a relevant diagnostic category, from the differential diagnosis. In the absence of additional information about the patient's past drug use, the provider's judgment is reasonable. The reasonableness of the provider's assessment—not the diagnosis per se—determines the basis for malpractice claims based on misdiagnosis.

As stated above, the plaintiff must establish harm as a result of the misdiagnosis. In psychiatry, many of the same medications are used to treat a variety of conditions.

Consider a patient who is started on an antidepressant medication for a misdiagnosis of depression. If that patient actually has post-traumatic stress disorder (PTSD), the prescribed antidepressant may be a reasonable and prudent treatment. If, however, the misdiagnosis caused the patient to forgo alternative or additional treatments, such as cognitive processing therapy for PTSD, the patient may have a legitimate claim of injury.

Negligent Treatment

In mental health fields, negligent treatment can be divided into somatic therapies (e.g., medications, transcranial magnetic stimulation, or electroconvulsive therapy) and the many types of psychotherapy. Medical malpractice actions against psychiatrists on the basis of negligent use of medications are similar to such actions against other physicians. Negligent medication prescribing may arise when a psychiatrist prescribes a medication that is not appropriate for the patient's psychiatric condition or other medical condition; prescribes an improper dose of medication; prescribes a medication without performing laboratory tests, physical examination, or other diagnostic tools when indicated; improper prescribing in combination with the patient's other medications or allergies; failing to assess for side effects; failing to assess response to treatment; creating medication dependence; and failure to obtain informed consent for the treatment.[23] Some jurisdictions require legal adjudication of a patient's capacity to consent to electroconvulsive therapy before it is administered.

A landmark case in psychiatric prescribing is *Clites v. Iowa* (1982).[24] Mr. Clites, a man with intellectual disability, was prescribed antipsychotic medication for aggressive behavior and developed tardive dyskinesia (involuntary body movements). Mr. Clites's father sued on his behalf, arguing that there was insufficient evidence of Mr. Clites's aggression, insufficient evaluation by a physician, use of the medication as a convenience for controlling behavior rather than as treatment, and failure to obtain informed consent. The court agreed with the plaintiff's position and explicitly recognized the right to informed consent for antipsychotic medication.

In cases alleging negligent prescribing, a psychiatrist's use of a medication approved by the Food and Drug Administration (FDA) but for an unapproved purpose is not necessarily negligence.[25] Physicians, including psychiatrists, are permitted to prescribe a medication as appropriate, once it has been approved by the FDA, even if it is used for an "off label" reason. Similarly, a psychiatrist's use of medication in a manner that differs from the instructions in the manufacturer's package insert or the *Physicians' Desk Reference* (PDR) does not constitute negligence, although it may create a rebuttable presumption of negligence in some jurisdictions, as it did, for example, in Illinois (*Ohligschlager v. Proctor*

Community Hospital, 1973).[26] In a leading nonpsychiatric case, *Ramon v. Farr* (1989),[27] the court clearly stated that the information in a drug manufacturer's package insert or the PDR may be considered as evidence of the standard of care, along with expert testimony, but that by itself, information from these sources cannot be used to establish negligence.

Several classes of medications used in psychiatry have "black box" warnings. Medications with such warnings are FDA-approved, but the FDA has issued the cautionary warning because of important potential risks associated with the medication. For example, antidepressant selective serotonin-reuptake inhibitors (SSRIs) have a black-box warning stating that they may cause suicidal thoughts or behavior in patients who are 24 years of age or younger. It is important for the prescribing clinician to understand the black-box warning and whether it applies to the patient, consider alternative medication choices without the warning when appropriate, and obtain informed consent that is consistent with the standard of care. Documentation of the physician's well-reasoned choice of medications is helpful as evidence against claims of medical malpractice.

In selecting a medication for a patient and informing the patient about its risks, clinicians should be mindful of foreseeable behaviors by the patient that might be influenced by the prescribed medication. Take, for example, a patient who falls asleep while driving and kills a third person after taking a prescribed sedative medication. Not only may the patient (the driver) face civil claims for wrongful death and criminal charges of homicide but also the patient and victim's representative may be entitled to bring civil legal action against the physician who prescribed the sedative medication. (The patient may have a defense against criminal charges of homicide on the basis of involuntary intoxication by the prescribed medication, if he can establish that he was not adequately informed about the medication and its risks.[28]) In *Coombes v. Florio* (2007),[29] the Massachusetts Supreme Judicial Court held that a physician owes a duty of reasonable care to third parties foreseeably put at risk by the physician's failure to warn the patient of the side effects of a prescribed medication. This case underscores the importance of informing the patient about potential side effects of the medication so that the patient can make informed decisions about whether to drive or engage in other activities.

Malpractice actions for negligent psychotherapy are rare. There are so many forms of psychotherapy, and providers may use more than one approach in their treatment with a patient. The standard of care is therefore often difficult to define. What is more, the therapy relationship is dependent on the patient's participation and investment in the therapy. Finally, the plaintiff must establish the causal nexus between the substandard therapy and harm to the patient. In recent years, there have been a number of cases against psychotherapists that concerned recovered memories of childhood sexual or physical abuse.[30] Several of these cases concern the adequacy of informed consent, including the adequacy of warnings about the risk of recovering false memories. Psychiatrists who provide treatment only with psychotherapy (and do not use somatic therapies) may face a malpractice action for delayed or ineffective treatment if they fail to explain to the patient that psychotropic medications, when appropriate, are another treatment option.

At issue in many claims of negligent treatment is the adequacy of the informed consent. The majority of jurisdictions rely on the "reasonable patient" standard, meaning that physicians shall disclose what a reasonable person would want to know in order to make a decision regarding the proposed treatment.[31] The reasonable-patient standard, articulated in *Canterbury v. Spence* (1972),[32] has replaced the "reasonable physician" standard in these jurisdictions and requires disclosure of "material information." Where the reasonable-patient standard is used, expert testimony is not needed to establish what a reasonable patient would want disclosed; the trier of fact assumes this role. Exceptions to the requirement for informed consent include emergency situations (requiring immediate treatment to prevent harm), the patient's incapacity to make medical decisions (prompting the use of a surrogate decision maker or adjudication), therapeutic privilege (pertaining to disclosures that would cause serious harm to the patient), and waiver by the patient.

Vignette 3: Informed Consent

Dr. B. prescribes a sedative hypnotic for her patient, Mr. H., for insomnia. Before prescribing the medication, she informs Mr. H. of the risks of sedation and disorientation. Dr. B. does not tell Mr. H. about the possibility of sleepwalking, but she tells him that patients may have a wide range of reactions and that he should use caution until he knows how he will respond. After taking the medication, Mr. H. falls down his staircase while sleepwalking, severely injuring his ankle. He sues Dr. B.

The adequacy of the informed consent is likely to be a basis of the plaintiff's case. In most jurisdictions, the standard for adequate informed consent is based on an objective-patient standard—what a reasonably prudent patient would want to know in order to make an informed choice under the circumstances—rather than what any patient subjectively deemed significant or what the clinician thought was important. The plaintiff must further demonstrate that a reasonable patient, had he or she been informed of the material facts, would have made a different treatment decision. Assuming that this case is heard in a jurisdiction that uses the reasonable-patient standard, Mr. H. must show that the risk of sleepwalking is material information that a reasonable patient would want to know and that a reasonable patient, if informed of the risk of sleepwalking, would not have taken the medication. In jurisdictions that use this standard, the issue of the adequacy of informed consent, unlike most other areas of medical malpractice, does not require expert opinion; the trier of fact assumes the role of a reasonable patient. (Informed consent is discussed in more detail in chapter 5.)

Boundary Violations

Boundary violations are interactions between clinicians and patients that blur the lines of the professional relationship. Although sexual relations between a patient and therapist are arguably the most egregious boundary violations, boundaries may be crossed, for example, when a provider discloses certain personal information, excuses a patient from payment, routinely extends a patient's appointment duration, enters into a business venture with the patient, or accepts gifts. (In one notorious example, a physician treating a famous musician for terminal cancer brought his son into the patient's hospital room, had the son perform for the patient, and then had the failing patient autograph, with some assistance, the boy's instrument.) In addition to actions in malpractice, boundary violations may be the subject of explicit state legal provisions. More so than in other health care disciplines, claims based on boundary violations are a substantial source of malpractice actions against mental health providers.

The topic of boundary violations may also be included in professional organization ethics guidelines. The American Medical Association (AMA) Code of Medical Ethics states that sexual contact with a current patient constitutes sexual misconduct.[33] When it comes to sexual or romantic relationships with former patients, the AMA cautions that the relationship is unethical if it exploits trust, knowledge, or emotions or is based on influence from the prior professional relationship. Under Sections 10.05 and 10.08 of the American Psychological Association's Code of Ethics, psychologists must not engage in sexual intimacy with former patients for at least 2 years after conclusion of the treatment relationship; sexual relationships with current patients are prohibited.[34] The American Psychiatric Association unequivocally prohibits sexual relationships with former as well as current patients.[35] Claims of boundary violations against mental health professionals emphasize the trust necessary in the treatment relationship and inequalities in power between the professional and the patient. The case of *Roy v. Hartogs* (1976)[36] is illustrative. Ms. Roy sued Dr. Hartogs for malpractice, alleging emotional harm as a result of engaging in sexual intercourse with Dr. Hartogs "as part of her prescribed therapy." The court emphasized the power differential between the parties in deciding in favor of the plaintiff.

In addition to malpractice suits, claims of sexual misconduct against mental health professionals may trigger disciplinary actions from professional organizations or licensing boards, other claims of civil liability (e.g., loss of consortium by spouse or battery), or criminal penalties in many jurisdictions. Medical malpractice insurance policies typically exclude coverage for claims of sexual misconduct and criminal activity. The insurance exclusions are based on the idea that these intentional actions do not fall within the scope of professional practice and therefore cannot be construed as general professional negligence.

Abandonment

Once a doctor–patient relationship exists, physicians and many other health care providers have an obligation to continue to provide care and not abandon the patient. Abandonment occurs when a health care provider unilaterally terminates treatment prematurely or at an unreasonable time (e.g., when the patient is in crisis) or without providing proper notice to the patient or obtaining the patient's consent to terminate the treatment relationship. A mental health provider who terminates the treatment relationship must give proper notice to the patient and give the patient sufficient time to seek care from an alternative provider. As with other types of malpractice, a plaintiff who claims malpractice on the basis of abandonment must prove that damages were sustained as a result of the abandonment.

Once the treatment relationship is established, mental health providers are not obligated to continue to see patients for an infinite duration. Health care professionals may discontinue services if they disagree with the patient about the course of treatment or the patient fails to comply with treatment. If a patient sees a psychiatrist but refuses to take recommended medications, for example, the psychiatrist may discontinue treatment by referring the patient to alternative services. It is not uncommon for patients to stop attending their appointments without explanation. A therapist cannot continue therapy with a patient who fails to attend appointments at regular intervals and would not be expected to keep scheduling appointments under these circumstances. However, the therapist would be expected to notify the patient that services were being terminated, with such notification including recommendations for treatment and a reasonable period of time during which the therapist would remain available if the patient had an urgent need for care or decided to reengage in the treatment plan. In this example as well, the prudent mental health provider would refer the patient to alternative sources of care. Some jurisdictions have specific legal requirements for how a clinician must notify a patient of termination, such as by certified mail.

Similarly, mental health providers do not have to continue to provide treatment if a patient fails to pay bills for services, in many cases if the patient threatens the clinician or a staff member, or if the patient fires the clinician. The provider may discontinue services after reasonable efforts have been made to remedy the situation or fee dispute. It is often helpful for the provider to work with the patient to identify the reasons for unpaid bills, threatening behavior, or the patient's discharge of the provider, as these discussions may correlate with treatment goals. When fired by a patient, the provider should take into account whether the patient had the requisite capacity to make such a decision. For example, a patient who fires his or her psychiatrist during a manic episode may lack capacity at the time to make that medical decision but later may be able (and expect) to reengage in care. As with other instances of termination, the provider should give reasonable notice and a time frame for the patient to obtain other services.

Battery and Assault

Battery is an intentional tort based on the right to freedom from unwanted bodily contact. The action must cause contact with the patient that is harmful or offensive to the patient. To establish the claim, the plaintiff must prove the defendant had the requisite intent. In civil battery, the defendant must have intended the act but not necessarily any resulting harm. Civil assault is an action that causes the plaintiff an unreasonable apprehension or fear of unwanted physical contact. The intent requirement for civil assault is that the defendant acted to purposely cause fear or acted with substantial certainty of causing apprehension.

An early and commonly cited case of medical battery is *Mohr v. Williams* (1905).[37] In *Mohr*, a physician obtained consent to perform surgery on a patient's right ear. The physician operated on the left ear because that ear appeared to be more seriously diseased. The court held that the physician's touching of the left ear without consent constituted battery.

In mental health, claims for battery and assault may arise, for example, from treatment of a patient with an injectable medication or electroconvulsive therapy without the requisite informed consent or from injuries sustained while a patient was in restraints. Like sexual misconduct, actions based on intentional torts are usually excluded from malpractice insurance coverage when the intentional act was not part of standard practice. For example, a physician accused of injuring a psychotic patient in the course of placing or maintaining restraints on the patient would probably be covered by malpractice insurance, but there would be no coverage if that same physician punched the patient in a fit of anger.

RISK MANAGEMENT

Malpractice lawsuits against mental health professionals are stressful experiences. For some, just the fear of being sued is stressful. Despite diligent clinical practice, no practitioner is immune from the possibility of a suit. Furthermore, there are no algorithms or specific steps providers can take to shield themselves from all suits brought by patients. Four broad principles of practice, however, are helpful to keep in mind in order to reduce the risk of malpractice liability: good clinical care, communication, documentation, and consultation.

Good Clinical Care

Even when concerns about malpractice risk run high, the guiding principle should remain the provision of good care for the patient. Clinicians should use their knowledge and clinical judgment to benefit the patient, be mindful of their scope of practice, and treat patients within their area of competence. Providing good clinical care may require a referral to another provider if the patient's concerns or symptoms are outside the clinician's scope of practice. It is important for providers not to promise or guarantee results. Some jurisdictions recognize a cause of action on the basis of breach of contract or warranty in the case of a provider who makes an express promise or guarantee for a particular result. For example, in a nonpsychiatric case, *Robins v. Finestone* (1955), the court ruled that the patient was entitled to bring a breach of contract claim against a physician who had "guaranteed" the cure of a growth by one procedure but instead had to perform another, more invasive, procedure to remedy the ailment.[38]

Communication

Careful communication with patients and, at times, family members fosters a therapeutic alliance and can reduce the risk of a lawsuit. Good communication—and adequate informed consent—includes informing patients about their disease and prognosis, treatment options, and what to expect for further management. Communication between providers and patients encourages mutual decision making. It can also serve as a means to address a patient's complaints, correct misconceptions, or correct unrealistic expectations that could prompt a future legal action.

Patients are more forgiving of errors when they believe their providers are honest with them and are looking out for their best interests.[39] In a survey of patients or relatives of patients who were filing malpractice claims, Vincent and colleagues[40] found that the majority of claimants filed suits because they wanted to prevent similar errors from occurring to others, wanted the doctors to admit their actions, and wanted an explanation for the cause of their injury. When there is an unintended outcome, providers may be advised to avoid disclosure of any mistake or error due to concern that such statements could be used as admissions in litigation. However, patients often seek an apology or expression of regret after an error has been made.[36,41]

Documentation

Maintaining timely and thoughtful records is a means for providers to document their clinical judgment. Having such records is often protective in malpractice cases when they demonstrate that the clinician adequately assessed the patient and developed a reasonable treatment plan. Medical chart notes help the trier of fact understand the clinician's decision-making process. Take, for example, the situation in which a patient reports having recent suicidal thinking. A provider's documentation of the patient's risk factors and protective factors for suicide, as well as the rationale for treatment decisions, provides evidence that the professional standard of care was met.

The flip side—failure to maintain careful documentation—can hinder the defense in a malpractice case. If there is no (or poor) documentation in the patient's records, the trier of fact may assume that the clinician failed to conduct an assessment or develop a treatment plan or that, if there was a plan, it was carried out ineffectively. Although the defendant clinician will be afforded the opportunity to explain his or her actions, any rationale provided after the malpractice claim has been filed may be viewed more skeptically by the trier of fact. Where there is no clear documentation, early dismissal of the case (e.g., a summary judgment dismissing the claim before trial) is rare because a genuine issue of fact exists regarding the provider's actions and decision-making process.

If a provider obtains additional information about a patient after an encounter with the patient, that information can be documented as an addendum to the medical chart notes. In contrast, altering or falsifying medical records after an adverse event has occurred weighs heavily against the clinician if discovered in the lawsuit and may result in punitive damages. Malpractice insurance policies commonly have clauses of noncoverage in cases in which a provider is found to have improperly altered a medical chart. Such actions are also likely to violate professional ethics standards.

Consultation

Consultation with colleagues about difficult cases or ethical challenges is protective in malpractice actions. At the least, it demonstrates the clinician's desire to secure appropriate care for the patient. More important, consulting opinions may also aid the clinician's decision making and improve the patient's care.

On a more practical basis, consulting opinions that agree with those of the requesting clinician help to establish that the requesting clinician's care is within the standard of practice. A concurring second opinion demonstrates that other providers would act in a similar manner, suggesting reasonableness of the action. When the opinions of a consultant differ from those of the requesting provider, it is advisable for the requesting clinician to seek additional consultation or document the rationale for the differing opinions.

CONCLUSION

Medical malpractice claims are a common concern, but a relatively uncommon occurrence, for mental health providers. Even the most competent clinicians, including mental health professionals, cannot prevent all injuries to patients. Nor can mental health professionals entirely eliminate the risk of malpractice litigation. However, by maintaining clinical competence, communicating with patients, keeping careful treatment records, and consulting with colleagues, mental health professionals can reduce the risk of malpractice liability.

FREQUENTLY ASKED QUESTIONS

What is medical malpractice?

Medical malpractice is a legal action based in negligence for an act or an omission by a clinician that falls below the standard of care and causes injury to a patient.

Why are medical experts retained by the parties in a malpractice case?

The plaintiff (the person filing the lawsuit, commonly the patient) must demonstrate that the clinician fell below the standard of care in rendering services to the patient. Medical experts are needed to demonstrate the applicable standard of care.

What is the standard of care?

Although the specific legal definition varies by jurisdiction, the standard of care is that level of care required by a reasonably prudent clinician in the same or similar circumstances. The standard of care does not require optimal care. Whether a clinician deviates from the standard of care is usually established by expert testimony.

Is misdiagnosis malpractice?

It depends. If a clinician makes an error in diagnosis and the misdiagnosis causes the patient harm, such as delayed treatment or improper treatment, the patient may have an action in malpractice. If the misdiagnosis does not cause harm, the clinician should not be held liable for malpractice, despite the error.

How long does it take for a malpractice suit to be resolved?

Most medical malpractice cases are settled or dismissed before going to trial. For cases that proceed to trial, the typical interval from the time the suit is filed until it goes is approximately 18 months to 2 years.

REFERENCES

1. Hafemeister TL, McLaughin LG, Smith J. Parity at a price: the emerging professional liability of mental health providers. *San Diego Law Review*. 2013;50(29).
2. Jena AB, Seabury S, Lakdawalla D, Chandra A. Malpractice risk according to physician specialty. *New England Journal of Medicine*. 2001;365(7):629–636.
3. Professional Risk Management Services (PRMS). *Psychiatric claims by cause of action, 1998–2005*. Washington, DC: PRMS; 2005.
4. Health Care Quality Improvement Act, 42 U.S.C. sec. 11101 (1998).
5. Reich JH, Maldonado J. Empirical findings on legal difficulties among practicing psychiatrists. *Annals of Clinical Psychiatry*. 2011;23(4):297–307.
6. Kim CJ. The trial of Conrad Murray: prosecuting physicians for criminal negligent over-prescription. *American Criminal Law Review*. 2104;51:517–540.
7. Simon RI, Shuman DW. The doctor-patient relationship. *Focus*. 2007;5(4):423–431.
8. *Stepakoff v. Kantar*, 473 N.E.2d 1131, 1134(Mass. 1985).
9. Shekelle PG, Eccles MP, Grimshaw JM, Woolf SH. When should clinical guidelines be updated? *British Medical Journal*. 2001;323:155–157.
10. American Psychiatric Association. *Practice Guidelines for the Assessment and Treatment of Patients with Suicidal Behavior*. Washington, DC, American Psychiatric Publishing; 2003.
11. Simon RI. Standard of care testimony: best practices or reasonable care? *Journal of the American Academy of Psychiatry and the Law*. 2005;33(1):8–11.
12. *Vede v. Delta Regional Medical Center,* 933 So.2d 310(Miss. Ct. App. 2006).
13. *Tarasoff v. Regents of the University of California,* 551 P.2d 334(1976).
14. *Siebert v. Fink,* 280 A.D.2d 661(N.Y.App. Div. 2001).
15. *Williamson v. Liptzin*, 539 S.E.2d 313(N.C. App. 2000).
16. Simon RI. Suicide risk assessment: what is the standard of care? *Journal of the American Academy of Psychiatry and the Law*. 2002;30:340–344.
17. Garvey KA, Penn JV, Campbell AL, Esposito-Smythers C, Spirito A. Contracting for safety with patients: clinical practice and forensic implications. *Journal of the American Academy of Psychiatry and the Law*. 2009;37:363–370.
18. Simon RI. The suicide prevention contract: clinical, legal and risk management issues. *Journal of the American Academy of Psychiatry and the Law*. 1999;27(3):445–450.

19. Knoll J, Gerbasi J. Psychiatric malpractice case analysis: striving for objectivity. *Journal of the American Academy of Psychiatry and the Law*. 2006;34:215–223.

20. *State v. Andring*, 342 N.W.2d 128 (1984).

21. Schouten R. Legal responsibilities with child abuse and domestic violence. In: Jacobson JL, Jacobson AM, eds. *Psychiatric Secrets*. Philadelphia: Hanley & Belfus; 1995.

22. Johnson MA, Persad G, Sisti D. The Tarasoff rule: the implications of interstate variation and gaps in professional training. *Journal of the American Academy of Psychiatry and the Law*. 2014;42:469–477.

23. Wettstein R. Specific issues in psychiatric malpractice. In: Rosner R, ed. *Principles and Practice of Forensic Psychiatry*, 2nd edition. London: Arnold; 2003:250.

24. *Clites v. Iowa*, 322 N.W.2d 917 (1982).

25. American Medical Association. *HR-115.994: Prescription product labeling*. https://www.ama-assn.org/ssl3/ecomm/PolicyFinderForm.pl?site=www.ama-assn.org&uri=%2fresources%2fhtml%2fPolicyFinder%2fpolicyfiles%2fHnE%2fH-115.994.HTM. Accessed June 14, 2015.

26. *Ohligschlager v. Proctor Community Hosp.*, 303 N.E.2d 392 (1973).

27. *Ramon v. Farr*, 770 P.2d 131 (Utah 1989).

28. Piel JL. The defense of involuntary intoxication by prescribed medications: practice pointers from appellate case review. *Journal of the American Academy of Psychiatry and the Law*. 2015;43:321–328.

29. *Coombes v. Florio*, 450 Mass. 182 (2007).

30. Cannell J, Judson JI, Pope HG. Standards for informed consent in recovered memory therapy. *Journal of the American Academy of Psychiatry and the Law*. 2001;29(2):138–147.

31. Studdert DM, Mello M, Levy MK, Gruen RL, Dunn EJ, Orav EJ, Brennan TA. Geographic variation in informed consent law: two standards for disclosure of treatment risks. *Journal of Empirical Legal Studies*. 2007;4(1):103–124.

32. *Canterbury v. Spence*, 464 F.2d 772 (D.C. Cir. 1972).

33. American Medical Association Code of Medical Ethics, Opinion 8.14, Sexual Misconduct in the Practice of Medicine, 1992.

34. American Psychiatric Association. Principles of Medical Ethics with Annotations Especially Applicable to Psychiatry, Section 2, Annotation 1, 2013.

35. American Psychological Association. Ethical principles of psychologists and code of conduct. *American Psychologist*. 2002;57:1060–1073. Also available (with 2010 amendments) from www.apa.org/ethics/code/index.aspx.

36. *Roy v. Hartogs*, 85 Misc.2d 891 (1976).

37. *Mohr v. Williams*, 80 N.W. 12(Minn, 1905), overturned on other grounds.

38. *Robins v. Finestone*, 308 N.Y. 543 (1955).

39. Huntington B, Kuhn N. Communication gaffes: a root cause of malpractice claims. *Baylor University Medical Center Proceedings*. 2003;16:157–161.

40. Vincent CA, Young M, Phillips A. Why do people sue doctors? A study of patients and relatives taking legal action. *Lancet*. 1994;343:1609–1613.

41. Wei M. Doctors, apologies, and the law: an analysis and critique of apology laws. *Journal of Health Law*. 2007;40:107–159.

9

CONFIDENTIALITY AND TESTIMONIAL PRIVILEGE

ROBERT SCOTT JOHNSON AND RONALD SCHOUTEN

CONFIDENTIALITY

Confidentiality refers to a clinician's duty not to disclose to others information learned from a patient in the course of treatment unless the patient has provided consent for such disclosure, the clinician is compelled by a proper legal authority to disclose the information, or one of several other exceptions applies (e.g., implied waiver, emergency, or incompetence). In contrast to disclosure, the mere receipt of patient information without more does not constitute a breach of confidentiality on the part of the recipient.

The foundation underlying our current model of confidentiality is an amalgam of many component parts, such as custom (which varies from one society to another), ethical principles, case law, some state constitutions, statutes, and pertinent regulations. Among the most common questions raised by students, trainees, and even seasoned practitioners are those concerning confidentiality. What constitutes a breach of confidentiality? When can I disclose otherwise confidential information? When must I? In this chapter, we attempt to clarify for the practitioner what can at times seem like an impenetrable morass of verbiage and apparently conflicting directives.

Ethical Bases for Confidentiality

The Hippocratic Oath refers to confidentiality, in part, as follows: "Whatsoever I shall see or hear in the course of my profession . . . if it be what should not be published . . . I will never divulge."[1] Furthermore, the American Psychiatric Association's *Principles of Medical Ethics, with Annotations Especially Applicable to Psychiatry, 2013 Edition* states, in section 4, "A physician shall respect the rights of patients, colleagues, and other health professionals, and shall safeguard patient confidences and privacy within the constraints of the law." Annotations 1 through 5 elaborate as follows:

1. Psychiatric records . . . must be protected with extreme care. Confidentiality is essential to psychiatric treatment.
2. A psychiatrist may release confidential information only with the authorization of the patient or under proper legal compulsion.
3. Clinical and other materials used in teaching and writing must be adequately disguised in order to preserve the anonymity of the individuals involved.
5. Ethically, the psychiatrist may disclose only that information which is relevant to a given situation.[2]

Similarly, the American Psychological Association's *Ethical Principles of Psychologists and Code of Conduct, 2010 Edition* provides, in section 4:

4.01 Maintaining Confidentiality: Psychologists have a primary obligation to . . . protect confidential information.
4.02 Discussing the Limits of Confidentiality: . . . Psychologists discuss with persons the relevant limits of confidentiality . . . and the foreseeable uses . . . .
4.04 Minimizing Intrusions on Privacy: . . . Psychologists include in written and oral reports . . . only information germane to the purpose for which the communication is made.
4.07 Use of Confidential Information for Didactic or Other Purposes: Psychologists do not disclose in their writings, lectures or other public media, confidential, personally identifiable information concerning their clients/patients.[3]

Lastly, the National Association of Social Workers' *Code of Ethics* states, in section 1.07:

(c) Social workers should protect the confidentiality of all information obtained in the course of professional service, except for compelling professional reasons. The general expectation . . . does not apply when exposure is necessary to prevent serious, foreseeable, and imminent harm to a client or other identifiable person. In all instances, social workers should disclose the least amount of confidential information necessary to achieve the desired purpose.

(e) Social workers should discuss with clients . . . the nature of confidentiality and limitations of clients' right to confidentiality.

(p) Social workers should not disclose identifying information when discussing clients for teaching or training purposes."[4]

Case Law Governing Confidentiality

Confidentiality is a well-established principle in every jurisdiction, including the federal courts. Each jurisdiction has its own seminal court decisions governing the topic, and so we mention just two such cases here that delineate the rules of patient confidentiality. *Doe v. Roe*,[5] a landmark case heard in the New York County (NY) Supreme Court in 1977, is often cited on the issue of patient confidentiality. In that case, a psychiatrist and her psychologist husband published a book that reported verbatim and extensively a patient's thoughts, feelings, emotions, fantasies, and life story. The patient sued, alleging an unlawful invasion of privacy. The court, in its holding, stated that a physician who enters into a treatment relationship with a patient implicitly covenants to keep in confidence all patient disclosures, as well as all matters discovered by the physician, in the course of treatment. The physician was held to have violated the patient's right of privacy, with the court rejecting the defendant's argument that the scientific value of the book outweighed the patient's privacy interests.

Pettus v. Cole[6] is a 1996 California case that describes how the duty of confidentiality applies when clinicians are asked to evaluate a person on behalf of a third party. The case is noteworthy in that the decision is based on the right to privacy established by the California state constitution, state statutes, and case law. Pettus, an employee of DuPont, was sent for a fitness-for-duty evaluation by his employer. Two psychiatrists, both retained by the employer, provided DuPont with detailed reports of their psychiatric examinations of Pettus. Relying on those reports, DuPont subsequently insisted that Pettus enter an inpatient rehabilitation program for alcohol abuse as a condition of retaining his job. When Pettus was terminated for refusing to comply, he brought suit against DuPont and the two psychiatrists, alleging, in part, wrongful termination and breach of confidentiality. In ruling in favor of Pettus, the court held that the psychiatrists had violated the California Confidentiality of Medical Information Act (CMIA) by providing DuPont a detailed report of their psychiatric examinations without a written authorization for such disclosure. The court held that DuPont had violated both the CMIA and the California constitutional right to privacy by terminating Pettus for refusing to enter an alcohol-abuse rehabilitation program. Various exceptions to confidentiality are discussed below.

Health Insurance Portability and Accountability Act

The Health Insurance Portability and Accountability Act (HIPAA)[7] of 1996 was fully implemented in April 2003. Originally envisioned as a way both to facilitate the medical information between providers and to ensure that patients with preexisting medical illnesses would continue to receive health insurance coverage when they changed employers, the law went beyond that initial goal. Ultimately, HIPAA led to the promulgation of new rules regarding how health sharing information is to be managed. These fairly complex HIPAA rules have given rise to a number of misconceptions among providers about their requirements.

The Health Insurance Portability and Accountability Act governs the management of protected health information (PHI) by providers and health plans. Protected health information is defined broadly as any information held by a covered entity that concerns health status, provision of health care, or payment that can be linked to an individual. While PHI is a technical term unique to HIPAA, we use it here to refer to all information that clinicians are required to hold in confidence.

Under the laws preceding HIPAA, doctor–patient confidentiality required a release-of-information form signed by the patient, or at least verbal consent, before one clinician or facility shared PHI with another for the purpose of treatment, but with multiple exceptions. The most common of these exceptions relate to breaches of confidentiality to prevent harm to the patient or others. Many clinicians worried that HIPAA would eliminate those exceptions and would prohibit the reasonable disclosure of information when it was clinically necessary. However, HIPAA provides multiple exceptions to facilitate the communication of PHI for legitimate purposes.

A component of HIPAA known as the HIPAA Privacy Rule allows for disclosure of PHI without the specific consent of a patient in multiple situations where disclosure is deemed to be for the greater public good. Examples include certain reports to law enforcement, the reporting of infectious diseases, the reporting of abuse and neglect, and disclosures to prevent imminent and serious harm from befalling others. Furthermore, under HIPAA, covered health care providers (including physicians) may break confidentiality with regard to a patient's PHI as long as the disclosure pertains to payment, treatment, or health care operations purposes. Treatment includes providing, managing, and coordinating care. In order to avail themselves of these HIPAA protections, providers need to have provided patients with a HIPAA Privacy Notice outlining the HIPAA rules at the outset of treatment. Importantly, while HIPAA allows information to be disclosed for treatment, payment, and health care operations, such disclosures are permissive, not mandatory. Therefore, providers are free to institute more stringent policies, such as requiring the patient's written consent.[8]

Thus, HIPAA can be seen as setting a minimum standard for privacy protection, serving as a floor, not a ceiling. State statutes and regulations may augment the protections of HIPAA by providing still greater protection of patients' privacy, and HIPAA explicitly states that state laws that provide greater privacy protection preempt it. For example, some states may afford patients greater protection than HIPAA with regard to protecting HIV status, sexually transmitted infections, psychotherapy notes, and genetic-testing results. As always, it is important to understand the specific laws and regulations in your own jurisdiction.

While there is no dispute that HIPAA does not create a private cause of action for patients to sue for breach of confidentiality, as of this writing, state courts in Connecticut and West Virginia have ruled that a patient can sue a medical office for negligence if the office releases medical records to a third party in violation of the requirements of the HIPAA regulations.[9,10] In addition, the U.S. District Court for the Eastern District of Missouri refused to accept jurisdiction over a malpractice case heard in a state court, in which the patient alleged, in part, that the clinician had failed to appropriately protect the patient's privacy, citing as an example the privacy protections required by HIPAA.[11] In essence, these courts have ruled that HIPAA can serve as the standard of care for the purposes of a civil negligence lawsuit brought by a patient in a state court.

Enforcement of HIPAA regulations themselves falls under the auspices of the Department of Health and Human Services Office of Civil Rights (OCR). Nevertheless, patients can still avail themselves of civil remedies afforded by state statutes and common law for breach of confidentiality. Enforcement of the HIPAA Privacy Rule by the OCR is likely to be corrective rather than punitive (i.e., imposing a nominal fine, if any, and requiring a plan to prevent any future violations) when physicians or other covered providers are deemed to have acted in good faith. Protection for PHI includes password protection of devices connected to the networks on which the records are stored, as well as encryption of all mobile devices, such as laptops, smart phones, and tablet computers used for patient-related functions, including email.

Medical records used in research constitute PHI, and those records must be carefully protected. While OCR rulings against individual physicians or small practices are rarely punitive, large research institutions have had much harsher penalties imposed for violations of HIPAA. For example, fines of over $1 million have been levied, with stringent corrective-action plans required, in cases in which unencrypted laptops used in research containing PHI were lost or stolen.

Under HIPAA, most psychiatric records are generally treated like any other medical records. However, HIPAA affords special protection for a subtype of psychiatric records deemed "psychotherapy notes," recognizing that they should always be private. Psychotherapy notes cannot be released for treatment, payment, or health care operations without specific consent by the patient. In order for psychiatric notes to be considered psychotherapy notes, they must be kept apart from the patient's medical record. However, certain elements of psychotherapy notes—those relating to test results, diagnoses, treatment plans, prescribed medications, progress to date, and prognosis—are not afforded special protection but instead are treated just like regular psychiatric records.[8] In other words, these aspects of documented psychiatric care do not fall within the narrow definition of psychotherapy notes.

Vignette 1

Dr. S., the treating outpatient psychiatrist for Mr. P., a new patient, seeks medical records from Mr. P.'s recent inpatient psychiatric hospitalization at State Psychiatric Hospital. Under HIPAA, may the hospital release records to Dr. S. without written permission from Mr. P.?

Yes. Under HIPAA a "covered entity" is not prohibited from mailing, emailing, faxing, or orally conveying Mr. P.'s PHI to Dr. S., as in this instance its use falls within the HIPAA exception for treatment. Of note, the hospital is not bound by the "minimum necessary" standard, which would have required the hospital to make reasonable efforts to limit the amount of PHI disclosed, because the "minimum necessary" standard does not apply when a physician discloses information to another provider for treatment purposes. That said, the hospital is responsible for implementing "reasonable and appropriate" security safeguards. For example, hospital office staff should verify the location (fax number, email address, or mailing address) to which the information is being sent. Furthermore, psychotherapy notes are subject to tighter restrictions and always require the patient's consent before they are shared between providers.

Vignette 2

Mr. B. is in a locked inpatient psychiatric unit under the care of Dr. S. Mr. B.'s wife, Ms. C., calls Dr. S., pleading for any information regarding how her husband is doing. How should Dr. S. proceed under HIPAA?

If Mr. B. has specifically asked Dr. S. not to share any information whatsoever, Dr. S. may not divulge any information. One caveat is that Mr. B. must possess the capacity to make treatment decisions in order to bind Dr. S. in that regard. Otherwise, his prohibition would arguably have no effect. If Mr. B. has not prohibited Dr. S. from sharing information (or lacks the capacity to do so), HIPAA permits Dr. S. to share information with his wife, if Dr. S. believes that Ms. C. has a role in caring for her husband and that such sharing of information is in his best interest. That said, Dr. S. may share only information that is directly relevant to Ms. C.'s care for her husband. An example of the sort of information that could be shared would be the fact that Mr. B. needs to take ziprasidone, 20 mg twice daily, and that it should be taken with food.

Vignette 3

Mr. B. is a patient in Dr. S.'s outpatient practice who recently died. His wife, Ms. C., calls Dr. S., asking for medical records detailing her late husband's psychiatric treatment. Do HIPAA protections survive the death of a patient?

Yes. HIPAA protects Mr. B.'s PHI following his death just as if he were still alive. Mr. B.'s directive that his information not be shared would also survive his death. However, HIPAA also provides that the deceased's "personal representative" (e.g., the executor of his estate) has a legal right to access the deceased's PHI. Additionally, covered entities such as Dr. S. are permitted but not required to disclose the decedent's PHI to persons who were involved in the care of the patient before he or she died or in paying for such care (e.g., a health care proxy or a person who has medical power of attorney).

Questions about whether and to what extent PHI may be shared with law enforcement personnel come up routinely. The most common and important situations in which PHI may be shared with law enforcement personnel are the following: to prevent or lessen a serious and imminent threat to an individual or the public; to report evidence of a crime that occurred on the physician's premises; to report a death suspected to have resulted from criminal conduct; to comply with statutory reporting laws (e.g., gunshot wounds treated in an emergency room), to comply with a court order, a warrant, a summons, or a subpoena issued by a judge, or to report child abuse or neglect.[12]

Clinicians should remember that HIPAA is a floor, and that states may provide more stringent privacy standards, which would then apply. Most states have laws that require either a court order or written consent by the patient for the release of psychiatric records, status with respect to human immunodeficiency virus (HIV) infection, records of treatment for substance abuse, or results of testing for sexually transmitted infections. Clinicians should familiarize themselves with the pertinent state laws in their jurisdiction.

As discussed in chapter 16, subpoenas are requests for information that require a response, but unlike court orders, do not require compliance. A clinician who receives a subpoena for a patient's mental health records should take the following steps:

1. Notify the patient that the subpoena has been received. The patient may be completely unaware of the request.
2. Discuss with the patient the implications of releasing records (e.g., what information is going to be released).
3. Contact his or her own legal counsel and let the attorney know that the subpoena was received. This is of particular importance if the request arises in the course of a potential malpractice proceeding. The attorney can respond to the subpoena on the clinician's behalf, including a refusal to comply if the patient declines to have the records released. Attorneys for the patient, the requesting party, and the clinician can attempt to sort out the conflict; if they are unsuccessful, a judge will decide whether to issue a court order for release of the records or instead to quash (i.e., void) the subpoena.

Occasionally, an attorney representing a clinician's patient will contact the clinician. The attorney may ask for a meeting to discuss the care that was provided to the patient. The attorney may even provide verbal assurances that the patient will not sue the clinician and that there is no cause for concern. In fact, the majority of such requests arise because the patient is pursuing a legal claim against someone other than the clinician or is seeking disability benefits. In such circumstances, the request is reasonable and the clinician can comply, so long as the patient consents to release of the records. Clinicians should not take these assurances at face value, however. Before arranging a meeting with the attorney or providing copies of the records, it is advisable for the clinician to discuss the request with his or her legal counsel.

On January 5, 2016, the Obama administration promulgated new HIPAA regulations making it clear that certain covered entities may disclose to the National Instant Criminal Background Check System (NICS)—the system used to regulate access to firearms--information about patients who are subject to one of the "Federal mental health prohibitors." The prohibitors include involuntary civil commitment and adjudication of a patient as "a mental defective" (i.e., a judicial determination that the patient lacks decision-making capacity, is incompetent to stand trial, or is not guilty by reason of mental illness). The rule expressly states that "only covered entities with lawful authority to make the adjudications or commitment decisions that make individuals subject to the Federal mental health prohibitor, or that serve as repositories of information for NICS reporting purposes, are permitted to disclose the information needed for these purposes."[13] A treating clinician, even one initiating a civil commitment of a patient to a psychiatric unit, is not a "covered entity" for purposes of this HIPAA regulation unless he or she has some designated administrative authority for civil commitment or data collection.

Exceptions to Confidentiality

There are numerous ethical and legal exceptions to the requirement of confidentiality. Each exception represents a weighing of the pros and cons of disclosure versus confidentiality. Ethical exceptions tend to be permissive in nature, allowing the clinician discretion in deciding whether to breach confidentiality, and are often based on common sense. The legal exceptions to confidentiality are also rooted in common sense. They protect clinicians from liability for sharing information without the patient's express consent and, in so doing, encourage the release of information when such release is deemed to be of greater benefit than the maintenance of confidentiality. These exceptions may continue to evolve over time as courts, legislatures, and public opinion shift in their views of society's best interests.

Express Waiver

Naturally, patients are free to control the release of their own medication information. It is their prerogative to release such information, if they choose to do so, although they may be charged a duplication fee if the medical records are voluminous. Similarly, a patient may give the clinician permission to verbally share medical information with specific individuals or an entire group (e.g., family members). A signed authorization for release of information is rarely required in such situations, although it is appropriate to document the patient's permission in the record.

Implied Waiver

Patients can waive confidentiality by their actions, as well as by their words. For example, when a patient brings a spouse into a consultation with a psychiatrist, even if the question of a confidentiality waiver is not specifically discussed, the spouse's presence implies that the patient chooses to waive confidentiality with regard to matters discussed during that session. If the spouse's visit is anticipated, it is advisable to talk with the patient beforehand to clarify the purpose of the visit and determine the patient's views on what information should or should not be shared. It is important for the patient to know that you will answer any questions honestly but that the decision about what information is disclosed to the spouse belongs to the patient. If the spouse's visit is unannounced, take a moment alone with the patient to explore this issue before the spouse joins the session. Such an approach is likely to build the patient's confidence in the treating clinician, provide assurance that the patient is in control of his or her own information, and prevent the clinician from inadvertently disclosing information that the patient would prefer to keep confidential.

Duty to Protect Third Parties

Of all the confidentiality exceptions, perhaps the most widely known is the duty to protect third parties from patients who threaten to harm them. Most, but not all, jurisdictions have some form of this duty.

The duty to act to protect third parties from one's patients had its origins in infectious disease cases.[14] Certain jurisdictions imposed liability on physicians for failing to disclose a patient's infectious disease status where third parties became infected. This body of law was further developed after *Tarasoff v. Regents of the University of California*,[15] a seminal 1976 California Supreme Court decision. In it, the court held that psychotherapists have a duty to protect third parties whom the therapist knows or should know, on the basis of professional standards, are at serious risk of harm from a patient. Like most confidentiality exceptions, the case represents a balancing of the needs of the patient for privacy with the broader needs of society to be protected from violent harm. In words that have become famous, the court wrote that "the protective privilege ends where the public peril begins."

States with statutes and case law imposing a duty to protect third parties generally have limited those duties in various ways, and there is considerable variation among jurisdictions. For example, a statute might state that the threat must be to a third party who is identifiable, as opposed to being a vague threat against the public or a particular subgroup of individuals. Other statutes provide that the duty has been fulfilled by notifying law enforcement, warning the victim, or both, or by hospitalizing the patient. In the absence of the patient's consent, warning the potential victim constitutes a breach of confidentiality, and the clinician is obligated to divulge as little information as possible in the process of adequately conveying the warning. Doing so clearly requires the clinician to strike a balance between competing interests.

The ideal solution to this balancing problem lies in the clinical realm, not the legal realm. By appealing to the healthy side of the patient, the clinician may be able to help the patient understand and manage the hostility toward the potential victim, as well as help the patient realize that acting on that hostility is not in his or her best interest. With this approach, the patient may agree to hospitalization or other treatment measures that minimize the threat, provide consent for the clinician to warn the potential victim, or decide to inform the potential victim directly.

In many cases, it is wiser and more protective of patient confidentiality for the clinician to hospitalize the patient than to divulge confidential information to the intended victim. This makes it possible to avoid disclosure if the patient no longer represents a threat at the time of discharge. If the clinician issues a warning on the basis of a belief in its necessity, many statutes relieve the clinician of liability on the premise that the clinician acted in good faith. Finally, some states have determined that there is no duty on the part of mental health professionals to act to protect third parties.

Table 9.1 provides an interpretation of each state's *Tarasoff* law as of August 2015, as it applies to physicians and/or psychotherapists. Statutory language has been simplified significantly for the purpose of this table's readability. For this reason, and because of the changeable nature of statutory and case law, clinicians should familiarize themselves with the law in their jurisdiction of practice and check for updates periodically.

TABLE 9.1. Summary of State *Tarasoff* Statutes[a]

State	Duty to Protect	Permissive or Mandated	Action to Be Taken
Alabama	Yes	Mandatory	Notify victim and police
Alaska[b]	Yes	Permissive	Notify victim or police
Arizona	Yes	Mandatory	Notify victim or police
Arkansas[b]	Yes	Permissive	Unspecified
California	Yes	Mandatory	Notify victim or police
Colorado	Yes	Mandatory	Notify victim and police or admit patient
Connecticut	Yes	Permissive	Unspecified
Delaware	Yes	Mandatory	Notify police or admit patient
Washington, DC	Yes	Permissive	Notify victim or police
Florida	Yes	Permissive	Notify victim or police
Georgia	Yes/no; varies by profession	Other	
Hawaii[b]	Yes	Mandatory	Unspecified
Idaho	Yes	Mandatory	Notify victim and police
Illinois	Yes	Permissive	Unspecified
Indiana	Yes	Mandatory	Notify victim or police or admit patient
Iowa	Yes	Mandatory	Unspecified
Kansas	No		
Kentucky	Yes	Mandatory	Notify victim and police or admit patient
Louisiana	Yes	Mandatory	Notify victim and police
Maine	No		
Maryland	Yes	Mandatory	Notify police or admit patient
Massachusetts	Yes	Mandatory	Notify victim or police or admit patient
Michigan	Yes	Mandatory	Notify victim and police or admit patient
Minnesota[b]	Yes	Mandatory	Notify victim (or police if victim unreachable)

TABLE 9.1. Continued

State	Duty to Protect	Permissive or Mandated	Action to Be Taken
Mississippi	Yes	Permissive	Notify victim or police
Missouri	Yes	Mandatory	Unspecified
Montana	Yes	Mandatory	Notify victim and police
Nebraska[b]	Yes	Mandatory	Notify victim or police
Nevada	No		
New Hampshire[b]	Yes	Mandatory	Notify victim or police or admit patient
New Jersey	Yes	Mandatory	Notify victim or police or admit patient
New Mexico[b]	Yes	Permissive	Unspecified
New York	Yes	Mandatory	Unspecified
North Carolina	No		
North Dakota	No		
Ohio	Yes	Mandatory	Notify victim or police or admit patient
Oklahoma[b]	Yes	Mandatory	Notify victim or police or admit patient
Oregon	Yes	Permissive	Notify police
Pennsylvania	Yes	Mandatory	Unspecified
Rhode Island	Yes	Permissive	Notify victim or police
South Carolina	Yes	Mandatory	Unspecified
South Dakota	Yes	Permissive	Notify victim and/or police
Tennessee	Yes	Mandatory	Notify victim
Texas	Yes	Permissive	Notify police
Utah[b]	Yes	Mandatory	Notify victim and police
Vermont	Yes	Mandatory	Unspecified
Virginia	Yes	Mandatory	Notify victim or police or admit patient
Washington, DC	Yes	Mandatory	Notify victim and police
West Virginia	Yes	Permissive	Unspecified
Wisconsin	Yes	Mandatory	Unspecified
Wyoming[b]	Yes	Permissive	Unspecified

[a]The information in the table is from several sources—notably, Johnson R, Persad G, Sisti D. The Tarasoff rule: the implications of interstate variation and gaps in professional training. *Journal of the American Academy of Psychiatry and the Law.* 2014;42(4):469–477; and National Conference of State Legislatures. Mental Health Professionals' Duty to Warn. 2015. Accessed November 1, 2015, at http://www.ncsl.org/research/health/mental-health-professionals-duty-to-warn.aspx.
[b]The statute does not specifically make reference to physicians, psychotherapists, mental health professionals, or mental health coordinators.

The circumstances in which a duty to protect arises are generally limited by state statute. As examples, a state may limit the duty to situations in which the patient has a known history of violence, there is a reasonable anticipation of violence, or the patient has made a specific threat to an identifiable third party. Additionally, state laws often delineate specific acts clinicians must take to discharge their duty to protect, such as reporting information to the police, informing the intended victim, voluntary admission to a hospital, or involuntarily hospitalizing the patient for further evaluation.

To complicate matters, some state *Tarasoff* statutes apply generally to all physicians, while others refer to mental health professionals, psychotherapists, or some other group entirely. To add a further wrinkle, certain states (e.g., Arizona,) have different reporting standards for various groups of clinicians, with some subject to permissive reporting and others subject to mandatory reporting.

Vignette 4

Dr. S. learns from her patient, Mr. G., that he is thinking of harming Ms. L. Dr. S. believes this to be a serious and credible threat and believes that Mr. G. is capable of following through on it. What should Dr. S. do at this point?

First, Dr. S. should make sure that she understands the pertinent statutory requirements in her jurisdiction. This can be accomplished by reading the statute herself or, perhaps more productively, consulting with legal counsel or clinical colleagues who are familiar with the statute and have experience with these situations. Before rushing to notify the police or Ms. L., Dr. S. should take as much time as reasonably necessary to elicit additional information from Mr. G. about his thinking. In such situations, clinicians should weigh their ethical and, in some jurisdictions, legal obligations to warn patients like Mr. G. of their duty to breach confidentiality if they believe the patient is a danger to himself or others. Dr. S. also should keep in mind that as long as Mr. G. is suffering from a mental illness, she may have the option in her jurisdiction of admitting him (either voluntarily or involuntarily) to a psychiatric unit in lieu of contacting the potential victim or the authorities. This action may, in essence, buy the treatment team time to further assess the veracity of Mr. G.'s claims of wanting to harm Ms. L., without having to breach his confidentiality. If Mr. G. is hospitalized, his risk to third parties can be assessed as part of the decision making with regard to discharge, which will include an assessment of whether Mr. G.'s recovery during his hospitalization has been sufficient to make notification of third parties unnecessary.

If Mr. G. continues to harbor aggressive impulses toward Ms. L. at the time of discharge, or is being managed as an outpatient, ideally, Dr. S. can work with him to get him to disclose his impulses to harm Ms. L., so that she will be aware and duly warned. In addition, such sharing can have a therapeutic effect and help diminish those impulses. Where the *Tarasoff* duty applies, the fact that the intended victim is aware that the patient poses a threat to him or her does not necessarily eliminate the clinician's duty to take steps to protect the victim. As an example, in the 1983 case of *Jablonski v. United States*,[16] the U.S. 9th Circuit Court of Appeals held that a foreseeable victim who was aware that Jablonski posed a threat to her nevertheless should have been warned about his potential for violence, even though she had not been specifically targeted by Jablonski. A professional's assessment that there is a credible risk of harm to the potential victim is likely to have a greater impact than the potential victim's own impressions or the opinions of friends or family members, and the clinician may still have a duty, even if the potential victim is aware of the risk.

What if Mr. G. is highly unlikely to have the ability to carry out his threat against Ms. L. (e.g., he is bedbound because of paralysis)? In this situation, knowledge of the jurisdiction's particular statute is imperative. Some states, such as Delaware and Massachusetts, require that Mr. G. have not only the intent but also the ability to carry out his threats of harm against Ms. L. If he cannot carry them out, then no *Tarasoff* reporting duty arises.

What if, instead, Mr. G. demonstrates that he has the intent and ability to commit a specific violent act but there are no identified individual targets? For example, he plans to plant a bomb in a subway station but has no specific intended victim (or victims). Again, Dr. S. must specifically refer to the statute in the jurisdiction at issue, as there is some variation regarding the need for a specified individual target in order for a *Tarasoff* reporting duty to arise. Some jurisdictions (e.g., Indiana and New York) require only the imminent risk of serious harm to others for a *Tarasoff* reporting duty to arise. In other jurisdictions (e.g., Massachusetts and Michigan), a "reasonably identified" victim is required. Nevertheless, even if a duty to protect third parties is technically not triggered under the state's *Tarasoff* statute, Dr. S. is still within her rights to commit Mr. G. involuntarily to a psychiatric unit for treatment, given his homicidal ideation. Furthermore, were Mr. G. to harm someone after Dr. S. decided not to commit him involuntarily, he would have a potential malpractice claim against Dr. S.

What if Dr. S. practices in a jurisdiction with no *Tarasoff* reporting duty, either mandatory or permissive? Here, Dr. S. is in a bit of a quandary. In most cases, the decision to admit the patient (involuntarily or voluntarily) would be the path of least resistance and would minimize the risk of least legal exposure. However, had Mr. G. disclosed his thoughts of harming Ms. L. during the course of an outpatient office visit and then rapidly departed before a psychiatric admission could be arranged, Dr. S. would have had to weigh the pros and cons of breaching confidentiality in light of the credibility of his threat, his ability to carry it out, and the nature of the target. It may be the case that even in states that do not have either a mandatory or permissive *Tarasoff* duty, Dr. S.'s legal exposure would be slight if she acted in good faith when the risk was serious and imminent, with a specified target. Several jurisdictions specifically articulate good-faith provisions in their duty-to-protect statutes.

Even in a jurisdiction that does not give Dr. S. permissive authority to break confidentiality, much less impose a duty, Dr. S. might still reasonably conclude that a warning or notification is appropriate. This conclusion could be based on an ethical obligation, as opposed to a legal one. The ethics codes for the American Psychiatric Association, American Psychological Association, and National Association of Social Workers all grant permission for a breach of confidentiality if it is necessary to provide protection in the case of a patient who poses a danger to self or others. Additionally, even in a state that would not permit Dr. S. to breach confidentiality, she might reasonably fear a lawsuit for wrongful death if her patient should kill a third party. In that context, it might be preferable to be sued for breach of confidentiality than for wrongful death.

Vignette 5

Dr. S. learns from her patient, Mr. W., that he is HIV-positive and is putting one or more unknowing sexual partners at risk. What obligation does Dr. S. have?

This scenario highlights the conflict between the competing demands of keeping sensitive patient information, such as HIV status, private and protecting third parties at risk. As noted above, *Tarasoff* had its origins in infectious disease cases. What makes the HIV situation somewhat different from a typical *Tarasoff* matter is that the general public has been exposed to considerable information about the risks of unsafe sex. Therefore, there is an element of caveat emptor here that argues against Dr. S.'s need to warn. While the answer may vary depending on the jurisdiction and is not always clear, physicians should be aware of such competing tensions within the law, as well as specific legal prohibitions against release of HIV-related information without the patient's consent. For example, Massachusetts has a *Tarasoff* duty that would arguably apply in situations in which an HIV-positive person refused to inform his sexual partner of his HIV status and expressed his intent to infect the partner. Yet Massachusetts also has a statute that prohibits the release of any HIV-related medical information without the patient's express permission.

Civil Commitment

As discussed in chapter 2 on civil commitment, there is a well-established exception to patient confidentiality for matters related to civil commitment. Although state statutes vary considerably, confidentiality can be breached for purposes of obtaining temporary involuntary hospitalization and civil commitment if a patient has demonstrated that he represents a risk of harm to himself or others. Additionally, states allow for breach of confidentiality for purposes of civil commitment if a patient meets criteria for being "gravely disabled" or displays a "need for treatment," as defined by statute.

Suspected Child Abuse

All 50 states and the District of Columbia have statutes mandating that certain professionals (referred to as "mandated reporters") file a report to state social service agencies when they suspect child abuse or neglect. The obligation to report in each jurisdiction generally only requires that the clinician have a "reasonable basis" to suspect child abuse. Statutes vary with regard to whether or not the child at issue needs to have been seen as a patient by the reporting clinician, and there is also variation with regard to the types of abuse that must be reported. For clinicians practicing in hospitals, the hospital attorneys or social service office should be able to provide contact information in addition to advice on when and how a report is to be made. State penalties for failure to report suspected child abuse generally involve a substantial fine as well as possible criminal penalties. Furthermore, failure to report could result in discipline from state agencies that regulate professional licensing. Mandated reporters are generally protected from liability by an exception to the confidentiality requirements when the reporting decision was made in good faith.

There are some interesting permutations of these rules of which practitioners should be aware. For example, while the duty to report arises when there is a suspicion of abuse or neglect of a minor, the obligation ends once that minor reaches the age of majority (whatever that age may be in any particular jurisdiction). However, if the mandated reporter is aware that minor children remain at risk at the hands of the alleged perpetrator who was involved in the initial abuse, there may be a reporting duty. Mandated reporter requirements are discussed in chapter 10, "Evaluation of Child Abuse and Neglect," and chapter 11, "Juveniles and the Law."

Vignette 6

Dr. S. learns from her patient, Ms. J. (now 18 years of age), that she was sexually abused by her uncle when she was 14 years old. Ms. J. has never told anyone of this abuse, and her uncle has never been brought to justice for his actions. What is Dr. S.'s reporting obligation, if any?

Given that Ms. J. is now an adult in every U.S. jurisdiction, Dr. S. is generally not under an obligation to report this purported child abuse, as that burden falls on Ms. J. However, if minor children remain in the home and Dr. S. has reason to believe that they may be at risk of abuse, then she generally will have an obligation to report, as noted above. Furthermore, had Dr. S. learned of the abuse while Ms. J. was still deemed a minor,

Dr. S. would not have been able to relieve herself of the duty to report suspected child abuse by simply waiting until Ms. J. became an adult. Dr. S. should work with the patient to determine whether, and if so how, disclosure would be of therapeutic benefit to her. Ultimately, it will be the patient's decision whether or not to report the abuse.

Vignette 7

Ms. N., a social worker, is informed by an adult patient that he abused a child many years ago. Is Ms. N. required to break confidentiality and report this information?

In most jurisdictions, past criminal acts are protected as confidential information between the clinician and the patient. However, if the patient informs Ms. N. that he is planning to abuse another identifiable child, then state laws regarding mandatory reporting of child abuse would apply, triggering a duty to report.

Suspected Abuse of Elderly or Disabled Persons

Many U.S. jurisdictions also have statutes aimed at protecting vulnerable members of the population, other than children, from abuse. While these statutes are not as universal as those for reporting child abuse, practitioners should make themselves aware of the legislation that applies in the jurisdiction where they practice. Statutes generally require notification of the appropriate social services agency when mandated reporters become aware of such abuse. In some jurisdictions, these reporting statutes can apply to the mentally or physically infirm, regardless of age, who are dependent on others for their care and well-being.

Vignette 8

Dr. S. learns from her patient that Mr. H., a cognitively impaired 20-year-old man, is being physically mistreated by his caregivers. What is Dr. S.'s obligation?

Depending on the jurisdiction where she practices, Dr. S. may be under an obligation to report this mistreatment, just as she would be under an obligation to report child abuse. The same would be true if Mr. H. were 80 years old and living in a nursing facility.

Nonaccidental Injuries and Suspected Intimate-Partner Violence

Most states have enacted mandatory clinician reporting laws for certain types of injuries and domestic violence or, as it is now more commonly called, intimate-partner violence. Unlike laws pertaining to abuse of elderly persons, vulnerable adults, or children, these laws pertain to all adults who receive treatment from a physician. The statutes generally fall into three categories: statutes that require reporting of injuries from weapons; statutes

that require reporting of injuries resulting from violation of criminal laws, injuries resulting from violence, or injuries sustained by nonaccidental means; and statutes that specifically address intimate partner violence. New York's statute[17] is fairly typical of the first
category, requiring the reporting by clinicians of injuries from guns or sharp objects, injuries likely to result in death, and significant burns. An example of the second category is
Michigan's statute, which adds to the list of injuries those "inflicted . . . by other means of
violence."[18] Colorado's statute is representative of the third category, requiring physicians
to notify local police of "injuries resulting from domestic violence."[19]

Intimate partner violence is a far greater problem than many clinicians realize.
Estimates vary, but the data suggest that in the United States, 1% of women report having experienced domestic violence in the past year, and 22% report having experienced
domestic violence at some time in their lives.[20] In 2013, 13% of calls to the National
Domestic Violence Hotline identified a male victim.[21]

When interviewing a potential victim of intimate partner violence, it is important to
avoid using judgmental terms such as "abused" or "battered." The person may deny abuse
despite obvious signs of violence, so one should not always take such denials at face value.
Furthermore, asking what the potential victim did to provoke the violence or why he or
she has not left the batterer is to be avoided, as such comments unfairly appear to put the
blame on the victim.

Vignette 9

*Dr. S. sees Ms. B. regularly in her outpatient psychiatric practice and has grown to suspect that
Ms. B. may be the victim of domestic abuse. She has been reluctant to discuss her bruises or
acknowledge an abusive relationship. How should Dr. S. proceed?*

First, if mandatory reporting laws for suspected domestic abuse apply in Dr. S.'s state,
then she is bound by those laws to report suspected abuse. As with reporting of child
abuse and neglect, compliance with mandatory reporting requirements can be challenging from the standpoint of the clinician–patient relationship. Colleagues familiar with
these situations can be a valuable resource for the clinician faced with the need to report.
Clinicians should be aware that the period of greatest risk for physical violence is immediately after an abused partner takes action to get out of the relationship.[20]

Other Exceptions to Confidentiality

There are a number of other exceptions to confidentiality, which may vary across jurisdictions. Chief among them is the emergency exception, which arises when the failure to
breach confidentiality would result in the likelihood of harm to the patient or others. For
example, if a patient has a heart attack in a clinician's office, and that clinician is privy to

information about the patient's health conditions that would be helpful to the emergency medical technicians, confidentiality may be breached, since withholding that information could harm the patient.

Other common exceptions include incapacity on the part of a patient who is being transferred from one health care facility to another, defense against a claim of malpractice, collection of unpaid fees, and civil commitment of a patient.[22] These exceptions are created either by statute or by case law. Since they vary from one jurisdiction to another, clinicians should familiarize themselves with the laws in their jurisdiction.

PSYCHOTHERAPIST–PATIENT TESTIMONIAL PRIVILEGE

Unlike confidentiality, which encompasses the clinician's ongoing obligation to maintain patient privacy, testimonial privilege concerns the patient's right to prohibit the clinician from answering administrative or judicial requests for that patient's clinical information or for testimony about such information in the context of litigation. The psychotherapist–patient privilege reflects a decision by society that the preservation of the privacy of the psychotherapist–patient relationship is more important than the benefit that would be derived from requiring testimony by the psychotherapist. In essence, the testimonial privilege provides for exclusion of otherwise valuable evidence from an administrative or judicial proceeding.

Whereas the duty of confidentiality is ongoing, the psychotherapist–patient privilege must be invoked before it can be applied. If the privilege is not invoked, the clinician can disclose the information, provided that disclosure is otherwise permissible under HIPAA or the exceptions to confidentiality. The privilege belongs to the patient, but in some limited circumstances, it can be invoked by the clinician on behalf of the patient.

Ethical Underpinnings

Some would argue that privilege merely blocks the truth from coming out in judicial proceedings. However, others contend that privilege prevents highly prejudicial information from swaying the jury unfairly. As an example, a patient engaging in cognitive-behavioral therapy with a psychologist might concede, "I feel guilty about what I did." A lay jury might interpret that statement as a confession regarding the patient's involvement in an alleged crime and subsequent guilt. However, the privilege serves to protect the jury, in some ways, from itself and its lack of understanding about the nature of talk therapy. As most mental health professionals are aware, expressions of guilt by patients are common, often indicating a general sense of guilt and responsibility rather than evidence of actual guilt or liability in the legal sense.[23]

Case Law and Statutory Basis

English common law (i.e., case law) has served as the foundation for much of U.S. law. Common law initially held that a court was entitled to "every man's evidence," with no restrictions on who could be called to testify or on what they could be compelled to disclose. However, the passage of time led gradually to the insight that it was of benefit to society to establish certain limits on these testimonial disclosures, called "privileges." Examples include attorney–client privilege, spousal privilege, priest–penitent privilege, and doctor–patient privilege, a subset of which is psychotherapist–patient privilege.

With regard to psychotherapist–patient privilege, state statutes broadly define a "psychotherapist" as a psychiatrist, psychologist, clinical social worker, or licensed mental health counselor. Through the psychotherapist–patient privilege, a patient has a right to prevent the psychotherapist from disclosing confidential communications made for the purpose of treating the patient's mental or emotional condition. The privilege itself is something of a misnomer, since it does not apply solely to interactions that would be deemed talk therapy. If a psychiatrist is involved, even if the treatment at issue is strictly medication management, that psychiatrist is deemed a "psychotherapist" for purposes of the statute.

Shortly after the creation of the psychotherapist–patient privilege, there was some debate about whether the psychotherapist could raise the privilege on behalf of the patient if the patient had not done so. The California Supreme Court addressed this question in the seminal 1970 case of *In re Lifschutz*,[24] in which a treating psychotherapist had been called to testify and asked to produce medical records. He refused to do so, asserting psychotherapist–patient privilege. In its holding, the court stated that it is the patient, not the psychotherapist, who has a constitutional right to privacy. Therefore, the psychotherapist–patient privilege belongs to the patient, not to the doctor, and cannot be invoked by the latter. If the patient is unavailable or otherwise unable to invoke the privilege, however, the clinician can raise it on the patient's behalf until the patient is able to do so.

After all 50 states enacted psychotherapist–patient privilege laws, the federal Courts of Appeal were split on the question of whether the privilege existed in federal courts. In *Jaffee v. Redmond*,[25] the U.S. Supreme Court considered the issue of psychotherapist–patient privilege and resolved this split among the Circuit Courts, holding that the privilege does exist in federal courts. Furthermore, in its holding, the Supreme Court extended the psychotherapist–patient privilege to apply to psychologists and social workers as well as psychiatrists. Writing for the majority, Justice John Paul Stevens wrote, "The psychotherapist privilege serves the public interest by facilitating the provision of appropriate treatment for individuals suffering the effects of a mental or emotional problem. The mental health of our citizenry . . . is a public good of transcendent importance."

Subpoenas

Privilege issues commonly arise when patients are involved in litigation, whether civil or criminal. In such a circumstance, a clinician may receive a subpoena to produce records or to appear for a deposition. A subpoena for the production of documents, or subpoena *duces tecum*, is a common form of subpoena sent to clinicians to request the production of treatment records for discovery purposes or potential use as evidence in litigation. Clinicians should be aware that a subpoena generally constitutes a mere request for information, as opposed to a court order with which the clinician must comply. Nevertheless, a response to the subpoena is required, and the prudent clinician will notify his or her attorney of the subpoena. The attorney should be asked to advise the clinician as to the appropriate response and to provide the response, (e.g., the records sought are confidential and can be produced only with a release from the patient). The attorney and the clinician have the option to file a motion to quash the subpoena or to limit the nature of the information to be produced, citing psychotherapist–patient privilege. When testimonial privilege is cited as a reason for not producing the requested records or limiting those that are produced, a hearing may be held in which the judge will rule on whether the subpoena must be enforced. As a result of that hearing, the judge may uphold the testimonial privilege or issue a motion to compel, ordering production of the treatment records. The judge may also order that the records be provided for review by the judge alone, for the purpose of determining which, if any, of the documents must be disclosed and can be used as evidence.[26]

Vignette 10

Dr. S. receives a subpoena requesting that she turn over PHI regarding Mr. T., a patient of hers. What are her obligations in this situation?

Dr. S.'s obligations depend on who issued the subpoena. All subpoenas require a response, although in some cases, that response may be a refusal to comply for stated reasons. If the subpoena was issued by a judge or administrative tribunal, then Dr. S. should respond once she has consulted with her attorney. In contrast, if a court clerk or an attorney issued the subpoena, that party is required to provide evidence to the physician that reasonable and good-faith efforts were made to notify Mr. T. in writing of the litigation and of his right to object to the release of PHI, and that the time for objection has now passed and no objection was filed. Dr. S. should never ignore a subpoena, even if it asks for information that she does not have or she believes that it fails to meet the requirements delineated above. She should instead respond, expressing any reservations that she might have, in order to avoid being held in contempt of court.

Vignette 11

Dr. S. receives a subpoena issued by an attorney representing Mr. R., one of Dr. S.'s psychiatric patients. The attorney assures Dr. S. that Mr. R. has waived his psychotherapist–patient privilege. Should Dr. S. comply with the subpoena and forward the requested medical records?

No. Dr. S. should not rely on verbal assurances from the attorney regarding waiver of privilege. She will need to see a signed waiver form before producing the requested documentation. Dr. S. should also talk with Mr. R. to ensure not only that he signed the form voluntarily but also that he understands the extent and nature of the information that will be submitted. Subpoenas are discussed in more detail in chapter 16.

Exceptions to Testimonial Privilege

Waiver

With regard to evaluations conducted in clinical situations, a patient retains the right to prevent the clinician from testifying and to prevent the records of those conversations from being used in an administrative or legal proceeding. However, all states allow the patient to waive this right. Waiver is deemed to occur when the patient acknowledges that communications between the patient and the therapist will not be confidential.

With regard to examinations conducted by clinicians for third parties, as opposed to those conducted for clinical purposes, all states provide that the examinee (the person being evaluated for a court proceeding) may voluntarily waive his or her right to the psychotherapist–patient privilege. Before starting the formal interview, the clinician should inform the examinee of the clinician's role as an evaluator on behalf of the court or attorney. There should be no "off record" conversation between the clinician and the examinee before the examinee agrees to waive testimonial privilege. The clinician should also inform the examinee that once the psychotherapist–patient privilege has been waived, communications during the examination will not be privileged and the clinician may be called on to prepare a written report for the court or attorney and may ultimately be called to testify. The examinee should also be informed of the right to not answer any questions that he or she does not wish to respond to.

The evaluating clinician should document the examinee's understanding of the conditions of the evaluation. Additionally, in the event that a written report is prepared incorporating information gleaned from an interview with an examinee, the clinician should clearly articulate in the written report the examinee's waiver of privilege.

Patient Puts Mental Status into Issue

In an often-quoted expression, a patient may not make his or her mental status simultaneously "a sword and a shield." A good-faith litigant, suing for mental distress or other psychiatric injury or pleading insanity in a criminal case should not object to the testimony of a treating or examining clinician. On the contrary, the patient should seek out that testimony. Moreover, in a case of alleged emotional injury, it would be unfair to deny the defendant the opportunity to challenge the claim by blocking access to medical records and treating clinicians. Therefore, it is a well-understood exception to the psychotherapist–patient privilege that when the patient "puts mental status into issue," the privilege is waived.[27] Nevertheless, the patient can ask the judge to exclude the information on the grounds that it is unnecessary or unduly prejudicial to the patient's claim. The judge will then review the requested information and determine whether the interests of justice outweigh the importance of protecting the privileged relationship.

Danger to Self or Others

The privilege statute in Massachusetts, like such statutes in other states, specifies that the threat of imminent danger to self or others constitutes an exception to the patient's right to testimonial privilege. In many ways, this mirrors the exception to confidentiality for civil commitment purposes. The applicability of psychotherapist–patient privilege in the civil commitment process is discussed in chapter 2.

CONCLUSION

The abundance of rules and exceptions pertaining to confidentiality and privilege requires the prudent practitioner to be familiar with his or her own jurisdiction's laws. While this chapter has laid out the current state of the law to the best of our understanding, case law and statutory changes will no doubt continue to modify and shape the concepts of confidentiality and privilege. Just as the physician–patient privilege has been limited gradually through the enactment of exceptions, the psychotherapist–patient privilege may slowly meet the same fate over time.

FREQUENTLY ASKED QUESTIONS

When a clinician receives a subpoena requesting a patient's medical records, what is the clinician's duty?

If the subpoena was issued by a judge or administrative tribunal, then the clinician should respond once she has consulted with her attorney. In contrast, if a court clerk or an attorney issued the subpoena, that party is required to provide evidence to the clinician that reasonable and good-faith efforts were made to notify the patient in writing of the litigation and of his or her right to object to the release of PHI, and to confirm that the time for objection has now passed and no objection was filed.

What is the Tarasoff duty?

It is the duty to protect third parties from patients who threaten to harm them. Most, but not all, jurisdictions have some form of this duty. Table 9.1 lays out the Tarasoff duty in each U.S. state.

What situations may require mandatory reporting other than the Tarasoff duty?

Some of the most common examples include suspected child abuse, suspected elder abuse, suspected abuse of the disabled and infirm, suspected intimate-partner violence, and nonaccidental injuries.

In the context of an oral or written academic presentation to colleagues, in what manner is it acceptable for me to present patient information without violating patient confidentiality?

Patient information must be sufficiently disguised and changed such that the patient cannot be identified.

If I have a patient who presents as being imminently suicidal, does HIPAA prevent me from disclosing that information?

There is an exception to HIPAA that permits a clinician to share patient information in the interest of having the patient evaluated by mental health personnel for the purpose of assessing whether the patient warrants admission to a psychiatric unit.

REFERENCES

1. Edelstein L. *The Hippocratic Oath: Text, Translation and Interpretation.* Baltimore: Johns Hopkins University Press; 1943.
2. American Psychiatric Association. The Principles of Medical Ethics with Annotations Especially Applicable to Psychiatry. Revised. Alexandria, Virginia: American Psychiatric Press; 2009.
3. Ethics Committee of the American Psychiatric Association. Ethical principles of psychologists and code of conduct. *American Psychologist.* 2002;57:14.
4. National Association of Social Workers Code of Ethics. 2008. Accessed October 3, 2015.
5. *Doe v. Roe,* 400 N.Y.S.2d 668(New York Supreme Court 1977).
6. *Pettus v. Cole,* 49 Calif. App. 4th 402(California Court of Appeals 1996).
7. Health Insurance Portability and Accountability Act of 1996, 110 Stat. 193 (1996).
8. Brendel RW, Bryan E. HIPAA for psychiatrists. *Harvard Review of Psychiatry.* 2004;12(3):177–183.
9. *Emily Byrne v. Avery Center for Obstetrics and Gynecology,* 314 Conn. 433(Supreme Court of Connecticut 2014).
10. *R.K. v. St. Mary's Medical Center,* 735 S.E.2d 715(West Virginia Supreme Court of Appeals 2012).
11. *I.S. v. Washington Univ., No. 4:11-cvv-00235-SNLJ, E.D. Missouri, 2011,* No. 4 SNLJ(U.S. District Court for the Eastern District of Missouri 2011).
12. United States Department of Health and Human Services. U.S. Department of Health and Human Services Guidelines. Vol 2015. When does the Privacy Rule allow covered entities to disclose protected health information to law enforcement officials? http://www.hhs.gov/ocr/privacy/hipaa/faq/disclosures_for_law_enforcement_purposes/505.html. Accessed November 15, 2016.
13. Health Insurance Portability and Accountability Act Privacy Rule and the National Instant Criminal Background Check System. In: Department of Health and Human Services, ed. *81 Federal Register 382 (6 January 2016).* Washington, DC: Office of the Federal Register, National Archives and Records Administration; 2016:382–396.
14. Schouten R, Brendel RW. Malpractice and Boundary Violations. Chapter 86. In: Stern TA, Fava M, Wilens TE, Rosenbaum JF, eds. *Comprehensive Clinical Psychiatry,* 2nd edition. New York: Elsevier; 2015.
15. *Tarasoff v. Regents of the University of California,* 17 Cal. App. 3rd 425(California Supreme Court 1976).
16. *Jablonski v. United States,* 712 F.2d 391(U.S. Court of Appeals 9th Circuit 1983).
17. New York Penal Law, Sec.265.25 (2010).
18. Michigan Penal Code, Act 328 of 1931, Sec.750.411 (2001).
19. Colorado Revised Statutes, Sec.12-36-135 (2015).
20. Tjaden P, Thoennes N. *Full Report of the Prevalence, Incidence and Consequences of Violence against Women.* Washington, DC: U.S. Department of Justice, Office of Justice Programs. 2000. https://www.ncjrs.gov/pdffiles1/nij/183781.pdf
21. National Domestic Violence Hotline. *Men Can Be Victims of Abuse Too.* http://www.thehotline.org/2014/07/men-can-be-victims-of-abuse-too/, 2014.
22. Younggren JN, Harris EA. Can you keep a secret? Confidentiality in psychotherapy. *Journal of Clinical Psychology.* 2008;64(5):589–600.
23. Schouten R. The psychotherapist-patient privilege. *Harvard Review of Psychiatry.* 1998;6(1):44–48.
24. *In re Lifschutz,* 2 Cal. 3rd 415(Supreme Court of California 1970).
25. *Jaffee v. Redmond,* 518 U.S. 1(1996).
26. Metzner JL. Confidentiality and privilege. In: Jacobson JL, Jacobson AM, eds. *Psychiatric Secrets,* 2nd edition. Philadelphia: Henry & Belfus; 2001:463–470.
27. Slovenko R. Confidentiality and testimonial privilege. In: Rosner R, ed. *Principles and Practice of Forensic Psychiatry,* 2nd edition. New York: Arnold; 2003:137–146.

10

EVALUATION OF CHILD ABUSE AND NEGLECT

MATTHEW SOULIER AND CATHERINE AYOUB

Any clinician working with abused and neglected children would find it hard to imagine that, at one time, child abuse and neglect were poorly understood and received little attention from clinicians and government officials. This inattentiveness was probably due in part to the fact that the majority of children who are abused or neglected are under the age of 5 years. Rates of abuse and neglect decline as children grow older and more independent. In 2011, 14.3 children per 1,000 who were 3 years of age or younger were victims of abuse, but the rate decreased to 4.8 per 1,000 for children who were 16 or 17 years old.[1] However, new or repeated acts of abuse and neglect may occur throughout adolescence.

Governmental and public interest in child maltreatment escalated in 1962, when C. Henry Kempe published the sentinel article, "The Battered-Child Syndrome,"[2] which identified and described physical abuse of children. Kempe's findings placed the onus on the medical profession to begin looking for cases of child maltreatment during encounters with patients. Until Kempe's identification of child abuse, it was too often missed or ignored by clinicians, educators, and even law enforcement. Many clinicians ignored the possibility that parents and other caregivers were capable of intentionally harming children in their charge, and many regarded children as unreliable reporters. Still others, laboring under the traditional notion that children are the property of their parents, believed that parents had the right to treat their children as they saw fit. In the decades since the publication of Kempe's article, the research into childhood trauma has significantly expanded and increased awareness within the medical community. It is now well established that caregivers sometimes hurt the children they are supposed to protect and that these young victims are able to accurately report what they have experienced, providing a basis for interventions by clinicians, educators, state agencies, and law enforcement. Vignette 1 illustrates the abuse that children can sustain and witness within their homes.

VIGNETTE 1: IMPACT OF TRAUMA

S. is a 14-year-old boy charged with assault and battery whose attorney questions S.'s competence to stand trial because of his negative attitude and unwillingness to cooperate. He is described by probation workers as irritable. He has been diagnosed with a mood disorder and attention deficit–hyperactivity disorder (ADHD) but refuses to take any medication. During a psychiatrist's evaluation of his competence, S. appears sullen, withdrawn, and distrustful. After a significant effort on the psychiatrist's part to establish a rapport with S., he reveals some of the chaos that he has endured, including severe violence in his home that ended only when his father disappeared. He recounts that his father was physically abusive, often slapping and whipping S. with a belt. His father also intimidated and was physically aggressive with S.'s mother. Although the father's abandonment of the family when S. was 12 years old was a relief in many ways, his family later became homeless, and he was left alone for long periods as his mother tried to make ends meet. The psychiatrist correctly concludes that trauma has had a significant negative impact on S. and accounts for many, if not all, of his symptoms.

Abuse and neglect can drastically alter a child's developmental trajectory. In S.'s case, his criminal patterns may represent a reenactment of the violence he witnessed and was subjected to earlier in his life. His impulsive and aggressive nature may reflect a heightened sense of danger in response to old scars from trauma. Alternatively, the neglect he experienced may have left him with insufficient emotional resources to develop his prosocial interests, leaving him vulnerable to negative influences. His history of trauma has the potential to psychologically burden S. throughout his life.

THE PROBLEM OF CHILD ABUSE AND NEGLECT

Despite the expansion of child welfare services and a greater understanding of child abuse and neglect since the publication of Kempe's report over 50 years ago, children continue to be victimized worldwide. According to a recent report[3] on child maltreatment in the United States:

- In 2013, an estimated 3.5 million reports were made to Child Protective Services (CPS) agencies;

- After investigation, reports of abuse or neglect were substantiated for approximately 679,000 children;
- Of these substantiated reports, 79.5% involved neglect, 18.0% physical abuse, 9.0% sexual abuse, and 8.7% emotional abuse;
- In 2013, 1,520 children died as a result of abuse or neglect.

Child abuse and neglect are not problems exclusive to the United States. They are significant problems in the United Kingdom, for example, where the Department of Education is responsible for developing procedures for agencies to safeguard children from abuse and neglect. These include child protection conferences, which are initiated if concerns about a child's safety are substantiated and the child is at continued risk. A total of 65,200 child protection conferences were conducted in 2013–2014, up by 8.5% from 60,100 in 2012–2013.[4]

THE LEGISLATIVE RESPONSE TO ABUSE AND NEGLECT

In addition to the medical community's response to Kempe's identification of the battered-child syndrome, government agencies took action. By 1967, all states had mandatory reporting laws. These laws require that persons designated as mandated reporters—physicians and other health care workers, including social workers and psychologists; educators; child care workers; and law enforcement personnel—are responsible for reporting suspected or actual abuse or neglect to state agencies. Failure to do so is a criminal offense, punishable with fines, incarceration, or both, depending on the jurisdiction and whether there is a record of prior offenses.

In addition to the adoption of mandated reporting, states established CPS agencies, which were charged with protecting children from abuse and neglect. These local agencies receive and investigate reports from mandated reporters, identifying victims and perpetrators of abuse and neglect. In 1974, about 60,000 cases of maltreatment were reported to CPS agencies in the United States. By 2000, the annual number of reported cases was nearly 3 million.[5]

State statutes determine the process for reporting abuse and neglect of children. These reports are generally handled by county CPS agencies, except for reports involving American Indian children residing on tribal reservations. When tribal children are abused or neglected, their parents are referred to Indian Child Welfare, a tribal organization.

The U.S. Congress took additional steps to prevent child abuse by passing the Child Abuse Prevention and Treatment Act of 1974 (CAPTA), which provided federal funds to the states to support the reporting and investigation of child maltreatment, including support for training investigators. And CAPTA has been amended and authorized multiple times, as recently as 2010.[3] More recent authorizations of this law have placed greater emphasis on preventing child abuse and neglect and supporting families that have been reported to CPS.

CHILD MALTREATMENT AND ITS FORMS

Child abuse and neglect are defined by federal laws and state criminal and civil statutes. The CAPTA defines child abuse and neglect as "any recent act or failure to act on the part of a parent or caretaker which results in death, serious physical or emotional harm, sexual abuse or exploitation or an act or failure to act that presents an imminent risk of serious harm."[6]

The CAPTA definition of child maltreatment highlights the role of parents and other caregivers. When reporting abuse, professionals are exposing caregivers whose actions may have resulted in harm or may pose an imminent risk of harm. Even when the custodial caregiver is not the primary perpetrator, that caregiver is reported for, at minimum, failing to protect the child from harm inflicted by another person. Reporting systems seek information about all alleged perpetrators, but the definitions of abuse and neglect refer to caregivers. Each state is responsible for establishing its own definitions of child abuse and neglect that meet federal minimum standards.

Neglect

The most common type of child maltreatment is neglect, defined as the failure to provide a child with the necessities required for the child's health and welfare. Neglect involves acts of omission, whereas other types of abuse are acts of commission against children. About three-quarters of cases reported to CPS are categorized as neglect.[1] While there has been a downward trend in cases of physical and sexual abuse in recent years, rates of neglect have not decreased.[7] Actual or suspected failure to provide essential care on the part of parents or other caretakers constitutes an appropriate basis for reporting to the responsible social service agency. There are multiple subtypes of neglect, including physical, medical, and educational. Children are entitled to basic shelter, clothes, and hygiene, whereas luxury items such as cellphones are not considered necessities. Neglected children are typically not neglected in only one area; rather, their care is likely to be deficient in multiple areas.

The classic picture of physical neglect is an unkempt child who arrives at school on a cold day without a coat and with no lunch or money for lunch. Children are considered to be medically neglected if they have illnesses or injuries that have not been attended to, if they do not receive proper treatment for medical conditions, or if they are not provided with appropriate preventive care. Some challenging cases warrant consultation with a seasoned colleague—for example, parents' refusal of medical treatment for a condition in their child that is not life-threatening, such as ADHD. In such cases, the lack of treatment might well have an adverse impact on the child, but there may be room for argument as to its absolute necessity.

Education is also considered a basic requirement for childhood development, and parents who do not support their child's education at least until age 16 can be reported for their disregard. School refusal or phobia is a challenging problem, but parents are required to support their child's presence at school. Parents should communicate with the school if their child experiences any impediment to academic progress. For instance, parents are expected to report to school officials, such as the principal and psychologist, learning challenges or social problems such as bullying that are limiting their child's educational welfare. Some parents struggle to advocate for their child at school, but it is also incumbent on the school to proactively develop plans for improving the performance of struggling students. Parents will be asked and expected to attend special education meetings and to consider any interventions that the school proposes to aid their child. If the parents feel insecure about their ability to work with the school, there are alternative resources, such as educational advocates, who can be hired to communicate with the school and represent the child's best interests. Vignette 2 concerns a child whose development is negatively affected as a result of neglect by a parent with serious psychiatric illness.

Vignette 2: Parental Depression

J. is a 14-year-old ninth grader and the only child of a severely depressed mother. Her mother has struggled chronically with bouts of depression, but the latest bout has lasted for 2 years. S.'s mother stopped psychiatric treatment, including antidepressants, several years ago, because she did not feel that she benefited from them. She is emotionally unavailable to her daughter. She spends most of the day lying in bed and fails to attend to her daily hygiene. Though S. is excited about being a high school freshman, her school attendance has been poor. She is consistently late and sometimes fails to show up at school entirely. She has over 20 unexcused absences in the first 5 months of school. The school reports S.'s mother for neglect because she has failed to respond to the school's demand for an explanation of the unexcused absences. A CPS worker subsequently visits S.'s home and finds S. cooking dinner. She tells the worker that her mother is not feeling well and "probably isn't feeling up to a visit right now." Her mother, not realizing that a CPS worker is in the home, calls to her daughter from the bedroom, "Can you turn off my *lights? I want to go to sleep."* S. looks extremely anxious and insists that her mother is normally up but that she is feeling sick. *The CPS worker insists on talking to her mother and discovers that she is not physically sick but profoundly depressed.*

Neglected children such as S. are often "parentified" and assume responsibility for fulfilling their parent's needs. S.'s mother is not able to provide for herself or her daughter, and S. has attempted to care for both of them, at the expense of her education and personal life. She has prioritized her mother's needs over her own. Such role reversal interferes with normal development because the child is preoccupied with the parent's needs. S. is not able to attend to her own developmental needs because she feels the need to care for her mother. In settings such as school or a clinical office, S. may seem superficially mature, but she lacks the support of a developed emotional framework. Neglected children are often emotionally fragile because their parentified role limits their ability to develop free of inappropriate concerns. S. should be nurtured so that her mother's emotional needs are not her primary concern. Children thrive socially, academically, and emotionally in a structured, safe, and predictable environment.

Physical Abuse

Physical abuse is defined as any nonaccidental physical injury to a child.[8] The physical harm can be inflicted out of a desire to hurt the child, or it can be a consequence of severe corporal punishment. Parents or other caregivers may use corporal punishment in an effort to change or control a child's behavior. While there may be pockets of cultural acceptance of some forms of corporal punishment, such as swatting a child on the seat of the pants, that form of discipline generally meets with disapproval if it is not developmentally appropriate or is overly harsh. Examples of overly harsh discipline include physical punishments that leave bruises or other marks on the skin.

Physical evidence of maltreatment is a clear-cut reason for a mandated reporter to notify CPS. However, physical evidence is not a requirement for reporting suspected abuse. Nonbruising physical punishments can be emotionally scarring, especially if the parent is chaotic, unpredictable, out of control, or using fear, domination, and humiliation as the primary tools for behavioral change in the home. Mandated reporters should not consider bruises or other physical marks the only evidence that a parent has crossed the line toward abuse. Parents can be physically inappropriate without leaving any physical evidence. Such physical abuse may not leave scars, but it is emotionally traumatizing. Vignette 3 illustrates the multiple deleterious effects of physical abuse.

Vignette 3: Physical Abuse

C. is a bright, engaging 12-year-old boy with ADHD who is being treated with stimulant medication by a psychiatrist. Lately, C.'s academic achievement has declined, and his teacher told his mother that her son seems "really off." During a medication evaluation, C. tells his psychiatrist that he is disappointed that he has to visit his father this week. His parents separated when he was younger, and he has since spent alternating weeks at their homes. When the psychiatrist inquires about C.'s relationship with his father, C. says, "He thinks I'm stupid." The psychiatrist asks C. how he knows that his father has this opinion. C. states, "Every time he walks by me, he raps me on the back of my head with his ring and calls me 'stupid.'" C. also says that his father snaps C.'s ear with his fingers. C. states that he has headaches and that he is scared of his father when he visits, but his father won't stop hurting him. The psychiatrist examines the back of C.'s head and his neck and ears but finds no bruising, bumps, or marks. Nevertheless, the psychiatrist correctly reports the situation to CPS because C.'s father is engaging in intentionally hurtful physical acts that serve to degrade C. and that are having adverse social and academic effects on him.

Mental health professionals should be watchful not only for overt physical abuse that leaves marks or bruises but also for aggressive and menacing physical behaviors, such as those that C.'s father engages in, which can also be emotionally detrimental. Suspected physical abuse should be reported to CPS, whether or not there are physical signs of abuse.

Emotional Abuse

Emotional abuse is injury to a child's psychological capacity or emotional stability.[8] Examples of emotional abuse include humiliation, frequent yelling, and calling a child belittling names, as in C.'s case. Children can be hurt by parents who ignore, reject, or refuse to talk to them. Children can also be vicariously scarred by exposure to other emotionally or physically abusive relationships in the home. The chaos and turmoil that are characteristic of these homes can leave the children feeling hopeless about any prospect of having control over their own lives. The emotional damage to children is manifested by cognitive, behavioral, and psychiatric impairments, such as depression, anxiety, and aggression.[9]

Sexual Abuse

The CAPTA defines sexual abuse but does not define other subtypes of abuse. In general, sexual abuse is the exploitation of a child for the sexual gratification of the offender. Acts of sexual abuse can also include showing pornographic images to a child and making a child engage in sexually explicit behaviors, as in sexual trafficking. According to the Violence Against Women Reauthorization Act of 2013 (to which the Trafficking Victims Protection Act was attached as an amendment),[10] any person who induces a child to perform a commercial sex act in order to receive anything of gain is a human trafficker. Sex traffickers often coerce, threaten, or lie to children, but physical force does not need to be proven. The critical factors are the age of the victim and the offender's control over the victim.

Munchausen's Syndrome by Proxy

In Munchausen's syndrome by proxy, a parent or other caregiver intentionally fabricates, exaggerates, or causes mental or physical illness in a child. The diagnosis for the child in this syndrome is child abuse by condition falsification. It should be suspected when there are unusual medical findings or the child does not respond to typical medical treatments. However, careful multidisciplinary assessment is required to establish the presence of Munchausen's syndrome by proxy. In most cases, the perpetrators of this form of abuse are female caregivers.[11] In these situations, careful documentation of the child's illnesses or conditions is important in order to uncover patterns of care that are suggestive of the syndrome. Often, separation of the caregiver and child is part of the diagnostic process. The diagnosis for the adult perpetrator is recognized in the fifth edition of the *Diagnostic and Statistical Manual of Mental Disorders* (DSM-5) as factitious disorder imposed on another. A caregiver with this disorder often remains convinced of the child's illness and the caretaker's essential role in dealing with it. In most cases, separation of the caretaker from the child and termination of parental rights are strongly considered.

CAUSES OF ABUSE AND NEGLECT

There is no single factor that is known to lead to child abuse or neglect. Rather, child victimization is the result of an interaction among biological, social, and psychological factors. Risk factors such as poverty increase the likelihood of all forms of abuse, although most impoverished caregivers do not abuse their children. However, as risk factors such as substance abuse, parental mental illness, and early childbearing multiply in settings of social stress and poverty, children are at greater risk for abuse and neglect.[12] Researchers are trying to better understand these factors and why children in some high-risk situations are not abused. Such knowledge may lead to earlier intervention and to prevention of abuse, in contrast to the current societal response, which relies on purely reactive measures.

Sometimes, parents may not have the means to properly provide for their children, despite their best intentions. Such parents can be reported for neglect, but their level of accountability will depend on their knowledge of and willingness to access local resources and support as determined during the CPS investigation. A finding of criminal liability is unlikely if the parents are genuinely concerned and trying to ensure the welfare of their children. Instead, provision of resources and social assistance are more appropriate interventions for such parents. In other cases, parental judgment may be impaired because of physical or mental illness or as a result of drug or alcohol use. The CPS will determine whether a parent's deficits preclude him or her from properly caring for the child or whether the deficits are amenable to rehabilitation. For instance, supporting a parent's sobriety may be sufficient to stop neglect of the child. If the parent fails to take advantage of offered resources or rehabilitation and the neglect continues, CPS will take more restrictive actions and may ultimately terminate the parent's legal rights to make decisions on behalf of the child.

THE CLINICIAN'S REPORTING ROLE

State statutes identify parties who are legally required to report suspected child abuse or neglect. All states and the District of Columbia require these identified reporters to inform the appropriate agency when they encounter potential cases of child maltreatment. Failing to do so may result in professional, civil, and criminal penalties. Most states define mental health professionals as mandated reporters, along with parents, teachers, health care providers, and other parties, although each state has its own statutory definition. See Box 10.1 for additional examples of mandated reporters.

Mandated reporters generally do not want their identities revealed to the suspected perpetrator of abuse or neglect, and many states protect the identity of the reporter. Absolute confidentiality is unlikely, but if this issue is of critical concern to the reporter, it should be conveyed to CPS. The Health Insurance Portability and Accountability Act (HIPAA) specifically permits reporting of suspected child abuse and neglect, including protected health information, without authorization from the patient or parents.[13] State laws regarding confidentiality contain exceptions for mandated reports of abuse and neglect. Mandated-reporting statutes include provisions by which reporters are granted immunity from civil and criminal liability if they act in accordance with their duty to report in good faith. Breach of confidentiality and liability issues in this situation are discussed in more detail in chapter 9.

BOX 10.1

Examples of Mandated Reporters

Parents and other caregivers
Clergy
Mental health professionals
Health care providers
Teachers
Principals and other school officials
Police and other law enforcement officials
Day care providers
Home visitors (e.g., visiting nurses or hospice workers)
All citizens (in many states)

A mandated reporter must notify CPS by telephone and subsequently in writing if the reporter has reasonable cause to *suspect* that a child has been subjected to abuse or neglect. Note that the emphasis is on suspicion, not on clinical evidence of actual abuse or neglect.

Vignette 4: Reasonable Cause for Suspicion

A. is a 14 year-old girl who sees a therapist for weekly counseling because of poor self-esteem and mild depression. She is especially quiet at the beginning of one session but ultimately tells her therapist that she had sexual intercourse for the first time with a 19-year-old boy whom she met on the Internet. A. says that it "seemed" consensual. As the therapist expresses concern about a number of considerations, including the age difference, A. clearly regrets having mentioned the encounter and says, "Promise you won't tell anyone; I lied about my age to him." The therapist is reluctant to answer, not really knowing if abuse occurred.

A.'s therapist does not need to know with certainty that A. was abused to consider reporting the incident to CPS. Waiting for proof may leave A. vulnerable to additional victimization or allow the suspected abuser to hurt other victims. If the therapist suspects that sexual abuse occurred, she should alert CPS.

EVALUATION OF CHILD ABUSE AND NEGLECT

The evaluation of child abuse and neglect begins with the observations of mandated reporters as they work with children. Reporters should inquire further when they witness potential signs of abuse or neglect. However, they should also remember that many child victims of abuse will not explicitly reveal their maltreatment or the identity of the offender. Few signs are pathognomonic of abuse, especially if there is no physical evidence. While this topic cannot be covered exhaustively here for each type of maltreatment, clinicians should be concerned when a child displays sudden changes in behavior, a sharp decline in academic performance, or emotional lability,[14] especially if there is no recognizable physical or psychological cause for these changes. Other common signs of abuse and neglect include lack of supervision by a caregiver and failure to appropriately address medical or other essential needs. Children may become withdrawn, sullen, aggressive, or preoccupied as they cope with abuse or neglect.

In the long term, abuse and neglect alter the attachment patterns of children. After repeated disappointment, neglect, and unpredictable chaos, children may resort to maladaptive means of getting their needs met. In the disinhibited form of reactive attachment disorder, children show little resistance to engaging with unfamiliar adults. These traumatized children appear overly friendly, affectionate, and trusting. Such children are indifferent to the identity of their caregivers because there is nothing special or unique about their actual parents. Conversely, in the inhibited form of reactive attachment disorder, children avoid their caregivers or have paradoxical reactions to comforting situations. For instance, a child may have an irritable reaction to warm attention from a caregiver or may not respond at all. Researchers have sought to better characterize the presentations of abused children, recognizing that child victims have major attachment and other emotional disturbances that may not be manifested as specific intrusive thoughts or nightmares. While DSM-5 does not recognize proposed diagnoses such as developmental trauma disorder,[15] mental health professionals working with children should be consistently looking for signs of abuse or neglect.

When a mandated reporter is concerned about the well-being of a child, the parents (or other caregivers) should be interviewed separately from the child. The reporter should explicitly ask the parents to address the child's allegations. The reporter may then follow up with the child on the basis of the parents' feedback but only for the purpose of clarification, not to determine whether abuse occurred. If the parents are hostile toward each other, or if one parent may not be aware of the other parent's possible abuse, each should be interviewed alone. Some clinicians will choose not to contact the alleged perpetrator of the abuse or neglect after allegations arise because they consider this role to be investigative or potentially dangerous. However, the advantage of contacting the allegedly offending parent is that the clinician has an opportunity to express concern about the child and family and to explain his or her reporting duty, emphasizing that the obligation is to report potential abuse or neglect. The mandated reporter should demonstrate respect for all the involved parties. No matter how the reporting clinician may feel about a parent who is suspected of maltreatment, this parent is likely to remain highly important to the child. Even if CPS substantiates abuse or neglect on the part of the parent, he or she may still view the clinician as a valuable resource if the matter was discussed honestly in a tone of respect and caring for the child and family.

Concern about possible abuse should be heightened if a parent is indifferent or defensive or denies the existence of any problems rather than expressing support for the child. If the nonoffending parent fails to completely support the child following an allegation of abuse, the child is likely to feel enormous pressure to recant,[16] especially if the relationship between the nonoffending parent and the child is disturbed. For example, if the nonoffending parent relies on the child for the parent's own emotional needs, the child may recant his or her allegations against the perpetrating parent after witnessing the emotional distress of the nonoffending parent in response to the CPS investigation. Children must balance their safety and needs against their desire to maintain relationships with their family members. Though children may not articulate such concerns, clinicians should be attuned to the developmental perspective of the child. Children often shoulder guilt, shame, or anxiety about the welfare of their family. A clinician should never underestimate the importance of a parent to a child, even if the child does not feel safe with the parent.

However the parent responds to concerns about the child, if the mandated reporter reasonably suspects abuse or neglect, it should be reported to CPS. Difficult cases warrant consultation with colleagues. Clinicians with access to organizational resources such as departmental conferences or ethics committees should take advantage of them to discuss challenging cases.

Clinicians should always report the abuse or neglect if a child discloses maltreatment. However, if the need to report suspected abuse or neglect does not appear to be clear-cut, even after consultation, it does no harm to express concerns to CPS, which will decide whether investigation is merited. The downside to reporting suspected abuse or neglect in good faith is that it may put at risk a future relationship with the parents or other caregivers as well as clinical treatment with the child. But concern about this risk should never supersede the mandate to report child abuse and neglect. Moreover, our experience is that relationships with families often continue following reports of suspected abuse or neglect. One should err on the side of overreporting rather than underreporting. Clinicians who avoid reporting suspected maltreatment increase the risk of harm to the children they're treating and set themselves up for both liability and the burden of regret at missing an opportunity to intervene.

Mandated reporters should continue to remain supportive of the child, and they should not pursue the allegations by repeatedly querying the child about them.

A mandated reporter will not have access to all of the information relevant to the abuse, and there is no reason to choose sides, especially in cases in which allegations arise during a time of conflict, such as divorce. In many cases, the clinician has not spent adequate time with all the relevant parties and is not in a position to offer opinions about the presence or absence of abuse in criminal, civil, or family court. If called to testify about the potential maltreatment of a child, the clinician should consult a colleague who has a similar clinical practice and perhaps also consult a lawyer. If testimony is required, the clinician should simply report facts about the circumstances of the treatment and refrain from offering an opinion about abuse or neglect.[17]

The reporting clinician may feel uncomfortable or even threatened in an encounter with the accused perpetrator. However, any trepidation can be overcome by recognizing that one has met a mandated duty by prioritizing the safety of the child. The clinician should emphasize his or her concern for the well-being of the child and avoid any discussion that blames the offender, while maintaining an honest and respectful attitude. An accused offender can often understand and appreciate the clinician's focus on and concern for the child.

The challenges of making treatment decisions for children when the parents are divorced, with various custody arrangements, is discussed at length in chapter 11. Parents, particularly if they are divorced, may disagree about medical treatment for their child, but only the parent with legal custody of the child has the authority to consent to medical treatment. If both parents have legal custody and disagree about treatment for their child, the clinician should encourage them to discuss their concerns in an attempt to resolve their differences. If they remain unable to reach an agreement, treatment should be deferred, assuming the child's medical condition is not life-threatening. If one parent remains resistant to treatment that would benefit the child, the clinician can consider reporting this parent for medical neglect. However, such decisions should be made judiciously, especially if there is no danger of direct harm to the child as a result of withholding treatment.

Parents have the authority to consent to medical treatment on behalf of their children, but they are not allowed to refuse life-saving medical treatment. In such difficult circumstances, medical providers should seek court intervention, requesting that the court serve as or appoint a proxy medical decision maker on behalf of the child. The procedures by which a court becomes an alternative decision maker may vary, but they usually begin with a mandated reporter reporting the neglect to CPS. This reporter should also consider consulting with personal or hospital legal counsel and risk management. If CPS determines that a child is endangered by the medical decision making of a parent or other caregiver, legal counsel on behalf of CPS will seek judicial review.

INVESTIGATIONS OF CHILD ABUSE AND NEGLECT

Suspected abuse or neglect of a child should be reported to the CPS agency that serves the area in which the child resides. When the local CPS agency receives such a report, a decision will be made whether to investigate the allegation. The actual investigation of suspected child abuse or neglect will be carried out not by the mandated reporter but by professionals with expertise in such investigations. The CPS, law enforcement, specially trained forensic interviewers, and medical professionals such as pediatricians will gather evidence that either confirms or disconfirms the presence of abuse or neglect. If there is sufficient evidence of maltreatment, criminal charges will be brought against the perpetrator.

If the CPS agency determines that the child's living situation is unsafe, the agency is empowered to place the child in a safe environment while the investigation is being conducted. The CPS may call the mandated reporter during the investigative process to inquire about further observations or obtain additional information, but the reporter's role should not extend beyond answering those questions and continuing to treat the child.[18] For example, a mandated reporter should not ask the child to forward incriminating email messages or texts that constitute evidence of abuse. Throughout the investigation, the treating clinician should continue to treat the child and provide support for the current caregivers, as well as maintain appropriate documentation. The clinician's role in proving any form of abuse or neglect will be restricted to being called as a witness in order to provide a factual narrative of the case.

With further scrutiny, including interviews and investigation by law enforcement, CPS will determine whether the report of abuse or neglect is substantiated, unfounded, or indeterminate. The CPS can substantiate that abuse or neglect has occurred according to the preponderance-of-the-evidence standard. Some counties notify the mandated reporter by mail of the CPS agency's actions.

Many cities and towns now have a multidisciplinary interview center (MDIC) to investigate claims of maltreatment, particularly sexual abuse. The MDIC employs forensic interviewers with training in child development and in the use of interviewing techniques and protocols that minimize suggestion when eliciting a child's report of abuse. In 1985, the National Child Advocacy Center, in Huntsville, Alabama, became the first MDIC. It was created to join together key stakeholders involved with child protection, including CPS, law enforcement, and medical and mental health professionals. This team approach was initiated in response to high-profile cases in which children had been found to have misidentified perpetrators of abuse, often because of flawed interviewing techniques that did not take into account a child's susceptibility to adult suggestion. There are now more than 900 child advocacy centers and MDICs in the world. These centers train professionals in interviewing techniques and set a high standard for investigating reports of abuse, with a primary focus on child sexual abuse.

Only mental health professionals with the necessary specialized knowledge and training should conduct forensic interviews of children to investigate their allegations. As is emphasized throughout this book, treating clinicians should not conduct forensic interviews of any type with their own patients (i.e., forensic interviewers should not be clinically involved with any of the parties in a case). In general, interviews with children should be conducted away from the suspected offender. An appropriately trained interviewer should ask open-ended questions in a nonbiased and developmentally appropriate manner.[19] Ideally, the interviewer would say to the child, "Tell me what happened to you" and then follow the child's lead, adopting the child's language, without implying that there is a right or pleasing answer. A less-skilled interviewer might begin an evaluation of sexual abuse by asking, "Did he take off your clothes or did you take off your clothes?" Such an introductory question could make the child feel obligated to choose one of the presented options, even if he or she had no memory of clothes ever being removed. The interviewer should avoid introducing material about the allegation until the child has freely recalled the events.

Policies and procedures vary by state, but if the abuse or neglect is substantiated, CPS will work to ensure that the child and any other potential victims are safe. The CPS will forward the results of the investigation to law enforcement, and the accused caregiver may be further investigated, arrested, and charged. The CPS will also initiate medical and mental health treatment for the affected child and family members. Depending on the severity or legal consequences of the abuse or neglect, CPS may formulate a plan to rehabilitate the caregiver and promote the reunification of the family. Unless the parents are found to be unfit to meet their responsibilities as caregivers, reunification of the family is the primary aim. The steps that are taken to achieve reunification are closely monitored to ensure the safety of the child. Supervised visitation is a method for restoring parental contact with the child while monitoring the behavior and attitudes of the parent. Should the parent repeatedly reject such help or continue to abuse or neglect the child, parental rights, including decision making (legal custody) and residing with the child (physical custody), can be legally terminated.

PITFALLS AND POTENTIAL CONSEQUENCES

Child abuse and neglect, whether suspected or established, is an area fraught with potential for missteps by clinicians, often with potential serious consequences.

Failing to Identify and Adequately Evaluate Signs of Potential Abuse or Neglect

Vignette 5 highlights some of the potential problems mental health professionals can encounter when confronting suspected sexual abuse. The vignette begins with a psychologist's reluctance to pursue potential signs of abuse during an appointment.

Vignette 5: Identifying Signs of Abuse

M. is an eight-year-old girl who visits a psychologist because she is struggling with some bullying at school. Her mother insists on attending all the sessions. During the third visit, M. is noticeably squeezing her legs together while she is sitting in the office and appears to be masturbating. The psychologist is disturbed by M.'s behavior but does not explicitly ask the child about any potential abuse. The psychologist asks M.'s mother if she has observed any behavior at home that concerns her. The mother becomes very defensive and flatly denies any concern, while staring at M. in a less-than-affectionate manner. The psychologist decides that she will assess M. further at the next visit.

Mental health professionals should inquire about possible abuse as a standard part of any evaluation process. Asking children about abuse reveals concern for their well-being and indicates to them that it is appropriate to tell the clinician about any acts of abuse or neglect in the future. Children at least need to be asked about abuse privately, not in the presence of a parent or other caretaker, especially if there are signs of possible maltreatment. For example, a hovering parent, like M.'s mother, who insists on being present during the evaluation and appears to be interfering with it should heighten clinical suspicion. The same is true when a child has obvious bruising or other physical signs of abuse and the parent attempts to answer questions put to the child or otherwise inserts himself or herself into the assessment.

Vignette 5, continued

M.'s mother cancels the next scheduled appointment with the psychologist but does bring M. to the rescheduled appointment, 3 weeks later. After several additional sessions, M. mentions that she has seen her stepfather's "privates," but she does not report any inappropriate sexual behavior on his part. When the psychologist asks M.'s mother about her relationship with the stepfather, she emphasizes the positive aspects of their marriage.

Failing to Recognize the Perpetrator of Abuse

Most acts of child sexual abuse are not perpetrated by strangers, people who drive around in vans or wait for children in parks. The more common offender is someone known to the child, even someone as close as a parent or step-parent. According to 2013 data, parents remain the most common perpetrators of child abuse and neglect.[20]

Children are often forced to live with a variety of caregivers. For example, Berger et al.[21] reported that CPS is more likely to become involved when a mother is living with a man who is not the child's biological father. Detection of abuse by a perpetrator known to the victim is not easy, because the dynamics of child abuse, including potential grooming, are extremely complex and multilayered. Children often keep the abuse secret to preserve family relationships or prevent whatever the perpetrator of the abuse has said will be the consequence of revealing it. As the child holds the shame and secret of abuse, the perpetrator often continues his or her life as an apparently good parent, spouse, coworker, or community member. When allegations of abuse arise, most coworkers and community associates are surprised and insist that they never knew the offender to be a potential child abuser. As a clinician, be vigilant and remember that an individual's potential for abuse or neglect is not negated by a polite demeanor in your office, good standing in the community, or good social skills.

Vignette 5, continued

Ultimately, M. reveals that her stepfather touched her inappropriately, but she discloses only minimal details and then recants her allegation. The psychologist ends the session and considers whether she should call CPS.

Failing to Report an Act of Abuse

Any mental health professional whose work involves treating children may find it necessary to periodically call CPS about a child in his or her care. Clinicians working with children who never contact CPS may want to consider whether they are sufficiently inquiring about and looking for abuse. Here is a helpful rule of thumb: if as a mandated reporter you seriously consider calling CPS regarding a potential act of abuse or neglect, don't wait; call CPS right away. Often, clinicians rationalize or minimize acts of abuse as they give further consideration to a child's allegations made during an appointment. Clinicians often forget that they are obligated to report a suspicion of abuse, not proof that abuse occurred. They may hesitate out of concern that reporting will hurt feelings or jeopardize their relationship with the patient's family. Clinicians also fail to call CPS because they wonder whether they have sufficient information to merit a report or whether they are dealing with a "real" act of abuse. These concerns, and reluctance to report, are common. It is important to remember that any professional can call CPS for a consultation to help make a decision about reporting.

Mandated reporters may wonder about their duty if the act was committed many years ago. Clinicians may be reluctant to report past acts of abuse, fearing that they do not have enough information to warrant a report or that they may be sued for breaching patient confidentiality. However, we believe that the duty to report extends even to acts of abuse in the distant past if they have never been reported. In every state, reporters are immune from liability and can breach confidentiality for reporting child maltreatment on the basis of whatever information has been gathered, so long as the report is made in good faith. The CPS will decide what to do with the information and whether an investigation is warranted. When CPS is notified, the receiver of the report is often willing to be a resource, answering questions about state laws governing abuse and whether the referral merits investigation.

Vignette 5, continued

After further consideration, the psychologist reports M.'s brief disclosure of abuse to CPS. Deciding to investigate the allegations, CPS arranges a forensic interview with M. at an MDIC and contacts law enforcement officials, who agree to send a detective to the MDIC. A CPS caseworker tells M.'s mother not to discuss the claims of abuse with M. but to explain to her that she is going to have an appointment with someone she can talk to about what happened to her. M.'s mother takes her to the MDIC at the appointed time, and the CPS caseworker is waiting for them. M. and her mother are introduced to the forensic evaluator, who is aware of some of the details of the allegations. The forensic evaluator accompanies M. to a room with toys and a video camera, where M. is asked about the suspected sexual abuse. The CPS caseworker and detective watch the interview, but M. cannot see them during the interview.

Failing to Distinguish between Reporting and Investigating Abuse or Neglect

Clinicians who treat children have an obligation to remain aware of the possibility of abuse or neglect, to inquire about it, and to identify potential acts of abuse or neglect. Each encounter with a child should include an assessment of the child's safety and well-being. When an allegation of abuse or neglect arises, clinicians should gather basic information, including the nature of the maltreatment, the potential for further abuse or neglect, and demographic information about the child, the child's legal custodian, and the perpetrator. Clinicians are not likely to have access to all the information they would like to have. The CPS and court investigators will be able to gather additional information from collateral witnesses. Mandated reporters are not required to prove abuse or neglect but rather are required to report a reasonable suspicion of maltreatment. Vignette 6 describes two medical professionals confronting new allegations of abuse and correctly reporting their concerns rather than conducting an extensive investigation.

Vignette 6: Reporting Concerns

D., a nine-year-old boy, is seen by a social worker for an assessment because the school where he is a student is concerned about his oppositional behavior, tantrums, and bullying of other children. As a central part of this assessment, the social worker asks D. about his daily routine and learns that he is often left to fend for himself, as his mother has two jobs and his older brother is his caretaker. D. states that his brother frequently pushes and punches him, hits him with a switch, and locks him in a small closet. D. has told his mother about this treatment, and his mother has talked to the older brother. However, she believes that D. is exaggerating. D.'s story leads the social worker to suggest that D.'s pediatrician perform a physical exam. The pediatrician finds several linear bruises on D.'s back and legs that raise further suspicion of abuse. The social worker and pediatrician each file a report to CPS.

Mental health professionals can do harm by overzealously investigating an initial claim of maltreatment. Some abused children may become distressed and engage in maladaptive coping strategies such as self-harm if encouraged to delve deeply into past acts of abuse. They may be unable to protect themselves from the emotional turmoil that such traumatic memories trigger. Other children may be defiant or passive, even in the case of extreme abuse or neglect. Never mistake a child's disposition as evidence that abuse has or has not occurred.

The importance of having trained evaluators use empirically based interviewing techniques is illustrated in multiple cases of child sexual abuse. There is an extensive body of research that has examined the influence of suggestion as a contaminator of child memory. Famous cases such as the McMartin Preschool case,[22] in which children falsely reported their teachers as sexual abusers, have led researchers to recognize the influence of even well-meaning adults on childhood memories of abuse.

While refraining from asking directed questions that might influence the child's recollections of events, the clinician should carefully and accurately document the interview with the child, keeping in mind that the child's medical records might be subpoenaed in a subsequent criminal investigation or a custody dispute. It is important to ask open-ended questions first and then move toward more specific questions as the child offers information. Clinicians should not fear showing appropriate care for a child reporting maltreatment, but they need to be mindful of their specific role and the boundaries that separate them from investigators. Mental health professionals should avoid assuming multiple roles and should clearly explain to every patient their duties and responsibilities. The problem of the treating clinician serving as a forensic evaluator of his or her own patient is discussed elsewhere throughout this book, including chapters 11, 13, 15, and 16.

CONCLUSION

Child maltreatment continues to be a substantial problem worldwide. As mandated reporters, mental health professionals have a duty to identify and report suspected child abuse or neglect. Each role is unique, with its own duties and responsibilities. Child abuse and neglect can have lifelong consequences for the victims. Abused and neglected children are at risk for cognitive delays, learning difficulties, and emotional problems, including major psychiatric illness. A subset of victims have a constellation of impairing symptoms encompassed by post-traumatic stress disorder, but many traumatized children do not. Instead, these children, like S. in the first vignette, often receive multiple diagnoses such as depression, ADHD, and anxiety without any recognition of abuse or neglect as the underlying problem. Clinicians should remain vigilant in their duty to identify and report suspected cases of abuse and neglect. By doing so, they may help change the lifetime course of an abused or neglected child.

FREQUENTLY ASKED QUESTIONS

What is the most commonly reported form of child abuse?

Of all the forms of child abuse, neglect is reported most often. Neglect involves the omission of necessary care for the welfare and benefit of the child.

Should mandated reporters notify CPS if they suspect maltreatment or wait until there is more time to confirm the suspicion?

A mandated reporter should report suspected abuse or neglect to CPS. Mandated reporters do not investigate abuse or neglect and should not delay notifying CPS of suspected maltreatment. Failure to notify CPS in a timely fashion could lead to professional and legal liability.

Who are the most common perpetrators of child abuse and neglect?

Biological parents are the most common perpetrators of child abuse and neglect. Children are least likely to be maltreated by strangers.

Do all parents have the right to make decisions about medical treatment for their children?

Only parents who have legal custody of their children can make decisions about their medical care.

Child advocacy centers or multidisciplinary interview centers (MDICs) serve what role in child abuse investigations?

Forensic interviewers at these centers have special training in asking children about abuse while minimizing suggestive questioning. Such centers eliminate the need for multiple interviews by videotaping the interview of the child. These video recordings can then be accessible to those adjudicating the offense. The MDICs were created in response to cases of children making false allegations of abuse in response to suggestive questions posed by investigators.

REFERENCES

1. IOM (Institute of Medicine) and NRC (National Research Council). *New Directions in Child Abuse and Neglect Research*. Washington, DC: National Academies Press; 2013.
2. Kempe CH, Silverman FN, Steele BF, Droegemueller W, Silver HK. The battered-child syndrome. *Journal of the American Medical Association*. 1962;181:17–24.
3. Child Welfare Information Gateway. *About CAPTA: A Legislative History*. Washington, DC: U.S. Department of Health and Human Services, Children's Bureau; 2011.
4. Department of Education. *Characteristics of children in need in England, 2013–2014*. October 29, 2014. https://www.gov.uk/government/uploads/system/uploads/attachment_data/file/367877/SFR43_2014_Main_Text.pdf. Accessed September 1, 2015.
5. Meyers JEB. *The American Professional Society on the Abuse of Children Handbook on Child Maltreatment*, 3rd edition. Thousand Oaks, CA: Sage; 2011.
6. CAPTA. The CAPTA Reauthorization Act of 2010, Public Law 111–320 (42 U.S.C. 5106a).http://www.acf.hhs.gov/programs/cb/resource/capta2010.
7. Finkelhor D, Saito K, Jones L. *Updated trends in child maltreatment, 2013*. Crimes Against Children Research Center. January 2015. http://www.unh.edu/ccrc/pdf/_Updated%20trends%202013_dc-df-ks-df.pdf. Accessed September 1, 2015.
8. Child Welfare Information Gateway. *Definitions of Child Abuse and Neglect*. Washington DC: U.S. Department of Health and Human Services, Children's Bureau; 2014.
9. Child Welfare Information Gateway. *Long-Term Consequences of Child Abuse and Neglect*. Washington DC: U.S. Department of Health and Human Services, Children's Bureau; 2013.
10. Violence Against Women Reauthorization Act of 2013, Act No. S. 47 of 2013.
11. Ayoub C. Munchausen by proxy. In: Shaw R, DeMaso D, eds. *Textbook of Pediatric Psychosomatic Medicine: Consultation on Physically Ill Children*. Washington, DC: American Psychiatric Publishing; 2010:185–198.
12. Slack KS, Holl JL, McDaniel M, Yoo J, Bolger K. Understanding the risks of child neglect: an exploration of poverty and parenting characteristics. *Child Maltreatment*. 2004;9:395–408.
13. Policy statement—child abuse and the Health Insurance Portability and Accountability Act. *Pediatrics*. 2010;125(1):197–201.

14. Child Welfare Information Gateway. *What Is Child Abuse and Neglect? Recognizing the Signs and Symptoms.* Washington, DC: U.S. Department of Health and Human Services, Children's Bureau; 2013.

15. van der Kolk B, Pynoos RS, Ciccetti D, et al. *Proposal to include developmental trauma disorder diagnosis for children and adolescents in DSM-V.* Trauma Center. 2009. http://www.traumacenter.org/announcements/DTD_papers_Oct_09.pdf. Accessed August 31, 2015.

16. Malloy LC, Lyon TD. Filial dependency and recantation of child sexual abuse allegations. *Journal of the American Academy of Child and Adolescent Psychiatry.* 2007;46(2):162–170.

17. Practice parameters for child custody evaluation. *Journal of the American Academy of Child and Adolescent Psychiatry.* 1997;36(10 Suppl):57S–68S.

18. American Professional Society on the Abuse of Children. *Practice Guidelines: Forensic Interviewing in Cases of Suspected Child Abuse.* www.apsac.org/practice-guidelines, 2012. Accessed November 16, 2016.

19. American Professional Society on the Abuse of Children. *Practice Guidelines: Code of Ethics.* Chaired by Jon R. Conte, www.apsac.org/practice-guidelines, 1997. Accessed November 16, 2016.

20. U.S. Department of Health and Human Services, Administration for Children and Families, Administration on Children, Youth and Families, Children's Bureau. *Child maltreatment 2013.* 2015. http://www.acf.hhs.gov/programs/cb/research-data-technology/statistics-research/child-maltreatment.

21. Berger LM, Paxson C, Waldfogel J. Mothers, men, and child protective services involvement. *Child Maltreatment.* 2009;14(3):263–276.

22. Schreiber N, Bellah LD, Martinez Y, McLaurin KA, Strok R, Garven S, Wood JM. Suggestive interviewing in the McMartin Preschool and Kelly Michaels daycare abuse cases: A case study. *Social Influence.* 2006;1(1):16–47.

/// 11 /// JUVENILES AND THE LAW

MATTHEW LAHAIE AND ROBERT KINSCHERFF

Juveniles are persons who have not yet reached the age of majority, typically defined as the age of 18 years.[1] The law justifies differential treatment of juveniles on the basis of a number of assumptions made by legislatures and the legal system. Juveniles are assumed to lack the maturity, experience, and capacity for judgment required to make difficult decisions.[2] Parents have traditionally been viewed as possessing the fundamental right to direct the upbringing of their children and are presumed to act in the best interests of their children.[2,3] With the recognition that the state also has an interest in children as future citizens who would contribute to society, laws evolved to protect that interest, such as mandated education to a certain age, child labor laws, and laws to respond to instances of child maltreatment within families. When parents are not available or have been judged unfit to parent, courts may designate an alternative legal custodian who is empowered to make decisions on the child's behalf, such as a legal guardian, or may place the child in the legal custody of a state child protection agency.[1] In some cases, on the basis of jurisdiction-specific criteria and/or designation by a court, minors may be legally emancipated and serve as their own guardians, as if they were independent adults.[1]

Regardless of a juvenile's developmental level or cognitive capacity, the legal system has traditionally treated all children on the basis of their common status as minors rather than their individual characteristics.[4] Persons must be a specified minimum age to obtain a driver's license, vote in elections, enlist in military service, enter into contracts, consent to sexual activity, marry, and legally purchase alcohol and cigarettes. Over time, however, courts and legislatures have increasingly recognized that juveniles may have their own interests that must be considered despite parental wishes,[5] most commonly in circumstances of divorce, child protection, and medical decision making. There has also been expanded recognition that juveniles in specific circumstances have the capacity to make some decisions on their own without relying on or even notifying their parents or guardians.

Issues of custody and informed consent are ubiquitous in clinical practice with juveniles. Prudent clinicians working with this population will familiarize themselves with the relevant laws in their jurisdiction. From the first moments of working with a juvenile, the clinician must identify the juvenile's legal custodian and obtain consent before providing care, unless the circumstances constitute an emergency or some other exception to the legal obligation to obtain informed consent before providing professional services. In circumstances involving divorce and complex psychosocial situations, such as cases in which a state child protection agency has custody of the juvenile, clinicians must be alert to possible alternative custody or guardianship arrangements. These circumstances are relatively common among juveniles who come into contact with medical and mental health professionals.

VIGNETTE 1: PARENTAL CONSENT

As the on-call mental health evaluator for a local community emergency department, you have been consulted on the case of J., a 15-year-old boy who was brought to the emergency department by his parents after he attempted to commit suicide by hanging himself in his closet with his belt. Fortunately, his older brother found J. during the attempted suicide and was able to intervene before J. was seriously injured. J. was brought to the emergency department and was determined to not require further medical evaluation or treatment. The emergency department has asked your recommendation for managing J. During your evaluation, J. reports that for several weeks he has been experiencing auditory hallucinations commanding him to kill himself. He describes a very depressed mood and ongoing thoughts of suicide. You recommend inpatient psychiatric hospitalization but J. declines. However, J. lives in a jurisdiction where parents may consent to mental health care, including inpatient psychiatric hospitalization, on behalf of their children. J.'s parents are therefore able to consent to inpatient treatment on his behalf, and he is transferred to an appropriate treatment unit.

If J.'s parents were unwilling to consent to the recommendation of psychiatric hospitalization, there might be additional mechanisms for seeking the recommended care. The jurisdiction might have a mechanism for involuntary psychiatric hospitalization that would not require consent from J. or his parents. Additionally, if failure to consent to psychiatric hospitalization could reasonably constitute medical neglect, a mandated report may be made to the state child protection agency charged with the protection and well-being of juveniles. That agency may determine that failure to consent to psychiatric hospitalization rises to the level of medical neglect. If so, the agency may take steps to temporarily assume legal and perhaps also physical custody of J. If the agency assumes legal custody, it could then consent to J.'s admission to an inpatient psychiatric hospital.

JUVENILES AND FAMILY LAW IN DIVORCE AND CHILD CUSTODY

Society's views on divorce and custody have evolved over time, as have attitudes as to the legal status of juveniles and whether they have independent interests that need to be acknowledged and protected.

From Parental Property to Best Interests of the Child

The law regarding juveniles and their relationship to their parents and family has evolved over time. Before the 19th century, English common law considered a child to be the property of his or her biological parents.[6] Women had limited legal rights during this period, so the biological father generally possessed absolute legal authority over his children. As a result, the biological father of the child would ordinarily be readily granted legal custody of the child in the event of divorce.

During the 19th century, society increasingly appreciated the important role of the mother in child development. In the early part of the century, Caroline Norton, a prominent British feminist and social reformer, campaigned to promote increased rights for women, especially in marriage and divorce.[7] The British Parliament passed the Custody of Infants Bill of 1839, giving the courts discretion to determine child custody in divorce cases, and established a legal presumption that a mother would retain custody of children under the age of 7 years, should the parents divorce.[7] Passage of this bill in Britain spurred adoption of the tender-years doctrine across the United States. This doctrine held that children, especially young children, would be best served by being raised by their mothers in cases of divorce. During much of the 20th century, the legal presumption that mothers should be awarded custody of children in divorce cases largely replaced the previous presumption that fathers should be granted custody.

The presumption of maternal preference in custody disputes has been replaced by the best-interests-of-the child standard.[7] This standard is rooted in the Custody of Infants Act of 1873, which allowed British courts to structure custody arrangements that the court determined to be in the best interests of the child. This standard has been adopted by all American jurisdictions, including the territories.[8] It is intended to ensure that the custody outcome selected is the one that best serves the interests of the child. However, this standard does not provide guidance in determining which outcome will serve the best interests of any individual child. Given the problematic vagueness of the standard, some jurisdictions have attempted to provide guidance by specifying criteria for the court to consider in making custody determinations.[9]

Types of Legal and Physical Custody

In recent decades, state courts in the United States have increasingly favored a presumption of joint custody in cases of divorce.[8] With joint custody, each parent shares some combination of legal custody and physical custody. The preference for joint custody recognizes a child's psychological need to maintain relationships with both parents and the better developmental outcomes for children when divorced parents can coparent without chronic or intense conflict.

With joint physical custody, the parents share the day-to-day lodging and care of the child according to a court-ordered custodial schedule. Examples of living arrangements for children under joint physical custody include alternating weeks between parental households, spending weekends and selected holidays at one parent's household while spending the remainder of time at the other parent's household, and spending extended periods of time at each parent's household.

With joint legal custody, the parents are equally responsible for making decisions about child rearing, including decisions concerning medical care, religious upbringing, and education. Thus, shared legal custody requires that both parents be involved in making important decisions involving key life domains such as medical or behavioral health care, manner of education, and religious upbringing. Parents with shared physical custody typically manage routine day-to-day matters during the periods when the child is in each parent's care.

The court may specify other arrangements for parental custody such as alternating custody, in which both physical and legal custody alternate between the parents; sole custody, in which one parent retains sole legal and physical custody of the child; identified specific custody, in which one parent has broad legal custody but the other parent retains status as a legal custodian for specified domains (e.g., education); and split custody, in which one parent has legal and physical custody of one child, while the other parent has legal and physical custody of another child. In some cases, legal and/or physical custody is awarded to a third party rather than to either or both of the parents. Note that married stepparents or unmarried domestic partners who live with a biological parent do not have legal or physical custody of a child unless the child has been legally adopted by the stepparent or partner or a court has specifically identified that person as a legal or physical custodian.

Vignette 2: Married Biological Parents

You are seeing B. for a follow-up psychopharmacology appointment. B. is a 13-year-old girl who suffers from depression with significant functional impairment. B. is accompanied by her mother. Her parents are married, and she is in their full legal and physical custody. You have been discussing the risks and benefits of initiating an antidepressant medication. The mother and patient provide informed consent, and you provide a prescription and follow-up appointment. Because the parents are married, live together, share full custody of B., and appear to be acting in good faith, you consider one parent's consent to be sufficient.

In the above vignette, if B.'s parents were divorced or separated, additional potential concerns would arise. If the father of the child shared physical and legal custody and was regularly involved in the care and rearing of B., a clinician would typically be advised to discuss treatment recommendations with both parents and obtain informed consent from both of them before initiating a treatment. Although the consent of one parent may be legally sufficient, failure to communicate with both parents may lead to bad feelings and mistrust of the treatment, which may create barriers to effective treatment. The parents might indicate that one parent is primarily responsible for managing the care of the child, and the clinician would typically follow this guidance from the parents. If one parent has long been uninvolved in the care and rearing of the child, the clinician would be better positioned to rely solely on the consent of the involved parent but should do so only after careful consideration of potential risks to clinical care should the uninvolved parent learn of the treatment and object. Especially if the uninvolved parent still has legal custody, it may be legally, ethically, and clinically prudent to at least attempt to communicate with this parent in order to seek consent and gather a history from this parent's perspective.

A more difficult scenario for clinicians, patients, and their families is a situation in which the parents share legal custody but are in disagreement on the proposed treatment. Consent from one parent is not sufficient when the clinician has a reasonable basis to be concerned that the other parent opposes the treatment. If relations between the parents are contentious, such as in an ongoing divorce case, the clinician should attempt to build consensus between the parents on a treatment plan and to document that effort. If the disagreement between the parents continues, the clinician cannot proceed to implement the recommended treatment, and the parents may have to take their disagreement to court to seek a judicial decision regarding the initiation of treatment.

In a related scenario of concern to clinicians, a juvenile patient is brought in for (non-emergency) treatment by a noncustodian such as a grandparent, aunt, uncle, or family friend. Although such individuals may be able to bring patients to appointments, they are not able to provide consent for initiating evaluation or treatment unless they have been granted some form of guardianship allowing them to do so.

The State's Interest in Child Welfare and Protection

As discussed above, English common law regarded children as the property of their parents. Property rights traditionally allow for the property owner to handle property in any manner that does not interfere with the rights of another. The past century has seen a growing recognition of the interests of the state in the collective well-being of children as future citizens, as well as the individual rights and interests of children.[10] This is most evident in the evolution of child welfare and protection laws intended to protect children against maltreatment from their parents and other caregivers. According to a 2013 report on child maltreatment from the Children's Bureau of the U.S. Department of Health and Human Services, more than 679,000 children annually are the victims of abuse or neglect.[11]

Before 1875, children in the United States had limited protections against maltreatment within families.[10] Abuse of children was typically addressed through criminal prosecution, which occurred rarely and generally only in cases of egregious or lethal abuse or neglect. Judges had the authority to stop abuse when it was brought to their attention, but few cases other than the most egregious were brought before them. A limited number of jurisdictions provided legal authorities the right to remove children from situations in which they were subject to abuse and neglect; however, intervention was sporadic.

Spurred by the rescue of a severely abused child from a New York City tenement in 1874, interested citizens the following year established the New York Society for the Prevention of Cruelty to Children, the first child protection organization in the world.[10] By 1922, approximately 300 such organizations had been established across the country. These charitable organizations would serve as the first child protection agencies and were integral in the recognition of children's rights and the development of state child protection services.

Another innovation in the protection of juveniles was the establishment of the first juvenile court in 1899.[12] Juvenile courts were concerned primarily with the rehabilitation of delinquent children but also dealt with instances of abuse and neglect of children. During the Great Depression, charitable giving declined, and many nongovernmental child protection agencies closed. Child protection became the province of the juvenile courts and the police, with state child protection agencies emerging during subsequent decades.

In the 20th century, the federal government and the states established agencies that addressed social, health, and labor issues.[10] Franklin Roosevelt's New Deal and the Social Security Act created the Aid to Families with Dependent Children program and expanded the role of the Children's Bureau, a federal agency that had been established in 1912. Aid to Families with Dependent Children provided millions of dollars to the states to help support children in poor families. The role of the Children's Bureau was expanded to collaborate with state public welfare agencies in protecting and caring for neglected and delinquent children.

Child abuse became a national focus in part as a result of the medical community's increasing recognition of instances of abuse. In 1946, pediatric radiologist John Caffey published a medical article describing six children with subdural hematomas and long-bone fractures suggestive of severe physical abuse.[13] This work drew physician attention to instances of abuse that had caused specific childhood injuries. In 1962, pediatrician C. Henry Kempe and colleagues published "The Battered-Child Syndrome," which brought national attention to the issue of child abuse.[14] The news media became increasingly interested in the issue and published accounts of child abuse.

In 1962, the Children's Bureau recommended state legislation requiring physicians to report suspected child abuse to state authorities, and all the states had reporting laws by 1967. In 1974, Congress passed the Child Abuse Prevention and Treatment Act, authorizing federal funds to improve state responses to physical and sexual abuse and neglect of children and creating the National Center on Child Abuse and Neglect.[15] The Adoption Assistance and Child Welfare Act of 1980 required states to make reasonable efforts to avoid removing children from maltreating parents and to make reasonable efforts to reunite families if removal was necessary.[16]

In addition to the ethical obligation to advocate for the well-being of patients, clinicians are legally mandated to report concerns about abuse or neglect of juvenile patients according to the law of the state in which they practice. When child maltreatment is reported to a state child protection agency, the state determines whether further investigation is warranted. If an investigation substantiates concerns about neglect or abuse, the state may take action to both protect the well-being of the child and promote family stability and functioning. Potential interventions range from providing the family with clinical or social services to taking emergency custody of the juvenile and perhaps subsequently seeking permanent custody and termination of parental rights. All U.S. jurisdictions have a version of this child protection system, and mental health clinicians should become familiar with the relevant reporting process.

Vignette 3: Assessing Concerns of Abuse

You are a therapist at a community health center, and you are conducting an intake interview with A., a seven-year-old girl. At the beginning of the appointment, you meet with the mother to discuss the policies and practices of the clinic and the limits of confidentiality, including manda-tory reporting of child maltreatment, and to obtain informed consent for the intake interview. You proceed with obtaining a history from the mother, and then you meet with A. individually. As part of the play during your session, A. has a figurine she calls the "daddy" strike a figurine she calls the "baby" with a stick because the "baby" is bad. When you ask her if anyone strikes her, she relates that her daddy sometimes hits her when she is bad. Given your concern about possible abuse, you ask her to describe these instances, and she describes being "spanked" as a punishment for bad behavior. You ask her whether she has ever been spanked with a stick or other object, which she denies, and whether she has been injured during a spanking episode, which she also denies.

You meet again with the mother to gain more history about the possible physical punishment of A. in the home. The mother states that the family does use spanking as discipline, although they do so rarely. She reports that they never use a stick or other object for spanking, and that they use the palm of their hand to twice strike the children on the seat of their pants, over their clothing. When asked about the necessity of the use of spanking in the home, the mother reports that both she and her husband were raised in households that used spanking for discipline. She says that they believe as parents that spanking is a necessary form of discipline in order to reduce problematic behavior. The mother denies that A. has ever been injured or hurt by the spanking, and that spanking is a form of discipline reserved for rare instances when the parents feel that A. has been disobedient and after she has received multiple warnings. You take the opportunity to educate the mother on the negative effects of spanking and discuss alternative disciplinary approaches. She is surprised to learn of the negative impact and long-term ineffectiveness of spanking and is receptive to information about other approaches to disciplining A. The mother says that she will discuss this with her husband and that she plans to forgo spanking and to implement alternative strategies for discipline.

A.'s initial report of being spanked as a form of discipline raises concern about possible child abuse. Further inquiry with the child and the parent suggests that the spanking is not excessive in its duration, frequency, implementation, or use of force. Additionally, the mother appears to be open to learning about the negative impact of spanking on both the well-being and behavior of A, and she reports that she will forego spanking and attempt to adopt alternative discipli-nary strategies. In this case, you are relatively reassured that the past spanking does not meet the criteria for mandated reporting.

Consider a different scenario, in which the mother or the child stated that A. had been spanked with an object such as a stick. This would raise concern about physical abuse, which is a criterion for mandatory reporting. Similarly, if spankings were being administered with great physical force or excessive frequency or if they caused injury to A., there would be concern about physical abuse, and reporting would be required. If there is a reasonable basis for suspecting child abuse or neglect, a full risk assessment is recommended to ensure the safety of the child and to provide for appropriate disposition. Is the child safe to return to the home after the assessment, or is the risk so significant and imminent that a child protection agency should be engaged immediately to consider emergency physical custody of the child?

An additional consideration is when and how to inform parents when the clinician has determined that reporting concern about abuse or neglect is mandatory. Disclosure of reporting to parents is typically easier and less disruptive to treatment when it is done by a clinician who has conducted a time-limited evaluation, such as an evaluation in the emergency department, than when it is done by a clinician who is providing ongoing care. The clinician in an emergency or inpatient clinical setting who determines that reporting is required should consider disclosing that information to the parents so that they will not suspect the outpatient clinician of having made the report. This may help preserve the therapeutic alliance, which could already be tenuous. If reporting is required in an outpatient setting, the clinician should carefully assess safety considerations, and if there is a concern that the parents may become agitated, clinic or hospital security personnel should be engaged. The clinician may also choose to disclose the reporting to parents using alternative means, such as the telephone. If there is a concern about personal safety, the clinician may decide not to disclose that the report, which is typically confidential, has been made.

If a child is being abused or neglected, there is a significant risk of domestic partner abuse as well. In the vignette above, if there was reason for concern about potential abuse of the child, the mother could be a victim herself and should be screened for domestic violence. A victimized parent may minimize the nature of the abuse to the child and herself. For this reason, clinicians need to be attuned to signs of possible domestic partner abuse and more carefully assess the situation. A lower threshold for mandatory reporting may be required if there is concern that the patient and/or parent may be minimizing the nature of potential abuse. A social work consultation and referral to a variety of resources, including domestic-abuse support services, may also be appropriate.

JUVENILES AND CRIMINAL LAW

Criminal law is the body of law that relates to crime and the punishment of persons who are found to have committed a crime. Juveniles have been given special consideration in criminal law because of their perceived lack of maturity, experience, and judgment. For a person to have committed a crime, he or she must have been aware of its wrongfulness (*mens rea*) and must have actually engaged in the unlawful act (*actus reus*). Ordinarily, no crime has been committed unless both factors are present.[17]

Prior to the establishment of juvenile courts, children too young to fully understand the consequences of their actions were considered incapable of committing a crime. Children under the age of 7 ordinarily were not prosecuted for misconduct, but children over the age of 14 were considered to be liable as adults for crimes they committed. Those between ages 7 and 14 were considered to be in a gray zone where immaturity and lessened culpability would often be presumed. However, a child could be tried and punished as an adult if it appeared that the child understood the wrongfulness of his or her action and the consequences of the misconduct.

Juvenile Courts

During the 19th century, special facilities were established for juvenile offenders to separate them from adult offenders and focus on rehabilitation rather than punishment.[10] This approach reflected the legal doctrine of *parens patriae*, which holds that the state has the power to serve as if it were the parent or guardian of vulnerable citizens in need. The first juvenile court in the United States was established in 1899, and within 25 years, almost all the states had established them.[18,19] The specific procedures the courts followed varied from state to state, but these courts usually had jurisdiction over all offenders under the age of 18 who were charged with violating criminal laws.

Juvenile courts differed from the traditional criminal justice system in several ways. These courts typically managed their own cases, had probation officers and other staff who were accustomed to working with children and families, and could consider a child's life circumstances in addition to specifically legal factors in adjudicating and managing cases. This included the ability to forgo prosecution and handle cases informally if a reasonable rehabilitative alternative was available. The juvenile courts attempted to focus on rehabilitation and the best interests of the child, often relying on an informal, nonadversarial, and flexible approach to juvenile offenders. The courts could order that children be removed from their home to live with a relative, in a foster home or group home, or in an institution, depending on the severity of the offense committed and the relative risks and potential costs of recidivism.[19]

Unfortunately, the juvenile courts often failed to achieve their aspirations. In the landmark 1967 U.S. Supreme Court case of *In re Gault*, the majority of the justices criticized the failure of the juvenile court system both to provide basic constitutional protections in delinquency cases and to achieve its goals.[20] Writing for the majority, Justice Abe Fortas observed, "[U]nder our Constitution, the condition of being a boy does not justify a kangaroo court."[20] Most procedural protections provided by the Constitution (e.g., the Sixth Amendment right to counsel and Fifth Amendment rights against self-incrimination) were subsequently extended to juvenile delinquency proceedings.

From the mid-1980s through the early 1990s, juvenile homicides and drug crimes significantly increased. In response to this surge in juvenile crime and in reaction to an anticipated rise of juvenile "superpredators," most state legislatures limited the jurisdiction of the juvenile courts. Some states required juveniles accused of certain violent crimes to be tried in adult criminal court and to be sentenced as adults. These laws led to a significant increase in the number of juveniles who were tried as adults and incarcerated with adults. The increased incarceration of juveniles intensified concerns about the disproportionate impact of these more punitive laws on minority youth, the fundamental fairness of the adult sentences imposed, and the increased recidivism rates among youth tried and punished as adults rather than as juveniles.

Limitations on Sentencing of Juvenile Offenders

With the turn of the new century, the Supreme Court began to address the constitutional jurisprudence governing laws diverting juveniles into the adult criminal justice system and sentences that juveniles were receiving. Recent holdings by the Supreme Court have created additional protections for juveniles who have committed crimes by limiting the severity of punishment. In *Roper v. Simmons*, the Court held that it is unconstitutional to impose capital punishment (the death penalty) for a crime committed by a person who was under the age of 18 at the time.[21] This overruled the previous Supreme Court holding in *Stanford v. Kentucky*, which had upheld capital sentences for offenders who were over the age of 16 at the time of the crime.[22] In *Graham v. Florida*, the Supreme Court held that juvenile offenders may not be sentenced to life imprisonment without parole for nonhomicide offenses.[23] In *Miller v. Alabama*, the Court extended the *Graham* decision by ruling that all mandatory sentences of life without the possibility of parole for juvenile offenders are unconstitutional, regardless of the offense.[24] In limiting the severity of sentencing, these three cases reflected the Court's view of the special constitutional status of juveniles.

While Supreme Court cases on the death penalty and the severity of sentencing for juveniles who have committed serious crimes may seem distant from the clinical practice of most licensed mental health professionals, these landmark cases reflect an increasing legal and societal appreciation of the developmental status of youth and the need to protect them from the most onerous consequences of misconduct while also acknowledging their emerging autonomy—and thus their responsibility and accountability for their decisions and actions.

Miranda and the Reasonable-Adolescent Standard

In *JDB v. North Carolina*, the Supreme Court held that age is a relevant objective factor in considering whether a juvenile would perceive that he or she is in police custody and therefore must be given a Miranda warning.[25] A Miranda warning requires that police inform a suspect who is not free to leave (in a "custodial" situation) of his or her rights regarding self-incrimination (e.g., the right to an attorney and the right to refuse to answer questions) before being interrogated. If a person in police custody is not given a Miranda warning before being interrogated, statements made during interrogation will ordinarily not be admissible at trial. The Supreme Court held that because of the differences between children and adults and because of differences among children of similar ages, juveniles may have different perceptions of their freedom to leave or to not respond to questioning by adults. The Court recognized that a juvenile's judgment is not the same as an adult's and that a juvenile and an adult may view an identical situation differently. The Court emphasized that age is an objective factor that should be considered by a trial judge in determining whether a juvenile would perceive that he or she is in police custody and therefore should be given a Miranda warning.

Parental Liability for Juvenile Misconduct

Parents may be found liable for the negligent or criminal acts of their children.[26] In all 50 states, parents have civil parental liability and may be found responsible for malicious or willful property damage inflicted by their children if the damage was the result of the parents' neglect of their duty to provide adequate parental supervision. If found liable, parents may be obligated to financially compensate the harmed person.

Most states have laws against contributing to the delinquency of a minor, which means that parents who are found to be grossly neglectful in their parental supervision or who have misguided their children into engaging in delinquent acts can be found guilty and punished by incarceration, fine, or restitution to the victimized party. In the majority of states, it is also illegal for parents to negligently leave a firearm accessible to their children. Additionally, there have been some Internet law cases that have found a parent responsible for crimes committed by the child online as a result of negligence in providing supervision of the child. For example, if an adolescent caused thousands of dollars of damage in online identity fraud, his or her parents could potentially be held liable for compensating the victims. If parents split physical custody, the parent with custody of the child at the time of the offense typically bears the responsibility for the child's actions.

SPECIAL DOMAINS OF AUTONOMY

As noted above, minors are presumed to lack the capacity to make independent, legally binding decisions. However, children may be deemed to have the capacity to make independent decisions in specific situations established by statute or if they meet certain criteria.

Emancipated Minors

Emancipated minors are juveniles who have been freed from the custodial control of a parent or guardian by the order of a court.[27] Conversely, the former custodians of emancipated minors are freed of their custodial responsibilities. Many states have statutes that define the status of an emancipated minor, and the specifics vary from state to state. Generally, juveniles are eligible for emancipation by a court only if they are a specified minimum age, are living separately from their parents, and are economically self-sufficient. Some jurisdictions will legally emancipate juveniles who are married, become pregnant or a parent, or serve in the military. To become emancipated in most jurisdictions, the minor must request a court to designate that he or she is legally emancipated.

Typically, emancipated minors are considered adults for most purposes, including providing consent for medical and mental health care. Emancipated minors forfeit the right to parental support. Even when a juvenile has been declared emancipated, some rights and privileges reserved for persons at an older age may remain restricted until the juvenile reaches that age (e.g., a license to drive at the age of 16, the right to vote at the age of 18, or the right to purchase alcoholic beverages at the age of 21). Emancipation typically requires a court proceeding in which the court declares a juvenile to be either fully emancipated or emancipated only for certain purposes.

Clinicians need to be familiar with the status of an emancipated minor in the jurisdiction in which they are licensed to practice. In dealing with a patient who is an emancipated minor, clinicians are advised to verify a claim of emancipation and any limits or conditions upon emancipation especially with regard to providing consent for health care. While it may not be common, a treating clinician might be asked to become involved in a court hearing regarding emancipation by providing information relevant to a juvenile's maturity and history of self-sufficiency. However, treating clinicians are cautioned against providing expert opinions so as not to blur the forensic and clinical roles.

Informed Consent for Mental Health Care and Medical Care

States traditionally have recognized the rights of parents to make health care decisions for their juvenile children, but exceptions to this rule have emerged over time.[28] These exceptions include a medical emergency in which the requirement to obtain parental consent would delay care and thereby seriously endanger the child, emancipation by marriage, and achievement of legal emancipation on other grounds.[29]

Additionally, some states have adopted the mature-minor rule, which allows for a minor to make medical decisions if he or she is intelligent and mature enough to appreciate the risks and benefits of a medical treatment and has capacity to provide informed consent independently of his or her parents. Treating clinicians who are asked to opine as to the capacities of minor patients to make medical decisions should be wary of doing so unless they have information that is specifically relevant to the issue and that comports with professional practice and legal standards in their specific jurisdiction for providing such an opinion. In addition to the mature-minor rule, many states have passed laws that authorize juveniles to consent to health care specifically related to sexual activity (discussed below), substance abuse (also discussed below), and mental health care. Prudent clinicians will be aware of relevant federal and state law regarding these exceptions.

Sexuality and Reproduction

With the exception of abortion, many jurisdictions allow juveniles to consent to reproductive health services.[29] These services may include contraceptive services, testing and treatment for pregnancy and sexually transmitted diseases, prenatal care, and labor and childbirth services. These policies are based on studies showing that because of privacy concerns, juveniles may not obtain needed sexual health care services if they have to involve a parent.[30,31] Legal precedent has established that juveniles have a constitutional right to privacy that encompasses many decisions regarding their sexual health, including the right to obtain certain reproductive health care services.[32]

Abortion is a notable exception to the overall expansion of juveniles' right to consent to and access sexual health services.[29] Approximately 7% of abortions in the United States are provided to minors, and this is a hotly debated and fast-changing area of law. A limited number of states allow juveniles to obtain an abortion on their own, while the majority of states have laws that require at least parental notification and in some jurisdictions also specific parental consent for abortion. The states with parental-notification laws are required to provide for a confidential alternative to parental involvement, ordinarily through a mechanism by which a pregnant juvenile may obtain consent from a judge without informing her parents.[33]

The majority of states requiring parental involvement for abortion permit the pregnant juvenile to decide to carry the pregnancy to term and consent to prenatal care without a parent's involvement or notification.[29] As discussed above in relation to emancipated minors, a juvenile mother is commonly considered to be able to make major decisions regarding the health care of her child, although the scope of this decision making varies by jurisdiction. Additionally, the majority of jurisdictions permit a juvenile mother to place her child for adoption without notification of or consent by a parent or legal guardian.

Substance Abuse Treatment

States vary as to whether juveniles may consent to substance abuse treatment without parental notification or consent.[34] More than half the states permit adolescents younger than 18 years of age to consent to substance use treatment without parental notification and consent. The remaining states require parental consent to be obtained for the juvenile to obtain substance abuse treatment. Clinicians providing substance abuse treatment need to be aware of jurisdictional policies regarding the right of minors to consent to treatment.

Federal statutes provide special protections for ensuring the confidentiality of substance abuse treatment records. Section 42 of the Code of Federal Regulations, Part 2, governs substance abuse treatment programs receiving any federal assistance and requires that they maintain confidentiality for all patient records.[35] In general, these programs must not disclose information without the written consent of the patient. This is a more restrictive protection against disclosure of health information than that provided by the Health Insurance Portability and Accountability Act (HIPAA) Privacy Rule, which allows disclosure of health information for the purposes of treatment, payment, and health care operations without written authorization by the patient.[36] Whereas the HIPAA Privacy Rule defers to other applicable state and federal laws governing the confidentiality of minors, Section 42 of the Code of Federal Regulations requires that a minor always sign the consent form for a program to release health information, even to a parent or legal guardian.

Vignette 4: Confidentiality and Privacy

S., a 15-year old girl, presents to the walk-in hospital clinic where you are one of the staff physicians. She is not accompanied by a parent or guardian. S. reports that she recently had unprotected sex and is seeking medical evaluation and testing for sexually transmitted diseases and possible pregnancy. She notes that her parents are not aware of her sexual activity and she does not want them to be contacted. S. asks whether an abortion would be an option, if she is pregnant, and whether her parents would have to be involved.

To answer S.'s questions, you must be familiar with your state's laws on sexual health consent by minors, abortion consent by minors, emancipated minors, and mature minors. Many states would allow S. to give consent for testing and would honor her request that her parents not be notified about the testing. However, if she were pregnant and planned to obtain an abortion, the state might require parental notification or consent. Even with this requirement, there would generally be a mechanism by which S. could obtain consent for an abortion from a judge without her parents' being informed, typically called judicial bypass.

KEY STRUCTURES OF LAW RELEVANT TO JUVENILES

In addition to the case law and statutes discussed above, a number of other bodies of law have significant implications for the rights of juveniles. For clinicians working with minors, familiarity with these areas of law will help clinicians provide optimal care, ensure best practices, and avoid running afoul of legal issues.

Protected Health Information

For juveniles, HIPAA provides important protections.[37,38] As discussed above, juveniles have been deemed to have the ability to provide consent for their own health care under some circumstances. With this expanded capacity to provide consent comes protection of their protected health information (PHI). Protection of PHI for adolescents is based on the recognition that some minors would not seek needed health care if they could not do so confidentially. Numerous studies support the assertion that privacy concerns influence juveniles' willingness to address health issues, especially sensitive health issues such as contraception and sexually transmitted disease testing and treatment.[30,31]

Further, HIPAA created new rights for persons with respect to their health care history, including the right to have access to their medical records, the right to have erroneous information corrected, and the right to determine whether or not to release medical information in specific instances. Under HIPAA, health information encompasses any information about health status, the provision of health care, or payment for health care that can be linked to a specific person and is broadly interpreted to include any part of a patient's medical record or payment history. The law applies to "covered entities," which are defined as health plans, health care clearinghouses, and health care providers who electronically transmit any health information.[39]

Under the HIPAA privacy rule, juveniles who are legally emancipated are able to exercise the same rights as adults. Specific HIPAA provisions address the management of PHI for juveniles who are not emancipated and are still under the care of a parent or guardian. A parent, guardian, or person acting *in loco parentis* (as a parent) is considered to be the "personal representative" of the nonemancipated juvenile. Parents generally may access their children's PHI; the exception is a parent who is not considered to be the personal representative of the child.

Also, HIPAA provides two important provisions that are applicable when a juvenile is considered to be his or her own representative. First, the juvenile may request that he or she be contacted in a confidential manner. Most commonly, this is a request to be contacted at some place other than the family home or by a specific form of communication such as personal email rather than a home telephone shared by family members.

The second provision allows the juvenile to request limitations on disclosure of standard information about treatment, payment, or health care operations if disclosing that information would result in an increased risk of a specific danger, such as maltreatment or abuse by an angry parent. For example, insurance records of treatment for a sexually transmitted disease might be disguised so that parents will not be aware of the specific nature and purpose of that treatment.

The privacy rule also allows clinicians the discretion to not recognize a parent as the juvenile's personal representative if the clinician has a reasonable basis for believing that the parent has subjected—or may subject—the minor to domestic violence, abuse, or neglect, or if treating the parent as the personal representative could otherwise endanger the juvenile. A licensed health care professional may similarly deny a parent deemed the minor's personal representative access to the juvenile's PHI if—in the professional's reasonable judgment—that parent's access to the PHI would be likely to result in substantial harm to the minor or someone else. Conversely, HIPAA allows clinical care providers to disclose a juvenile's PHI in order to prevent or reduce an imminent threat to the health and safety of a person or the public.

In all these circumstances, clinicians are advised to seek consultation whenever practicable and to carefully document the basis for the decision that they made, the alternatives they considered, why they made the decision which they made, and why they decided against the alternatives they considered.

As noted elsewhere, state laws preempt HIPAA under specific circumstances, usually when those laws provide greater privacy protection than that provided under HIPAA. However, complications arise when state laws governing disclosure of health care information to the parents of minor patients are at odds with HIPAA. For example, if a non-emancipated juvenile has been allowed to provide consent for treatment without the involvement of a parent or legal guardian, should the clinician be able to disclose information relevant to the treatment to the parent or guardian? To address this question, HIPAA describes four potential scenarios involving state laws and HIPAA. First, if the state law explicitly requires that information be disclosed to the parent or guardian, then HIPAA allows the health care provider to comply with that law and to disclose the information. In the second scenario, if the state law explicitly permits, but does not require, that the information be disclosed to the parent or guardian, then the provider may exercise discretion in determining whether to disclose the information. In the third scenario, if the state law prohibits disclosure without the consent of the juvenile, the provider is required to obtain the permission of the juvenile before disclosing information to the parent or guardian. In the fourth scenario, if the state law is silent on parental access or notification, the provider may use his or her discretion to determine whether to disclose information to the parent or guardian.

Unfortunately, HIPAA leaves clinicians with unanswered questions regarding the privacy rule and interactions with "state and other applicable laws." Such laws include those relating to the provision of consent by minors, medical records, and health privacy; Title X of the Public Health Service Act; Medicaid; and the Family Educational Rights and Privacy Act (FERPA). Clinicians are advised to become familiar with HIPAA and with the laws in their own jurisdiction that are most likely to interact with HIPAA (i.e., laws governing consent and privacy) and to seek consultation should they have questions or concerns about how to proceed under specific circumstances.

Vignette 4, continued

S., the teenage girl who wants to be tested for sexually transmitted diseases and pregnancy, requests that she be contacted through her personal cell phone rather than her home address and telephone number. Under HIPAA's privacy rule, Jill has the right to be contacted in the manner that she prefers in order to maintain her privacy.

Educational Rights and Privacy

In 1974, FERPA was enacted to protect the privacy of students' educational records by placing restrictions on the disclosure of information to other parties, including law enforcement agencies and mental health clinicians.[40] The FERPA applies to all schools that receive funds under any applicable program of the U.S. Department of Education (including federally backed student loans). Also, FERPA provides that parents or eligible students have the right to inspect and review their educational records, the right to have inaccurate or misleading information in the records corrected, and with some exceptions, the right to give or withhold permission for the release by the school of any information from the student's education record.

Health information that is protected under HIPAA excludes any information governed by FERPA. This is likely to be relevant when health care is delivered in a school setting (e.g., by a school nurse or at a school-based clinic) or when there is communication with a school about a student's physical or mental health. In general, information in a student's record at a school-based health center is not considered part of his or her educational record and would therefore be afforded HIPAA protections. In the case of information that is less clearly part of a student's health record, a careful analysis should be conducted to determine whether the information is more appropriately covered by HIPAA or FERPA.

In October 2007, the U.S. Department of Education released clarifications on the limitations of FERPA in instances relevant to student health or safety.[41] These clarifications held that FERPA applied only to educational records, not to information that is known about a student by school staff. Therefore, in the event of a potential safety threat, school staff may disclose their observations of a student to law enforcement agencies, emergency medical services, and mental health clinicians. Additionally, schools can maintain "law enforcement units" of administrative or disciplinary staff members who keep separate investigative reports and other records apart from the formal educational records of the students. As a result, information related to an investigation of a potential threat by a student can be recorded in an investigative file rather than in an educational record protected by FERPA. Also FERPA allows for disclosure of information in an emergency in order to protect the health and safety of individuals. Again, when practicable, clinicians are advised to seek consultation from a seasoned professional and/or legal counsel familiar with laws and professional practice in their jurisdiction, if they are uncertain about how they should proceed.

Special Education

The Individuals with Disabilities Education Act (IDEA) is a federal law that ensures the provision of services to children with disabilities throughout the United States by guaranteeing that all students with disabilities have access to free and appropriate public education.[42] The IDEA governs how states and public agencies provide early intervention, special education, and related services to infants, toddlers, children, and youth with disabilities. The law is aimed at providing educational services that are individualized to meet the specific needs of students with disabilities and are provided in the least restrictive environment. Specialized educational interventions may include individual or small-group instruction, modified curricula, assistive technologies, and specialized forms of therapy, such as speech, physical, and occupational therapy. For each student, a specialized education plan, called an individualized education program (IEP), is developed to meet the student's specific educational needs and ensure that the student is able to access the individualized services. Mental health clinicians may become involved in the creation of these plans, especially if there are social and emotional considerations that need to be addressed.

Equal Access for Juveniles with Disabilities

The Americans with Disabilities Act (ADA), passed in 1990, is a comprehensive civil rights law that prohibits discrimination against people with disabilities and guarantees that they have access to the same opportunities that are available to people without disabilities.[43] To be protected by the ADA, a person must have, have had, or be perceived as having a disability (defined as a physical or mental impairment) that substantially limits one or more major life activities. A mental or physical impairment may be considered a disability even if it is not severe or permanent. The ADA requires that persons with disabilities have equal access to employment opportunities (which is of less relevance to juveniles than to adults) and educational opportunities, such as school programs, as well as physical access to public buildings and accommodations. Clinicians working with juveniles with disabilities need to be aware of the protections that the ADA affords them.

GUIDELINES FOR CLINICIANS

The following guidelines should assist clinicians as they navigate the difficult medical-legal issues that can arise when treating juveniles.

Knowing the Law Where You Practice

As discussed in detail in chapter 1, while federal laws apply to all U.S. jurisdictions, laws and regulations relevant to clinical practice often vary widely from state to state, especially when it comes to the evaluation and treatment of children and adolescents. Two clinicians confronted with a similar situation in different states will have to consider and apply relevant standards of law and professional practice that may lead to different decisions or outcomes. Even states that adhere to principles such as acknowledging the emerging autonomy of adolescents may craft laws and regulations that vary in their details, such as the ages at which certain decisions can be made by juveniles or the legal processes required. As a clinician, it is imperative that you familiarize yourself with the applicable laws, regulations, and practices of the specific jurisdiction in which you practice. If you fail to do so, you risk running afoul of important legal obligations or not recognizing opportunities for the exercise of professional discretion. Most important, failure to familiarize yourself with relevant law can have adverse consequences for your patients, including compromised clinical care and legal rights or interests, as well as potentially dire consequences for you as the clinician.

Clinicians practicing in new jurisdictions can familiarize themselves with local practices, laws, and regulations by consulting local clinicians, state professional societies, professional publications, hospital legal departments, and attorneys specializing in laws governing clinical practice. When a clinician faces a legally ambiguous circumstance, consultation with a hospital legal department or attorney is recommended to clarify the legal issues at hand and to protect the patient, clinician, and clinical practice organization from unintended consequences.

Knowing To Whom You Owe a Duty of Care

Your first consideration as a clinician is to clearly identify the person for whom you are working and, accordingly, the person to whom you owe your primarily legal and ethical obligations. As the treating clinician, you establish a duty of care to the patient.

As a clinician providing health care services to a juvenile patient, the client to whom you owe an ethical obligation is the identified juvenile patient, and your primary obligation is to give priority to the welfare of the patient over competing interests.[44] However, your primary legal client is usually the parent or guardian who has the legal capacity to authorize, guide, and terminate the clinical relationship. In situations in which juveniles are legally deemed to have authority to consent to their own clinical care, such as in the case of an emancipated minor, the juvenile is the primary legal client.

When an agency, court, school, or other organization engages the consultative, educational, or research services of a clinician, then that organization is the clinician's presumptively identified legal client, and the clinician has primary legal and ethical obligations to that organization, unless otherwise clarified. However, while the clinician has primary legal and professional obligations to the client organization, he or she also has ethical and legal obligations to the juvenile for whom the clinician's professional services have been engaged, including obligations to both parties to provide competent professional services.

Vignette 5: Legal, Professional, and Ethical Obligations

You are a child psychologist who has been retained by a school to evaluate the aggressive behavior of B., a student at the school, because staff members are concerned that B. may pose a risk of harm to others. You have an obligation, first, to explain your role and the purpose of the evaluation to B. and his parent(s) or legal guardian; second, to be clear about what will happen with any report that you generate and who owns that report; third, to clearly obtain informed consent from B.'s legal custodians and seek to obtain "assent" from B. himself for B. to undergo the evaluation; fourth, to explain your role and the purpose of the evaluation to any school personnel or other parties who may be interviewed as part of the evaluation; and finally, to provide competent professional services in the course of conducting the evaluation.

In this situation, the school's goal of ensuring the safety of other students and staff may conflict with the goal of B. and his parent(s) or legal guardian to maintain the status quo, and the clinician will need to be careful to avoid slipping into a dual-agent role, which could entail conflicting obligations. Similarly, a therapist for a juvenile patient might be asked by school personnel to provide consultation in managing the patient's aggressive behavior in school. If the therapist agrees to the consultation, the result may be conflicting roles that undermine the therapist's primary obligation as the treating clinician for the patient.

A clinician who conducts a forensic evaluation of a juvenile (i.e., an evaluation that is intended to be used in a legal or administrative proceeding or determination) has a different role from that of a clinician who has established a therapeutic relationship with a juvenile patient or a clinician who provides professional consultation regarding a juvenile.[45] Forensic evaluations are intended to generate forensically sound and defensible information, opinions, and recommendations for courts, attorneys, or others who are parties to legal cases. For example, a court may order a forensic evaluation of a juvenile in a delinquency case or a custody evaluation in a divorce case involving conflict over child custody. The client in a forensic evaluation is typically the court or attorney who has requested the evaluation.

Considering the Context in Which You Are Providing Care

It is critically important that clinicians clearly understand their role and the context in which they are working. For clinicians who work with juveniles and their families, the role and context can be complicated. Are you providing clinical care to a juvenile patient in a clinical setting? In the course of providing clinical care to a juvenile patient, have you received a subpoena or court order to submit records or testify in a legal proceeding involving the juvenile? Have you been retained by an attorney to perform a custody evaluation of a family that is involved in divorce proceedings? Each of these contexts presents the clinician with challenges in identifying, clarifying, and managing legal, ethical, and professional practice obligations to the minors involved, their parents or legal guardians, and often, other third parties. An understanding of your role, responsibilities, and legal, ethical, and clinical obligations is paramount in conducting your work professionally and responsibly and is essential if you are to avoid common legal, ethical, and clinical practice pitfalls.

Understanding Your Role in Legal Proceedings

Clinicians must be alert to their roles when they participate in legal proceedings involving juvenile clients. If a clinician is retained by an attorney to conduct an evaluation that will assist the attorney in representing the child, then the work is protected by attorney–client privilege. The clinician is well advised to clarify whether, in his or her jurisdiction, the attorney–client privilege or the mandated reporting requirement takes precedence, as information may be obtained that would normally trigger mandated reporting. For example, California case law holds that a mental health professional's mandated reporting duties are trumped by the attorney–client privilege. In most states, however, there is no law that clearly resolves which would prevail. In the absence of a clear law, the clinician is advised to clarify with the attorney, before beginning work on the case, how the clinician would respond in the event that he or she became aware of information that would ordinarily trigger a mandated reporting obligation.

The work product created by a clinician who has been retained by an attorney belongs to the attorney. For example, a clinician might conduct a psychological test of a juvenile, resulting in a report, and later, the parents of the youth might want to sign a release-of-information form for the clinician to release the report to a school, a treating clinician, or another party. In these cases, only the attorney can authorize release of the test report; the parents cannot do so because they were not the legal clients for whom the testing was done.[46]

The same is true if the clinician is ordered by a court to conduct an evaluation, except that in this case the court is the identified client. Courts ordinarily do not stand in the way when a third party requests release of a court-mandated report, if the request is warranted; however, explicit prior court authorization for its release is generally required. Clinicians are advised to clarify these expectations before performing the evaluation.

In the case of a subpoena or court order to provide records and/or testify before the court about the clinical evaluation or treatment of a juvenile, the clinician should consult an attorney to make certain that he or she responds appropriately but does not improperly disclose information. Particularly complex situations can arise, such as those involving contested child custody proceedings. For example, an attorney might suggest that a juvenile undergo an evaluation or receive treatment as part of a legal case without disclosing the legal context to the treating clinician. Or the law might not be clear about whether testimonial privilege (discussed below) can be waived in the case of a juvenile patient's communications with a clinician.

Vignette 6: Testimonial Privilege

You provide therapy to C., a 13-year-old girl with a history of depression, self-injury by cutting, and suicidal ideation that has prompted multiple inpatient psychiatric hospitalizations. Her parents are engaged in a contentious divorce proceeding and an intense dispute over the custody of their daughter. The wife alleges that her husband has significant psychiatric issues that impair his fitness as a parent. During the course of your treatment of C., her mother asks you to provide a letter recommending that C. be placed in the sole physical and legal custody of her mother, severing her father's parental rights. You explain to the mother that your primary role is as C.'s treating clinician and that offering opinions about custody determinations in a divorce proceeding would inevitably conflict with your obligation to maintain a therapeutic relationship with C. In addition to this conflict between therapeutic and forensic roles, it is uncertain whether you have sufficient training and experience to render forensic opinions about child custody in this case. Finally, an individual therapist's scope of knowledge is typically limited and falls far short of the thorough knowledge of the family, its individual members, and their respective relationships and functioning that is required to render a sound forensic opinion about custody determination.

Distinguishing between Confidentiality and Testimonial Privilege

Confidentiality is the ethical duty of the clinician not to disclose any information that is learned from or about a patient in the course of conducting a clinical evaluation or providing ongoing care. Barring a few important exceptions (e.g., mandated reporting, information disclosed under emergency circumstances, or information disclosed in an effort to secure involuntary civil commitment), consent is required from the patient—or if the patient is a juvenile, from the patient's parent or legal guardian—for a clinician to disclose protected information. (Confidentiality is discussed in detail in chapter 9.)

The physician–patient privilege (or the psychotherapist–patient privilege, if the clinician is not a physician) is a testimonial privilege that states have created that prohibits physicians and other designated licensed clinical professionals from disclosing during the course of a legal proceeding any "protected communications" or other confidential information that was learned during the course of patient care. In some jurisdictions, a parent or legal guardian of a juvenile may be able to waive this privilege on behalf of the juvenile, whereas such a waiver is not allowed in other jurisdictions. Some states have created statutes allowing judicial discretion in waiving the physician–patient privilege in child custody disputes. (See chapter 9 for a full discussion of testimonial privilege.)

CONCLUSION

For mental health clinicians working with juveniles, the law intersects the lives of and our work with juvenile patients in multiple ways and may raise many issues relevant to their care. These issues include custody disputes, involvement in the criminal justice system, and minors seeking medical evaluation and treatment without the consent of their legal custodians. Clinicians need to be familiar with the laws and regulations that are relevant to their practice, which vary among jurisdictions. Where uncertainty exists, clinicians are advised to seek additional resources or expert counsel, including possible legal consultation, to better understand the situation and applicable rules so as that they can take the most appropriate actions.

FREQUENTLY ASKED QUESTIONS

Why does the legal system give special consideration to juveniles?

Juveniles are presumed to be less mature, to have less experience, and to be less emotionally and cognitively developed than adults. As a result, the law gives special consideration to juveniles, providing multiple legal processes that are intended to take into account the immaturity and vulnerability of juveniles while recognizing their developing capacities and autonomy. For example, the law protects most (but not all) juveniles from prosecution and sentencing as adults for misconduct but also acknowledges their autonomy for making certain kinds of decisions regarding their clinical care.

What are the different custody statuses for juveniles?

Juveniles are typically considered to be in the legal and physical custody of their parents. However, when parents divorce, legal and physical custody may be shared equally by the parents (joint custody) or split by a court between the parents in a variety of ways. Some states now encourage or require a court in a divorce child custody matter to learn and take into consideration the custody preferences of adolescents. Juveniles who are not in the custody of their parents may be in the legal or physical custody of a guardian or state agency.

Clinicians should know the custody status of a juvenile patient. For example, children in the custody of a state child welfare agency will ordinarily—but not necessarily always—have all decisions about their care made by a representative of that agency, such as a caseworker. Juveniles placed in the custody of a state juvenile justice authority can have their physical placement decided by that authority (e.g. incarceration, residential placement, or community-based placement), but a parent or other legal guardian may still have to authorize any medical or mental health assessment or care. Juveniles who have been legally emancipated from their parents and are not in the legal custody of an agency or other party (e.g., a guardian) are essentially their own guardians, as if they were adults.

Are nonemancipated juveniles allowed to make decisions regarding their own health care?

Traditionally, parents made all decisions regarding the health care of juveniles unless a court specifically determined that a different arrangement was warranted in individual cases. However, the federal government and the states have increasingly recognized that juveniles of a certain age or level of maturity are capable of making their own decisions about at least some aspects of their health care. Many states have statutes that allow for juveniles of a certain age or maturity to make decisions regarding sexual and reproductive health care, mental health care, and substance abuse treatment. All states require some form of parental notification or consent in cases in which a juvenile seeks an abortion, unless she requests that a court approve the abortion without parental notification, which the court may do if the safety of the juvenile would be jeopardized by informing her parents. This exception to parental notification is known as a judicial bypass.

REFERENCES

1. Benedek E, Ash P, Scott C, eds. *Principles and Practice of Child and Adolescent Forensic Mental Health*. Washington, DC: American Psychiatric Publishing; 2010.
2. *Parham v. J.R.*, 442 U.S. 584, 602(1979).
3. *Pierce v. Society of Sisters*, 268 US 510(1925).
4. Horowitz R. Legal rights of children. *Child and Adolescent Psychiatric Clinics of North America*. 2002;11:705–717.
5. *Tinker v. Des Moines*, 393 US 503, 511(1969).
6. Gould J, Martindale D. *The Art and Science of Child Custody Evaluations*. New York, NY: Guilford Press; 2007.
7. Wroath, J. *Until They Are Seven: The Origins of Women's Legal Rights*. Winchester, UK: Waterside Press; 1998.
8. American Psychological Association. Guidelines for Child Custody Evaluations in Family Law Proceedings. *American Psychologist*. 2010;65:863–867.
9. Child Custody Act of 1993, Michigan Compiled Laws. § 722.
10. Meyers J. A short history of child protection in America. *Family Law Quarterly*. 2008–2009;42:449–464.
11. Administration on Children, Youth and Families, Children's Bureau. *Child maltreatment 2013*. http://www.acf.hhs.gov/programs/cb/research-data-technology/statistic-research/child-maltreatment. Accessed September 29, 2015.
12. American Bar Association Division of Public Education. *The history of juvenile justice*. http://www.americanbar.org/content/dam/aba/migrated/publiced/features/DYJpart1.authcheckdam.pdf. Accessed September 27, 2015.
13. Caffey J. Multiple fractures in the long bones of infants suffering from chronic subdural hematoma. *American Journal of Roentgenology*. 1946;194:163–173.
14. Kempe CH, Frederic N, Silverman MD. The battered-child syndrome. *JAMA*. 1962;181:17–24.
15. 42 U.S.C. 67(2012).
16. 42 U.S.C. 670(1996).
17. Blackstone W. *Commentaries on the laws of England*. The Avalon Project at Yale Law School. http://avalon.law.yale.edu/subject_menus/blackstone.asp. Accessed November 10, 2015.
18. U.S. Department of Justice Office of Justice. *Juvenile justice: a century of change*. http://www.ojjdp.gov/publications/PubAbstract.asp?pubi=3911. Accessed March 10, 2016.
19. American Bar Association Division of Public Education. *The history of juvenile justice*. http://www.americanbar.org/content/dam/aba/migrated/publiced/features/DYJpart1.authcheckdam.pdf. Accessed September 27, 2015.
20. *In re Gault*, 387 U.S. 1(1967).
21. *Roper v. Simmons*, 543 U.S. 551(2005).
22. *Stanford v. Kentucky*, 492 U.S. 361(1989).
23. *Graham v. Florida*, 560 U.S. 48(2010).
24. *Miller v. Alabama*, 567 U.S. ___ (2012).
25. *J.D.B. v. North Carolina*, 564 U.S. ___ (2011).
26. Tomaszewski A. From Columbine to Kazaa: parental liability in a new world. *Ill L Rev*. 2005;2005(2):573–579. http://www.illinoislawreview.org/article/from-columbine-to-kazaa-parental-liability-in-a-new-world/. Accessed March 10, 2016.

27. Maradiegue A. Minor's rights versus parental rights: review of legal issues in adolescent health care. *Journal of Midwifery and Women's Health.* 2003;48(3):170–177. http://www.medscape.com/viewarticle/456472_5. Accessed September 27, 2015.
28. Hill BJ. Medical decision making by and on behalf of adolescents: reconsidering first principles. *Journal of Health Care Law and Policy.* 2012;15:37–73.
29. Boonstra H, Nash E. *The Guttmacher Report on Public Policy, special analysis: minors and the right to consent to health care.* http://www.guttmacher.org/pubs/tgr/03/4/gr030404.html. Accessed November 11, 2015.
30. University of Chicago School of Medicine Section of Family Planning and Contraception Research. *Youth awareness of a minor's right to access reproductive health services.* http://familyplanning.uchicago.edu/policy/publications-resources/Teen%20Knowledge%20of%20Minor%20Consent%20Laws.pdf. Accessed November 10, 2015.
31. Jones RK, Purcell A, Singh S, Finer LB. Adolescents' reports of parental knowledge of adolescents' use of sexual health services and their reactions to mandated parental notification for prescription contraception. *Journal of the American Medical Association.* 2005;293:340–348.
32. *Planned Parenthood v. Matheson,* 582 Supp. 1001, 1009(D. Utah 1983).
33. Dennis A, et al. *The impact of laws requiring parental involvement for abortion: a literature review.* Guttmacher Institute. https://www.guttmacher.org/pubs/ParentalInvolvementLaws.pdf. Accessed November 9 2015.
34. Brooks MK. Legal and ethical issues. In: *Treatment of adolescents with substance use disorders.* http://www.ncbi.nlm.nih.gov/books/NBK64357/. Accessed October 29, 2015.
35. Confidentiality of Alcohol and Drug Abuse Patient Records, 42 Code of Federal Regulations Part 2. http://www.ecfr.gov/cgi-bin/text-idx?rgn=div5;node=42%3A1.0.1.1.2. Accessed November 14, 2015.
36. Substance Abuse and Mental Health Administration. *The confidentiality of alcohol and drug abuse patient records regulation and the HIPAA Privacy Rule: implications for alcohol and substance abuse programs.* http://www.samhsa.gov/sites/default/files/part2-hipaa-comparison2004.pdf. Accessed November 8, 2015.
37. Health Insurance Portability and Accountability Act of 1996, 110 Stat. 193 (1996).
38. English A, Ford C. The HIPAA privacy rule and adolescents: legal questions and clinical challenges. *Perspectives in Sexual and Reproductive Health.* 2004;36(2);80–86. https://www.guttmacher.org/pubs/journals/3608004.html. Accessed October 29, 2015
39. National Institutes of Health. *To whom does the privacy rule apply and whom will it affect?* https://privacyruleandresearch.nih.gov/pr_06.asp. Accessed September 29, 2015.
40. Family Educational Rights and Privacy Act, as amended 2010. 20 U.S.C. § 1232g; 34 CFR Part 98 and 99.
41. U.S. Department of Education. *Safe schools and FERPA: FERPA guidance on emergency management.* http://www2.ed.gov/policy/gen/guid/fpco/ferpa/safeschools/index.html. Accessed September 30, 2016.
42. 20 U.S.C. 33(2012).
43. 42 U.S.C 126(2009).
44. American Academy of Child and Adolescent Psychiatry. *Code of Ethics.* https://www.aacap.org/App_Themes/AACAP/docs/about_us/transparency_portal/aacap_code_of_ethics_2012.pdf. Accessed November 8, 2015.
45. Buratto S, Dinwiddie SH. Virtual mentor: health law, juvenile forensic evaluations. *American Medical Association Journal of Ethics.* 2013;15:860–865.
46. National Academy of Neuropsychology. *Independent and court-ordered forensic neuropsychological examinations.* https://www.nanonline.org/docs/paic/pdfs/nanimepaper.pdf. Accessed March 3, 2016.

/// 12 /// MENTAL HEALTH PROFESSIONALS AND THE CRIMINAL JUSTICE SYSTEM

REENA KAPOOR AND ALEC BUCHANAN

The criminal justice system has little relevance to the daily practice of many mental health clinicians. They are more familiar with courtrooms from television and movies than from clinical experience, and they rarely see patients who are involved with the courts. However, since more than 7 million Americans are under criminal justice supervision on any given day,[1] even clinicians working in private practice are likely at some point in their careers to treat a patient who is charged with a crime, on probation or parole, or mandated by a court to receive mental health treatment. In those circumstances, a basic understanding of the criminal justice system can be invaluable.

In this chapter, we provide clinicians with a framework for understanding how persons with mental illness typically progress through the criminal courts, from arrest to reentry into the community.

We begin by explaining how clinicians should handle a patient's disclosure of criminal activity. We then review the different roles of a treating clinician and a forensic evaluator with regard to patients who are involved with the courts. We use one case vignette throughout the chapter, following a patient through the criminal justice system as he undergoes common psychiatric evaluations: competence to stand trial, criminal responsibility, and eligibility for mental health diversion programs. For each type of evaluation, we review the legal standards and relevant landmark court decisions. Finally, we offer helpful tips for clinicians interacting with the criminal justice system.

HANDLING A PATIENT'S DISCLOSURE OF CRIMINAL BEHAVIOR

In some cases, a clinician first learns that his or her patient has been involved in a crime only after the patient has been arrested. However, it is not uncommon for patients to disclose their involvement in criminal activity, ranging from petty theft to serious violence, during the course of psychotherapy or an appointment for medication management. Consider the following case example:

Vignette: Disclosure of a Crime

Dr. A., a psychiatrist, has been treating Mr. X., a 21-year-old college student who was diagnosed with schizoaffective disorder a year earlier, with psychotherapy and medication. During a routine outpatient appointment, Mr. X. tells Dr. A. that he suspects his roommate of spying on him and trying to "steal secrets from my mind." Two weeks ago, Mr. X. punched his roommate in the mouth after accusing him of spying. The roommate had cuts and bruises on his face, but he did not report the episode to the school or police, considering it just a freakish thing that happened. Mr. X. says that "everything is fine now" and that he is focused on studying for final exams.

In this situation, Dr. A. may not know what to do. He may feel revulsion and fear toward his patient. For many clinicians, the first impulse is to call the police or encourage the patient to do so in the office. After all, the patient has committed a crime, so shouldn't the authorities be involved?

Dr. A.'s main task in this instance is not to facilitate punishment for an alleged crime but rather to assess and manage the risk of further harm. Mr. X. has engaged in an act of violence that was seemingly motivated by delusional beliefs. Now, 2 weeks after the violent episode, Dr. A must determine whether Mr. X. currently poses a risk of harm to self or others. A full discussion of violence risk assessment can be found in chapter 4. In this case, Dr. A.'s assessment will focus on determining whether Mr. X. is still having violent thoughts toward his roommate, whether the delusional beliefs are still present, and whether Mr. X. poses an imminent risk of harm. In addition to the risk of violence toward other persons, Dr. A. will assess the risk of suicide, as Mr. X. may also be a danger to himself.

Performing these assessments is the first step, but if a risk is identified, the clinician's task has not been completed. The risk must be managed. Generally, a clinician in this type of situation will need to decide first whether the patient's condition is serious enough to warrant hospitalization. For example, in some cases, untreated psychotic symptoms and a recent violent act would meet criteria for involuntary admission on the basis of dangerousness to others. In the case of Mr. X., the decision is more difficult, since the violent act occurred 2 weeks ago and the patient is now denying any violent plans or intent. He still has delusional thoughts, but he is willing to make medication changes and return as often as necessary for follow-up. He is also willing to allow Dr. A. to contact his parents and dorm monitor. After speaking with the dorm monitor and parents, who agree that Mr. X. will live at home temporarily rather than at the college, Dr. A. decides not to hospitalize the patient.

In the aftermath of a patient's disclosure of criminal behavior, whether violent or not, clinicians may have questions about exactly what their obligations are. They may fear that they will he held liable for the patient's actions if the patient harms another person and may think that a *Tarasoff* warning is necessary. (See chapters 3 and 9 for an explanation of the clinician's duty to warn or otherwise protect identifiable third parties, established by *Tarasoff v. Regents of the University of California*.) Having heard the terms "misprision of a felony" and "accessory after the fact," clinicians may believe that they face criminal charges, not just civil liability, if they do not report the patient's actions. Before acting on these thoughts, consultation with an attorney, risk management professional, or forensic psychiatrist is well advised. Each state has its own laws regarding criminal conspiracies, clinician–patient confidentiality, mandated reporting, and discretionary disclosures to law enforcement personnel. After discussing the relevant laws in the local jurisdiction, the clinician should decide on a course of action and carefully document the reasons for the decision in the patient's chart.

WHEN A PATIENT IS ARRESTED

A few days later, Mr. X.'s roommate decides to report the assault to the police. After taking a statement from the roommate, the police arrest Mr. X. and charge him with assault in the second degree. Mr. X.'s parents call Dr. A. to tell him about the arrest. They are very worried about their son because they believe he "won't make it in prison." They ask for Dr. A.'s help in getting their son out of this predicament.

Persons who have been arrested are typically taken to the police station for booking, fingerprinting, and interviewing (if they agree to be interviewed) and are held there until the scheduled court appearance for arraignment. In some jurisdictions, they stay in lockup at the police station until the court appearance, and in other jurisdictions, they are taken to the county jail. In either case, persons who have been charged with relatively minor criminal offenses have the option of posting bail and being set free until the court appearance.

For a person with a mental illness, the first few hours and days of confinement in jail or police lockup can be a harrowing, high-risk period. Suicide rates during the first 7 days of incarceration are roughly four times higher than the rate for the general U.S. population.[3] Several factors contribute to the high risk of suicide, including drug or alcohol withdrawal symptoms, difficult conditions of confinement, difficulty adjusting to new life circumstances after the crime, and (in some cases) lack of access to prescription medications. Suicides in correctional settings generally occur by strangulation, typically with the use of clothing or bed sheets. A smaller number of suicides result from cutting or medication overdose.[4]

Because of the high risk of suicide, police departments and county jails have an obligation to attend to the serious medical and psychiatric needs of their detainees. Many police departments do not have the resources to provide health care in the jail or lockup, so they use local emergency departments for urgent medical evaluations. In some large cities, where local jails can house several thousand inmates, the jail medical staff may offer evaluation for and treatment of mental health disorders at the correctional facility. Whether health care is provided on site or at a local hospital, the initial evaluation at the jail should include screening for suicide, treatment of drug or alcohol withdrawal, and continuation of outpatient prescription medications—tasks that can sometimes take several days to complete.

Clinicians who learn of a patient's arrest should communicate the patient's urgent medical needs to the jail or police lockup, since sharing this type of information can often hasten the patient's access to necessary treatment. This task can be tricky, since the patient did not sign a release-of-information form in advance of the arrest that would have allowed communication with the police. Instead, the clinician must determine whether local laws permit nonemergency communication between facilities without the patient's consent for the purpose of diagnosis and treatment (as many states do), or whether the patient's situation is enough of an emergency to warrant disclosure of clinical information without consent. Consultation with an attorney or forensic psychiatrist can be helpful in these cases.

In the case of Mr. X., Dr. A. or the patient's parents could let the jail know what medication Mr. X. takes at home, whether he has ever attempted suicide, and whether he uses illicit drugs. Some correctional facilities will allow a patient to take his or her own supply of medications, if they are properly labeled and verified as authentic. Other facilities will obtain the medications (or a therapeutic substitute) from their own pharmacy because they consider outside medications a risk for illicit drug abuse.

MENTAL HEALTH COURTS AND JAIL DIVERSION PROGRAMS

All persons in the criminal justice system appear in court and are arraigned (formally charged with a crime) within a few hours to days after their arrest. After arraignment, the defendant will have another opportunity to post bail. He or she may also be eligible for a hearing in a specialty court, such as a drug court or a mental health court, or participation in a jail diversion program, depending on the circumstances of the case. Referral to a specialty court or diversion program generally occurs as outlined in our case vignette:

Mr. X.'s parents hire a criminal defense attorney to represent their son, and they tell the attorney about Mr. X.'s history of mental illness. The attorney notifies the court's jail diversion staff and requests an evaluation of Mr. X., since she hopes that he can avoid incarceration by agreeing to undergo mental health treatment. A member of the jail diversion staff interviews Mr. X. in the courthouse lockup, with the aim of presenting a treatment plan for the court to consider at the time of arraignment. If the court agrees, Mr. X. can participate in mental health treatment rather than serve time in jail. If he successfully completes the treatment program as stipulated by the court, his criminal charges will be dismissed.

Mental health courts and jail diversion programs were developed in the 1990s, largely in response to the growing population of mentally ill persons in jails and prisons. An estimated 15% of prisoners have a serious mental illness, and correctional facilities are difficult environments in which to provide treatment. In addition, many persons with mental illness are caught in a cycle of drug abuse, noncompliance with treatment, arrests for petty crimes, short incarcerations, and homelessness. Alternative strategies such as jail diversion and mental health courts arose from a desire—on the part of both the courts and mental health professionals—to create a more effective system for serving the needs of these people.

Two models of diversion for persons with mental illness were initially developed: separate mental health courts and jail diversion programs housed within the regular criminal courts.[5] The two models used slightly different procedures to accomplish the same objective. The jail diversion programs placed mental health clinicians in the criminal courthouse to work with patient-defendants, prosecutors, defense attorneys, and judges in order to facilitate treatment as an alternative to incarceration. The mental health courts operated as a completely separate court system for persons with mental illness, purportedly with a more therapeutic focus. Creating a separate court system had the advantage of fostering specialized expertise, though it also potentially increased the stigma associated with participation.

Early data from jail diversion programs and mental health courts were promising. These approaches reduced the number of days that mentally ill persons spent in jail and in most cases resulted in a high rate of retention in mental health treatment after 1 year. There was no adverse effect on public safety as a result of diversion, even for persons with significant histories of violence.[6] Cost estimates were also favorable. Jail diversion programs resulted in savings from reduced arrest and booking costs, jail days, court costs, and emergency room visits.[7] As a result, jail diversion programs and specialty courts expanded rapidly. By 2015, hundreds of jail diversion programs and mental health courts had been developed around the country.

Since mental health courts and jail diversion programs were successful, reform efforts next focused on diverting persons with mental illness at other junctures in the criminal justice process. Police officers received crisis intervention training to identify signs of mental illness so that they could divert mentally ill persons to treatment programs instead of arresting them.[8] In addition, community reentry programs were developed for persons with mental illness who were released after a long incarceration, with the aim of providing support and increasing their chances for successful reintegration into the community. Together with traditional jail diversion programs, these additional efforts make up the Sequential Intercept Model of criminal justice diversion,[9] which has become a national standard for how to manage persons with mental illness in the criminal courts.

A key feature of all jail diversion programs is that the patient-defendant must agree to participate. No one can be forced into a diversion program or specialty court instead of proceeding to trial. This arrangement is necessary to protect the rights of defendants, but it can be problematic when persons with mental illness do not understand that they are ill or are simply too symptomatic to participate in the evaluation process. Under these circumstances, the patient-defendant cannot be diverted, and the usual course of events in the criminal trial process continues. One such example is described in Mr. X.'s case:

Mr. X. refuses to speak at length with the jail diversion clinician, telling her that he "isn't going to agree to any more spying and mind games." He paces back and forth in the lockup cell, mumbling under his breath about "secrets" and "mind control." His attorney tries to speak with him before the arraignment, but he refuses. During the arraignment, he is mute, rocking back and forth slowly in his chair. The attorney for Mr. X. tells the judge that she is concerned about her client's symptoms of mental illness, and she asks the court to order an evaluation of his competence to stand trial. The judge agrees.

Differing Roles of Treating Clinicians and Forensic Evaluators

Mr. X. has now entered the part of the criminal justice system in which mental health treatment and evaluation are more formally separated. This separation can be confusing for those without experience in criminal proceedings. For example:

Mr. X.'s parents, who were in the courtroom for the arraignment, contact Dr. A. to update him on their son's situation. They explain that the court ordered an evaluation of their son's competence to stand trial, and they ask Dr. A. to perform the evaluation, since he knows Mr. X. better than any other mental health clinician.

The reasoning that Mr. X.'s parents use when asking Dr. A. to perform the evaluation is intuitive; why wouldn't the doctor who has known the patient for years be best situated to perform an evaluation of their son's competence for the court? However, as discussed in other chapters, treating clinicians and independent forensic experts have very different roles. The treating clinician has an ethical duty to act in the patient's best interest, which typically means advocating for the patient's health and welfare when necessary. In the context of the criminal justice system, the clinician may think that the patient is very ill and that the court proceedings are exacerbating his condition. If Dr. A. were to write a report for the court, he might feel pulled toward providing an opinion that would relieve his patient of the burdensome court proceedings. For example, he might opine that the patient is very sick and doesn't belong in jail. Assuming that this was truly his opinion, he would be acting ethically in advocating for his patient's improved health.

Criminal courts have no such mandate to act in the best interest of the patient-defendant. When courts request a psychiatric evaluation, they are seeking an objective answer to the question being posed. Therefore, courts generally request that the evaluation be performed by a mental health professional who is not treating the patient. In most cases, the evaluator is a forensic psychiatrist or psychologist.

Forensic evaluators have a different ethical mandate from that of treating clinicians, with a focus on truth-telling, respect for persons, and objectivity, as opposed to advocacy for the patient.[10] When performing a forensic assessment, the evaluator has a primary obligation to answer the question being posed truthfully, recognizing that some harm may come to the evaluee as a result. For example, if the forensic evaluator opines that the defendant is competent, he or she may then be exposed to severe criminal penalties as the trial progresses. If the evaluator opines that the defendant is dangerous to others, the judge may impose a longer prison sentence or additional conditions of probation. Conversely, the evaluator's assessment may benefit the evaluee by mitigating or delaying punishment.

The forensic evaluator strives to be objective, regardless of the consequences for the evaluee, but also maintains respect for the evaluee during the process, avoiding pejorative language and graphic descriptions of criminal behavior. The evaluator strives to be a neutral party who objectively uses his or her expertise to help the court answer questions.

In most cases, mental health professionals are encouraged not to wear two hats, acting as treating clinician and forensic evaluator for the same patient.[11] There are some circumstances in which this may be unavoidable—for example, a trial in a rural location with limited access to forensic evaluators. However, the ethical conflict posed by attempting to serve as both the treating clinician and the forensic evaluator is substantial, and testifying in court about a patient can also damage the therapeutic relationship. Therefore, mental health professionals should strive to separate treatment and forensic evaluation to the greatest extent possible.

Evaluation of Competence to Stand Trial

After seeking consultation from a colleague who is a forensic psychiatrist, Dr. A. explains to Mr. X.'s parents that he cannot perform the evaluation of their son's competence to stand trial, since it was ordered by the judge and must be completed according to state statute. Instead, Mr. X. is evaluated by a court-appointed psychologist, Dr. B.

The question of competence to stand trial is most often raised by the defendant's attorney, typically when he or she is having difficulty working with a client who appears to be mentally ill. The judge and the prosecutor, however, may also raise the issue. Courts tend to have a low threshold for acceding to requests for competency evaluations because the examinations are relatively easy to arrange, and justice is not served by trying a defendant who does not understand what is happening. If the defendant is in jail, the competence evaluation takes place there, or if the defendant is out on bail, it occurs in a community setting, such as a psychiatric outpatient department. There is no fixed formula for deciding who will conduct the evaluation. Some states use teams comprising a psychiatrist, psychologist, and social worker, while others use individual practitioners.

Wherever the evaluation is conducted, the main questions being addressed are whether the defendant understands the proceedings and whether the defendant is able to assist his or her attorney. These "understand and assist" criteria were outlined in the 1960 U.S. Supreme Court decision *Dusky v. United States*[12] and are used, with only minor variation, in all U.S. states. Collateral sources are used as in any other psychiatric evaluation, and Dr. A. may be contacted for details of Mr. X.'s history, diagnosis, and treatment. Since the information is not being requested for the purposes of treatment, Mr. X.'s permission will always be required before Dr. A. can release clinical information to the evaluator. The consent to this release is usually obtained by the forensic evaluator at the time of the evaluation and forwarded to the treating clinician along with the request for information.

The report of a defendant's competence to stand trial focuses on functional abilities, including the defendant's memory, concentration, and reasoning ability. It usually does not contain details about what the defendant says happened during the alleged criminal offense. The purpose of the evaluation is to establish whether the defendant can participate in the proceedings, not whether he or she is guilty or innocent.

Psychiatric symptoms can affect competence to stand trial in many ways. Most commonly, symptoms distort a person's understanding of the court proceedings. For example, a defendant with schizophrenia may have a delusional belief that the judge is a member of the Illuminati, and all trial proceedings are therefore a form of religious persecution rather than an effort to resolve a criminal charge. In a smaller number of cases, persons are found to be incompetent to stand trial because they are unable to assist in their own defense, despite an adequate understanding of the criminal proceedings. For example, a defendant with bipolar disorder may be so manic that he or she cannot sit still or stop talking when instructed to do so by the court. Defendants often "fail" both aspects of the competence test. Intellectual deficits, psychotic symptoms, or a severe affective disorder, for example, may interfere with a defendant's abilities both to understand the proceedings and to assist in his or her defense.

It is important to note that the forensic evaluator's opinion about the defendant's competence is just that—an opinion. Competence to stand trial is a legal determination, and the judge is the ultimate fact finder in the court. The judge listens to all the evidence presented and decides whether the defendant is competent. In the majority of cases, the judge agrees with the court-appointed mental health expert, but this not always so. Some cases are contentious, particularly when serious criminal charges are involved and the experts on the two opposing sides differ widely in their opinions. The judge serves as final arbiter, deciding which expert testimony is most credible.

After finding a defendant incompetent to stand trial, the judge must next decide whether there is a substantial probability that the defendant's competence can be restored with treatment. The judge looks to a forensic mental health evaluation for guidance on this matter. For example, if the defendant has lifelong, severe intellectual disabilities, there is little chance of successful restoration of competence. However, if the defendant has a psychotic illness that is likely to respond to medication, restoration of competence will be attempted. Depending on the severity of the illness, the likelihood that the defendant will cooperate with treatment, and the specific treatment needs, the judge can order that such treatment be provided in an inpatient forensic hospital or an outpatient setting.

Some states also have the option of in-jail competence restoration because of a lack of available hospital beds.[13]

In a small number of cases, competence cannot be restored, even with the best available treatments. In *Jackson v. Indiana*, the Supreme Court ruled that defendants cannot be held in the hospital indefinitely for the purpose of competence restoration, even when charged with very serious crimes.[14] If competence has not been restored after a "reasonable" period of time, they must either be released from the hospital or civilly committed. A defendant who does not meet the civil commitment criteria in the local jurisdiction (see chapter 2) must be released.

Evaluation of Criminal Responsibility

Once a defendant is found competent to stand trial, the criminal case proceeds. In the case of Mr. X., the trial process continues to unfold:

The forensic evaluator, Dr. B., concludes that Mr. X. is competent to stand trial, since he received consistent medication while in jail, and his delusions and paranoia have subsided. The court agrees with Dr. B.'s findings, and Mr. X.'s criminal case proceeds. Mr. X.'s attorney retains a forensic psychiatrist to perform an evaluation of Mr. X.'s sanity at the time of the crime because the attorney suspects that Mr. X. assaulted his roommate while under the influence of psychotic symptoms.

Before a defendant is convicted and punished, most courts want to know whether the defendant was to blame for what happened. So-called general defenses are one of the ways in which systems of criminal justice achieve this. Persons who cause harm by accident, unless their carelessness itself makes them blameworthy, are not usually convicted or punished. In addition to the intentionality of the criminal conduct, the presence or absence of psychiatric symptoms can be relevant in determining the extent of blame. For instance, a psychiatric condition such as schizophrenia or an intellectual disability may make it difficult for someone to control his or her behavior. In these situations, the court may wish to mitigate or reduce the punishment. In rare cases, a person may have been so ill that no punishment seems fair.

In these rare instances, most U.S. states have statutes that allow the defendant to be acquitted of the crime and provided with psychiatric treatment in lieu of punishment. Usually, these statutes require that the defendant suffer from a "mental disease or defect" that affected his or her behavior at the time of the crime. The statutes are typically referred to as NGRI statutes because they allow for acquittal on the grounds that a defendant is "not guilty by reason of insanity." However, the older label, "insanity defense," is still widely used.

An insanity plea must be raised by the defense, and a competent defendant may make his or her own choice of plea, even against the advice of an attorney. Thus, a mentally ill defendant who was found to be competent to stand trial but has since deteriorated clinically may choose, as a result of illness, not to plead insanity as a defense. Courts faced with this situation will sometimes order a mental health evaluation in order to establish whether the defendant is competent to make the decision regarding how to plead.

The criteria for the insanity defense vary depending on the state in which the defendant is being tried. A typical statute would excuse a defendant who failed to "appreciate the difference between right and wrong" or who "was unable to conform his behavior to the requirements of the law." In some states, only the first of these criteria is used. In others, an older formulation applies, which is derived from the trial of Daniel M'Naghten in England in the 1800s. M'Naghten was accused of trying to assassinate Prime Minister Robert Peel (although he mistakenly killed the prime minister's assistant). His NGRI acquittal caused much public controversy, and as a result, the House of Lords asked the justices to explain the basis for the insanity defense. The judges reviewing the case noted that M'Naghten should have been acquitted if he did not "know the nature and quality of the act he was doing; or if he did know it, he did not know he was doing what was wrong."[15] One U.S. state (New Hampshire) permits acquittal if the criminal act was the "product" of a mental disease or defect. Problems in defining behavior that is a product of mental illness have limited this standard's usefulness, and it has fallen out of widespread use.

To summarize, the standards for NGRI defenses used in the United States are as follows:

- the M'Naghten test: an inability to know right from wrong,
- the Model Penal Code (a.k.a. American Law Institute) standard:[16] a lack of substantial capacity to appreciate the wrongfulness of conduct or to conform conduct to the requirements of the law, and
- the Durham rule:[17] behavior that is a product of mental disease or defect.

Most states have adopted one of these tests of criminal responsibility. However, the Supreme Court clarified in *Clark v. Arizona* that the U.S. Constitution does not guarantee the right to an insanity defense or to any particular legal standard of insanity.[18] In fact, a handful of states—Idaho, Utah, Kansas, and Montana—have abolished the insanity defense altogether.[19]

In conducting an evaluation of criminal responsibility for the court, the forensic evaluator interviews the defendant to gather data but also typically obtains a large amount of collateral information. Part of the reason is that courts are usually difficult to persuade when the only evidence of abnormality in a defendant's mental state comes from the defendant. The forensic evaluator must therefore look beyond the defendant's account of his or her psychiatric history and the arrest incident, seeking to reconcile data gathered from multiple sources: the defendant, police records, medical records, accounts from family and friends, witness and victim statements, and psychological testing results.

As with an evaluation of competence to stand trial, the treating clinician often receives a request from the forensic evaluator for treatment records or verbal communication. The defendant's permission to release the records is required. The defendant's family may also be contacted, and here the ethical issues are more complicated. Because the information that the family members are being asked to disclose is not part of any medical record, statutes written to protect the privacy of such records do not apply. Mental health clinicians conducting forensic evaluations approach these questions in different ways. Many will contact family members only after obtaining the defendant's permission, as their concern in such instances is to show proper respect for the defendant. Others will contact family members even without the defendant's permission if they think that the collateral information is essential and that the assessment would be incomplete without the perspectives of family members.

Many evaluations of criminal responsibility lead to a plea that is accepted by the prosecution and the court. Occasionally, the court holds a trial in which the defense presents evidence that the defendant meets criteria for an NGRI defense, and that evidence is challenged by the prosecution. Rules for the standard of proof (e.g., beyond reasonable doubt) and also for the burden of proof (whether it lies with the prosecution or the defense) vary from one jurisdiction to another. In Massachusetts, once the insanity defense has been raised by the defense, the burden is on the prosecution to prove sanity beyond a reasonable doubt. In Connecticut, the burden is on the defense. In contrast to popular belief, only a small fraction of criminal defendants present an insanity defense, and a minority of those defenses are successful.

Also in contrast to popular belief, defendants who are found not guilty by reason of insanity do not "walk away free" from the courthouse. They are not admitted to a community hospital, with a typical length of stay of only a few days, but instead are usually committed to a forensic psychiatric hospital for evaluation and treatment. Many persons who have been acquitted on grounds of insanity spend months or years in the hospital after the court proceedings have ended because they are deemed too dangerous for release to the community. In some states, such as Connecticut, treatment progress and community placement are overseen by the Psychiatric Security Review Board (PSRB), which must approve each step of the acquittee's journey from hospital to freedom. Persons under the purview of the PSRB typically spend longer in the hospital after an insanity acquittal than they would have spent in jail had they pled guilty to the crime. Even when released to the community, they live under many restrictions, affecting their ability to travel, work, date, use computers, enter bars, and attend school. Thus, defendants who are facing a relatively short sentence if convicted will frequently forgo an insanity defense, even if they are good candidates for it, since they are likely to face more restrictive conditions if they have been found not guilty by reason of insanity than if they had pled guilty.

Presentencing Evaluations for Mitigation

A defendant who is not acquitted on the grounds of insanity may still be able to have his or her condition taken into account at sentencing, since the court can alter the sentence in response to its perception of the defendant's abnormality. Mr. X.'s case proceeds along these lines:

The forensic psychiatrist concludes that Mr. X. was suffering from delusions and paranoia at the time of the crime but that he appreciated the wrongfulness of his conduct and did not meet the state's criteria for an insanity defense. Despite the lack of a viable insanity defense, Mr. X.'s attorney asks the forensic psychiatrist to write a report about her findings. The attorney hopes that the report can be used to negotiate with the prosecutor and mitigate the sentence imposed on Mr. X.

The courts are interested in culpability, and culpability is not all-or-nothing. First, mentally ill persons who know what they are doing when they commit a crime and know that it is wrong may nevertheless be less culpable because of their mental state. Second, the court takes into consideration whether treatment may make it less likely that the defendant will commit another crime. Both these factors are highly relevant in determining an appropriate punishment, and forensic evaluators are often asked to opine about these issues before sentencing.

In addressing these factors, the forensic evaluator will usually be expected to address the question of what risk, if any, the defendant poses to other people. Formal rating scales and risk assessment instruments, such as the Violence Risk Appraisal Guide (VRAG)[20] and the Historical Clinical Risk–20 (HCR-20),[21] are available to help the psychiatrist address this question. However, the courts are usually looking not for a number or score on a scale but rather for an assessment of whether any risk that the defendant poses can be managed in the community. The courts are seeking reassurance that the public will not be placed at risk if the defendant is given a reduced punishment or prescribed a combination of treatment and punishment. Often, a defendant's response to treatment in the past will be helpful in assessing the likelihood that subsequent treatment will be successful.

Community Supervision and Mandated Mental Health Treatment

The last step in a person's progression through the criminal justice system is often an order for community supervision during probation or parole. A supervision order can come after a period of incarceration, or it can be imposed in lieu of incarceration. Here is what happens in Mr. X.'s case:

After reading the forensic psychiatrist's report on Mr. X., the prosecutor offers a plea bargain: 6 months in jail (which Mr. X. has already served) and 2 years of probation. One of the conditions of probation is that Mr. X. must comply with mental health treatment. On the advice of his attorney, Mr. X. accepts the offer. He is released from jail, and he begins outpatient treatment.

When a court orders psychiatric treatment as a condition of probation or parole, the defendant may be required to participate in a particular court-affiliated program or may be allowed to receive treatment from his or her former treatment provider. Clinicians considering whether to accept a patient back into treatment under these circumstances are often concerned that they have no experience working with the criminal justice system. However, the courts are not usually asking mental health clinicians to provide treatment that they would not otherwise provide. They are seeking to use a resource that is available and that they believe may be helpful.

Although clinical treatment is largely unchanged when a person under criminal justice supervision returns to his or her provider for treatment, some aspects are slightly different. The first difference is that the court will expect to be informed, either directly or more often through the probation officer, about the progress of treatment. To allow this to happen, defendants sign a document agreeing to the release of details of their treatment to the court. Without such an agreement to disclose treatment information, the court will usually not grant probation, ordering the defendant to receive a custodial sentence (i.e., jail time) instead. Defendants usually know this when they agree to participate in treatment, and they may feel slightly coerced. They may also be reluctant to disclose details about their history or current symptoms, out of fear that such disclosure will have adverse legal consequences. An open, frank discussion about the limits of confidentiality between clinician and patient at the outset of treatment can be very helpful in quelling fears and building a therapeutic alliance.

Second, the court's mandate for the patient to participate in treatment, usually for a specified duration, may affect the treatment's progress over time. A patient who fears being incarcerated will usually be more likely to keep appointments, but this is not the same as active participation in a treatment program. A court mandate is not necessarily damaging to the therapeutic relationship, however. Regardless of whether they are subject to a criminal sentence, patients attend treatment sessions for many reasons, not just one. A patient may have an interest in staying out of prison and may also have a genuine interest in becoming well.

TIPS FOR MENTAL HEALTH PROFESSIONALS

Mr. X.'s case illustrates just one of many situations that mental health clinicians can encounter when their patients are involved in the criminal justice system. There is no one-size-fits-all approach to handing these situations, but a few guiding principles can be helpful to keep in mind.

> *Seek consultation when possible.* Clinicians working in hospitals can always consult with risk managers, forensic psychiatrists, and/or hospital attorneys, even on an emergency basis. In private practice, finding an appropriate consultant may be more difficult, but consultation should still be pursued. Cases in which a patient is charged with a crime can have multiple layers of complexity, involving both criminal and civil law, so they should not be tackled alone.
>
> *Remember that a clinician's responsibility is to the patient, not to the criminal justice system.* Treating clinicians often want to be helpful or to act as "good citizens" by placing the needs of the police or courts (i.e., solving crimes and enforcing the law) above the needs of their patients. However, the clinician's primary responsibility is to the patient, which means assessing risk and taking appropriate clinical steps, not acting as an agent of law enforcement. In some cases, a disclosure may be warranted in order to protect the patient or others from imminent risk, but notification of the police should never be undertaken lightly.
>
> *Keep good records and document clinical reasoning.* It is important to document interactions with the patient, family, and court personnel carefully. When clinical decisions are made, the reasoning behind those decisions should be explained as fully as possible. This documentation may be very important in the future, either for the patient in his or her criminal case or for the clinician in the unlikely event of a civil lawsuit.
>
> *Maintain separation between the roles of treating clinician and forensic evaluator.* Treating clinicians have valuable information about the patient that the criminal justice system may wish to know. However, for the reasons outlined in this and other chapters, clinicians should separate themselves from the role of forensic

evaluator, instead allowing (where possible) for an independent, nontreating mental health professional to perform assessments of competence to stand trial, criminal responsibility, and presentencing mitigation. In most cases, the treating clinician's involvement in the criminal case will be as a provider of collateral information about the patient's past treatment, which may include appearing in court as a fact witness (as opposed to a forensic expert).

Understand the limits of confidentiality when providing treatment to a person under criminal justice supervision in the community. As described above, a person who agrees to undergo mental health treatment as a condition of probation or parole is generally required to grant permission for the treating clinician to report on the progress of treatment. The limits of confidentiality should always be made clear to the patient. The nonconfidential nature of treatment may affect its progress, but therapeutic work can still take place.

CONCLUSION

Persons involved in the criminal justice system must navigate a complex and often unfamiliar set of rules and procedures in order to resolve the charges successfully. For persons with mental illness, the task is even more challenging. As a first step, many persons with mental illness are offered an opportunity to participate in treatment in the community as an alternative to incarceration, but not all of them are willing to engage in or are eligible for these programs. If they are not diverted from the criminal courts, they often undergo one or more evaluations by a forensic mental health professional—evaluations of competence to stand trial, criminal responsibility, and presentencing—before the criminal case is adjudicated. Adjudication may result in incarceration, mandated mental health treatment in the community, or both. Mental health professionals have important roles at many junctures in the criminal justice process, helping to provide guidance for both the courts and the persons with mental illness who pass through them.

FREQUENTLY ASKED QUESTIONS

What should I do if my patient tells me he committed a serious crime?

Most states provide exceptions to medical confidentiality so that clinicians can address the risk of harm to others. Typically, these exceptions allow patient information to be shared with third parties, including with the police, when there is an "imminent" or "serious" risk. Sometimes the relevant statutes require that the person or group at risk be identifiable. Other exceptions to confidentiality derive from statutes that mandate the reporting of child or elder abuse, irrespective of any ongoing risk. The clinician whose patient reports that he has committed a crime should establish whether disclosure of this information is permissible or required. If disclosure is not required, the usual course is to address the reported information clinically and to ensure, where relevant, that the patient has access to legal advice.

If my patient commits a crime, will I have to testify in court?

Possibly. A treating clinician is unlikely to be asked by the court to perform a forensic evaluation or give testimony as an expert witness. However, the clinician may be called to testify as a fact witness, providing the court with information about the defendant's treatment history, diagnosis, and symptoms around the time of the alleged criminal offense. The clinician may disclose this information with the patient's permission or when ordered by a court to do so. The psychiatrist should consult with an attorney or a forensic psychiatrist before testifying or releasing confidential records.

If a person refuses to participate in a specialized mental health court or a jail diversion program, can he or she be forced to do so?

No. Participation in programs and specialized courts is voluntary. If a defendant does not want to participate or is unable to give consent, the case proceeds in the regular criminal court.

If a defendant has active psychotic symptoms, can he or she be found competent to stand trial?

Yes. In order to be found competent to stand trial, a defendant must be able to understand the court proceedings and assist his attorney in his defense. In some cases, psychotic symptoms will have a direct impact on the defendant's understanding of court proceedings (e.g., the defendant may think that the judge is part of a conspiracy against him or her). In other cases, the psychotic symptoms remain separate from the defendant's understanding of the proceedings (e.g., the defendant may have religious delusions that are unrelated to the criminal charges). In the latter situation, the defendant may have active psychotic symptoms but still be found competent to stand trial.

Does every defendant who has been diagnosed with a serious mental illness meet the criteria for an insanity defense?

No. An insanity defense (more formally known as not guilty by reason of insanity, or NGRI, defense) is a legal determination that courts must make on the basis of specific criteria. These criteria vary by jurisdiction. In some states, the defendant must show that mental illness was so severe that it impaired his or her capacity to know right from wrong. Other states use different criteria, such as whether the criminal behavior was a "product" of mental illness or whether the influence of mental illness was so strong that the defendant could not conform his or her behavior to the requirements of the law. Each case is evaluated individually, and defendants with psychiatric diagnoses may or may not meet the legal criteria for insanity.

REFERENCES

1. Bureau of Justice Statistics. *Correctional populations in the United States, 2013.* http://www.bjs.gov/content/pub/pdf/cpus13.pdf. Accessed October 27, 2015.
2. *Tarasoff v. Regents of University of California,* 17 Cal. 3d 426(1976).
3. Bureau of Justice Statistics. *Mortality rates in local jails and state prisons, 2000–2012.* http://www.bjs.gov/content/pub/pdf/mljsp0012st.pdf. Accessed October 4, 2015.
4. Shaw J, Baker D, Hunt IM, Moloney A, Appleby L. Suicide by prisoners: national clinical survey. *British Journal of Psychiatry.* 2004;184:263–267.
5. CMHS National GAINS Center. *Practical Advice on Jail Diversion: Ten Years of Learning on Jail Diversion from the CMHS National GAINS Center.* Delmar: Author; 2007.
6. TAPA Center for Jail Diversion. *What Can We Say about the Effectiveness of Jail Diversion Programs for Persons with Co-Occurring Disorders?* Delmar: Author; 2004.
7. Massachusetts Department of Mental Health Forensic Services. *Pre-Arrest Law Enforcement-Based Jail Diversion Program Report July 1, 2011 to January 1, 2014.* http://www.mass.gov/eohhs/docs/dmh/forensic/jail-diversion-program-2014.pdf. Accessed August 25, 2015.
8. Compton MT, Bahora M, Watson AC, Oliva JR. A comprehensive review of extant research on Crisis Intervention Team (CIT) programs. *Journal of the American Academy of Psychiatry and the Law.* 2008;36:47–55.
9. Munetz MR, Griffin PA. Use of the Sequential Intercept Model as an approach to decriminalization of people with serious mental illness. *Psychiatric Services.* 2006;57:544–549.
10. Appelbaum PS. A theory of ethics for forensic psychiatry. *Journal of the American Academy of Psychiatry and the Law.* 1997;25:233–247.
11. Strasburger LH, Gutheil TG, Brodsky A. On wearing two hats: role conflict in serving as both psychotherapist and expert witness. *American Journal of Psychiatry.* 1997;154:448–456.
12. *Dusky v. United States,* 362 U.S. 402(1960).
13. Kapoor R. Commentary: Jail-based competency restoration. *Journal of the American Academy of Psychiatry and the Law.* 2011;39:311–315.
14. *Jackson v. Indiana,* 406 U.S. 715(1972).
15. *M'Naghten's case,* All ER Rep 229(1843).

16. American Law Institute. *Model penal code* (proposed official draft). Philadelphia, PA: Executive Office, American Law Institute, 1962.

17. *Durham v. United States,* 214 F.2d 862(1954).

18. *Clark v. Arizona,* 548 U.S. 735(2006).

19. *Insanity defense among the states.* Findlaw. http://criminal.findlaw.com/criminal-procedure/the-insanity-defense-among-the-states.html. Accessed August 10, 2015.

20. Quinsey VL, Grant TH, Rice ME, Cormier CA. *Violent Offenders: Appraising and Managing Risk.* Washington DC: American Psychological Association; 1998.

21. Webster CD, Douglas KS, Eaves D, Hart SD. *HCR-20: Assessing Risk for Violence.* Vancouver: Simon Fraser University; 1997.

13

DISABILITY EVALUATIONS

MARILYN PRICE

Psychiatric impairment has become an increasingly common basis for disability payments in the United States. When a patient files a disability claim based on psychiatric impairment, the role of his or her treating clinician is to provide information about the impairment and how it affects work capacity. This clinical information will be considered in the determination of disability, but the determination will be dependent on the definitions, rules, and criteria used by the various disability agencies[1] and will be made by the agency or insurer, not the treating clinician. Unfortunately, few mental health professionals have received sufficient training in participating in the disability application process.[2] This lack of training is especially problematic considering the prediction that demand for mental health disability evaluations will continue to grow in the coming years.[1]

This chapter introduces mental health professionals and trainees to the concepts of functional impairment and disability and the usual contexts in which they might arise in mental health practice. The chapter describes the most common types of disability evaluations: Social Security, workers' compensation, private insurance (e.g., long-term disability coverage), the Americans with Disabilities Act, fitness for duty and return to work, and disability in the context of litigation (e.g., assessments for psychic harm in a personal injury case).

Ethical implications may arise when a clinician is asked to perform dual roles (i.e., the role of the treating clinician and the role of a forensic evaluator providing an independent opinion regarding work-related functioning). Trying to separate these roles is especially problematic in the context of disability.[3] Clinicians often feel pressured by their patients to support their applications for disability. Special consideration must be given to questions of confidentiality and how much information can or should be shared with others.[1]

TYPES OF DISABILITY EVALUATIONS

As the American Academy of Psychiatry and the Law (AAPL) notes in its *Practice Guideline for the Forensic Evaluation of Psychiatric Disability*, "[t]he disability evaluation is the most common psychiatric evaluation requested for nontherapeutic reasons."[4] Estimates of the prevalence of disability in the United States vary, but most estimates are around 10%. In 2013, 12.6% of the U.S. population reported being disabled,[5] and in 2014, 8.4% of the population between the ages of 18 and 64 years had a work limitation due to disability.[6] Psychiatric impairments are usually among the top 10 causes of disability in adults,[4] and the World Health Organization has predicted that "depression . . . will be the second leading cause of disability [worldwide] after heart disease by 2020."[4]

Social Security Evaluations

Vignette 1: Disability Benefits

Ms. T. is a 34-year-old day care worker with a diagnosed bipolar disorder who has had eight psychiatric hospitalizations within the past 2 years for either depression or mania. While manic, Ms. T. is typically very irritable with the children and her coworkers; she fails to document when she has fed or diapered each infant and sometimes omits a scheduled feeding. When depressed, she is often late for work, and her personal hygiene deteriorates. She has difficulty organizing and performing scheduled tasks in a timely manner and becomes overwhelmed by her responsibilities in caring for the children. As a result, she is unable to attend to their physical needs. When she is stable, Ms. T. is able to function at work, but her rapid cycling has resulted in an inability to hold a job for any length of time. Ms. T. worked full-time for 12 years before developing symptoms of bipolar disorder. She does not have any private disability coverage and wants to apply for Social Security disability benefits.

Social Security Disability Insurance (SSDI) and Supplemental Security Income (SSI) are the two most common sources of disability coverage for which disability evaluations are performed.[1] Both programs are administered by the Social Security Administration (SSA), which is "the largest supplier of disability benefits in the country."[7] Social Security Disability Insurance, in particular, is the source of most disability compensation.[8] Almost a third of all approved SSA disability claims are awarded on the basis of mental illness,[8] and "psychiatric disturbances have become the largest single reason for disability awards by the SSA, accounting for 22% of all claims."[7] As noted in the AAPL practice guideline, a "mental disorder that prevents substantial gainful employment is the leading reason why individuals receive SSDI," and such disorders "form the largest single diagnostic category among SSDI recipients."[4]

Under Title II of the Social Security Act, SSDI pays benefits to persons who have worked for a statutorily determined minimum period and have contributed to the Social Security trust fund through the Social Security tax on earnings, as well as paying benefits to certain disabled dependents of these persons.[9] Title XVI provides for SSI benefits to be paid to persons, including those under the age of 18 years, on the basis of financial need.[9] For example, a person with chronic psychosis who was unable to complete high school because of recurrent hospitalizations and who has never been able to work might apply for SSI, while someone who developed a disabling psychiatric illness after years of paid work would be eligible to apply for SSDI. After receiving SSDI payments for 24 months, the disabled person becomes eligible for Medicare. In most states, persons who have qualified for SSI would also qualify for Medicaid.[9]

In order to qualify for Social Security disability, the applicant must meet a relatively demanding standard: "the inability to engage in any substantial gainful activity (SGA) by reason of any medically determinable physical or mental impairment(s) which can be expected to result in death or which has lasted or can be expected to last for a continuous period of not less than 12 months."[10] Supplemental Security Income and SSDI do not provide benefits for partial disability.

The documentation that needs to be provided for the SSDI disability application is identical to the documentation required for the SSI disability application.[10] The SSA considers nine diagnostic listings for mental disorders:

> organic mental disorder;
> schizophrenic, paranoid, and other psychotic disorders;
> affective disorders;
> intellectual disability;
> anxiety-related disorders;
> somatoform disorders;
> personality disorders;
> substance addiction disorders; and
> autism disorder and other pervasive developmental disorders.

For each listing, other than intellectual disability and substance addiction disorder, the SSA describes the disorder and enumerates the criteria for the set of medical findings (paragraph A criteria) and the set of impairment-related functional limitations (paragraph

B criteria). Paragraph C criteria, which are used when paragraph B criteria are not met, reflect additional considerations given to a documented history of past acute symptoms or repeated episodes of decompensation. The category of substance addiction disorders is really just a reference listing of other listed mental or physical impairments that must be used to evaluate the behavioral or physical manifestations resulting from regular use of addictive substances.[10]

The SSA determines the severity by assessing functional limitations using four criteria described in paragraph B of the listing. These include activities of daily living (ADLs); social functioning; concentration, persistence, or pace; and episodes of decompensation. The SSA website provides guidance concerning information that is useful in determining each of the functional limitations. For ADLs, consideration would be given to deficits in the areas of cleaning, shopping, cooking, taking public transportation, paying bills, maintaining a residence, caring appropriately with respect to grooming and hygiene, using telephones and directories, and using the post office.

Some patients, such as Ms. T., have psychiatric disorders characterized by multiple episodes of decompensation and relatively short periods of stability. The SSA determinations take into account the frequency of decompensation in considering whether an applicant meets the criteria for severity of functional limitations. Episodes of decompensation are exacerbations or temporary increases of symptoms and signs associated with a loss of adaptive functioning, as indicated by difficulties in performing ADLs, maintaining social relationships, or maintaining concentration, persistence, or pace (i.e., the four functional-limitation criteria). To qualify as an episode of decompensation, the symptoms or signs would generally have resulted in increased treatment or placement in a less stressful situation or some combination of both.[10]

Decompensation can be inferred from the need for a significant change in medication or for more structured support, such as that provided on an inpatient unit, in a halfway house, or in a highly structured and directing household. Supplemental Security Income defines the term "repeated episodes of decompensation" as at least three episodes of decompensation within a year, or an average of one every 4 months, each lasting at least 2 weeks. Fortunately, the SSA does not rigidly adhere to this requirement and may consider whether more frequent episodes of shorter duration can be used to demonstrate equal severity.[10]

For applicants who are 55 years of age or older, the only requirement is that the disability makes the applicant unable to perform work similar to the work he or she did in the past,[7] but for younger applicants, the inquiry focuses on whether the applicant can work at all. A 35-year-old who is unable to return to a former job manufacturing fine instruments because of a loss of visual acuity might nonetheless be able to work in a different occupation and therefore might not qualify for SSDI. In contrast, a 55-year-old in the same job and with the same loss of visual acuity might be considered disabled. The SSA typically relies heavily on information provided by the treating clinician in making disability determinations.[8] In fact, treaters are considered by the SSA to be the "preferred source" for performing the examination or test of their own patient.[10]

A mental health professional whose patient applies for SSDI or SSI benefits is not asked to determine whether the patient is disabled or qualified to receive benefits; that determination is made by the SSA. But the mental health professional will be asked to complete a questionnaire regarding the diagnosis and functional impairment.[8] Because SSDI and SSI applications require the involvement of the treater, it is important for most mental health professionals to have some familiarity with the application process so that they know where to turn for more information and resources before encountering a patient like Ms. T. This section describes the process briefly.

The SSA's disability assessment process is guided by a manual called the Blue Book, which is available online.[10] According to the Blue Book, application for SSDI or SSI benefits follows a five-step "sequential evaluation process," characterized by review of the following factors: "(1) the claimant's current work activity, (2) the severity of his or her impairment(s), (3) a determination of whether his or her impairment(s) meets or medically equals a listing ... (4) the claimant's residual functional capacity, his or her past work, (5) and his or her ability to do other work based on age, education, and work experience."[10] The SSA requires the use of several standardized forms to support the disability application, and these forms can help guide the disability evaluation process for the clinician. A psychiatric diagnosis by itself is insufficient. There must be evidence that the psychiatric impairment affects work capacity.

Occasionally, the SSA also requests evaluations of residual functional capacity (RFC). These evaluations are performed when there is insufficient medical evidence to justify an award of benefits and when the SSA needs more information about what the applicant is (or is not) still able to do in a work environment.[4] If a patient needs to be evaluated for RFC, the treating clinician might find the AAPL practice guideline's section on RFCs (as well as the references in that section) helpful.[4] The SSA may also request a consultative examination (CE), which is a paid, independent assessment specific to the Social Security disability review process. Consultative examinations require a level of expertise and an impartiality or objectivity that some treating clinicians are unable to provide.[4] Mental health professionals who are asked to perform CEs for the SSA should be familiar with the Blue Book guidelines regarding the content of a CE report,[10] as well as the AAPL practice guideline.[4]

The SSDI application process can be time-consuming and invasive for the applicant. Typically, SSA requires the submission of voluminous medical records, and Levin notes the critical importance of forewarning patients about the likely loss of confidentiality and the potential for intrusive inquiries about the applicant's mental health treatment.[1] Before initiating an application for SSDI or SSI benefits, the patient should be encouraged to deliberate about these and other potential negative consequences of the application, including the possibility that it will be rejected. Rejections can be appealed, but the appeals process is no less arduous or stressful than the initial application. If the patient decides to proceed with the application, it is important for the clinician to respond promptly to documentation and paperwork requests from the SSA.[1]

Let us return briefly to Vignette 1 to see how Ms. T.'s application for disability benefits might be analyzed.

Vignette 1, continued

Ms. T. would apply for SSDI rather than SSI because her work history exceeds the statutory minimum. She has a qualifying diagnosis (bipolar disorder) and has had work-related impairments. She has been fired because her impairing psychiatric symptoms have affected her job performance. While Ms. T. does have very short periods of stability, her repeated hospitalizations and medication changes would be consistent with a finding of repeated episodes of decompensation. Her illness has already lasted for about 2 years without substantial improvement.

Requests for assistance with SSDI and SSI disability applications are relatively common in the practice of clinical psychiatry. Readers are encouraged to consult additional resources[8,9,10] for more detailed information about the SSA and the disability application process as it pertains to mental health professionals whose patients are applying for (or receiving) benefits.

Workers' Compensation Evaluations

Vignette 2: Trauma at Work

Mr. S. was working as a waiter when a gunman opened fire in the restaurant where he worked. The intended target, a guest celebrating his birthday with his family, was killed. Several stray bullets hit Mr. S. in the chest and abdomen. He suffered life-threatening internal injuries and underwent emergency surgery. He had a complicated postoperative course resulting in a 4-month hospitalization. Although Mr. S. recovered from the physical injuries, he has developed severe symptoms of post-traumatic stress disorder (PTSD). He avoids leaving his home because he fears being shot. He has flashbacks precipitated by loud noises or by being in a restaurant or other public places. He is in treatment but thus far has made little progress.

Workers' compensation is a system designed to protect workers from the financial consequences of injuries suffered or disabilities acquired through the performance of work. In order for the claimant (patient) to succeed, he or she need not demonstrate that the employer was negligent, only that an unanticipated or accidental event caused an injury (or disability) that arose from and occurred in the course of work performed for the employer.[4] Claims for full or partial disability are considered.

Workers' compensation laws vary from state to state, but all 50 states and the District of Columbia have some form of workers' compensation program in place. As noted in the AAPL practice guideline, workers' compensation claims for mental injury fall into one of three categories of injury: physical-mental injury, in which a physical injury precedes the mental injury (as in the case of Mr. S.); mental-physical, in which a mental injury leads to physical harm, such as unusual stress at work leading to a heart attack); and mental-mental (e.g., machinist is physically unharmed but develops severe anxiety after witnessing a coworker dying in an accident on the assembly line).[4] States vary regarding which of these categories of mental injury will be compensated. Similar programs cover federal employees.[4] The confidentiality of psychiatric evaluations in workers' compensation cases differs from one jurisdiction to another and is regulated by state laws.[4] Recent years have seen an increase in workers' compensation claims based on mental impairment.[7]

In order for Mr. S. to prevail in a workers' compensation claim, he merely has to show that the injury or disability resulted from an event or exposure that occurred while he was performing his employment duties. A labor or industrial board holds an administrative meeting to make the ultimate determination of whether the injury or disability was work-related. In claims for psychiatric disability, the question of causation can be complicated; "[w]hen a mental disorder is claimed . . . the causal relationship between the psychiatric disorder and the workplace may be more aggressively questioned" by a workers' compensation tribunal.[4]

In workers' compensation cases, the treating clinician is typically asked to complete a standardized form called the Attending Physician's Statement of Disability.[1] The form requests brief information about the history of the current disability, diagnostic information, treatment dates, a description of the nature of the treatment provided, information about the patient's progress and functional limitations, a ranking of the severity of physical impairment (similar to the Axis V Global Assessment of Functioning scale used for diagnostic formulations in the *Diagnostic and Statistical Manual of Mental Disorders*, fourth edition), a definition of stress as applied to the claimant (for mental or nervous impairment), and the prognosis. A rating based on the American Medical Association (AMA) *Guides to the Evaluation of Permanent Impairment*[11] may be required, depending on the jurisdiction in which the case arises.[12] The *AMA Guides* for assessing and rating disability represent the most common system in use for workers' compensation cases.[4,12] The treating clinician may be asked to specify whether the disability is temporary and partial, temporary and total, permanent and partial, or permanent and total.[4,7,12,13] Clinicians whose patients are involved in workers' compensation cases are strongly encouraged to consult additional resources specific to workers' compensation.[12]

Vignette 2, continued

Mr. S. initially received workers' compensation for his physical injuries. His claim for workers' compensation for PTSD was approved. Mr. S. had never suffered from a psychiatric condition before his injury, so his psychiatric symptoms were determined to be due to his injury at work. He was considered to have a temporary and total disability.

Private Disability Insurance Evaluations

Vignette 3: Long-Term Disability Benefits

Mr. J. is a help desk supervisor at an engineering firm whose symptoms of depression recently began causing impairment in functioning both at work and at home. After receiving phone calls from several engineers expressing concern about Mr. J. (who appeared to be distracted and confused and grew tearful during a recent service call), and after he had missed work for two consecutive days, the manager of information technology services suggested that Mr. J. take some time off from work and talk to Human Resources about using his short-term disability (STD) benefits. Mr. J. has now exhausted those benefits and would like your help as his treater in applying for benefits under his long-term disability (LTD) policy. Although his depression has begun to improve with treatment, he does not feel that he is "back to normal," and he is concerned that if he returns to his job prematurely, he will continue to make mistakes and may end up being fired.

Many employers provide their workers with options for STD and LTD insurance coverage. In addition, STD and LTD policies can be purchased independently from a private insurance company; these policies are sometimes called independent disability insurance (IDI).[14] A large and growing percentage of claims for private disability insurance benefits are based on psychiatric disability.[4] The benefits provided vary significantly from one policy to the next. Some policies provide coverage in the event that the insured becomes unable to perform the work that he or she was doing at the time the policy was purchased (own-occupation policies), while others define disability as the inability to perform any gainful occupation (any-occupation policies).[7] It is not uncommon for LTD policies to limit coverage for psychiatric impairments to a 2-year period (as opposed to coverage provided up to age 65 for physical or general medical impairment), despite concerns about parity and discrimination.[14] Such limitations are often called "mental/nervous" (MN) benefits limitations.[14]

Typically, STD leave involves coverage for disability periods usually starting from 1 month of claiming impairment and lasting up to half a year.[14] Because the coverage period is short, the treating clinician, rather than an independent forensic specialist, is often the medical professional who provides information to the insurer (with the patient's permission). There is an internal review of the claim by the insurer's medical consultants before it is approved.[14]

Typically, LTD policies pay the covered individual a monthly benefit when he or she is unable to work due to accident or illness, and coverage usually begins after an initial waiting period (called an elimination period), the duration of which varies from one policy to the next.[14] Policies with shorter initial waiting periods tend to have more expensive premiums than those with longer periods. The benefit period typically lasts until the age of retirement or eligibility for Social Security; however, some policies provide lifelong benefits and others have a time limit, such as 5 years.[14] Applications for LTD benefits usually require extensive documentation to support the policyholder's claim. When a patient applies for STD or LTD benefits, the treater is asked to complete an Attending Physician's Statement of Disability, which is similar to the form used in workers' compensation cases.[1]

The paperwork that must be completed or filed by the treating clinician whose patient is receiving or applying for LTD benefits will vary; however, merely releasing treatment records (with the patient's consent) is often sufficient.[14] As Anfang and Wall note, "[t]reating mental health clinicians will rarely be asked to do more beyond completing initial claim forms, providing a copy of the actual treatment records, and then providing updated physician statements and records and speaking with the claims adjustor or medical professional employed directly by the insurance company."[14]

Private insurance carriers sometimes request an independent medical evaluation (IME) from a physician other than the patient's treatment provider. For claims involving psychiatric disability, IMEs are generally performed by experienced forensic psychiatrists.[4] The physician who performs an IME must maintain objectivity and independence, qualities that are often unrealistic to expect from the patient's treating clinician. Disability carriers may request an evaluation when there are inconsistencies in the record and they want to determine whether the claimant remains disabled. Disability carriers may seek to ensure that the claimant is receiving proper treatment for his or her condition and that the focus is on a return to work. Being in treatment is often a condition for receiving benefits. An IME may also be requested when the claimant seeks to settle the claim with a one-time payout. When a settlement of a claim is being considered, an IME might be requested to ensure that the request is not motivated by suicidal ideation and also to assess whether the claimant is competent to handle a large settlement or whether a conservatorship would be necessary. Mental health professionals who are asked to perform a disability evaluation such as an IME should consult additional resources tailored to forensic specialists.[4,14]

Vignette 3, continued

Mr. J. and his treating clinician should explore Mr. J.'s perception of how his current impairments would affect his ability to perform his essential job functions. In addition, there should be discussion of the ramifications should Mr. J. not return to work. He does not know how long his specific job will be held open for him versus any available job with his employer. He may face termination if he does not return within a set period of time, as defined in his employment contract. He has not yet looked at his LTD policy to see whether it is an own-occupation policy and whether there are limited benefits for a mental health condition. Mr. J. may have difficulty reentering the workplace should he be out of work for a prolonged period, especially if he is not keeping up with new technological developments.

Family and Medical Leave Act Evaluations

Patients may need to apply for leave on the basis of the Family and Medical Leave Act (FMLA) in order to protect their job and health insurance benefits during a period of disability, and they may need some assistance from a treating clinician to support the application. The FMLA of 1993[15] is a law that enables employees to take up to 12 weeks of unpaid, job-protected leave in the event of disabling illness or certain family events (e.g., the birth or adoption of a child or the illness of a close relative who requires the employee's care).[16] The leave can be continuous or intermittent, depending on the requirements for treatment or care. The documentation required from the clinician for an FMLA leave is relatively minimal and straightforward as compared with the requirements for other disability benefit programs.[1] Family and Medical Leave Act leave is unpaid and aimed at protecting a worker's current job and health insurance benefits while he or she is undergoing treatment, recovering from a disabling period of illness, or tending to covered family responsibilities. In the case of psychiatric illness, the mental health professional would typically be asked to help the patient complete an FMLA certification form. Clinicians who are asked to help a patient apply for FMLA leave will find the Department of Labor's website helpful.[16]

Veterans Administration Evaluations

Clinicians employed by the Veterans Administration (VA) may also perform disability evaluations to determine a veteran's or service member's eligibility for VA benefits for a service-connected disability. Veterans Administration disability benefits are tax-free, and in 2013, roughly 21% of veterans in the United States reported a service-connected disability.[5] To apply for VA disability compensation, the veteran or service member must submit a package of documents, including any relevant reports from doctors or hospitals. To obtain sufficient documentation and prevent abuse of the system by persons who are not disabled, courts have required *diagnosis* of the claimed condition, that is, a trained professional clinician must have made the diagnosis of the condition that forms the basis of the veteran's disability claim.[17,18] The timing of the onset of the disorder and its connection (or lack thereof) to the patient's active-duty service are important factors in the VA's determination of eligibility for benefits. A condition that arose spontaneously after an honorable discharge and that is not directly related to the patient's military service would not be covered. Consider the following two examples.

Vignette 4: Service-Connected Disability

Mr. G., 28, comes to you for an evaluation and report (required documentation) to support his application for VA disability benefits for a service-connected disability. He explains that since his discharge from active duty 3 years ago, he has been fired from two civilian jobs because of problems related to what he believes might be PTSD. He recounts having been in the third car in a convoy in which the first vehicle was destroyed by a roadside bomb that exploded while the convoy was en route to a secure location. Mr. G. reports that since his return to the United States, he has suffered from nightmares, insomnia, and flashbacks that have resulted in exhaustion, distractibility, and irritability at work. On the basis of this information, it seems possible that he may indeed have a service-connected disability that could qualify him for VA disability compensation.

Vignette 5: Non-Service-Related Disability

Mr. W., a 57-year-old veteran who receives his medical care at the VA, comes to you for a disability evaluation, claiming that he should be eligible for VA compensation for an injury that occurred in the past year. While riding his motorcycle, he had an accident resulting in a brain injury, with residual cognitive impairment and behavioral problems due to frontal-lobe damage. Mr. W. completed rehabilitation for his injuries from the accident, but the behavioral disinhibition and cognitive problems are severe enough to render him unable to work in his former occupation as a loan originator. Although Mr. W. is a veteran and may be disabled, his disability does not appear to be service-related, since he was discharged from military service over 20 years ago, and the injury that gave rise to his disability was unrelated to his service and unrelated to any VA medical care that he received.

For the veteran or service member who wants to apply for VA disability benefits, the application process is fairly straightforward and can be completed online (http://www.benefits.va.gov/compensation/). For the clinician treating a patient who is applying for VA disability, it may be helpful to learn about the VA benefits system. During the evaluation process, it is important to explore any connection between the patient's current impairment and his or her military service, as this inquiry is relevant for eligibility determinations.

Americans with Disabilities Act Evaluations

Vignette 6: Returning to Work

Your patient, Ms. B., is a schoolteacher who was forced to leave her position because of poorly controlled depression. For a period of several months, she was completely unable to work. However, her symptoms have since improved, and she wishes to return to gainful employment. While the school administration is sympathetic and willing to work with Ms. B., there are doubts about whether she could effectively perform in the cognitively and socially demanding role of a high-school chemistry teacher. With the help of her family, Ms. B. has hired an attorney specializing in the Americans with Disabilities Act (ADA) and employment law, who has begun negotiations with the school department to avoid an ADA lawsuit. As a compromise, the school department is willing to offer Ms. B. a different position in the high school but requests further information about the nature and extent of her impairments and how they might be manifested in the workplace, as well as information about accommodations that would be necessary in order to mitigate the impact of her impairments on her work performance.

While most disability evaluations occur in the context of a temporary or permanent inability to work, evaluations for ADA cases typically involve a person who wishes to return to work or to remain working despite a disability. The ADA[19] was enacted in 1990 and amended in 2008 by the Americans with Disabilities Act Amendments Act (ADAAA).[20] The ADAAA significantly expanded the scope of conditions that may be considered disabilities for ADA protection, but not all impairments are ADA-covered disabilities. The ADA specifically excludes active illegal substance abuse,[21] and the Equal Employment Opportunity Commission (EEOC) has also clarified that personality flaws (e.g., abrasiveness or arrogance that is unrelated to mania or other mental illness) and certain diagnoses are not disabilities under the ADA.[22] However, the ADA does prohibit discrimination against persons who have a history of being disabled or who are regarded as being disabled,[20] which is important for patients who have been victimized or singled out because of stigma and stereotypes about persons with mental illness.

Treating clinicians should familiarize themselves with several of the terms involved in ADA disability law. These terms are defined by statute or by regulations released by the EEOC, which is tasked with implementing the ADA. The terms include impairment, disability, substantial limitation, major life activity, reasonable accommodation, essential job function, undue hardship, and direct threat. To meet the ADA standard for being disabled, a patient must have a substantial limitation in one or more major life activities (MLAs),[19] which are similar to, but not synonymous with, ADLs. Once it is determined that an employee or job applicant *is* disabled within the meaning of the ADA, the inquiry turns to whether he or she can perform the essential job functions (EJFs) with or without reasonable accommodation. The EJFs are determined by the employer. An employer is not required to retain a disabled employee if the employee poses a direct threat in the workplace.[23]

Reasonable accommodations are defined as changes in job requirements or structure that would enable a disabled employee to perform the EJFs and thereby enjoy the same benefits and privileges of employment as those available to nondisabled workers.[23,24] Examples of such accommodations are changes in job-application processes, the work environment, and the benefits and privileges of employment.[23] Such changes are reasonable as long as they do not impose an undue hardship on the employer and do not represent an attempt to exempt the employee from performing EJFs.[25,26] While an evaluating clinician can suggest accommodations that may be necessary for the employee to be able to perform the essential functions of the job, the reasonableness of the accommodations is determined by the employer as a business matter. Common accommodations for mental disabilities include flexible work schedules and allowance for the employee to take paid or unpaid leave.[27] The employer's determinations of the EJFs and the reasonableness of accommodations are often the subject of review by the EEOC or the courts in the course of disability discrimination claims.

Fitness-for-Duty and Return-to-Work Evaluations

A psychiatric fitness-for-duty evaluation (FFDE) is an examination requested by an employer to assess whether an employee suffering from a psychiatric disorder or other medical condition is able to perform EJFs.[4] An FFDE may be requested if an incident or complaint has raised suspicion of impairment because of mental illness that compromises the ability to safely and/or effectively perform essential work functions. Assessment may also be requested to determine whether the employee represents a threat to the workplace. When a patient seeks to return to work after a leave of absence for treatment of psychiatric illness, the patient's employer may require an FFDE in order to ensure that the employee is able to perform his or her job safely. These evaluations are referred to as return-to-work evaluations. The FFDEs are most commonly requested for employees whose job performance has serious implications for the health, safety, and well-being of others (e.g., police officers, physicians, pilots, and teachers).[4] Courts have upheld administrative decisions to fire professionals whose impairments can jeopardize the safety of others, even when those impairments were directly caused by an ADA-covered disability.[28,29]

In some situations, a treating mental health clinician may be asked for a letter clearing his or her patient to return to work, and doing so may be appropriate. However, when public safety is a consideration, the clinician should consider the alternative of an FFDE performed by a mental health professional who does not have a treating relationship with the patient and has access to information from the workplace.[30] The ethical issue that arises when the treating clinician assumes a role that calls for an independent, objective expert is discussed below, as well as in chapters 15 and 16. Formal psychiatric FFDEs are performed by forensic specialists, not by treating clinicians, with some exceptions.[31]

An FFDE can result in one of the following assessments of the employee's fitness for duty:[31]

1. fit: the employee is able to perform his or her job without danger to self or others without any limitations or restrictions;
2. temporarily fit;
3. fit subject to work modifications: if the evaluator's modifications can be accommodated by the employer, then the employee is considered fit for the modified job; if the recommendations cannot be reasonably accommodated, then the employee could be considered either temporarily unfit (i.e., with improvement modifications may no longer be needed) or permanently unfit;
4. temporarily unfit;
5. unfit.

Psychiatric impairments may have special implications for patients employed in certain professions in which public safety is at stake. An FFDE of a law enforcement officer, for example, must take into consideration the additional implications related to the officer's ability to safely use a firearm.[4] In addition to being subject to FFDEs over the course of their employment, law enforcement officers and firefighters may undergo a pre-employment psychological screening examination. The pre-employment screening is usually performed by a psychologist and is followed by a full pre-employment FFDE if concerns are raised.[31] The International Association of Chiefs of Police, Psychological Services Section, has ratified pre-employment and fitness-for-duty guidelines, which include information about conducting these evaluations.[32,33]

The evaluator may recommend that the employee's return to work be conditioned on verified treatment compliance and workplace monitoring or supervision. The evaluator should also be alert to the possibility that an employer may have ordered a psychiatric FFDE for inappropriate, punitive reasons. The AAPL characterizes such evaluations as "a misuse of psychiatry."[4]

Psychiatrists who are asked to perform psychiatric FFDEs of physicians are encouraged to review the American Psychiatric Association's *Resource Document on Guidelines for Psychiatric Fitness-for-Duty Evaluations of Physicians*[34] and other publications specific to this type of specialized disability evaluation.[35–37] Similarly, psychiatrists who perform FFDEs of police or corrections officers will find specialized resources on evaluating fitness for duty and disability in law enforcement professionals particularly helpful.[4,38–42] Additional, less specialized resources regarding psychiatric FFDEs are also available.[4,43,44]

Other Evaluations of Impairment

The clinician may be asked to provide information about a patient's impairment in the context of personal injury or other types of civil litigation, such as workplace sexual harassment. When disability or impairment is relevant to civil litigation, the issue of causation is often of critical importance. In a personal injury case, can it be shown that the accident gave rise to the patient's current impairment, or is it possible that the patient's difficulties are unrelated to the accident? Such questions represent complex inquiries and will vary depending on the facts in an individual case. Treating clinicians may also be asked to assist in designing individualized education plans (IEPs) for children protected by the Individuals with Disabilities Education Act.[45,46]

DISCUSSING DISABILITY APPLICATIONS WITH PATIENTS

Mental health professionals are very likely to be approached by patients to support their applications for disability benefits. Levin offers a helpful, seven-step, systematic approach to discussing the disability application procedure with patients.[1] This approach begins with a discussion about the reasons for the disability application and potential outcomes.

The patient and the clinician then discuss the application process, especially the issue of confidentiality.[1] Levin notes that there will be times when the clinician does not believe that the patient's symptoms are disabling. He recommends that in such cases, the clinician not avoid informing the patient of this opinion but rather focus on achieving the goals of treatment and return to work.[1]

The clinician clarifies the criteria that will be used to determine whether the patient is eligible for disability benefits and gathers clinical information about how symptoms have caused work-related impairment. The next step is to translate the findings into the appropriate administrative language for the entity in question (e.g., SSA or a private insurer), usually by completing a form. Final steps include processing the outcome with the patient, providing support and further documentation through the appeals process, and considering the possibility of recommending that an independent medical evaluation (IME) be performed by a mental health professional who is not the patient's treating clinician.[1]

ETHICAL ISSUES

Several ethical issues may arise in the context of disability evaluations. The AAPL practice guideline lists role conflict, honesty and objectivity, confidentiality, and forced employee evaluations as the most salient ethical issues for psychiatrists performing these assessments.[4]

Experts have identified role conflict as one of the major ethical issues for psychiatrists and psychologists who perform disability evaluations.[3,4,47] This topic receives additional attention in chapters 15 and 16. Role conflict occurs when, for example, the clinician is torn between duty to the patient (as treatment provider and advocate) and duty to the party requesting the evaluation (as an objective observer). Candilis and Neal discuss how the American Psychological Association's ethics codes can be applied to forensic work and the issue of dual agency.[48]

Bias is a common problem for clinicians whose patients request assistance in applying for disability benefits. Because the role (and ethical responsibility) of the treating clinician is to help the patient as much as possible, mental health professionals frequently avoid questioning or challenging a patient's firm belief that he or she is disabled. Furthermore, some clinicians may avoid confronting or challenging a patient's self-perception in order to preserve the therapeutic alliance.[7] This type of bias can lead the clinician to overlook important factors such as probable secondary gain, which is an indirect benefit from illness or disability. While in the context of a disability application, secondary gain often refers to monetary or disability payments, other indirect benefits may include increased personal attention and sympathy, or avoidance of adverse situations or responsibilities.

Conversely, mental health professionals who regularly perform disability evaluations for compensation can be vulnerable to advocacy bias and the desire for continued employment by insurers and other third parties to perform assessments. This financial incentive may lead to evaluations that are biased in favor of the party that requested the evaluation.[4]

The importance of honesty and the associated ethical implications are closely related to potential problems relating to role conflict and bias in treating patients who are applying for disability protection. As Levin explains:

> When clinicians do not believe the symptoms are disabling they should not avoid sharing this appraisal with the client. In these instances the clinician can utilize the discussion as an opportunity to focus on treatment goals and return to work. If they feel they cannot or should not be involved in the client's disability benefits application either because they lack sufficient information, lack expertise related to the client's condition, or feel unable to be objective, clinicians should consider referring the client to another mental health provider specifically for purposes of a disability assessment or evaluation.[1]

There can be several reasons why a patient's beliefs about his or her disability do not match the clinician's opinion. Some patients may attempt to feign a disability or exaggerate an impairment in order to "game the system" and obtain secondary gain from disability benefits. Others may genuinely believe that they are incapable of returning to work. Clinicians should be careful to monitor knee-jerk judgmental reactions; the desire to file for disability may truly be directly related to the patient's illness and may signal important changes in therapeutic status and the need to review or change treatment plans. The therapeutic alliance may suffer from the conflicting views of a patient who believes he or she is disabled and a clinician who thinks that the patient is able to work but is choosing not to do so. A similar problem occurs when patients with poor insight do not view themselves as disabled, despite evidence of severe impairment in the workplace, and want to return to work prematurely.[4] Malingering and deception are discussed in chapter 14.

A related concern is that of consistency. Weber[46] addressed the problem that may arise when a clinician treats or evaluates a patient who is applying for disability status protections under multiple programs—for example, applying for SSDI while maintaining that return to work would be possible with accommodations under the ADA. Weber notes, "If an examiner provides data supporting the conclusion that the person is unable to engage in previous work or substantial gainful work that exists in the national economy, it may be hard to support the position that the individual is nevertheless able to perform the essential functions of a job that he or she has applied for or seeks to be restored to."[46] Unfortunately, patients who apply for disability coverage are often in difficult circumstances, prompting them to seek help from multiple programs. When this happens, the clinician should be alert to potential conflicting opinions. Upholding the ethical standard of honesty can help to prevent or resolve such conflicts.[12]

Clinicians should also be aware of and frank about the limitations of their professional expertise. Some impairments may require specialized or additional assessment from other medical or psychological specialists, such as a neuropsychologist or a rheumatologist. Most disability programs require a physician to sign the application,[46] so mental health professionals who do not have medical degrees (e.g., licensed clinical social workers or psychologists) may need to refer cases to a psychiatrist or other physician. When impairment involves both physical and mental symptoms (e.g., chronic pain), evaluation of physical impairment should be performed by a different medical specialist.[1]

Additional ethical concerns are related to confidentiality. As the AAPL practice guideline and other sources note, disability evaluations are not confidential.[4,7] The evaluating clinician has an ethical duty to ensure that the patient is aware of the loss of confidentiality associated with the disability application process. How much confidentiality will be lost is likely to depend on the context of the application or evaluation, but patients should be warned beforehand. The clinician helping a patient apply for disability or performing a disability evaluation for a third party should nonetheless aim to protect the patient's or examinee's confidentiality to the maximum extent possible under the circumstances.[4] The AAPL practice guideline recommends obtaining a signed release from the examinee or patient, including a Health Insurance Portability and Accountability Act (HIPAA) disclosure if the evaluator is covered by HIPAA.[4] For clinicians who are interested in learning more about HIPAA and its application to psychiatric disability cases, the AAPL practice guideline may be helpful.[4] Readers will also find chapter 9 of this volume helpful for clarifying legal and ethical aspects of confidentiality in the provision of mental health treatment. Chapter 15 discusses broader ethical issues at the interface of clinical practice and the law.

DIFFERENCES IN THE ROLES OF TREATING CLINICIAN AND INDEPENDENT EVALUATOR

Failure to appreciate the differences between the role of the therapist and the role of the independent medical evaluator can threaten the validity of a disability evaluation.[49] There are concerns about trying to wear two hats, or acting as both the treater and the independent evaluator.[3] The role of the treating clinician is to provide information regarding level of functioning to the disability program. At times, the treating clinician may be asked by the patient or the patient's attorney to provide an opinion regarding impairment. Since the treating clinician's role is to establish the diagnosis and provide appropriate treatment, it is understandable that the clinician will rely heavily on the patient to provide accurate information during a diagnostic assessment and will generally not question the validity of that information. In contrast, the independent medical evaluator will attempt to assume an objective stance and will not make any assumptions about the reliability of the examinee's report.

Instead of emphasizing diagnosis, the independent psychiatric examiner will emphasize functional capacity and will compare "the examinee's presentation and circumstances to a legal standard defined by contract, statute or administrative ruling."[49] The examinee's functional capacity will be tied to a specific context.[4,49] Treating clinicians may fail to appreciate that an examiner's role is not to determine whether the evaluee is entitled to receive benefits but rather to describe the functional limitations in such a manner that the decision maker can make an informed decision.[49]

Since the aim of a clinical evaluation is to collect information in order to arrive at a diagnosis and recommend a treatment plan, the treating clinician is not generally focusing on the legal standard for disability when assessing functional capacity. The objectives of an independent evaluation are quite different:

> The assessment of disability requires establishing the existence of a condition and identifying the associated symptoms and manifestations that are present in the examinee. The examinee's specific job duties must be determined and translated into measurable functional capacities, so that the examiner can assess the relationship between the examinee's psychological condition and symptoms, and his or her lack of ability to perform the relevant occupational duties. These links between condition, symptoms, functional capacity and occupational duties must be clearly established and logically connected.[49]

During an IME, the forensic evaluator, in contrast to the treating clinician, will be provided by the referral source with access to multiple sources of information, which may include medical and psychiatric records from multiple providers, pharmacy records, results of psychological and neuropsychological testing, surveillance data, employment records, academic records, and personal records such as tax returns.[1] After obtaining consent, the evaluator may conduct collateral interviews to gather information about the level of functioning.[49]

A psychiatric interview conducted as part of a disability claim, like a clinical interview, should be comprehensive but with a greater focus on occupational functioning.

It is helpful to obtain a detailed written job description and to refer to specific aspects of the person's job tasks when conducting the interview, especially if the person has an own-occupation policy. Patients or examinees will often say that they are "disabled." The interview affords the examinee the opportunity to provide a perspective on his or her occupational impairments. It also allows the examiner to perform a mental status examination and correlate observations with claimed deficits.[4,49]

During the interview, a forensic evaluator will review a typical day in the examinee's life to obtain more detailed information about a claimed impairment and its impact on the examinee's level of functioning. As Levin notes, if an examinee reports a full schedule of demanding personal activities, this can challenge the claim of an impediment to work.[1] Furthermore, a review of daily job tasks and specific examples of ways in which the examinee's impairment affects job performance is important; this understanding helps the mental health professional to connect a examinee's mental health to his or her real-world occupational functioning so that the disability opinion will be tailored to the claimant's situation. The degree to which a particular symptom poses a problem in the workplace often depends on the nature of the work that the person must do; functional impairments resulting from severe depression, for example, could be more of a problem in a job with frequent deadlines than in a job with greater flexibility.[7] Anfang and Wall suggest asking disability claimants to describe both a typical good day and a typical bad day, since symptoms and impairment are often not static.[14]

A longitudinal approach to the psychiatric history is helpful for determining whether there has been a response in the past to treatment and whether there have been periods of improved functioning. A longitudinal occupational history may reveal whether psychiatric impairment has contributed to poor job performance.[4]

A common error of treating clinicians and even forensic evaluators is the failure to consider the specific demands of a job.[4] For a 35-year-old applying for SSDI benefits, general functional abilities needed to perform any gainful activity would be relevant, such as ADLs, social functioning, and concentration, persistence, and pace.[10] In the case of an own-occupation policy, however, a disability carrier could determine that one person is disabled while another person with the same diagnosis and severity of impairments is not disabled because of differences in how the impairments affect each person's ability to perform his or her own core job duties. Matching core job duties to functional impairment is essential. A job description will aid in this process.[4,49]

Treating clinicians are less likely than independent forensic evaluators to consider the possibility of exaggeration or malingering. However, forensic evaluators may be more likely to view any evidence of inconsistency as indicating that there is no basis for the claim of disability.[49] No disability evaluation is complete until the evaluator has considered the possibility that the patient or claimant might be malingering or exaggerating. Experts have estimated that rates of malingering or exaggeration may be as high as 30% among persons applying for disability benefits.[50] It is important to keep in mind that persons with genuine symptoms may exaggerate them in an effort to ensure compensation. Thus, an exaggeration of symptoms does not necessarily negate the existence of an underlying condition. Because the potential for malingering is significant among disability applicants, readers will find it helpful to review the detailed discussion of malingering in chapter 14.

Psychological testing can be helpful in the disability evaluation process, but the results are not dispositive of the disability issue and must be viewed in the broader context of the evaluation. As Piechowski points out, psychological testing is "vulnerable to methodological limitations, including those related to the psychometric properties of the test itself such as the test validity and reliability, sensitivity and specificity, and rate of false positives and false negatives. In addition the selected tests must be appropriate to the referral questions, administrated in accordance with standard procedures and valid for the purposes for which they are used."[49] Nevertheless, psychological testing can confirm impressions gained from the interview, collateral interviews, and records. If psychological testing is inconsistent, then further inquiry may be necessary.

A forensic examiner will have more experience than the average treating clinician in integrating complex and at times conflicting data in order to provide an accurate estimate of functional capacity.[42] The AAPL practice guideline provides sample reports that illustrate how information is presented and then synthesized to support the opinions regarding the level of impairment and work capacity.[4]

Readers are strongly encouraged to consult additional sources to help prepare for and conduct successful disability evaluations. The *Clinical Guide to Mental Disability Evaluations*[51] is especially helpful, and it contains chapters on specific topics, including SSDI,[8] workers' compensation,[12] LTD,[14] the ADA,[23] fitness for duty in general,[43] and fitness for duty in the case of specific professions, including health care[36] and law enforcement.[38] The AAPL practice guideline[4] is available online at no cost (http://www.aapl.org/practice.htm). As Drukteinis notes,[12] the AMA's *Guides to the Evaluation of Permanent Impairment*[11] is helpful when a psychiatrist is asked to provide a numerical value for estimated psychiatric disability. Clinicians who have to testify in court and those who must file reports for patients or evaluees in the context of disability applications should consult chapter 16.

CONCLUSION

When a patient is first seeking to apply for disability benefits, he or she is at a crossroads. There are positive benefits derived from working, especially for persons suffering from a mental illness. Work can provide a sense of stability and accomplishment and can promote social well-being. Living on disability payments can have negative consequences, including experiencing difficulty when later trying to reenter the workforce.[7] Care should be taken in discussing the consequences of applying for benefits.

The determination of disability rests on the specific definition of disability used by the agency or company to which the patient has applied for benefits. Each source of benefits is subject to a specific set of contractual obligations, laws, statutes, or regulations. Private disability insurance companies, federal entitlement programs such as SSDI and SSI, and worker's compensation evaluate claims in relation to their own criteria and definitions in order to determine whether an applicant is eligible for disability benefits.[7,51]

Clinicians should understand that a psychiatric diagnosis, no matter how serious, does not equate with disability, because a determination of disability rests on how psychiatric impairment affects functional capacity and occupational functioning.[4] In completing documentation for programs such as SSDI and SSI, it is helpful for clinicians to describe how psychiatric signs and symptoms translate into impairment in the workplace or in social functioning. This may require further questioning of the patient. The focus should be on functional capacity in relation to core job functions rather than on diagnosis.

FREQUENTLY ASKED QUESTIONS

Is there a difference between disability and impairment?

Yes. Impairment is defined as "a significant deviation, loss, or loss of use of any body structure or body function in an individual with a health condition, disorder, or disease."[11] Impairment is not synonymous with disability. The threshold for having an impairment is usually lower than that required for having a disability, but some impairment is a necessary prerequisite to being disabled.[11] Disability is a legal term or status whose exact definition varies depending on the context.

Is there a difference between Social Security Disability Insurance (SSDI) and Supplemental Security Income (SSI)?

While both programs are administered by the Social Security Administration, SSDI pays benefits to persons who have worked for a statutorily determined minimum period and have contributed to the Social Security trust fund through the Social Security tax on earnings, as well as providing benefits for certain disabled dependents of the insured person.[9] Title XVI provides SSI benefits for persons, including those under the age of 18, on the basis of financial need.[9]

Does a worker need to show that the employer was negligent in order to collect workers' compensation benefits?

No. Workers' compensation protects workers from the financial consequences of injuries suffered or disabilities acquired through the performance of work. There is no requirement that the claimant demonstrate that the employer was negligent, only that an unanticipated or accidental event or exposure caused an injury (or disability) that arose from and occurred in the course of work performed for the employer.[4]

Do some insurers allow claims for partial disability?

SSI and SSDI do not provide payments for partial disability. However, worker's compensation and, depending on the policy, private disability carriers do allow partial-disability claims.

Are there advantages to having an own-occupation disability policy?

Yes. An own-occupation private disability policy provides coverage in the event that the insured becomes unable to perform the work that he or she was doing at the time the policy was purchased. Other policies may define disability as the inability to perform any gainful occupation.[7] This difference in the definition of disability can have consequences. A surgeon with arthritis that impairs his or her ability to perform surgery would be considered disabled under an own-occupation policy. However, if the definition of disability is an inability to perform any gainful occupation, then this surgeon may not be considered disabled because the arthritis would not interfere with the ability to work at a medical clinic.

REFERENCES

1. Levin AP. What should I do? When clients seek disability documentation. In: Gold LH, Vanderpool DL, eds. *Clinical Guide to Mental Disability Evaluations.* New York, NY: Springer; 2013:75–94.
2. Christopher PP, Boland RJ, Recupero PR, Phillips KA. Psychiatric residents' experience conducting disability evaluations. *Academic Psychiatry.* 2010;34(3):211–215.

3. Strasburger LH, Gutheil TG, Brodsky A. On wearing 2 hats: role conflict in serving as both psychotherapist and expert witness. *American Journal of Psychiatry*. 1997;154(4):448–456.
4. Gold LH, Anfang SA, Drukteinis AM, et al. AAPL practice guideline for the forensic evaluation of psychiatric disability. *Journal of the American Academy of Psychiatry and the Law*. 2008;36(Suppl 4):S3–S50, p.S4.
5. Erickson W, Lee C, von Schrader S. *Disability Statistics from the 2013 American Community Survey (ACS)*. Ithaca, NY: Cornell University Employment and Disability Institute (EDI). http://www.disabilitystatistics.org. Accessed July 5, 2015.
6. VonSchrader S, Lee CG. *Disability Statistics from the Current Population Survey (CPS)*. Ithaca, NY: Cornell University Employment and Disability Institute (EDI), 2015. http://www.disabilitystatistics.org/. Accessed July 5, 2015.
7. Drukteinis AM. Disability. In: Simon RI, Gold LH, eds. *Textbook of Forensic Psychiatry*, 2nd edition. Washington, DC: American Psychiatric Publishing; 2010:283–301, pp.287–288.
8. Williams CD. Social Security Disability Income claims: treating mental health clinicians and consultative mental health examiners. In: Gold LH, Vanderpool DL, eds. *Clinical Guide to Mental Disability Evaluations*. New York, NY: Springer; 2013:185–213.
9. *Benefits for people with disabilities*. Social Security Administration. http://www.ssa.gov/disability/. Accessed June 21, 2015.
10. *Disability evaluation under Social Security*. Social Security Administration. http://www.ssa.gov/disability/professionals/bluebook/general-info.htm. Accessed June 23, 2015.
11. Cocchiarella L, Landersson GBJ, eds. *Guides to the Evaluation of Permanent Impairment*, 6th edition. Chicago, IL: American Medical Association; 2008.
12. Drukteinis AM. Workers' compensation evaluations. In: Gold LH, Vanderpool DL, eds. *Clinical Guide to Mental Disability Evaluations*. New York, NY: Springer; 2013:215–239.
13. Metzner JL, Struthers DR, Fogel MA. Psychiatric disability determination and personal injury litigation. In: Rosner R, ed. *Principles and Practice of Forensic Psychiatry*. London: Arnold; 1994:232–241.
14. Anfang SA, Wall BW. Long-term disability evaluations for private insurers. In: Gold LH, Vanderpool DL, eds. *Clinical Guide to Mental Disability Evaluations*. New York, NY: Springer; 2013:241–257.
15. 29 U.S.C. §§ 2601 *et seq.*(1993).
16. Family and Medical Leave Act. United States Department of Labor. http://www.dol.gov/whd/fmla/. Accessed June 23, 2015.
17. Dube AR, Sadoff RL. Veterans Affairs entitlement for service-connected disability caused by posttraumatic stress disorder. *Journal of the American Academy of Psychiatry and the Law*. 2015;43(2):239–240.
18. *Young v. McDonald,* 766 F.3d 1348 (Fed. Cir. 2014).
19. Americans with Disabilities Act, Pub. Law No. 101-336, 104 Stat. 327(1990), 42 U.S.C. §12101 et seq. (1990).
20. Americans with Disabilities Act Amendments Act, Pub. Law No. 110-325, 122 Stat. 3553 (2008), 42 U.S.C. §12101 et seq.
21. U.S. Equal Employment Opportunity Commission, U.S. Dept. of Justice, Civil Rights Division. *EEOC enforcement guidance: the Americans with Disabilities Act and psychiatric disabilities*. EEOC Notice No. 915.002, 1997. U.S. EEOC. http://www.eeoc.gov/policy/docs/psych.html. Accessed June 23, 2015.
22. U.S. Equal Employment Opportunity Commission, U.S. Dept. of Justice, Civil Rights Division. *Regulations to implement the equal employment provisions of the Americans with Disabilities Act, as amended.* 29 C.F.R. Part 1630, RIN 3046-AA85. 2011; Fed. Reg. 76(58): 16978–17017.
23. Recupero PR, Harms SE. The Americans with Disabilities Act (ADA) and the Americans with Disabilities Act Amendments Act in Disability Evaluations. In: Gold LH, Vanderpool DL, eds. *Clinical Guide to Mental Disability Evaluations*. New York, NY: Springer; 2013:259–289.
24. 29 CFR§1630.2(0);2011.
25. Smith DM. The paradox of personality: mental illness, employment discrimination, and the Americans with Disability Act. *George Mason University Civil Rights Journal*. 2006;17:79–156.

26. *Samper v. Providence St. Vincent Medical Center,* No. 10-35811, 2012 U.S. App. LEXIS 7278(9th Cir., April 11, 2012).

27. Gold LH, Shuman DW. *Evaluating Mental Health Disability in the Workplace: Model, Process and Analysis.* New York, NY: Springer, 2009.

28. *Jakubowski v. The Christ Hospital, Inc.,* No. 09-4097 (6th Cir., Dec. 8, 2010).

29. Regenbogen A, Recupero PR. The implications of the ADA Amendments Act of 2008 for residency training program administration. *Journal of the American Academy of Psychiatry and the Law.* 2012;40(4):553–561.

30. Meyer DJ, Price M. Forensic psychiatric assessments of behaviorally disruptive physicians. *Journal of the American Academy of Psychiatry and the Law.* 2006;34(1):72–81.

31. Granacher RP. Employment: disability and fitness. In: Buchanan A, Norko MA, eds. *The Psychiatric Report.* New York, NY: Cambridge University Press, 2011:172–185.

32. IACP Police Psychological Services Section. *Psychological fitness-for-duty guidelines.* Philadelphia. 2013. http://www.theiacp.org/psych_services-section/pdf/psych. Accessed June 20, 2015.

33. IACP Police Psychological Services Section. *Preemployment psychological evaluation guidelines.* Orlando 2014, http://www.theiacp.org/psych_services-section/pdf/psych. Accessed June 20, 2015.

34. Anfang SA, Faulkner LR, Fromson JA, Gendel MH. The American Psychiatric Association's Resource Document on guidelines for psychiatric fitness-for-duty evaluations of physicians. *Journal of the American Academy of Psychiatry and the Law.* 2005;33(1):85–88.

35. Foote WE. Forensic evaluation in Americans with Disabilities Act cases. In: Goldstein AM, Weiner IB, eds. *Handbook of Psychology: Forensic Psychology.* Vol. 11. New York, NY: Wiley; 2003:279–300.

36. Price M, Meyer DJ. Fitness-for-duty evaluations of physicians and health care professionals: treating providers and protecting the public. In: Gold LH, Vanderpool DL, eds. *Clinical Guide to Mental Disability Evaluations.* New York, NY: Springer; 2013:337–367.

37. Dilts S, Sargent DA. The law and physician illness. In: Rosner R, ed. *Principles and Practice of Forensic Psychiatry,* 2nd edition. Boca Raton, FL: Taylor & Francis; 2003:173–179.

38. Pinals DA, Price M. Fitness-for-duty of law enforcement officers. In: Gold LH, Vanderpool DL, eds. *Clinical Guide to Mental Disability Evaluations.* New York, NY: Springer; 2013:369–392.

39. Pinals DA, Price M. Forensic psychiatry and law enforcement. In: Simon RI, Gold LH, eds. *Textbook of Forensic Psychiatry,* 2nd edition. Washington, DC: American Psychiatric Publishing, Inc.; 2010: 413–450.

40. Rostow CD. Psychological fitness for duty evaluations in law enforcement. *Police Chief.* 2002;9:58–66.

41. Miller L. The psychological fitness-for-duty evaluation. *FBI Law Enforcement Bulletin.* 2007;76(8):10–22.

42. Rostow CD, Davis RD. *A Handbook for Psychological Fitness-for-Duty Evaluations in Law Enforcement.* New York, NY: Haworth Clinical Practice Press; 2004.

43. Wettstein RM. Fitness-for-duty evaluations. In: Gold LH, Vanderpool DL, eds. *Clinical Guide to Mental Disability Evaluations.* New York, NY: Springer; 2013:309–336.

44. Anfang SA, Wall BW. Fitness-for-duty evaluations. *Psychiatric Clinics of North America.* 2006;29(3):675–693.

45. 20 U.S.C. § 1400–1482(2006).

46. Weber MC. AAPL Guideline for forensic evaluation of psychiatric disabilities: a disability law perspective. *Journal of the American Academy of Psychiatry and the Law.* 2008;36(4):558–562.

47. Allan A. Ethics in psychology and law: an international Perspective. *Ethics and Behavior.* 2015;25(6):443–457.

48. Candilis P, Neal T. Not just welfare over justice: ethics in forensic consultation. *Legal and Criminal Psychology.* 2014;19:19–29.

49. Piechowski LD. Identifying examiner-related threats of validity in the forensic assessment of disability. *International Journal of Law and Psychiatry*. 2015. http://dx.doi.org/10.1016/j.ijlp.2015.08.010. Accessed July 21, 2015.

50. Mittenberg W, Patton C, Canyock EM, Condit DC. Base rates of malingering and exaggeration. *Journal of Clinical and Experimental Neuropsychology*. 2002;24(8):1094–1102.

51. Gold LH, Vanderpool DL, eds. *Clinical Guide to Mental Disability Evaluations*. New York, NY: Springer; 2013.

14

MALINGERING AND FACTITIOUS DISORDER

SCOTT R. BEACH AND MATTHEW LAHAIE

Clinicians in all disciplines rely on their patients to provide them with accurate histories and accounts of their symptoms. This is particularly true for physicians, who are responsible for diagnosing and treating a wide array of medical conditions, as well as for mental health professionals, who diagnose and treat conditions that often involve subjective rather than objective symptoms. Though patients may sometimes be limited in their ability to provide an accurate history because of cognitive deficits, psychiatric illness that affects their thought processes, or physical ailments that limit their ability to communicate, we expect that our patients will provide us with correct information to the best of their abilities. Patients who engage in deception shatter this expectation by willfully deceiving medical providers, even going so far as to feign illness. This chapter explores deception syndromes in detail, using case examples to illustrate key points.

MALINGERING

Malingering involves the conscious feigning, induction, or exacerbation of symptoms for conscious gain. Malingerers lie about their symptoms and diagnoses in order to achieve a tangible goal and are aware of their motivation while doing so. This so-called secondary gain is the hallmark of the phenomenon and can take a variety of forms. Secondary gain often involves obtaining something desired, such as food, shelter, or medication, especially controlled substances. For example, a patient may lie about being suicidal in order to gain admission to the hospital, where he will be provided with "three hots and a cot" (i.e., three hot meals a day and a place to sleep). In the outpatient setting, a patient may falsely claim to have symptoms in order to qualify for disability payments. Another variety of secondary gain is avoidance of responsibility, such as missing a court date or obtaining time off from work, release from the military, or relief from child care or elder care obligations.

Malingering is taken extremely seriously in the military, given the potential for reducing the number of available troops and the understandable attraction of avoiding combat. Article 115 of the U.S. Uniform Code of Military Justice makes it an offense to intentionally feign or induce an illness, potentially subjecting the accused to court martial proceedings.[1] Feigning an illness in order to avoid duty can result in forfeiture of all pay and allowances and confinement for 1 year. Intentional self-infliction of injury to avoid duty in a hostile fire zone or time of war is punishable by dishonorable discharge, forfeiture of all pay and allowances, and confinement for 10 years.

In addition to outright lies about symptoms, malingering can involve exaggeration of the nature and severity of real symptoms, simulation of new symptoms, or false imputation of symptoms. As an example of false imputation, a patient with chronic neck pain may attribute the pain to a recent accident in order to pursue litigation against another party in the hope of obtaining financial compensation.

Patients who malinger by reporting physical symptoms most commonly choose symptoms that cannot be objectively measured, such as pain. Psychiatric symptoms are often easier to fake than physical symptoms, and patients may claim that they are suicidal or are suffering from hallucinations or delusions.

Malingering behavior tends to be more common in men than in women. Though malingering is traditionally associated with antisocial personality disorder, the behavior has also been detected in otherwise psychologically normal adults.

While the true prevalence of malingering is unknown, studies suggest that it is common and that the rate of malingering depends on the clinical setting. An estimated 1% of civilian mental health patients may be malingering, as compared with 5% of military mental health patients.[2-4] Malingering is thought to be especially prevalent in the medicolegal context, with some studies estimating that up to 40% of personal injury, worker's compensation, and disability claims may have elements of malingering.[2-4] The prevalence of malingering in different psychiatric settings probably varies widely, with studies suggesting that 13% of psychiatric patients in urban emergency departments, 10% to 12% of psychiatric inpatients presenting with suicidality, and 32% of patients in forensic psychiatric units are malingerers.[5-8] Clinicians should keep in mind that malingering can involve nearly any condition and can be found in any clinical setting or patient population.[2,3]

Although the total costs of malingering in the United States are unknown, the burden of unnecessary medical care delivered in terms of both dollars and time is probably great. In 2010, the total estimated fraud of Medicare and federal Medicaid funding was estimated at $70 billion.[9] Malingering threatens patient safety because of the risk of iatrogenic injury to the malingering patient. Conversely, patients who have previously been identified as malingerers may not receive appropriate care when they actually need it. Clinicians who encounter malingering may become distrustful of patients, including those who are not malingering, causing damage to the clinician–patient relationship and potentially leading to burnout. On treatment units, malingering behavior may disrupt clinical teams if some team members trust the patient's reports of symptoms and others do not.[9] A patient on the medical unit who reports suffering from bipolar disorder and feeling suicidal, for example, may win the sympathy of the nursing staff and primary team. If the consulting psychiatrist later determines that the patient is exaggerating symptoms to avoid an upcoming court date and recommends discharge rather than psychiatric hospitalization, members of the primary team may become angry with the consulting clinician and advocate strongly for psychiatric hospitalization. The consulting clinician, in turn, may feel that the primary team is being duped by the patient. In its worst form, this difference of opinion results in a "chart war," in which the two sides attempt to justify their opinions by using the medical record as a forum for debate.

Malingering is a practice that has been documented throughout history. In the Old Testament of the Bible, David feigned insanity in order to escape the King of Cath (I Sam 21:10-15). The Roman physician Galen documented two cases of malingering: a case of colic that he thought was feigned to avoid attending a public meeting, and a knee injury that was thought to have been feigned by a slave in order to avoid going on a trip with his master.[10] Many persons have feigned illness to avoid military service in times of war and peace. As noted above, the U.S. Uniform Code of Military Justice makes malingering a court martial offense.[1] In the criminal justice system, illness may be feigned to avoid prosecution or secure a more favorable outcome. Vincent "The Chin" Gigante, an alleged member of the American Mafia and boss of the Genovese crime family, notably feigned psychotic illness from 1967 to 1997 in order to avoid prosecution.[11]

Though there have been no controlled studies of malingering, many commentators over the years have proposed specific signs that point to a greater likelihood of such behavior. Involvement in the legal system is a risk factor for malingering, particularly among patients who are referred for examination by an attorney.[12] In general, patients who malinger tend to have poor coping skills and to use immature defense mechanisms. As a group, they tend to seek medical or psychiatric care frequently, but they vary in terms of their personalities. Some exhibit the charming and glib personality of a con artist and may demonstrate an overfamiliarity with hospital staff, calling doctors by their first names and greeting nursing staff as though they were long-lost friends. Others appear to be dependent and needy, playing to the clinicians' sympathies, and still others are irritable and demanding. Regardless of the style of presentation, the goal is to convince the clinician that the patient has an illness that warrants intervention or compensation.

Another common feature of malingering is a long list of claimed allergies. Multiple allergies have also been described in patients with borderline personality disorder. Malingerers tend to have a list of allergies that precludes the use of whole classes of medications and is structured to guide the physician toward prescribing desired medications. For example, a malingerer who presents with pain may report allergies to ibuprofen, acetaminophen, and aspirin, insisting that opiate narcotics are the only option. Similarly, someone who fakes psychosis may report allergies to all antipsychotic medications and insist that only benzodiazepines are helpful in mitigating her symptoms.

Because they are desperate to have their needs met, patients who malinger frequently exhibit the "black cloud" phenomenon, in which the number and degree of bad things that have happened to them recently may strike the interviewer as implausible. The patient who reports that he is feeling suicidal because his mother, stepfather, two brothers, and childhood pet all died under separate circumstances in the past 2 weeks should be evaluated for malingering. Finally, perhaps the most consistent telltale sign of malingering is the escalation of symptoms in response to not having demands met. The patient who initially reports pain ranked as 5 on a scale from 1 to 10 may gradually increase the severity of the pain over the course of an emergency room visit until her request for opiates is heeded.

Though the presence of secondary gain is necessary for the diagnosis of malingering, it is insufficient by itself. Many patients with true medical or psychiatric illness stand to benefit in other ways from treatment, but this does not always indicate that they are malingering. Because clinicians have such a negative visceral reaction to being deceived by patients, it is important to ensure that malingering behavior is actually present before acting on that impression. Clinicians who have encountered a malingering patient recently are likely to be even more suspicious of possible malingering, putting themselves at risk of overcalling that diagnosis and a possible malpractice claim if the patient is harmed as a result of a treatable condition that is missed.

Vignette 1: Suspicion of Malingering, Example 1

Mr. A. is a 25-year-old homeless man with a history of alcohol use disorder. He presents to the emergency department reporting that he feels unsafe in the community and requests admission to a locked inpatient unit. A review of recent records shows that Mr. A. has had multiple similar presentations in the recent past, resulting in a series of brief hospitalizations, each ending with his leaving the hospital against medical advice when his demands for benzodiazepines went unmet. In the emergency room, he is initially charming with nursing staff and with other patients in the waiting room. When interviewed, Mr. A. says that his mood has worsened over the past day, but he does not report any obvious stressors. When initially asked about suicidal ideation, he says that he has no specific plan or intent but that he "doesn't feel safe." Though he doesn't offer the information spontaneously, when asked about legal involvement, he reports an upcoming court date, stating, "I think it might be sometime this week." He remains calm and pleasant throughout the interview, complimenting the resident interviewer on her outfit. In view of the information he has presented and his recent records, the resident psychiatrist decides that Mr. A. does not meet criteria for locked inpatient care and would benefit more from referral to a partial hospitalization program and outpatient follow-up. When Mr. A is presented with this recommendation, his demeanor abruptly changes. He disparages the interviewer and shouts at her, "If you don't lock me up, I'm going to cut my wrists as soon as I leave here. I told you I was suicidal!" On the basis of his history and presentation, the resident strongly suspects that Mr. A. is malingering.

Vignette 2: Suspicion of Malingering, Example 2

Mrs. B. is a 54-year-old widow who has been admitted to the hospital with recurrent cellulitis of her abdomen, for which she has been hospitalized four times within the past year. The psychiatry service is consulted because of significant worsening of her cellulitis on the day of planned discharge. Given that this has also happened during prior admissions, concern has been raised about the possibility of intentional self-harm. During the initial interview, Mrs. B. appears comfortable in her room, which is decorated with personal effects from home. She mentions several times that her primary care physician is a well-known figure in the hospital. She spends much of the interview lamenting her situation. Asked casually if there is anything good about being in the hospital, Mrs. B. replies, "Not even the money is good." Asked to explain this statement, she reports in a matter-of-fact manner that her late husband purchased a hospital indemnity insurance policy for her, which pays her $100 for every day spent in the hospital. She also has a separate medical insurance policy that pays her hospital bills. The diagnosis of malingering is suggested by the consultant and confirmed when the patient is later caught in the act of deeply scraping at her wound site with her fingernails.

FACTITIOUS DISORDER

In contrast to malingering, factitious disorder involves intentional feigning, induction, or exacerbation of symptoms for an unconscious gain. In other words, patients are aware that they are feigning symptoms but are unaware of their motivation for doing so. Unlike malingering, factitious disorder is regarded as a mental disorder in the *Diagnostic and Statistical Manual of Mental Disorders* (DSM). The unconscious gain that underlies factitious disorder, called "primary gain," is adoption of the sick role. An obvious secondary gain is not present. As in malingering, the specific symptoms in factitious disorder can be physical or psychological in nature. Psychological symptoms may include suicidality, hallucinations, dissociation, and bizarre behavior.

Whereas patients who are malingering typically report symptoms but do not actually induce symptoms, patients who have factitious disorder with physical features often engage in specific behaviors to injure or sicken themselves or to perpetuate an illness. In a classic example, a patient with an infected knee may surreptitiously inject fecal matter or other contaminated material into the wound to prevent healing and prolong the infection. The patient obviously maintains awareness of this behavior but remains unaware of his motivation for doing so. While this behavior is similar to the case of Mrs. B., described above as an example of malingering, the distinction is that Mrs. B. had a tangible reason for prolonging her illness or even creating new medical problems (receiving additional payment for being in the hospital), whereas the motivation for a patient with factitious disorder is the intangible sick role.

The prevalence of factitious disorder is unknown but may account for up to 5% of all outpatient physician visits.[13,14] Specialists may see an even higher percentage of these cases.[14]

Though the term "Munchausen's syndrome" is often used interchangeably with factitious disorder, it actually refers to a specific variant. The syndrome is named after Hieronymus Karl Friedrich, Freiherr von Münchhausen. The real-life Münchhausen was locally famous for telling larger-than-life stories about his experiences in the Russo-Turkish War, and his tales were later turned into a collection of fictional stories. In the stories, the fictional Münchhausen claimed to have traveled thousands of miles across the Russian countryside and described exploits that included riding a cannonball and traveling to the moon. Hallmarks of the Munchausen variant of factitious disorder, which is thought to account for 10% of cases and has a strong male predominance, are peregrination (traveling from one hospital to another to seek treatment) and pseudologia fantastica (telling fantastic stories to support the patient's claims).

Travel between hospitals allows patients with factitious disorder to present the same symptoms repeatedly and decreases the likelihood that new providers will have access to their old medical records. Pseudologia fantastica is thought to serve the purpose of drawing clinicians into the patient's story and engendering empathy for his plight, which in turn reinforces the symptoms. It is a form of pathological lying with interweaving of fact and fiction, repeated frequently and often with the patient assuming the role of victim.

In addition to those symptoms seen specifically in the Munchausen variant, a common feature of factitious disorder is impostorship. Patients may claim to be a decorated war hero or the survivor of a well-known disaster. After the Boston Marathon bombing, there were several reports of patients presenting with vague, unconfirmed symptoms, who claimed to have been at the finish line when the bomb exploded. Such cases also occurred after the 9/11 attacks, with people claiming that they were in or near the Twin Towers when the planes struck. Like pseudologia fantastica, this symptom may serve to align the clinician, and others, with the patient and increase the likelihood that the patient's reported symptoms will be taken seriously.

A common feature of factitious disorder with psychological features is pseudohallucinations—perceptual disturbances that the patient recognizes as unreal and explicitly describes as hallucinations. Though some patients with chronic psychosis gain insight into their hallucinations, most still describe them as "voices" rather than "hallucinations." Thus, factitious disorder should be part of the differential diagnosis in the case of a patient who reports hallucinations, especially in the absence of other symptoms suggestive of psychosis.

Another common feature of factitious disorder is factitious bereavement, in which patients repeatedly present reporting acutely depressed mood in the setting of the loss of a loved one. For example, a patient may present to the emergency room seeking admission for suicidality and report that her mother died 2 days ago. A review of prior records reveals that the patient reported her mother's recent death in 2011, 2004, 1999, and 1982. In some cases, the person reported dead may still be living or may have played only a very minor role in the patient's life. This phenomenon was also noted after the 9/11 attacks. In such cases, the purported death of the loved one is often described with a peculiar lack of affect.

As with malingering, some features of factitious disorder may be predictive. Patients with so-called common factitious disorder (as distinct from the Munchausen variant) are most commonly women and typically have a history of emotional deprivation or physical or sexual abuse. This is particularly true in cases of factitious disorder imposed on another (see below). Like patients with malingering, those with factitious disorder generally have a history of numerous hospital admissions and presentations to the emergency room, and many patients have multiple medical-record numbers at the same hospital under different names. Factitious disorder should be high on the list of differential diagnoses for any patient who arrives at the hospital wearing identification bracelets from other hospitals. Many persons with factitious disorder also meet criteria for borderline personality disorder, with poor identity formation and rigid psychological defenses. Many also have features of masochistic personality, which include rejecting opportunities for pleasure, refusing or rendering ineffective offers for help, and surrounding themselves with people who treat them poorly. A large percentage of patients with factitious disorder have backgrounds in the medical field (e.g., nursing, assistance with patient care, or pharmacy work), and may use their medical knowledge to feign illness more convincingly. In the Munchausen variant, antisocial personality disorder is common, as are strong dependency traits and confusion regarding sexual identity. Most patients have an average or above-average IQ.

Patients with factitious disorder frequently have a characteristic pattern in their presentation. They often arrive at the emergency room overnight, on the weekend, or on a holiday, when staffing is decreased and senior-level staff are likely to be absent, presumably to increase the likelihood of successful deception. They are typically familiar with the requirements for admission or intervention and will frequently report an acute illness of dramatic nature, often using medical jargon in their description. These patients typically request specific treatment, either directly or indirectly. Once admitted, they begin demanding increasing attention and express anger and frustration when their demands go unheeded. In many cases, the patient correctly predicts worsening of the disease and complains to the staff about mistreatment or misdiagnosis. The patient may play on the clinician's fear of liability to drive further unnecessary testing and treatment. Eventually, the deception may be uncovered, often by a chance finding, which typically results in anger on the part of the staff, with the patient either being discharged or signing out against medical advice. Shortly after discharge, the patient may present to another facility with a similar history and set of symptoms.

Factitious disorder is frequently debilitating to patients, with serial hospitalizations making it impossible to achieve meaningful and sustained employment or relationships. Some patients die from unnecessary medical interventions.

While patients with factitious disorder most commonly feign their own illness, a variant exists, formerly called factitious disorder by proxy and now termed factitious disorder imposed on another, in which persons falsify symptoms or induce illness in another person. Almost always, the victim is someone who is dependent on the person engaging in the deceptive behavior. Children are the most common victims, although siblings or parents, especially if infirm or intellectually disabled, may also be targeted. In contrast to standard factitious disorder, the motivation here is to satisfy the caregiver's psychological need to care for a chronically or severely ill child. Dr. Roy Meadow, a pediatric nephrologist, first described this phenomenon in 1977, when he reported two cases of children with fictitious illness, a boy with "hematuria" who was found to have his mother's blood in his urine and a child who died of poisoning with salt.[15]

This disorder has two characteristic forms. The classic form involves a parent or caregiver intentionally inflicting injury or inducing illness in a child while deceiving treating clinicians with false or exaggerated information. The other, perhaps more common and potentially insidious, involves a caregiver embellishing or fabricating symptoms in order to cause overly aggressive medical evaluations and interventions. While factitious disorder imposed on another is the psychiatric diagnosis applied to the caregiver, the harm inflicted on the child by medical interventions can be classified as medical child abuse. As many clinicians may have difficulty appreciating that a caregiver could intentionally induce or cause harm to a child, these presentations may go unrecognized and unaddressed, allowing for continued suffering of the child and potentially resulting in substantial morbidity or even death. The incidence of factitious disorder imposed on another is unknown, but it is widely believed to be underreported. When these cases are discovered, they become appropriate subjects for mandatory reporting of abuse and neglect, as described in chapter 10.

In the past two decades, a new variant of factitious disorder has emerged, known as Munchausen by Internet. Although not included in the fifth edition of the DSM (DSM-5), the syndrome has been described in several journal articles.[16,17] Rather than present to hospitals with symptoms, sufferers seek attention from other Internet users by feigning illness in chat rooms or on blogs or social media sites. The expansion of the Internet has made it much easier for persons to gain a nuanced understanding of certain medical diseases in order to appear more convincing. Classic patterns of behavior in this variant of the syndrome include verbatim recapitulation of textbook descriptions of illnesses, with a description of recurrent, worsening illness followed by miraculous recovery, and a reported duration of severe illness that conflicts with the Internet user's behavior, such as blogging about being in the intensive care unit with septic shock. Some patients even fake their own deaths in this syndrome as the ultimate ploy for sympathy.[18]

Vignette 3: Factitious Disorder, Example 1

Mr. C., a 32-year-old man, is admitted to the hospital with hypertension and episodic attacks that suggest a possible pheochromocytoma. He describes episodes consistent with that diagnosis, and laboratory testing reveals elevated levels of vanillylmandelic acid. Early in his hospital stay, inconsistencies are noted, such as lack of diaphoresis during episodes, low metanephrine levels in relation to other test results, and several episodes that are reported to have happened in the hospital but were unwitnessed. A psychiatric consultation is requested to rule out panic disorder, but the patient refuses the consultation. Suspicious of the situation, the nursing staff find evidence of unused antihypertensive medication in his nightstand drawer and later find an empty bottle of vanilla extract. When confronted with this evidence, the patient remains calm and unconcerned. He declines psychiatric follow-up. Records obtained from other hospitals reveal previous negative workups for pheochromocytoma.

Vignette 4: Factitious Disorder, Example 2

Mr. D. is a 57-year-old man with multiple medical problems and a history of repeated psychiatric hospitalizations who presents to the emergency room seeking psychiatric treatment. He reports that earlier that evening, he had been walking along the river, when he felt an overwhelming urge to kill himself. He reports that he jumped off a bridge into the river, noting that he is unable to swim. Just as he was gasping for his last breath, a bystander dove in and pulled him to safety. After the rescue, the bystander and his wife brought the patient to their home, where they fed him and gave him clean clothes. They then brought him to the emergency room. Asked by the interviewer where this couple was now, the patient replies that they left and that he doesn't have any contact information for them. Nursing staff at triage report that the patient arrived by himself. It is also noted that the patient's clothes were soiled, despite his report that the couple gave him clean clothes. A call to the local police department reveals no reports of anyone jumping from the bridge. A review of medical records reveals multiple similar presentations over the years. It is also noted that the patient occasionally claims to have been on the roster of a local professional sports teams several decades ago, but no record of this has ever been found. On the basis of the patient's pseudologia fantastica, inconsistencies, and past impostorship, a provisional diagnosis of factitious disorder is made.

Vignette 5: Munchausen

Ms. E. joins an online forum for patients with terminal brain cancer. She presents herself as a 21-year-old college student, recently returned from a mission trip to build houses in Ecuador, who has just been diagnosed with glioblastoma multiforme, after suffering from increasingly painful headaches for several weeks. She describes visits to various emergency rooms, each time being sent home, with the diagnosis finally made only because she insisted on head imaging. She reports that her tumor "crossed the midline" and that she has therefore been given a prognosis of 6 months to live. Over the next 3 months, she describes frequent appointments, side effects of steroid treatment, and several visits to the emergency room. Eventually, she reports that she has been hospitalized on the neurology unit of a specific prominent metropolitan hospital. When another forum member writes excitedly that she happens to be on the same unit and wonders whether they could visit each other, Ms. E. immediately replies that she has just been moved to the intensive care unit and is not allowed any visitors. Over the next 4 days, she continues to post twice-daily updates, including a detailed explanation of having an intracranial pressure monitor inserted. On the fifth day, Ms. E. poses as a family member of the patient and reports that the patient has passed away. Following an initial outpouring of sympathy, group members become suspicious when the details of the funeral reported by the family member are not verified by the funeral home and no record of an obituary is found on an Internet search. The following day, Ms. E. joins the forum under a different name, reporting that she is a 14-year-old boy recently diagnosed with brain cancer.

GANSER'S SYNDROME

Ganser's syndrome was once thought to be a variant of malingering or factitious disorder but in recent years has been linked more closely to dissociative disorders. The hallmark of the syndrome is the provision of approximate answers to questions. For example, if asked, "How many legs does a chair have," a patient might respond, "three," thus providing the correct set or category, but an incorrect, though close-to-correct, reply. Other features of Ganser's syndrome include clouded consciousness, somatic symptoms, and pseudohallucinations. The syndrome has also been reported in patients with organic brain injury.[19]

EVALUATING PATIENTS FOR MALINGERING OR FACTITIOUS DISORDER

When interacting with patients who are suspected of being untruthful with providers, the clinician should bear in mind that many patients lie to clinicians for nonpathological reasons. This "lying" may include exaggeration or minimization of symptoms or distortion of sequences of events. Many patients engage in this behavior because they fear the possible consequences of telling the truth. This is particularly true in interactions with psychiatric providers. Some patients fear that telling the full truth will result in involuntary hospitalization, and they may even have extreme fears about what such a hospitalization would entail (e.g., being injected with medications against their will or being placed in a straightjacket and a padded room). Other patients may believe that unless they exaggerate the truth, they will not be taken seriously and will be dismissed. Still others, especially those who have grown up in totalitarian regimes and have learned to both fear and deceive authority figures, will distort the truth when talking to hospital personnel who have control over the patient and the treatment.

The desire to be liked by providers is another common reason why patients lie. They may choose to minimize shameful and stigmatizing symptoms, such as the extent of alcohol consumption, in order to appear more normal, or they may report what they think the provider wants to hear. This is quite common, even among psychologically healthy patients. For example, many of us tell our primary care physicians that we exercise three times per week and confirm with our dentists that we floss after every meal, when in fact, most of us do not fully adhere to these recommended practices.

Patients who deceive health care providers can be broadly divided into those who "lie bad" and those who "lie good." Modified from the "faking bad" and "faking good" validity scales that are embedded in personality tests such as the Personality Assessment Inventory (PAI) and the Minnesota Multiphasic Personality Inventory–Second Edition (MMPI-2), the terms "lying good" and "lying bad" were coined by George Murray, M.D., S.J., former chief of the Massachusetts General Hospital Psychiatry Consultation–Liaison Service, as a more inclusive and descriptive means of classifying patients who feign, exaggerate, or minimize symptoms. For example, a psychiatric patient who lies bad might rank his depression as "the worst it's ever been," when in reality, the severity is fairly mild as compared with past episodes. Conversely, patients who lie good tend to minimize their symptoms in order to present themselves in a better light. For example, a patient might report that she hasn't used heroin for 9 months despite having used it earlier that day.

The pattern of deception can often be predicted by paying attention to certain elements of the patient's presentation. In the emergency room setting, patients who arrive on their own, especially those who walk into the hospital, are more likely to lie bad. They tend to be seeking medical or psychiatric services and therefore may exaggerate symptoms in order to obtain such services. Patients who are brought into the emergency room by family members, referred from a doctor's office, or especially brought in by police, are more likely to lie good and minimize their symptoms. This is particularly true of patients who present in that manner for psychiatric services. For patients likely to lie good, obtaining and reviewing collateral information becomes even more essential before making a decision regarding disposition. For example, a patient brought to the psychiatric emergency room by her sister might state that she is doing well except for occasional "relationship stress" and decline treatment. Her sister, however, advocates strongly for inpatient admission. She explains that the patient's "stress" is related to her stalking and threatening a former college professor whom she believes is in love with her, and the sister fears for the safety of the professor.

Predicting the pattern of deception can be helpful in informing the appropriate approach to the interview. For patients who are likely to lie good, it may be helpful to normalize and contextualize behavior before asking about it. For example, when inquiring about suicidal ideation, the interviewer might note, "When people are as depressed as you have described, they sometimes have bothersome thoughts about wanting to harm themselves," before asking the patient whether she has ever experienced such thoughts. Another technique that can be used with patients who tend to lie good is that of gentle assumption. In this approach, rather than asking a yes-or-no question about suicidal ideation, the interviewer might ask, "When was the last time you had thoughts of harming yourself?" The phrasing of this question assumes that those thoughts are present and may make it less likely that the patient will falsely deny having experienced such thoughts. In this situation, it can also be useful to ask about high frequency, commonly experienced symptoms, such as brief episodes of sadness. The more of these symptoms such a patient denies having experienced, the more likely she is to be minimizing her symptoms.

For patients who may be likely to lie bad, alternative techniques can be used. In these cases, it is imperative that the interviewer pay close attention to possible inconsistencies in the patient's history. Asking repeatedly about details may serve to highlight some of these inconsistencies. With the so-called Columbo method, the interviewer feigns naiveté regarding details that don't seem to connect logically, in a strategy similar to that used by Peter Falk's detective character in the Columbo television series. For example, rather than confront the patient about a discrepancy between the medical record and the interview regarding the timing of his mother's death, the interviewer might say, "I'm sorry to be so confused about this. You said your mom just died, but I read an old note stating that your mom died in 2009. Did you have two mothers?" Such an approach is less antagonistic than direct confrontation and may allow the patient to save face while still making it clear that the interviewer is aware of the inconsistency.

When a patient is suspected of malingering, gentle assumption can also be used to ask casually about secondary gain. For example, rather than asking a patient if they have any legal charges, the interviewer who is aware that the patient is involved in the legal system could simply ask, in a casual manner, "When is your next court date?" Asking about low-frequency, unlikely symptoms can also be useful in interviewing a patient who may be lying bad, particularly if the patient claims to have all the symptoms that the interviewer asks about. Such overreporting of symptoms, especially when they span multiple bodily systems, is often referred to as a "positive review of systems." Patients who claim to have multiple, very-low-frequency psychotic experiences such as visual hallucinations of speech bubbles emerging from people's mouths or concerns about a conspiracy in which cars would take over the world are likely to be exaggerating their symptoms.

In addition to the above interviewing techniques, formal psychological or neuro-psychological testing may be useful in determining whether a patient is attempting to deceive health care providers. As noted above, personality inventories, such as the PAI and the MMPI-2, have embedded validity scales for both faking good and faking bad. Faking-bad scales ask about low-frequency, unlikely experiences, whereas faking-good scales ask about high-frequency, near-universal experiences. Patients who answer "no" to multiple faking-good questions or "yes" to multiple faking-bad questions are likely to be minimizing or maximizing their symptoms, respectively. Alternatively, the Psychopathic Personality Inventory Revised (PPI-R) is a 154-item self-report measure of global psychopathy and specific traits that may be administered when malingering behavior is suspected. It also contains validity indexes for inaccurate reporting. An additional test for patients who may be reporting cognitive deficits as a form of malingering is the Test of Memory Malingering (TOMM), a 50-question, visual-recognition memory test that is scored on the basis of cutoffs for chance and for response patterns by patients with head injuries or cognitive impairment.[20]

MAKING THE DIAGNOSIS OF FACTITIOUS DISORDER

When factitious disorder is suspected, information from collateral sources is essential. Available friends, relatives, and prior treaters should be contacted, and outside medical records reviewed, as well as all internal medical records. In obtaining this information, it is important to keep in mind the ongoing duty of confidentiality. While a clinician can always receive information about a patient, disclosure of information about the patient (including the very fact that the person is a patient) can only occur with the patient's permission or if the disclosure falls within one of the exceptions to confidentiality, as discussed in chapter 9. Verification of the history presented by the patient via laboratory studies or imaging is also of paramount importance in the workup for factitious disorder.

Technology may be making it easier for clinicians to detect factitious behavior. The expansion and unification of medical records through centralized databases means that many practitioners have access not only to records in their own hospital system but also to records in hospital networks and community health services. In addition, central monitoring programs, such as the Prescription Monitoring Program in Massachusetts, allow physicians to see all prescriptions for controlled substances that patients have received, regardless of the prescriber or pharmacy.

Early suspicion is important to avoid colluding with the patient in ordering unnecessary tests and subjecting the patient to further risk of iatrogenic injury. Patients may play on the fear of liability in convincing physicians to order unnecessary tests and procedures, and clinicians must constantly balance what they consider to be due diligence in the workup against the perceived risk of iatrogenesis. While observation of the patient engaging in self-infliction of symptoms or the discovery of medical paraphernalia among the patient's belongings may be diagnostic of factitious disorder, searching the patient's room or videotaping the patient without consent may be considered an invasion of privacy. Advice from legal counsel is recommended before using such measures. Most experts recommend avoiding confrontation until the diagnosis is nearly definitive. Premature confrontation is likely to result in hostility, defensiveness, increased secrecy, or elopement. Even if the diagnosis has been established or the patient has been "caught red-handed," confrontation rarely results in an admission of deceptive behavior.

Clinicians are advised to monitor their own countertransference when working with patients who are suspected of malingering or factitious disorder, since acting out of hostility is never useful and is always risky. Attention should be paid to keeping emotionally charged comments out of the medical record. Instead of describing a patient as "hostile" or "belligerent" in the chart, for example, it may be more useful to report specific, objective examples of behaviors or comments that were made. Strategies for gentle confrontation include reframing the desire for medical attention as an indicator of psychological distress and discussing the full range of possible diagnoses, including factitious disorder, with the patient. Because factitious disorder is extremely difficult to treat, the approach should focus on management rather than cure. While it may be tempting to retaliate against a patient's deception by dismissing him or discharging him without follow-up, such practices may constitute abandonment, opening the door to possible malpractice complaints. Instead, the focus should be shifted from workup and treatment of the reported ailment to enhancement of the patient's available psychological and social resources in order to minimize the psychological distress underlying the disorder.

MAKING THE DIAGNOSIS OF MALINGERING

The diagnosis of malingering should be made only after other potential causes have been ruled out. Given the medical professions' revulsion toward "cranks," premature closure in such cases carries a significant risk that the patient's complaints will be immediately dismissed by future providers, setting the stage for a potential malpractice claim based on misdiagnosis. The diagnosis of malingering is ultimately based on a combination of inconsistencies in the history, the presence of secondary gain, a history of suspected deception, and other associated features outlined above. Patients with a history of malingering remain at risk for real medical or psychiatric illness and should be granted a reasonable evaluation at each visit.

There is debate about whether it is useful or therapeutic to confront someone believed to be malingering. Certainly, confrontation is likely to damage the therapeutic relationship and is often met with defensiveness and denial. Some recommend a gentle confrontation that allows the patient to save face, though this may be difficult to achieve if the deception is blatant. Because malingering may not only harm the patient by generating unnecessary tests and workup but also jeopardize the care of other patients through misallocation of limited resources, others advocate direct confrontation in cases where the diagnosis is clear. If the provider chooses to confront the patient about his behavior, it may still be possible to engage the patient in a discussion of motivations for the deception and alternative options for further treatment, including psychotherapy in the case of factitious disorder and referrals to outpatient resources such as homeless shelters and substance abuse hotlines in the case of malingering.

DISCHARGE IN DECEPTION SYNDROMES

In some cases, a decision may be made to discharge the patient who has been diagnosed with factitious disorder or malingering. The term "therapeutic discharge" is sometimes used to describe the circumstance in which continued hospitalization is felt to be countertherapeutic and detrimental with respect to resource management. Because factitious disorder and malingering are diagnoses of exclusion, this approach is typically reserved for patients who have repeatedly engaged in deceptive behavior. If a patient is being seen for the first time and is suspected to be deceiving the provider, it is advisable to document carefully any inconsistencies that may be present, as well as the suspicion of deceptive behavior, in the record but to avoid confrontation and treat the patient as though his reports are truthful (although refraining from ordering any unnecessary or dangerous tests and procedures). Such a practice provides protection against premature closure and abandonment of the patient.

If the patient has repeatedly engaged in deceptive behavior and a decision has been made to discharge the patient, it is imperative that all members of the team be made aware of that decision and that discharge procedures be organized before informing the patient. The goal is to minimize the time between informing the patient about the plan for discharge and the actual discharge, so as to limit any opportunity for disruption or further manipulation on the unit. The primary team should confirm that no other workup is planned and should be instructed to prepare discharge paperwork. Be prepared for opposition and protest from family members, including litigation, and consultation with hospital attorneys may be helpful as part of this process. Nursing staff working with the patient should be asked not to mention the discharge plan to the patient ahead of time and should have discharge instructions printed and ready to review with the patient. Security should be notified of the plan and should always be standing by, even if the patient has no history of violence, given the often contentious nature of the discharge. If the patient has belongings in a secured space, these should be gathered and ready at the bedside. Once all parties are assembled, either the consulting psychiatrist or a member of the primary team should inform the patient of the plan for discharge. Nursing staff should review the discharge paperwork, and the patient should be given an opportunity to change into appropriate clothing for discharge.

If the patient protests the discharge, the spokesperson should reiterate the plan, focusing on any additional resources that will be offered to the patient. Such resources should always be a key component of any discharge plan in this setting and may include referral to outpatient medical or psychiatric resources and information about housing and local shelters. It is recommended that providers not engage in a debate with the patient or in a lengthy confrontation, as this is unlikely to be useful and has the potential to result in the provider expressing anger and negative emotion toward the patient. All participants should be clear that the discharge will take place regardless of how the patient behaves when presented with the plan. In this way, lengthy engagement with the patient becomes unnecessary, because nothing that the patient might say would reverse the decision that has been made. One possible approach is to explain the decision for discharge to the patient by briefly highlighting the inconsistencies in current and past presentations, noting that the history provided is not clinically realistic or logical. In other circumstances, the provider may simply state that the workup has been completed and that there is no further indication for hospitalization. Ultimately, the patient should be escorted out of the hospital by security, with a request to security personnel that they remain with the patient until he or she is off the premises.

Documentation is a vital component of any contentious discharge and should include several key components. As with all discharge reports, documentation should include a discussion of the diagnosis of malingering or factitious disorder, with as much supporting evidence as is available. Documentation should always include a detailed risk assessment for harm to self or others. In addition to the standard practice of listing risk factors and mitigating factors, it may be prudent to discuss the reasons for giving apparent risk factors less weight and the analysis of clinical risks and benefits that has informed the decision to discharge the patient. For example, one might say, "Although the patient has reported multiple prior suicide attempts, which would typically elevate her risk for future self-harm, it is important to note that none of these prior attempts have ever been verified, none have apparently resulted in medical hospitalization, and, in fact, the patient has provided conflicting accounts of several of these attempts." Emphasis should also be placed on future orientation, which is often present to a significant degree in patients exhibiting deceptive behavior and which strongly argues against imminent self-harm. Documentation should include a summary of the events surrounding discharge, with an emphasis on the resources that were offered to the patient at the time of discharge.

CONCLUSION

Deception syndromes are common in medical and psychiatric populations. Clinicians must be aware of these syndromes and prepared to consider them as part of a broad differential diagnosis. While recognition of malingering and factitious disorder can tempt treaters to retaliate against the patient for willfully deceiving those trying to care for him, it is essential to maintain professionalism in these situations and focus on providing adequate care, avoiding unnecessary workups, and encouraging the patient to seek treatment for the deceptive behavior itself, when appropriate.

FREQUENTLY ASKED QUESTIONS

What is the difference between malingering and factitious disorder?

In cases of malingering, patients intentionally feign symptoms to meet specific conscious goals, or secondary gain, such as obtaining money from legal settlements, disability payments, food, or shelter or being excused from work or military service. In cases of factitious disorder, patients intentionally feign symptoms in order to meet unconscious psychological needs, typically assuming the sick role.

How common are factitious disorder and malingering?

The true prevalences of malingering and factitious disorder are unknown. However, they are both thought to occur commonly in multiple clinical settings. Malingering is thought to occur more frequently in correctional, military, and medicolegal settings, such as disability evaluations, criminal prosecutions, and civil litigation for monetary damages.

What are the complications of factitious disorder and malingering?

Factitious disorder and malingering result in unnecessary medical evaluations and treatments, which can cause harm to patients and sap the health care system of significant financial resources. Malingering also incurs significant cost to the economy because of decreased productivity and false claims for benefits. Clinicians who encounter cases of factitious disorder and malingering may experience significant frustration, anger, and bewilderment, and frequent exposure to such cases may result in burnout.

How are factitious disorder and malingering diagnosed?

Aside from a patient's frank admission of deception, malingering and factitious disorder are diagnoses of exclusion. Making a diagnosis of either one requires a reasonable medical evaluation as well as a critical analysis of the total circumstances.

REFERENCES

1. Uniform Code of Military Justice: U.S. Code Chapter 47. 10:801–946.
2. Peebles R, Sabella C, Franco K, Goldfarb J. Factitious disorder and malingering in adolescent girls: case series and literature review. *Clinical Pediatrics* 2005;44(3):237–243.
3. Stutts JT, Hickey SE, Kasdan ML. Malingering by proxy: a form of pediatric condition falsification. *Journal of Developmental and Behavioral Pediatrics.* 2003;24(4):276–278.
4. LeBourgeois HW, 3rd, Foreman TA, Thompson JW, Jr. Novel cases: malingering by animal proxy. *Journal of the American Academy of Psychiatry and the Law.* 2002;30(4):520–524.
5. Rissmiller DJ, Wayslow A, Madison H, Hogate P, Rissmiller FR, Steer RA. Prevalence of malingering in inpatient suicide ideators and attempters. *Crisis.* 1998;19(2):62–66.
6. Rissmiller DA, Steer RA, Friedman M, DeMercurio R. Prevalence of malingering in suicidal psychiatric inpatients: a replication. *Psychological Reports.* 1999;84(3 Pt 1):726–730.
7. Yates BD, Nordquist CR, Schultz-Ross RA. Feigned psychiatric symptoms in the emergency room. *Psychiatr Services.* 1996;47(9):998–1000.
8. Pollock PH, Quigley B, Worley KO, Bashford C. Feigned mental disorder in prisoners referred to forensic mental health services. *Journal of Psychiatric and Mental Health Nursing.* 1997;4(1):9–15.
9. King K. *Medicare and Medicaid fraud, waste, and abuse: effective implementation of recent laws and agency actions could help reduce improper payments.* Testimony before the subcommittee on Federal Financial Management, Government Information, Federal Services, and International Security, Committee on Homeland Security and Governmental Affairs, U.S. Senate. 2011. http://www.gao.gov/new.items/d11409t.pdf. Accessed September 16, 2015.
10. Lurid F. Galen on malingering, centaurs, diabetes, and other subjects more or less related. In: *Proceedings of the Charaka Club.* Vol. X. Williams & Wilkins; 1941.
11. Newman A. Gigante says he was crazy . . . like a fox. *New York Times,* April 8, 2003.
12. American Psychiatric Association. *Diagnostic and statistical manual of mental health disorders: DSM-5* (5th edition). Washington, DC: American Psychiatric Publishing. 2013.
13. Wallach J. Laboratory diagnosis of factitious disorders. *Archives of Internal Medicine.* 1994;154(15):1690–1696.
14. Fliege H, Grimm A, Eckhardt-Henn A, Gieler U, Martin K, Klapp BF. Frequency of ICD-10 factitious disorder: survey of senior hospital consultants and physicians in private practice. *Psychosomatics.* 2007;48(1):60–64.
15. Meadow R. Munchausen syndrome by proxy: the hinterland of child abuse. *Lancet.* 1977; 2(8033):343–345.
16. Feldman MD. Munchausen by Internet: detecting factitious illness and crisis on the Internet. *Southern Medical Journal.* 2000;93(7):669–672.

17. Feldman MD, Bibby M, Crites SD. "Virtual" factitious disorders and Munchausen by proxy. *Western Journal of Medicine*. 1998;168(6):537–539.
18. Johnson B. The short life of Kaycee Nicole. *The Guardian*. Sunday May 27, 2001.
19. Dalfen AK, Anthony F. Head injury, dissociation and the Ganser syndrome. *Brain Inj*. 2000;14(12):1101–1105.
20. Tombaugh TN. The Test of Memory Malingering (TOMM): normative data from cognitively intact and cognitively impaired individuals. *Psychological Assessment*. 1997;9:260–268.

15

ETHICS AT THE INTERSECTION OF MENTAL HEALTH AND THE LAW

PHILIP J. CANDILIS AND NAVNEET SIDHU

While Hippocratic principles inform medical ethics to some degree today, contemporary medical ethics is often traced to the English physician Thomas Percival at the turn of the 18th century. In 1847, the fledgling American Medical Association (AMA) adopted its first code of ethics, using Percival's 1790s treatise *Medical Ethics* as a key source.[1] It endorsed honor as an important foundation in elevating the treatment of patients above physicians' self-interests and advocated for the separation of law and medicine. An abiding element of this work was the sense that the profession ought to be free from societal oversight.

As society evolved, however, so did the guidelines by which physicians conducted themselves. The regulatory capacity of licensing boards and hospitals grew, and ethics codes were revised to help meet the goals of expanding access to health care and improving public health. By the 21st century, specialty associations such as the American Psychiatric Association were required to adhere to the AMA code of ethics.[2] Because psychiatrists often meet patients when they are at their most vulnerable, the principles and guidelines laid out in the AMA ethics code are thought to provide an important foundation for clinical practice in psychiatry. Similarly, psychologists and social workers receive guidance from the ethical codes adopted by the American Psychological Association and National Association of Social Workers, respectively.

This important guidance notwithstanding, psychiatrists and other mental health professionals often encounter complex situations in which medical ethics may not offer unequivocal answers. Throughout our work, we gather sensitive information that may be reportable to legal authorities; obtain informed consent from patients with conditions affecting impulse control, sexuality, thoughts, and mood; and offer treatments that can be complex and even controversial. As practitioners whose responsibilities extend to the legal system and society as a whole, we may be required to evaluate dangerousness or competence to stand trial for a court, workplace risk for an employer, or disability for an insurer. Mainstream medical ethics may provide guidance that is inadequate in dealing with such issues and sometimes may be in direct conflict with our societal duty.

Using the commonly applied Hippocratic ethic of "First, do no harm," for example, clinicians will immediately find themselves at odds with the potential consequences of a court-ordered evaluation or one conducted for a third party, such as a disability insurance company. After all, the opinion arising from an evaluation of the patient's responsibility for a crime or disability status may lead to adverse legal, emotional, and financial repercussions for the evaluee. The clinician's opinion that the patient is competent to stand trial, criminally responsible, or able to work may be at odds with the evaluee's views about his or her best interests. Professional ethics codes alone are consequently not sufficient for many of the issues that arise at the intersection of mental health practice and the law.

Deciding what is ethical when a clinician's assessment has legal implications is complicated by the intersection of these two different endeavors—clinical care and law. Rules that govern professional behavior in clinical medicine, psychology, and social work, for example, fail to capture the nuance of society's police power and "state as parent" (*parens patriae*) standards, both of which are discussed throughout this book (e.g., see chapters 1, 2, and 5). These societal mechanisms require psychiatrists to consider duties to the community as well as to the patient. The community may be interested in detaining a dangerous patient (police power) or protecting a patient who cannot survive on the streets (*parens patriae*). In fact, the ethics of the law differ enough from clinical ethics that patients are often called "evaluees" or "interviewees," terms that establish a distance between the practitioner and the person being evaluated. The language, combined with an express explanation of the clinician's role, signals that the role of the practitioner is that of evaluator, not treater, and that the traditional clinician–patient relationship does not exist under the circumstances. Let us look first at this special kind of practice—called forensic mental health—and then apply its lessons to clinical mental health practice and the law in general. We will be considering the underlying moral basis of this important work.

FORENSIC EVALUATIONS

Derived from the Latin term for public setting or forum, "forensic" refers to assessments conducted for the purposes of the law, to assist the law, or otherwise to advise a legal party. Forensic mental health practice is informed by a literature that is different from clinical practice and makes use of an interview framework that has become routinized for the specific population being examined. Forensic evaluations include assessments for decision-making capacity, competence to stand trial, criminal responsibility (the absence of which is the basis for the insanity defense), malingering, fitness for duty, and the like. It is a special kind of ethics that governs interactions of this kind. Let us start by scrutinizing the complex position and role of the psychiatrist who is asked to conduct a forensic evaluation. It will help us unpack the obligations of all clinicians interacting with society's rules.

In a forensic setting (e.g., courtroom, prison, or state or forensic hospital), clinicians face several ethical dilemmas. On the one hand, they provide a service to the court and society as a whole. On the other hand, they have duties to the individual. While it is generally agreed that the forensic psychiatrist or psychologist and evaluee are not in a typical doctor–patient relationship, some of the same principles of medical ethics ground the interaction. Indeed, prior to 2005, the American Academy of Psychiatry and the Law (AAPL) explicitly stated that the same ethics that guide clinical psychiatry should apply to forensic psychiatry. Since then, however, AAPL has taken a course we endorse: supporting a greater balance between the needs of the individual and those of society.

In mental health and the law, we find authors on both sides of the equation. Appelbaum,[3] for example, describes a nonmedical, hierarchical approach in which legal values such as truth and justice drive the forensic encounter. In contrast, Weinstock and colleagues[4] prefer an approach that advocates the balancing of conflicting medical and legal values. More broadly, Candilis and Martinez[5] recognize that society expects medical experts in the legal system to retain many medical values. Consider the following common forensic situation:

Vignette: Competence to Stand Trial

Ms. A. is a 49-year-old immigrant who has been accused of disturbing the peace, a misdemeanor. She allegedly jumped the turnstile at a station in the city's subway system and caused enough of a commotion to be arrested by transit police. She refers repeatedly to her lost baby but does not appear to have given birth recently. Recognizing that Ms. A. may be suffering from a mental illness, the arraigning judge (the judge who sees her for the first time) refers her to the court's mental health clinic for assessment of competence to stand trial. The court, like many of the courts in large U.S. cities, enlists clinicians to assist the judge in making decisions about disposition.

Evaluation for competence to stand trial is a common clinical undertaking at the intersection of law and mental health practice. As a matter of fairness, U.S. law does not permit defendants who are not competent to stand trial (i.e., those who are not capable of understanding the judicial process) to enter the legal system (*Dusky v. United States*).[6] For detailed information on competence to stand trial, see chapter 12.

What are the obligations of the evaluating clinician in these circumstances? Do the usual clinical obligations of care and cure apply, or do the setting and circumstances require application of a different ethic? It may be clear that the judge is referring the defendant to the clinician not for treatment but for legal purposes that are beyond the usual framework of mental health practice. The defendant's mental state matters to the judge but not in the same way that it matters to the clinician. Consequently, the clinician's assessment follows different rules about what is right or appropriate. Granted, if the person requires urgent medical assistance, the psychiatrist or other clinician has an obligation arising from core professional expectations to provide it. But the clinician's primary responsibility is not to establish a diagnosis and provide treatment.

THEORIES OF ETHICS

Distinctions between classic medical ethics and other ethical frameworks are not unusual in mental health. Competing obligations in forensic practice, psychiatric research, correctional health, military psychiatry, managed systems of care, and even school counseling generate different priorities and outcomes. Consequently, ethicists have developed a number of frameworks for assessing the ethical requirements of a clinical case, many of them now well known and widely practiced. Because psychiatrists, like all physicians, work the entire breadth of health care, societal expectations are strong and the statuses of patient and physician are easily recognized. For the most part, the same is true of the relationship between other mental health practitioners and their patients or clients. But when the context, role, or setting is different, the rules may be different as well—a fact that may be difficult for many patients, and clinicians, to grasp.

In applying ethics to the practice of medicine and other clinical fields, professionals can be guided by different viewpoints. These are the theories of morality that help professionals reconcile the world of principles and rules with the complex and ambiguous world of human interactions.[7] Just as principles provide a basic framework for ethical decision making, ethical theories provide an opportunity to vary our perspective. This flexibility can be highly valuable in addressing the ethical questions that arise in mental health and the law.

In some influential writings, such as those by Nagel,[8] ethical theories are presented explicitly as ways to view complex problems from another angle. This applies to the issues addressed by mental health professionals, including some of the most controversial, from paraphilias, illicit drug use, and violence to free will and moral responsibility. The values of individual actors, their institutions, and communities will all have an influence on the outcome. For example, as clinicians, we are often concerned about access to weapons among suicidal or aggressive persons seeking mental health treatment. However, this concern may conflict with the prevailing view in states that curtail questions about the right to bear arms or among persons who view gun ownership as a citizen's duty.

Each ethical issue generally involves a moral agent, a choice or action, a consequence or outcome, and the context of that outcome. In mental health, the moral agent is the health care professional, the action or choice involves a health care decision, and the anticipated and potential outcomes are embedded in the moral perspective. Together, these offer a multifaceted approach to analyzing ethical problems.

Principles

The dominant theory for medical ethics in the past decades has been the principlism of Thomas Beauchamp and James Childress.[9] These ethicists have identified a series of principles (or clusters of principles) that seem to govern the majority of health care issues: autonomy, beneficence or nonmaleficence, and justice. Based on a vast body of knowledge from moral philosophy and social and medical sciences, these principles have become a mantra for students of medicine and clinical ethics: autonomy, beneficence/nonmaleficence, and justice.

Autonomy, or self-rule, is a bulwark of Western legal thought and carries with it a respect for the individual (called respect for persons) that recognizes the importance of personal freedom and the damage caused by interference from others. Western culture holds autonomy as a core value that defines the intrinsic worth of the individual, protects individual rights, and is a means of personal advancement. When applied to health care, this principle guides requirements of confidentiality, truth telling, and informed consent. Individual patients cannot make autonomous decisions without these foundational elements of ethical theory. For example, clinicians must offer alternatives to patients seeking a procedure or treatment and must outline the risks as well as the benefits so that the patient can make an informed decision.

Beneficence (the state or quality of doing good) and its variant, nonmaleficence (avoidance of harm), are for many the grounding principles or purpose of all health care. The World Health Organization's primary goal, for example, is the "attainment by all people of the highest possible level of health." This beneficence-based ethic requires health care professionals to provide competent service and exhibit compassion for patients, and it underscores the patient's well-being as a fundamental goal of health care professionals. In addition, clinicians must truthfully present their professional limitations and make the necessary referral when they cannot be helpful. This ensures that clinicians do not practice beyond the scope of their knowledge

Justice in medical ethics refers to fairness in the distribution of resources, in the treatment of like cases alike, and in the procedures used to assess and treat patients, no matter who they are. In the management of scarce resources—such as health care services in rural areas or new technologies in remote regions—justice requires that physicians avoid waste and manage limited resources carefully. Although it differs from the justice of health care, criminal justice follows similar tenets; we address the distinctions below.

These principles alone do not provide enough guidance to resolve complex human interactions such as those that occur when mental health practice and the law collide. The questions of how to balance the requirements in these two spheres, to whom we owe the primary duty and how we choose the criteria for making decisions, persist. In mental health law, for example, clinicians worry about the obligation to breach confidentiality when a patient is considered to pose a danger to self or others—the common requirement for civil commitment. It may seem clear that the harm to others carries more weight than the privacy of the patient, tilting the balance in favor of the obligation to breach confidentiality, but that decision may have a chilling effect on patients seeking help with mental health issues (although this has not, in fact, been proven to be the result of confidentiality warnings).

Beauchamp and Childress[9] describe a hierarchical construction of ethics, with principles and rules for day-to-day practice beneath them. Consider the example of a social worker who must decide whether the one available placement in a group home should be assigned to a young pregnant woman or an elderly diabetic man? Using the principles of beneficence, nonmaleficence, and justice, she will have to determine whose situation would be improved more and who stands to lose more. She must consider how to distribute the limited resource justly. How much good will her decision do, and how much harm will be done to the person she does not place in the group home? Can she decide fairly, using the same process and criteria for each case? Overall, a familiarity with many theories will allow her to develop a richer approach to such difficult questions.

Virtue Theory

Virtue theory focuses on the moral agent's character and sets up both practical and aspirational expectations for professionals. Aristotle defined virtue as "the excellence of a thing."[10] For clinicians, caring and compassion are central virtues, along with other virtues, such as protecting the community and acting honorably. Virtue theory assumes that people want to do what is right and good but that good intentions alone cannot guarantee good decisions. Knowledge and practice are required to establish habits of virtuous action. Thus, for a virtuous mental health professional, this might include learning cross-cultural approaches, and being aware of the inequities of the mental health and judicial systems. Professional integrity and ethical habits in the clinical practice of medicine owe much to commentators on virtue and character.

The obvious weakness of this theory is that virtuous and well-intentioned people can make bad decisions. In addition, two people who are equally well intentioned may take positions that are diametrically opposed to each other. For example, in the debate over outpatient commitment (see chapter 2), people who disagree on the right balance between individual freedom and state interference can be equally well meaning and virtuous. Some want to protect individual rights and reject mandated outpatient treatment, while others want to protect patient welfare and press patients into treatment. A single theoretical approach is therefore, insufficient for addressing the problem.

Deontology

Deontological, or duty-based, theories (*deon* means duty in ancient Greek) do not focus on the moral agent but rather on the rightness of the decision itself. This theory assumes that actions are right or wrong in and of themselves, which means that an act can be inherently bad even if it brings about a good result. As the philosopher Immanuel Kant, probably the most well-known deontologist, observed, "The ends do not justify the means."[11] A classic modern-day example is that of a surgeon who can save five people with the organs of one person but who is not justified in killing that one person. According to Kant's categorical imperative (which is very much like the Golden Rule), moral acts must be generalizable to all situations; if they are not, they are unethical.

Even so, duty-based theories cannot handle all real-world ethical dilemmas. For example, telling the truth is a moral act because it has universal properties of the good, but what if truth telling causes harm? The Nazi-at-the-door scenario (i.e., "Is Anne Frank here?") is traditionally used to argue against the universality of even the most basic moral assumptions. Acknowledging that a Jewish refugee is hiding in the attic completely over-whelms any good that comes from telling the truth.

A more recent example is physician-assisted dying. The definitions of harm and ben-efit are at the core of this controversial topic, particularly since the general rule that physi-cians should not kill is so compelling. However, as many have argued, a patient's suffering may require considering the ending of life as an act of mercy. Deontological theories are often too crude to resolve such agonizing questions.

Consequentialism

Consequentialism focuses on the consequences or outcomes of actions, with "good" gen-erally defined as that which benefits the greatest number of people. The best-known ver-sion of consequentialism is the utilitarianism of John Stuart Mill and Jeremy Bentham.[12,13] Utilitarianism assumes that all people have equal moral worth and guides us to actions that will produce the greatest net good for the greatest number, a view that is particularly useful in public health discussions. From this perspective, consequentialism maximizes utility, happiness, or efficiency in health care decisions.

The most common criticism of consequentialism is that some persons are harmed in the quest for the greater good. In working with vulnerable populations, as we do in men-tal health care, or with members of minorities whose beliefs are not valued in the domi-nant culture, the most ethical course of action may be to protect the smaller group. Thus, there may be no calculus that provides a tidy ethical answer. In psychotherapy in particu-lar, critics cast doubt on the ability of clinicians to predict the desired consequence for anyone, let alone the greatest number of people. Modern societies are not homogeneous, and one set of values does not govern all decisions.

Social Contract Theory

Social contract theory focuses on the expectations of society and how governments and professionals must respond to the community. Social contract theorists developed mod-els for how people consent to live peacefully together, with French philosopher Jean-Jacques Rousseau emphasizing the importance of the people's "general will" in guiding societal leadership.[14] These theorists proposed the development of rational agreements between political authorities and the masses, and such agreements form the basis for the open democratic process in many modern societies.

In everyday practice, clinicians often face situations in which the expectations of their patients differ from their own—the contract is unclear. This may arise during a discussion of vaccinations with a family that resists them or during the warnings on the limits of confidentiality with a patient who expects complete privacy. A recent example is the discussion with patients who are reluctant to divulge information because of the fear of losing their firearms. As we have seen, a number of states limit these gun discussions in service to the right to bear arms. For example, the 2014 Florida case of *Wollschlaeger v. Governor of Florida*[15] prohibited doctors from inquiring about guns or documenting such information in the medical chart, unless it was specifically relevant to the patient's health. The classic criticism of social contract theory, as may be obvious from the contentious political climate of recent years, is that leaders may assume that they know the will of the people better than the people themselves do.

Communitarian Ethics

Even though the major theories discussed thus far offer valuable perspectives on issues in mental health practice and the law, none of them completely addresses the individual's relationship to the community. It is communitarian ethics that describes the context of many ethical dilemmas by emphasizing the moral connection between individuals and their community. Such theories focus on the duties and obligations that arise from the nature of specific relationships. For example, the duty we owe to a police officer is different from the duty owed to a neighbor.

Examples of communitarian ethics can be seen in several modern ethical and political movements, especially environmentalism and feminism.[7] In health care, the feminist perspective is represented in the "ethics of care." This approach, grounded in the work of Harvard psychologist Carol Gilligan,[16] assumes that human beings are interdependent and that their identity requires interconnection, not simply a contract to leave each other alone. On the basis of her work exploring the moral thinking of girls, Gilligan argued that moral decisions cannot be made fairly and wisely just by applying universal rules impartially. Instead, an emotional stance that integrates the moral actor with her relationships is warranted.

As an example of the dilemma that Gilligan addresses, consider the case of mothers who are incarcerated. Should justice be applied regardless of dependent relationships, or should the needs of the children at home be considered as well? How might persons diagnosed with eating disorders be affected by the unreasonable standards of beauty that the community has established? How does the community's valuation of traits such as assertiveness and autonomy over interdependence, community, and sharing influence views of gender and illness?

Narrative Ethics

Many aspects of the ethical principles and social contract and communitarian theories have been incorporated in narrative ethics, which focuses on storytelling as a framework for understanding the patient's experience of illness, including his or her values, beliefs, and cultural practices.[17,18] The narrative starts with the patient's presenting symptoms and unfolds as the patient tells the story of his or her illness in the context of broader life experiences, with the clinician engaging in the narrative from a position of empathy, compassion, and professional expertise. The joint telling and retelling constitute the doctor–patient relationship. The beliefs and biases of both the patient and the clinician, the choices made, and the outcomes are all part of the narrative.

When the patient's story is examined as part of an evaluation for involuntary hospitalization, for example, narrative ethics challenges us to consider the nuances of patients' reports and to counter the tendency to impose simple and absolute standards. Combined with the application of ethical principles (e.g., beneficence) and the practice of virtues (e.g., cultural awareness), the narrative perspective leads to an understanding of the more subjective and existential values of the patient's story, which in turn provides a basis for assessing the need for hospitalization. For example, a clinician should not assume that someone who refuses to eat is in need of involuntary commitment. In the context of the patient's story and cultural practices, the refusal to eat may actually be a religious fast in the Hindu or Buddhist tradition rather than a symptom of a serious mental disorder.

Familiarity with narrative alongside other ethics approaches can help avoid the moral relativism of the pure patient account or the pure certainty of the trained clinician. It is not enough for one's story to justify one's actions; ethics would then be related entirely to one's personal perspective. A patient who believes that marijuana is a safe remedy may come up against a clinician who believes that it only interferes with prescribed medication. An appreciation of the patient's narrative and the offer of potential alternatives may provide an acceptable resolution. Similarly, a deeply religious clinician may struggle with her atheist patient's refusal to attend Alcoholics Anonymous because of its reliance on a "higher power." Acknowledging the patient's story and consulting on other group options (e.g., Rational Recovery or Smart Recovery) increases the likelihood of satisfactory outcomes for both the patient and the clinician.

Overall, even the telling of the patient's truth must have some kind of objective context. Consider the patient in group therapy who extols the virtues of benzodiazepines (a controlled substance) for anxiety. The therapist must be aware of the effect of the patient's narrative on those group members who are struggling with addiction.

An understanding of the merits and limitations of ethics theories fosters sensitivity to the complexity of human behavior. Since we lack full neutrality and objectivity, we must strive to appreciate the value of multiple perspectives, develop habits and skills of ethical practice, and practice with the humility that a diverse society requires.

APPLYING ETHICS THEORIES

What do these approaches to ethics mean for Dr. Z.'s evaluation of Ms. A.?

Ms. A. waits impatiently for the court clinician. The officer at the door makes it clear that she is not free to go, but he says she will be seeing "the doctor." When Dr. Z. arrives, he is wearing a jacket and tie, not a white coat. "Who are you?" she demands. "Are you gonna help me?"

What are the requirements of this interaction, especially in light of the patient's expectation? She believes she is in a clinic to see the doctor and has experience with clinicians who have cared for her in the past. But Dr. Z. is working for the court; he is not the patient's advocate. His job is to assess her capacity to understand the judicial process and work with her attorney. Truth telling requires that he inform Ms. A. of this, yet he must behave in a compassionate and caring manner. He must not treat her unprofessionally just because she is under court control.

In Ms. A.'s mind, a patient tells the doctor what ails her, and the doctor heals her. Therefore, she views Dr. Z. as someone who will extend a helping hand; he is not someone aligned with the law, a system that seeks to punish her. Appelbaum[3] argues that "subjects of forensic evaluations will assume that an evaluating psychiatrist is playing a therapeutic role and, therefore, that the usual ethics of the clinical setting apply."

Perhaps Dr. Z.'s training will allow him to reflect on Ms. A.'s vulnerability in a system that controls her. Since she is from an oppressed cultural group—let's say she is Uzbeki or Chechnyan—he may be more sensitive to her experiences with the legal system or society in general. Immigrants, especially those who are women, are not always welcome in their adoptive communities. And they may have experienced considerable discrimination in their homeland. In addition, Ms. A. may be reluctant to speak her mind with a male physician because of her cultural beliefs and experiences. Dr. Z. should encourage her to tell her story so that he can understand the path that led her to court and she can express her symptoms in a way that does not presuppose Western categories or labels.

Dr. Z. explains the purpose of the evaluation and informs Ms. A. that he is a court-appointed examiner who is not involved with her in a typical doctor–patient relationship. What they discuss may not be kept confidential from the court.

An explanation of the limits of confidentiality is a requirement of truth telling and transparency in all professional actions. It is actually a requirement for all mental health encounters, since clinicians are required to report suicidal and homicidal patients, as well as child and elder abuse. However, this explanation may widen the gap Dr. Z. has to bridge in order to put Ms. A. at ease. He must establish some kind of rapport with her. But Ms. A. has the common expectation that because Dr. Z. is a doctor, he will help her. His apparent denial of the beneficence principle puts the physician in an adversarial position as far as Ms. A. is concerned, adding to her distress.

"Get out! Just take me to the judge!" she exclaims. As Dr. Z. explains his position and the importance of the evaluation, he asks, "Is there anything you need before we begin?" Ms. A. shakes her head and says, "You don't understand." She starts sobbing and mumbling to herself. After a few minutes, it is evident that she will not be able to cooperate with the evaluation until she calms down.

Although Dr. Z. is not Ms. A.'s treating psychiatrist, he legitimately attempts to establish a rapport with her in order to relieve her distress. His effort to do so reflects both the principle of beneficence and the virtue of compassion. But it may confuse Ms. A., who has an expectation of doctors as a whole that is based on her culture and personal history, reflecting a communitarian concern.

Ms. A. opens up. She says that she has been searching for her baby, believing she gave birth last week. Although Dr. Z. finds this unlikely, given her age and lack of supporting evidence, he expresses sympathy while redirecting her to the purpose of the evaluation.

On the surface, Dr. Z.'s response may seem callous, but he has been appointed by the court to evaluate Ms. A.'s competence to stand trial. He therefore has an obligation to fulfill a social contract that serves the interests of justice for his community. He has been entrusted with a societal mission: to assess Ms. A.'s ability to be tried.

Alternatively, it may seem as if Dr. Z. is feeding Ms. A.'s delusion when he expresses sympathy for her loss. Yet, while Ms. A.'s behavior is based on her delusional belief system, her distress is real. If Dr. Z. completely disregards it in order to move the wheels of justice, he will fail to establish a connection that is essential to the narrative. He will be unable to understand or acknowledge Ms. A.'s perspective, her thoughts, and her account of the event. He will be unable to engage in her story, the essential telling and retelling, and the alliance building. As a result, she will not be able to reveal her story; her voice will not be heard. In light of common social expectations, Dr. Z. will fail the professional ethic that requires sensitivity to the plight of vulnerable persons. Here, utilitarian thinking (consideration of the greater good) falls short if it serves simply to extract information, without attention to the ethic of care that is an essential aspect of clinical ethics. Indeed, pure medical ethics would forbid the desertion or abandonment of a person in distress.

This situation highlights the conflicting roles and responsibilities of the practitioner caught between clinical and forensic ethics, which can present an impossible dilemma. Dr. Z. serves medicine when he uses the skills he has learned as a clinician to put Ms. A. at ease. Yet he applies those skills in an effort to obtain information that may help ease her way into a potentially punitive system. This presents a challenge to common role theory, which typifies the expectations of doctor and patient. We are back to weighing benefi- cence against justice in the clinician's work. Instead, it may be that a virtuous sensitivity to Ms. A.'s plight takes us beyond mainstream ethical thinking and provides the compassion, transparency, and honesty the situation requires.

Ultimately, Dr. Z. is able to ask whether Ms. A. knows the charge she is facing. "No, I didn't do anything wrong," she responds. Dr. Z. follows his usual practice of reading the police report to Ms. A.

By reading the police report to Ms. A., Dr. Z. may appear to be coaching her or dis- regarding her account. But it is often part of the educational aspect of court evaluations. Even while he is engaged in the relatively simple task of providing information, Dr. Z. has to think about how he delivers the information and how he thinks Ms. A. can hear it. In adjusting to her individual needs, Dr. Z. has to be mindful of her vulnerability due to mental illness and account for her cultural expectations or biases, educational level, and intellectual ability.

Communitarian ethics, which focuses on the interdependence of the community and the individual, comes into play here. For example, having lived most of her life as a mem- ber of an oppressed minority under Soviet rule, Ms. A. may distrust authority figures, and men in particular.

Ms. A. understands the major elements of the police report, even though she does not know the specific name of the charge itself. Satisfied, Dr. Z. asks Ms. A. about her previous experiences with the legal system. She reveals a recent history of minor charges such as trespassing, for which "my lawyer told me to say I was guilty and I went home." It appears to Dr. Z. that Ms. A. is unable to appreciate the significance of pleading guilty, incurring a criminal record, and risking harsher penalties because of past infractions. When Ms. A. explains that she was chasing the people she thinks stole her child, Dr. Z. grows more concerned. He realizes that Ms. A. does not recognize the authority of the police in her situation, although she clearly describes jumping the turnstile and otherwise behaving erratically.

Although Dr. Z. now recognizes that a psychotic illness is interfering with Ms. A.'s understanding of her situation and the legal ramifications, he has elicited seemingly incriminating information. She has acknowledged the observations in the police report and reported behavior consistent with the charges. Ms. A. may not have retained Dr. Z.'s earlier explanation of the limits of confidentiality. She may not appreciate that she is protected from self-incrimination. At the same time, the information is relevant to her competence to stand trial. Dr. Z. needs to know not only whether Ms. A. has an understanding of the charges but also whether she has a coherent and rational narrative.

In such situations, it is standard practice to exclude incriminating information from a competence report but to include the observation that the defendant has a recognizable explanation. This standard reflects a specific protection in the U.S. Constitution (the Fifth Amendment protection from self-incrimination) and the cardinal element of the principle of justice. Under some state statutes, such as those in Massachusetts and the District of Columbia, self-incriminating statements made in the course of court-ordered mental health evaluations may not be used to establish guilt.

Overall, Ms. A.'s story may be incriminating, but it also betrays a serious lack of understanding of the legal process. How Dr. Z. balances these factors takes into account both individual protections (nonmaleficence) and community obligations (communitarianism and beneficence).

When Dr. Z. follows up with questions about courtroom personnel, Ms. A. immediately responds, "I know my attorney is in it with the judge."

Dr. Z. must determine whether this is delusional thinking or part of Ms. A's cultural perception. Perhaps her previous experiences with the legal system have been less than fair. He recognizes that this may be part of the oppressive history of her culture at the hands of the Soviets. Taking cultural experiences into account, which reflects both narrative ethics and cultural sensitivity, increases the complexity of the diagnostic assessment. Dr. Z. can acknowledge Ms. A.'s previous experiences and her distrust but nonetheless educate her about the nature of the U.S. legal system, her attorney's role as her advocate, and the neutral role of the judge.

Despite his explanation, Ms. A. remains suspicious of her attorney and the judge. There may indeed be an element of cultural history in this too, as a phone call from Ms. A.'s frantic sister quickly makes clear. Ms. A was harassed by local police in her homeland, largely because of her mental illness. Without a robust defense or patient advocacy in her homeland, she has developed beliefs that are the result of both past experience and mental illness.

This brings Dr. Z. to another critical component of ethical perspective: the perspective of women as a nondominant group (part of narrative and communitarian ethics). The ethics of care, for example, asks us to consider a feminist perspective. This is a view not simply of political activism, as in the feminist movement, but of the manner in which women handle ethical dilemmas. In 1992, for example, Alison Jaggar[19] brought attention to the limitations of traditional ethics in considering matters of concern to women. Traditional ethics overrates culturally accepted masculine traits, she observed, such as "independence, autonomy, intellect, will, hierarchy, domination" while it underrates culturally feminine traits such as "interdependence, community, sharing, emotion, absence of hierarchy, nature, peace, and life." Also, it favors "male" ways of moral reasoning, which emphasize rules, rights, universality, and impartiality, over "female" ways of moral reasoning, which emphasize relationships, responsibilities, particularity, and partiality. Other authors have also discussed the differences between the "communal woman" and the "autonomous man." Although Carol Gilligan notes that the respective languages of care and justice are not gender-correlated in an ironclad way, common societal perspectives assign the values of care to women and justice and autonomy to men.

As a savvy practitioner, Dr. Z. is aware that women, like minority groups, are at a disadvantage in the legal system by virtue of their gender. The American Civil Liberties Union, for example, notes that over 64% of incarcerated mothers lived with and cared for their children before being sent to prison.[20] In 2005, 75% of women in New York State prisons were mothers, and two-thirds of these women lived with minor children before they were incarcerated.[21]

For Dr. Z., this more recent social commentary suggests that he must be careful to integrate the concerns of his female evaluees into his assessments. The child-rearing aspect of Ms. A.'s presentation is certainly psychotic, but it is grounded in a well-known role for women worldwide. Discounting it because it is psychotic does more than simply diagnose a symptom; it subverts an important social role for a person in distress.

If Ms. A. were in a better state of mind, her strategy for the case, her willingness to plea bargain, and her consideration of sentencing options would probably be influenced by her relationships with family and others. Narrative ethics and feminist ethics recognize that personal relationships lie at the center of any moral question.

Dr. Z. assesses Ms. A. as incompetent to stand trial and recommends hospitalization for treatment and restoration to competence. She is unwilling to be hospitalized, so Dr. Z. recommends a commitment order.

Although Dr. Z. may appear to be assuming the clinical role by recommending hospitalization, the court order will be for restoration of competence; treatment is a sidelight. Many jurisdictions keep treatment separate from restoration. In fact, to preserve the right to refuse treatment, some jurisdictions do not permit treatment for the express purpose of restoring competence. The conflict persists between the clinician's duty to the patient to provide treatment and the forensic evaluator's duty to the court to assess the defendant's competence.

A few months later, Dr. Z. encounters Ms. A. while covering an inpatient unit for a colleague. She recognizes him and waves cheerfully. The treatment team has diagnosed schizophrenia and a long-standing marijuana addiction. Her history also reveals multiple miscarriages in her 20s and 30s. Ms. A. is taking medications now, has shown progressive clinical improvement, and has been assessed as competent to stand trial. During the team meeting, she challenges Dr. Z.: "I feel good when I smoke weed. Haven't you ever taken drugs?" Briefly taken aback, Dr. Z. responds, "This is not about me. I want you to understand that marijuana can affect your illness. Let's focus on that." Ms. A. is not yet ready to change gears. She places a hand on Dr. Z.'s arm, saying, "Marijuana is fun, I could show you."

Dr. Z. relies on his training regarding the need to maintain firm boundaries, as proposed by Gutheil and Gabbard.[22] Their model divides the problem of crossing personal and professional lines into two groups: boundary violations and boundary crossings. Traditional ethical theories governing boundary theory in psychotherapy developed from serious concerns about professional sexual misconduct.[23] Over the last few decades, rules and guidelines regarding such boundary violations have been widely accepted and incorporated into the laws of some states, as well as the policies of professional organizations. These rules and regulations are actually quite instructive on how mental health professionals interact with society's rules.

Gutheil and Gabbard define boundary violations as activities that are harmful to patients and clearly outside the usual behaviors that characterize the patient–professional relationship. These are actions that result in clear exploitation. Often, violations fall under the guise of personal disclosures, physical contact, gifts, business transactions, and sexual relationships.[24] Violations represent a significant abandonment of ethical principles and usually lead to substantial harm. In responding to Ms. A.'s provocative remark, Dr. Z. has to maintain boundaries while preserving a rapport with Ms. A. for the benefit of her treatment in the hospital. In doing so, he must take into account Ms. A.'s history, culture, illness, and resulting vulnerability.

Let us take this a step further:

Two years later, an engaging, professional-looking woman approaches Dr. Z. at a restaurant. Dr. Z. is alone, going through a divorce, and feeling rather lonely. The woman turns out to be Ms. A., who is now fully recovered and offers her profuse gratitude for his help. She invites him to join her and her friends for dinner.

Should Dr. Z. accept the invitation? What ethical principles or theories come into play? At its core, this appears to be a classic boundary violation that exploits a prior professional relationship. It may seem superficially innocuous because Ms. A. is not alone, but Dr. Z. is being invited into a setting where her past vulnerability and his power over her disposition confer great danger. Personal disclosures, violation of the patient's privacy ("How do you know each other?"), and physical contact are significant risks. He must refuse her invitation.

While Dr. Z. had to maintain compassion, establish rapport, and employ a nuanced approach in his previous interactions with Ms. A., he must now retreat from her expectation of greater familiarity. He is not a cardiologist who can go for a round of golf with a former patient. He must recognize the coercive influences of the previous setting, his own personal motivations (and virtues), and the potential harm to the patient and the community from exploiting past vulnerabilities.

Boundary crossings are the other side of this coin. These are behaviors that may be acceptable because they are not exploitative and are in the service of treatment. Common examples include giving the patient a ride in a snowstorm and visiting a patient at home as part of clinical outreach. These behaviors may cross personal–professional boundaries but are clearly supportive of the patient and the treatment.

Savin and Martinez[25,26] define boundary crossings more liberally than previous commentators, as transactions within the therapeutic encounter. They may require sensitivity to the cultural meaning of the boundary crossing—say, a gift—and the potential benefit or harm to the clinical relationship. Savin and Martinez discuss acceptable forms of gift-giving, for example, as those that may help the patient regain a sense of empowerment or resonate with a cultural practice that fortifies care.

The graded-risk model for boundary crossings proposed by these authors considers carefully whether the crossing may benefit the patient as well as the patient–physician relationship. This nuance raises similar questions for the ethics of mental health practice in general, which may frequently be challenged by classic boundary theory. Consider, for example, whether a unit social worker or nurse working with Ms. A. should hold her hand to comfort her? Brief human contact may offer support and hope to a hospitalized patient. What if Ms. A. asked the clinician to pray with her? When do personal and professional values join to help the patient, and when do they collide, resulting in confusion and exploitation?

ROBUST PROFESSIONALISM

We call the model that integrates numerous ethical approaches to such difficult questions a robust professional ethics. This is an ethics for mental health as a whole that takes into account the patient or evaluee, the practitioner, and the community as well. The model considers the harms to an individual under the control of a system or institution and applies practices and skills that encourage honesty, transparency, and self-reflection. These principles, perspectives, and virtues together offer the greatest likelihood of success and consistency in negotiating difficult mental health dilemmas—ones that are too often assigned a simple role- or job-dependent solution.

The AMA ethicist Matthew Wynia and his colleagues[27,28] have carefully distilled professional ethics into the question of whether the work is "a structurally stabilizing, morally protective force in society." Does it embrace the elements of "devotion to service, profession of values, and negotiation within society"? Since the mental health professional has responsibilities in many directions, it may be clear by now that a comprehensive ethical approach is necessary to answer such questions.

Whether to accept a gift, a stock tip, or a date with a patient requires answering these important unifying questions: Is my behavior structurally stabilizing and morally protective? Does it serve the patient or the community? Is it part of a transparent negotiation between members of society? If the behavior is exploitative, forbidden by common theories of ethics, or frankly self-serving, it cannot be ethical. And to be clear, dating a current or former patient is the third rail of psychiatry, psychology, and social work.

Although it is always tempting to apply a single principle or theory to a clinician's work, or to abandon clinical precepts entirely if one is working in a courtroom, a prison, or a military installation, careful analysis indicates that many ethics sources, perspectives, and tools are necessary to accomplish the task at hand. Mental health practice is not a matter of wearing different hats as we navigate through the system but of recognizing the underlying moral basis of the work in all settings. Deciding whether what we do is stabilizing and protective may be the simplest way of testing whether we have learned the many lessons of ethics as they are applied in mental health, law, and society at large.

CONCLUSION:

As shown in each chapter of this book, clinicians routinely encounter issues at the interface of clinical care and the legal system. These encounters give rise to unique ethical dilemmas for which no clear solutions are found in the ethical codes proffered by professional associations. Rather, the path towards resolution lies in taking a robust professional ethics approach, which allows the practitioner to consider multiple ethical approaches and arrive at a solution that prioritizes various professional duties and optimizes the outcome.

FREQUENTLY ASKED QUESTIONS

May I accept an expensive gift card from a patient or patient's family?

Gifts of any monetary value are potential traps for clinicians. They may be accompanied by an expectation of special favors in return and may interfere with clinical objectivity. This is especially important in mental health practice, where the patient or evaluee may anticipate an outcome that differs from the clinician's. Examples include disability cases and the prescription of controlled substances. Expensive gifts are usually boundary violations. However, token gifts fall under the rubric of boundary crossings or culturally approved practice. These are potentially beneficial to the therapeutic encounter because they enhance rapport and express cultural sensitivity. When there is any doubt, the clinician should consult with colleagues or refer to hospital policy.

How can I work with a new patient in my practice who has fired several other providers and written negative comments about them on Yelp and other websites?

Patients may certainly have legitimate cause for complaint. But in the case of a patient who is confrontational and has publicly expressed dissatisfaction with previous providers, it is best to share your concerns about the posting of the patient's private information (and about the impact on the clinician's reputation) to encourage an open dialogue. You may also ask to speak with the patient's previous providers.

As a practitioner in a small town, I often find myself in social situations with patients I have counseled. How should I conduct myself?

In serving patient confidentiality through beneficence and respect for persons, you must ensure that the reason you know each other and the work you have done together remain private. Politely responding to a patient's greeting is appropriate, but at no point should the discussion become a social encounter or an opportunity for self-disclosure. "I come to this swimming pool often" or "Meet my wife" is too much information under classic rules for preserving boundaries. It is important to maintain professionalism both inside and outside the office.

Are intimate relationships with family members of patients ever acceptable?

No. Virtuous practice, the social contract, and respect for patients dictate that it is unethical and unprofessional to be involved in intimate encounters with family members of patients. It is a form of exploitation that takes advantage of the clinician's position of power. The Opinions section of the psychiatric code of ethics contains a specific prohibi-tion against personal third-party relationships.

How much information must I disclose if I'm worried the patient will turn down treatment he or she needs?

The patient's autonomy requires information disclosure as part of the informed-consent process. Clinicians do often exercise professional judgment in censoring information that may be provocative or overly upsetting, but exercising this privilege requires a clear docu-mentation of the reasoning behind it. In addition, because consent is part of the narrative process and is not limited to a single point in time, the clinician must continue to assess and provide information that the patient finds relevant (or "material," in legal terms). This comes from knowing the patient's values, culture, and preferences.

REFERENCES

1. Percival T, Percival E. *The Works, Literary, Moral and Medical: To Which Are Prefixed Memoirs of His Life and Writings and a Selection from His Literary Correspondence.* London: J. Johnson; 1807.
2. American Medical Association. *History of AMA ethics.* https://www.ama-assn.org/about-us/code-medical-ethics.
3. Appelbaum PS. A theory of ethics for forensic psychiatry. *Journal of the American Academy of Psychiatry and the Law.* 1997;25:233–247.
4. Weinstock R, Leong GB, Silva JA. In: Rosner R, Weinstock R, eds. *Ethical Practice in Psychiatry and the Law.* New York: Plenum Press; 1990:Chapter 3.
5. Candilis PJ, Martinez R. Commentary: the higher standards of aspirational ethics. *Journal of the American Academy of Psychiatry and the Law.* 2006;34:242–244.
6. *Dusky v. United States,* 362 US 402 (U.S. Supreme Court 1960).
7. Candilis PJ, Weinstock R, Martinez R. *Forensic Ethics and the Expert Witness.* New York: Springer; 2007.
8. Nagel T. (1986). *The View from Nowhere.* New York: Oxford University Press; 1986.
9. Beauchamp TL, Childress JF. *Principles of Biomedical Ethics.* New York: Oxford University Press; 2001.
10. Aristotle. *The Nicomachean Ethics* (trans. H. Tredennick). London: Penguin; 2004.
11. Kant, I. *Groundwork of the Metaphysics of Morals,* revised edition (trans. M. Gregor, J. Timmermann). Cambridge: Cambridge University Press; 2012.
12. Mill JS. *Utilitarianism,* 1st edition. London: Parker, Son & Bourn, West Strand; 1863.
13. Bentham J. *Introduction to Principles of Morals and Legislation.* 1907 Reprint of the 1789 edition.
14. Rousseau JJ. *On the Social Contract* (trans. G Cole). New York: Dover; 2003.
15. *Wollschlaeger v. Governor of Florida,* 760 F.3d 1195 (11th Cir. 2014).
16. Gilligan C. *In a Different Voice: Psychological Theory and Women's Development.* Cambridge, MA: Harvard University Press; 1982.
17. Griffith EEH. Ethics in forensic psychiatry: a cultural response to Stone and Appelbaum. *Journal of the American Academy of Psychiatry and the Law.* 1998;26(2):171–184.
18. Candilis PJ, Martinez R, Dording C. Principles and narrative in forensic psychiatry: towards a robust view of professional role. *Journal of the American Academy of Psychiatry and the Law.* 2001;29:167–173.

19. Jaggar AM. Feminist ethics. In: Becker L, Becker C, eds. *Encyclopedia of Ethics*. New York: Garland Press; 1992:363–364.

20. American Civil Liberties Union. Fact Sheet. *Women in Prison Project of the Correctional Association of New York*. Published March 2006.

21. American Civil Liberties Union. Fact Sheet. *Women in Prison Project of the Correctional Association of New York*. Published March 2002.

22. Gutheil GT, Gabbard GO. Misuses and misunderstandings of boundary theory in clinical and regulatory settings. *American Journal of Psychiatry*. 1998;155:409–414

23. Gabbard GO, Nadelson C. Professional boundaries in the physician-patient relationship. *Journal of the American Medical Association*. 1995;273:1445–1449.

24. Gutheil GT, Gabbard G.O. The concept of boundaries in clinical practice: Theoretical and risk management dimensions. *American Journal of Psychiatry*. 1993;150(2):188–196.

25. Savin, D., Martinez, R. Cross-cultural boundary dilemmas: a graded-risk assessment approach. *Transcultural Psychiatry*. 2006;43(2):243–258.

26. Martinez R. A model for boundary dilemmas: Ethical decision-making in the patient-professional relationship. *Ethical Human Sciences and Services*. 2000;2(1):43–61.

27. Wynia MK, Latham SR, Kao AC, Berg J, Emanuel L. Medical professionalism in society. *New England Journal of Medicine*. 1999;341:1612–1616.

28. Wynia MK, Papadakis MA, Sullivan WM, Hafferty FW. More than a list of values and desired behaviors: a foundational understanding of medical professionalism. *Academic Medicine*. 2014;8(5):712–714.

16

CLINICIANS IN THE LEGAL SYSTEM

Records, Requests for Information, and Testimony

RONALD SCHOUTEN

This final chapter addresses important topics at the interface of the law and clinical practice that do not fit neatly into one of the other chapters or require an entire chapter themselves. Readers who want to learn more about the details of these issues, especially as they relate to practice in their own jurisdictions, will benefit from contacting their institutional or personal attorneys, their malpractice insurers, or state professional societies. For those who would like to look more closely at these issues from a medicolegal perspective or explore the possibility of a subspecialty forensic practice, advanced texts for both clinicians and forensic specialists,[1-3] journals,[4] and training[5,6] are available.

MEDICAL RECORD KEEPING

Clinicians are required to maintain treatment records under a variety of state and federal requirements.[7] Massachusetts, for example, requires that physicians maintain adequate records for each patient and retain those records for 7 years from the date of the last patient encounter.[8] If the patient is a minor, the record must be kept for a minimum of 7 years or until the patient reaches the age of 18, whichever is longer. An "adequate" record is one that has enough information to enable a physician to provide effective continuing care to the patient and to be able to look back and see what a patient's condition was like at a given point in the past. In addition, there must be sufficient information to allow a consulting physician or new physician to take over the care of the patient.

Most states, including Massachusetts, have similar requirements for psychologists[9] and social workers.[10] Massachusetts requires that psychologists retain records for only 5 years. The American Psychological Association, on the other hand, suggests retaining records for 7 years.[11] States may specify the data that must be included in the record. Since these specifications differ from one state to another, readers are encouraged to check the requirements in the jurisdiction where they practice. Clinics and hospitals are generally required to maintain records for longer periods than individual practitioners.

REQUESTS FOR PATIENT INFORMATION AND RECORDS

Clinicians commonly receive requests for information about patients. Many people may have an interest in obtaining information about a given patient, and that interest may be appropriate (e.g., a concerned family member seeking information about a loved one) or completely illegitimate (e.g., a fan or a media reporter trying to learn the medical status of a celebrity patient). Requests for information can come from sources as diverse as disability insurance companies; attorneys representing the patient or the patient's estate, or opposing counsel; government agencies; guardians ad litem appointed by a court; or law enforcement officials. Requests can be conveyed informally, such as a telephone call to an inpatient unit or an email to the treating clinician asking, "How is my husband doing?" At the opposite extreme, formal requests may arrive in the form of a subpoena "commanding" the production of records or deposition testimony.

When information about a patient is requested, the clinician must determine whether the request is legitimate or illegitimate and whether he or she must or should comply with the request. Guidance on these questions can be found in the rules surrounding confidentiality and privilege, which are covered in chapter 9. The focus here is on the various types of requests from patients and third parties, and how to handle them.

Regardless of the type of request for information, clinicians will be well served by observing two basic rules when responding to the request. First, the patient must consent to the disclosure of information or must have waived his or her right to prevent disclosure. (See the discussion of the psychotherapist–patient privilege in chapter 9.) Second, the clinician should not attempt to answer questions that are outside his or her knowledge, skills, and role as a treating clinician. (See the discussions of the conflicting roles of independent experts and treating clinicians in chapters 13 and 15.)

Notes Excusing Patients from Work or School

It is not unusual for patients to ask their clinicians to write a note excusing them from work or school. Such notes should be short and to the point, containing as little medical information as is necessary to accomplish the task. The same is true of notes authorizing a return to work or school. For these purposes, employers and educational institutions do not need (and generally do not want) to know about diagnoses or treatments being provided. If a diagnosis is to be included, it should be as general as possible. Consider this example:

To whom it may concern:

Mr. Jones has been in treatment with me for three months and has suffered an exacerbation of his symptoms. I recommend that he stay out of work for two weeks as we address his symptoms.

Thank you for your consideration.

Yours truly,

Dr. Smith

Fitness-for-Duty Evaluations

As discussed in chapter 13, these are formal work- or school-related evaluations that require an objective assessment and reliance on collateral sources of information. As such, they are inconsistent with the role and duties of a treating clinician and should be left to an independent evaluator with experience in performing such assessments. The role of the treating clinician, as described in chapters 13 and 15, is to provide relevant information as a collateral source, so that the independent evaluator can make the assessment as comprehensive, objective, and accurate as possible.

Notes Excusing Patients from Jury Duty

Notes excusing patients from jury duty generally require more clinical detail than notes excusing patients from work or school, and there are often specific jurisdictional requirements. Massachusetts, for example, provides for two types of excuses or disqualifications: standard and permanent. A person is considered to be qualified for jury duty if "such person is able to perform a sedentary job requiring close attention for six hours per day, with short work breaks in the morning and afternoon sessions, for three consecutive business days."[12]

The standard disqualification, which is good for 3 years, requires a note on a physician's letterhead indicating that the patient suffers from a medical condition that prevents him or her from serving as a juror. The medical condition can be described generally (e.g., "a chronic psychiatric condition"); no specific diagnosis is required. A sample letter for standard disqualification in Massachusetts is provided in Appendix 1.

The permanent disqualification is good for the life of the patient and requires an opinion from the physician that the patient suffers from a chronic condition and will never be capable of performing jury duty. Like the letter for a standard disqualification, it requires only a general description of the medical condition, not a specific diagnosis. A sample letter for permanent disqualification in Massachusetts is provided in Appendix 2.

Family and Medical Leave Act and Disability Forms

Under the federal Family and Medical Leave Act (FMLA), eligible employees who have a qualifying medical condition, are caring for a family member with such a condition, or have a child by birth, adoption, or new foster care placement are entitled to up to 12 weeks of unpaid leave from work. If the requested leave is for a qualifying medical condition, the employer has the right to require certification of the condition by a physician and also has the right to request a second and third opinion about the condition. According to the U.S. Department of Labor, the certification should provide the following information:

> contact information for the health care provider; the date the serious health condition began and how long it will last; appropriate medical facts about the condition; for leave for the employee's own serious health condition, information showing that the employee cannot perform the essential functions of the job; for leave to care for a family member, a statement of the care needed; for intermittent leave, information showing the medical necessity for intermittent or reduced schedule leave and either the dates of any planned leave or the estimated frequency and duration of expected incapacity due to the condition.[13]

While a specific diagnosis is not required, provision of one is usually helpful in establishing that a serious health condition exists. With or without a diagnosis, the clinician must describe the symptoms that make the condition serious and interfere with the patient's ability to perform his or her job duties. Ultimately, it is the patient's decision as to what information is disclosed and how much of his or her medical condition to share with the employer, if any.

Patients who apply for short-term or long-term disability are required to authorize release of their medical records to the disability insurance carrier in order to establish the existence of the disability initially, document that it has continued or abated, and document ongoing treatment. Clinicians are usually asked to complete an Attending Physician's Statement (or a similarly named form), even if the responsible clinician is not a physician. This form should always be accompanied by a signed release from the patient. Before completing the form, however, the clinician should confirm that the patient agrees to the release of information and understands its purpose and potential consequences.

One of the challenges with such forms is that they often ask the clinician to opine about the patient's daily activities or work capacity. In most cases, the clinician will not have had a chance to obtain any objective data to answer the question and must rely almost entirely on the patient's report. The clinician should feel free to indicate that he or she has no direct knowledge of the patient's activities or work capacity and is therefore unable to answer the question. If the insurer or other requesting party wishes to have an objective answer, an independent medical evaluation, as discussed in chapter 13, can be pursued.

Fitness to Drive

Patients who have certain health conditions may be required to obtain certification of their fitness to drive, usually from their treating physician or another clinician. When such requests are made, the clinician must determine whether he or she is qualified to conduct the assessment and offer an opinion.[14] Does the clinician have expertise with driving assessment? Has the clinician personally observed the patient drive? The answer to these questions is "no" in most cases. While some medical specialists (e.g., ophthalmologists or neurologists) may be able to gather objective indicators of fitness to drive or the lack thereof, behavioral health specialists are usually working with more subjective criteria. In some cases, where symptoms are extreme, the clinician can make a determination of fitness. Where the symptoms and their impact on fitness to drive are less clear-cut, it is appropriate for the clinician to indicate that he or she cannot offer an opinion and to suggest alternative resources for assessment. Depending on jurisdictional rules and resources, driving ability can be assessed by state police, driving instructors, or occupational therapists, with the assessment serving as a primary evaluation or as an adjunct to the clinician's assessment.[15] States vary with regard to whether clinicians are obligated to report patients they believe to be impaired in their ability to drive. In some states, clinicians may be held liable for reporting a patient to the Department of Motor Vehicles without the patient's permission.[16]

Fitness to Carry a Firearm

Individuals with mental illness can be prohibited from possessing and carrying firearms. Federal law prohibits possession of a firearm by or transfer of a firearm to a person who "is an unlawful user of or addicted to any controlled substance" or "has been adjudicated as a mental defective or has been committed to any mental institution."[17] Unless the person has been convicted of a felony, the ban is not permanent, and the person can petition for reversal of the prohibition. For example, in Massachusetts, five years after a person has been discharged from a commitment to an institution for mental illness or alcohol or substance abuse, he or she can reapply for a firearms license. That application must be accompanied by

> an affidavit of a licensed physician or clinical psychologist attesting that such physician or psychologist is familiar with the applicant's mental illness, alcohol or substance abuse and that in the physician's or psychologist's opinion, the applicant is not disabled by a mental illness, alcohol or substance abuse in a manner that shall prevent the applicant from possessing a firearm, rifle or shotgun.

Alternatively, the patient in question can petition a court for relief. A person who has been disqualified from firearms ownership on the basis of adjudication as an incapacitated person who is unable to manage his or her own affairs can petition the probate court for relief from the restriction (i.e., ask the court to declare that he or she is no longer incapacitated).[18]

As with driving requests, patients generally first turn to the treating clinician to complete the necessary forms and provide a favorable opinion regarding their fitness to own and carry a firearm. Emotions around weapons ownership run high, and the question of fitness to own and carry firearms is among the most serious and contentious that clinicians are asked to address. Few issues pose as much potential for conflict between the clinician's duty as an advocate for the patient and his or her obligation to the public. Many clinicians, including those who are otherwise comfortable writing notes and completing forms for their patients, are reluctant to commit themselves to an assessment that could have such serious ramifications and regarding a subject with which they are not familiar. In such cases, it is appropriate to refer the patient for an independent evaluation, usually to another clinician with forensic experience specifically related to violence risk assessment.

States have specific requirements for assessing the risk of violence, and clinicians who elect to perform such an assessment should understand the requirements in their jurisdiction. Clinicians must also ask themselves whether they have the requisite skills and ability, including the ability to make a decision that is contrary to what the patient hopes to hear. This is particularly true in the case of patients who are employed in law enforcement or security services and are required to carry a weapon as part of their duties.[19,20] Chapter 3 provides a more detailed discussion of violence risk assessment.

Patients' Requests for Their Own Records

Pursuant to the Health Insurance Portability and Accountability Act (HIPAA) and statutes or regulations in most states, patients are entitled to copies of their own medical records, except under certain circumstances.[7,21] This is usually a straightforward request. In some cases, however, the information in the record may be distressing to the patient or subject to misinterpretation. For example, behavioral health records documenting certain symptoms and diagnoses may upset or offend the patient, and the technical terms in psychological and neuropsychological testing reports can easily be misinterpreted. Confronted with a patient's request for medical records, the clinician should discuss with the patient the risks and benefits of having a copy of the full record. The clinician can offer to provide a summary of the record, if release of the entire record is considered problematic. If the patient still insists on receiving the entire record, the clinician can provide a copy of the actual record to the patient's current clinician or legal representative. If the record is to be given to the patient, it is generally beneficial for the clinician and patient to review it together so that the clinician can explain any technical terms, put the information in context, and answer any questions the patient might have.

Telephone or In-Person Requests from Third Parties

These requests are common and can arise spontaneously or when a clinician attempts to gather more information about the patient's status from family members, friends, coworkers, employers, or schools. Unless the requesting party is the legally appointed representative of the patient or the patient has signed a release for that person to obtain information, the appropriate response to such requests is "I'm sorry, but I'm not authorized to comment on whether a person is or is not a patient here." In many cases, the requesting party will already know that the person in question is a patient at the facility or practice. If so, a similar response is appropriate: "I'm sorry, but I don't have permission to share any information about that person without his [or her] permission." In both situations, however, it is appropriate to ask the party making the request whether there is anything the clinician or facility should know about the person in question. As discussed in chapter 9, confidentiality is an obligation that relates to disclosing information and does not prevent clinicians from receiving information. Also, there are exceptions to confidentiality that allow for the sharing of information without the patient's consent.

Requests for Information by Letter, Email, or Other Electronic Means

Written requests for information come in many forms, with varying levels of formality. Such requests are often made by a clinician performing an independent examination of the treating clinician's patient. Whether the request is made by letter, email, or other electronic communication, it should be treated just like oral requests unless it is accompanied by a release of information signed by the patient and the patient's consent to release can be verified. Even with a signed release, before providing any information, the clinician who receives the request should confirm with the patient that he or she:

1. is aware of the request,
2. understands the reasons for the request,
3. understands the substance of the information that will be released,
4. can weigh the risks and benefits of releasing the information,
5. has discussed release of the information with his or her attorney, if litigation is involved,
6. is aware of the psychotherapist–patient privilege and his or her right to exercise it (if applicable), and
7. consents to the release or agrees to waive the privilege.

This list also applies to written requests from attorneys representing the patient or a former patient. Additionally, the clinician should report the request to his or her malpractice attorney or the attorney for his or her practice or institution, as such requests may be the first sign of a pending malpractice action against the clinician.

Subpoenas

Another form of written request for information and records is a subpoena, as shown in Appendix 3. A subpoena is a summons to appear in court or at a deposition and to bring certain documents or simply to supply the documents. Subpoenas are legal documents containing intimidating legal terminology that convey authority, using phrases such as "hereby commanded" and warning of dire consequences for failure to comply. They tend to strike fear in the hearts of clinicians, who may comply with them automatically. That is almost always a mistake.

Subpoenas cannot be ignored; the penalties for doing so include a finding of contempt, monetary fines, and on occasion, incarceration. However, even though subpoenas are official requests, backed by the authority of the court, they are open to resistance and do not require automatic compliance. Possible responses to a subpoena include a request for a delay or refusal to comply for a stated reason (e.g., the subpoena is unduly burdensome), with a judge subsequently ruling on the appropriateness of the subpoena. A subpoena is often accompanied by a token monetary payment, which is less than $10 in some jurisdictions.

The first thing for a clinician to do after receiving a subpoena is to call his or her personal or institutional legal counsel for advice and assistance in responding to the subpoena. The attorney will inquire about the case and explore any bases for refusing to comply, or asking the court to void or quash the subpoena. If the attorney advises compliance, the clinician should still wait until he or she has had a chance to review the items listed above with the patient in question before providing any information.

A discussion with the patient about the psychotherapist–patient privilege is even more important when a subpoena is involved, because a subpoena signals that the patient is involved in litigation, and waiving the privilege may compromise his or her legal interests. If the patient chooses to allow the clinician to comply with the subpoena, it is best to make sure that the patient and his or her attorney know what information is in the record and how that information might affect the patient and the patient's claim. If the patient chooses to exercise the psychotherapist–patient privilege, the clinician's attorney will indicate that in the response. The dispute will be resolved between the parties, but for the time being, the clinician will have fulfilled his or her obligation to respond to the subpoena. Patients who realize that highly sensitive material will be revealed if they waive the psychotherapist–patient privilege and allow the clinician to submit records or testify have been known to drop their claims for emotional distress damages rather than allow the information to be exposed in legal proceedings. An overview of privilege issues related to subpoenas is provided by Gutheil and Drogin.[22]

When a subpoena for records is received, or even anticipated, the clinician should never alter the records except to add information with appropriate notation of the date and time of any alteration. Destruction of records or deliberate alteration of information in the record to conceal evidence can result in charges of spoliation of evidence. In addition, evidence of that destruction or alteration can be admitted to attack the credibility of the clinician as witness or defendant.[23] The advent of electronic medical records has made it increasingly difficult to alter records without detection, but those who would attempt to do so should note that hard drives can be subpoenaed and subjected to forensic computer analysis. Even well-meaning attempts to alter or create records after the fact (e.g., creating notes retroactively in an attempt to assist a patient when contemporaneous treatment notes were not taken) can lead to consequences ranging from severe embarrassment to licensing-board complaints.

Court Orders

A court order, issued by a judge, is different from a subpoena. A judge's order that a clinician produce records may be appealed but otherwise requires compliance. Such an order can be issued after a patient has raised the psychotherapist–patient privilege, the parties have argued the issue before a judge, and the judge has ruled against the patient. Failure to comply with a court order carries a higher risk of a contempt finding, fines, and incarceration than failure to comply with a subpoena. Individuals who fail to comply with a court order to appear before the court are subject to arrest in criminal cases and to a form of civil commitment in civil cases (with civil commitment in such cases referring to confinement in a facility like a jail or house arrest rather than a psychiatric hospital).[24]

Consider the following vignette, which is divided into two parts.

Vignette 1: Court Orders

Mr. B. died of an overdose of pain medications, sedative hypnotics, antidepressants, and alcohol on the last night of a gambling junket with his friends. Mrs. B. brought a lawsuit against Mr. B.'s psychiatrist, Dr. W., alleging that her husband's death was a suicide that could have been prevented but for Dr. W.'s malpractice. Mrs. B. did not claim emotional distress damages but did sue for her husband's pain and suffering and the value of his lost earnings and household services. Dr. W.'s defense attorney sent a subpoena to Mrs. B.'s social worker therapist, requesting her psychotherapy notes for Mrs. B. Intimidated by the formality and legal language of the subpoena, Mrs. B.'s therapist immediately photocopied all her notes and sent them to the defense attorney. Reviewing the notes, the defense expert found documentation that Mrs. B. believed her husband's death was an accident, not a suicide, and that she was only suing because her sister-in-law was pressuring her to do so. The case was settled shortly thereafter for a small amount of money.

As discussed in chapter 9, Mrs. B. could have raised the psychotherapist–patient privilege to prevent the records from being released. She had not claimed emotional distress damages, nor had she otherwise made her mental state an issue in the case. Dr. W.'s attorney simply went on a very successful fishing expedition that resulted in a favorable settlement for his client when the social worker, incorrectly believing that she had to comply with the subpoena, sent out the record without talking to legal counsel or the patient. If

Mrs. B. had been notified about the subpoena and her attorney had had a chance to raise the psychotherapist–privilege on her behalf, the outcome might have been quite different, as illustrated in an alternative version of Vignette 1.

Vignette 1, alternative version

Mrs. B.'s social worker did the right thing and consulted both her attorney and Mrs. B. However, Mrs. B. had also put her mental state at issue by claiming emotional distress damages. In response to the subpoena, Mrs. B. and her therapist raised the psychotherapist–patient privilege, seeking to block release of the therapist's records and testimony. The parties argued about whether Mrs. B. had truly waived the privilege; the judge ruled that she had and held that the subpoena was valid. However, he agreed to review the records in camera (in chambers) to determine what material in the record would be admitted into evidence. Mrs. B. still refused to turn over the records and instructed her therapist not to release them. Dr. W.'s attorney obtained a court order directing the therapist to release the records. At this point, Mrs. B.'s therapist was legally obligated to turn over the records. Failure to do so could have resulted in a fine or jail time for contempt of court.

Clinicians may appear in one of several roles when testifying at a deposition or in court. As discussed in chapter 1, the main distinction is between the role of fact witness and the role of expert witness. Since this book focuses on the interface between clinical practice and the legal system, the discussion in this chapter primarily addresses the fact witness role.

THE CLINICIAN AS FACT WITNESS

As discussed in chapter 1, a fact witness is someone who has firsthand knowledge that is relevant to the matter at issue in a court case, administrative proceeding, or legislative hearing. Anyone with such knowledge may be called to testify at a deposition, trial, or hearing so long as the testimony is relevant to the matter at hand and the person possesses testimonial capacity.

A clinician may be called to testify as a fact witness if his or her patient is involved in litigation and the patient's mental status is at issue in the case. This can occur, for example, in a civil case in which the patient is claiming emotional distress damages or in a contract, guardianship, or conservatorship matter in which the patient's decision-making capacity is being questioned. In criminal cases involving competence to stand trial, criminal responsibility, or aid in sentencing, the treating clinician may be called to enter the patient's medical records into evidence and to describe the patient's clinical history, condition at the time of an alleged crime, and prognosis. The treating clinician has an obligation to provide information when called as a fact witness for the patient or in a matter in which the patient has put his or her mental status at issue. Compliance with that request may be voluntary, but if the clinician declines, a subpoena or court order may follow.

The clinician's role as a fact witness is to describe what the clinician knows about the patient. Unlike an expert witness, the clinician as fact witness can testify only to what he or she observed or heard from the patient. In other words, the clinician may not testify as to hearsay: information heard from others about the patient that is used to establish the truth of what the third party is saying. Clinicians are given a bit more leeway if the hearsay evidence, such as reports of symptoms from a patient's family members, was used as part of the clinician's evaluation and treatment of the patient. Even then, it can be used only to support the clinician's diagnosis, not to establish the fact at issue. The clinician as fact witness cannot offer expert opinion testimony, except under limited circumstances in which the treating clinician has specific expertise in the matter at hand. Consider the following case.

Vignette 2: Clinician's Testimony

Mr. S. was charged with assault with a dangerous weapon and was hospitalized after the alleged assault. The defense attorney asked Mr. S.'s psychiatrist, Dr. M., to testify as a fact witness and at trial called him to testify that Mr. S. was exhibiting symptoms of mania at the time of the alleged crime and was not criminally responsible. Dr. M. had seen Mr. S. in a manic state on several occasions but was out of the country at the time of the alleged crime and learned about the onset of the manic episode and its course from Mr. S.'s sister. The prosecution objected to Dr. M.'s proposed testimony on both issues (whether the defendant was manic at the time of the alleged crime and whether he was criminally responsible), and the judge sustained both objections.

The judge upheld the first objection because Dr. M. had no firsthand knowledge of any manic symptoms exhibited by Mr. S. at the time of the offense. Mr. S.'s sister would have been the appropriate fact witness to testify to that issue. However, Dr. M. would have been allowed to testify about Mr. S.'s clinical condition before and after the event, if he had such knowledge on the basis of their treatment relationship. For example, he could have testified that he had observed hypomanic symptoms in Mr. S. in the weeks before the event and that descriptions of him offered by others (including Mr. S.'s sister) were consistent with Mr. S.'s past manic episodes, which Dr. M. had witnessed. He would also have been allowed to testify about reports of symptoms from Mr. S.'s sister, if he had used those reports as part of his diagnostic process, and to offer an opinion as to Mr. S.'s diagnosis and prognosis in his role as a treating expert (i.e., a treating clinician with expertise regarding bipolar disorder).[25,26]

The judge would probably have had several reasons to sustain the objection to Dr. M.'s offering an opinion regarding criminal responsibility. First and foremost, the defense did not list Dr. M. as an expert witness before the trial. Treating and other clinicians called as fact witnesses should be aware of the very real possibility that they have been listed as expert witnesses, without their knowledge. If Dr. M. did not have documented expertise in forensic matters and had not conducted a forensic evaluation, including a review of other information related to the case, the judge would probably have excluded his expert testimony. On the other hand, the judge might have acknowledged Dr. M.'s role as a treating expert if he did have some training and experience in criminal forensic matters, leaving it to the prosecution to attack the basis for his opinion.

Depositions

As discussed in chapter 1, the discovery phase is an important part of the litigation process. It allows each side to obtain information about the claims or defenses of the opposing party outside the courtroom, so that they can be more specific in their claims, tailor their arguments, and, in many cases, eventually decide to settle the dispute out of court.

Depositions are a key part of the discovery process. They usually take place in a lawyer's office or occasionally in a clinician's office and involve testimony given under oath, with a court reporter making a record of what is said, just as if the testimony were in a courtroom. The rules governing depositions are a bit different from those for courtroom testimony. The attorney conducting the deposition can ask a wide range of questions, many of which might not be admissible in court. The attorney representing the deponent (the person giving the testimony) can object, but the deponent is still expected to answer. The objection is preserved for the record and, if necessary, will be the basis for an argument before the judge that that information cannot be introduced into evidence at trial.

A clinician may be subpoenaed for a deposition, either because his or her patient is involved in litigation or because the clinician is involved as a party in malpractice or other litigation. As noted above, the subpoena may be accompanied by a token monetary payment. Requesting, and receiving, an hourly fee for the deposition or trial testimony is ill advised because it places the clinician at risk of converting his or her role from fact witness to expert witness. The potential consequences of that conversion can include attacks on the clinician's opinion and overall credibility because a forensic evaluation was not done. Ultimately, this may damage rather than help the patient's cause.

The deposition is used as an opportunity to assess the basis and strength of the deponent's knowledge and opinions and to explore the opinions the deponent would offer at trial. On the basis of what is learned at the deposition, opposing counsel may raise an objection to all or part of the deponent's proposed trial testimony.

The request for the deposition usually comes from the attorney for the plaintiff (e.g., the patient or the patient's estate) in an action against the clinician or the attorney for someone with whom the patient is engaged in litigation. In some cases, deposition testimony is obtained because the deponent will not be available to testify in court when the case is expected to go to trial.

A clinician who receives a deposition subpoena should keep the rules regarding all subpoenas in mind: first, the clinician's personal or institutional attorney should be notified of the subpoena, and second, if information is to be revealed about a patient, then the patient must agree to the disclosure or have waived the psychotherapist–patient privilege. A patient who sues his or her clinician is deemed to have waived the privilege by putting his or her mental status at issue, although the patient can still object to the release of specific information on the grounds that it is irrelevant or unduly prejudicial (i.e., presents the patient in a bad light).

A subpoena for a deposition triggers anxiety in virtually everyone. In addition to the two basic rules above, there is another one that applies to depositions: don't panic! A deposition is one of those medicolegal events for which the clinician's attorney can prove to be a best friend. Listening to and accepting the advice of the attorney will do much to allay anxiety and get the clinician through the process. Here are some things to expect at the deposition:

1. The attorneys in the room will introduce themselves for the record and agree to ground rules about how objections will be handled and how the transcript will be managed after the deposition (e.g., whether the deponent wants to review the transcript and make any corrections or waive the review).
2. The clinician being deposed will be sworn in: "Do you swear or affirm to tell the truth, the whole truth, and nothing but the truth?"
3. The deponent will be asked to speak loudly enough for the court reporter to hear, to say "yes" or "no" so that the court reporter can record the answer, rather than saying "uh-huh" or nodding or shaking his or her head. The deponent will be instructed not to speculate and only to answer a question if he or she can do so without guessing.

4. The substantive portion of the deposition usually begins with background questions about the deponent's personal background and educational and work history.

5. The deposition then moves on to the deponent's knowledge about the issue at hand in the litigation. If the clinician is being deposed because his or her patient is involved in litigation, the questions will focus on how long the clinician has known the patient, the treatment relationship, the treatment that has been provided, the diagnosis or diagnoses, the prognosis, and any impairment. If the clinician is being deposed as a defendant in a malpractice suit, he or she will be asked similar questions, but there will be a greater focus on questions related to the allegedly negligent treatment that is the subject of the litigation.

6. Attorneys have different styles, and the approach used by a given attorney may differ according to the specific witness or type of case. An attorney may be very pleasant to the deponent at the deposition, engendering a false sense of security, and then become much more aggressive at trial or may take the opposite approach, with aggressive questioning at the deposition and a more measured tone at trial.

7. As with courtroom testimony, there is direct examination and cross-examination during a deposition. Unlike direct examination in trials, however, more leeway is given for leading questions on direct examination in depositions (e.g., "Isn't it the case, Doctor . . .").

8. One or more of the attorneys will interrupt the questioning periodically with an objection. This is often stated as, "Objection to the form," which is a way to note that the question was leading or otherwise improperly posed. This is usually followed by an instruction that the deponent may answer the question.

9. If the deponent's attorney strongly objects to a given question, he or she may instruct the deponent clinician not to answer. The opposing attorneys will then argue about this, and there may be talk of suspending the deposition in order to ask a judge to resolve the issue. In the interests of time and expense, this rarely happens, and the question is reserved for discussion with the judge at a later date, with possible introduction of the question at trial.

10. Once the direct examination is completed, any attorneys representing other litigants in the case will be offered an opportunity to ask questions. This will be followed by cross-examination, and potentially by redirect examination and recross-examination.

11. At the end of the deposition, the witness is often asked if he or she wants to review and sign the final transcript, if this has not been addressed earlier.

Courtroom Testimony

While depositions trigger anxiety for most clinicians, the prospect of testifying in court induces near-terror for many, especially for those who are testifying in their own defense. All eyes are on the clinician who is sworn in and takes the stand, whether as a witness or the defendant. The trier of fact—either a judge alone or a jury—considers not only the verbal testimony of the witness but also the witness's behavior and appearance. Demeanor evidence, as it is called, helps to determine the witness's credibility and in many cases will determine the fact finder's view of the witness's reliability, expertise, and reasonableness. This is less important at a deposition, although the examining attorney will certainly be noting the witness's demeanor in anticipation of the trial.

Tips for Clinicians Testifying during a Deposition or Trial

1. Be well rested before giving testimony. Sleep deprivation is never beneficial.
2. Remain as calm as possible and avoid becoming defensive.
3. Listen carefully to each question. If you can answer the question, do so. If you cannot remember, do not know the answer, or do not understand the question, say so. Do not attempt to construct facts to fill in the gaps in memory.
4. Answer the question asked and stop. On direct examination, the attorney will ask you to expand your answer if he or she feels it will be helpful. Consider this example: Question: Doctor, are you familiar with Mr. Smith's medical history? Answer: Yes. Question: Please tell the jury what you know of Mr. Smith's history. On cross-examination, it is best to answer the questions by saying "yes," "no," "I don't know," or "I'm sorry, but I can't answer the question as it is worded." In carefully considered situations, it may be worthwhile to expand on your answers, but beware that anything you add may lead to additional questioning.
5. If you leave something out of an answer, your attorney will have an opportunity to elicit that testimony on redirect examination.
6. Avoid humor or attempts at it.
7. Dress professionally (i.e., conservatively). This is particularly important at trial.
8. When responding to questions at a deposition, look at the attorney asking the questions. At trial, look at the judge if it is a bench trial; if it is a jury trial, look at the jury or alternate between looking at the jury and looking at the judge.
9. Speak so that those in attendance, either at a deposition or trial, can both hear and understand you. Pay close attention to the speed of your speech. The court

reporter can be a good barometer of this; if he or she asks you to repeat yourself or to slow down, apologize and make the appropriate change.

10. Avoid professional jargon, but if it is unavoidable, explain the term you have used.
11. If there is an objection to the question, wait to answer until you are instructed to do so.
12. Don't argue. If you disagree with the way you are being questioned, leave it to your attorney or the judge to intervene.

Gutheil and Drogin offer additional advice regarding clinicians in court.[22]

CONCLUSION

This chapter has covered a number of topics at the interface of clinical practice and the law that are commonly encountered by clinicians of every discipline. All clinicians keep records (or should), and requests for copies of those records are common, whether from the patient, from the patient's employer or school, from a disability insurer, or from an attorney with whom the patient is involved in some sort of litigation. The patient may request a letter excusing him or her from jury duty or work or attesting to his or her fitness to carry a firearm. To respond to such requests, clinicians must understand the rules and procedures for releasing information, as well as the limits of their ability to answer the question being posed. If the requisite ability is lacking, clinicians are permitted, and arguably obligated, to limit their involvement and to refuse to answer technical questions that are outside their expertise. In these matters, clinicians have some control over whether and, if so, how they fulfill the request. There is less leeway when it comes to subpoenas, court orders, and testimony at depositions and trial. Clinicians are advised to make use of the legal resources available to them for understanding the extent of their obligations and protecting their own interests.

FREQUENTLY ASKED QUESTIONS

Your patient is in an automobile accident and is planning to sue the other driver. Her lawyer asks you for her medical records and provides you with a signed release. You have been treating this patient for 10 years in weekly psychotherapy, and long ago, once her acute symptoms had resolved, you stopped taking notes after each session. Your state license statute requires that you keep a record sufficient to provide good clinical care and to allow another clinician to take over treatment should you no longer be available. The lawyer wants the entire record, which you know

consists of weekly notes for the first 3 years and an occasional note entered when there was a significant incident in the patient's life. What do you do?

The first step is to inform your malpractice insurer of the request. The insurer may assign an attorney to advise you and help negotiate the process with the patient's attorney. In any case, you will need to inform the patient's attorney of the situation and offer to provide a treatment summary. Ultimately, if the case goes to deposition or trial, you may be asked why there are no contemporaneous records. Explain the reason, even if it is not a particularly good one or exposes you to criticism. Under no circumstances should you manufacture records where there were none. It is much better to confess the omission than to be caught in a deception.

Mr. J. has been in treatment with you for bipolar disorder for 5 years. During a manic episode, he is involved in a high-speed car chase with police, which ends in a collision and the death of a pedestrian. He is charged with vehicular homicide, and his attorney asks you to testify that Mr. J. is not criminally responsible. Should you agree to testify on this issue?

As with many medicolegal issues, the answer is "It depends." If you have expertise regarding the insanity defense and have knowledge of Mr. J.'s behavior during previous manic episodes, you might testify as a treating expert that he was likely to have met the criteria for the insanity defense if he was manic at the time. This is true, even though you have not conducted a formal forensic evaluation. It will be important to state the limitations on the information you have reviewed. As discussed elsewhere in this book, you should agree to serve only as a fact witness, not as Mr. J.'s expert witness.

Mr. J. in the example above is found not guilty by reason of insanity and is hospitalized in a forensic hospital for 1 year. He is discharged at the end of that time and returns to treatment with you. His license is suspended for a minimum of 1 year. At his first visit after that year is up, he asks if you will write a letter to the Department of Motor Vehicles stating that he is fit to drive. What do you do?

Again, the answer is "It depends." If Mr. J. is still symptomatic and exhibiting poor judgment or side effects of medication, you should tell him that you cannot write the letter and explain why. If he is not symptomatic, but you do not have the capacity to make the assessment, you can proceed in one of three ways. First, you can write a letter stating that Mr. J. is not actively symptomatic and that you see no obvious evidence of an inability to drive but that you are not in a position to make the determination. Second, you can refer

Mr. J. to the state police, a driving school, or other testing facility for evaluation and then incorporate that assessment in your letter. Third, you can tell Mr. J. that you do not have the capacity to conduct the assessment and that doing so would interfere with your clinical relationship, and then refer him to one of the above assessment resources.

You receive a subpoena from an attorney claiming to represent your patient, Mr. Y., in connection with a personal injury case. She requests copies of all your treatment records for Mr. Y. and your appearance at a deposition. What should you do?

You should first inform Mr. Y. of the request and then confirm that this is his attorney, that he wants the records released, that he understands the psychotherapist–patient privilege, and that he understands the risks and benefits of releasing the records.

REFERENCES

1. Melton GB, Petrila J, Poythress NG, Slobogin C, Lyons PM, Otto RK. *Psychological Evaluations for the Courts, Third Edition: A Handbook for Mental Health Professionals and Lawyers*, 3rd edition. New York: Guilford Press; 2007.
2. Appelbaum PS, Gutheil TG. *Clinical Handbook of Psychiatry and the Law*, 4th edition. Philadelphia: Lippincott Williams & Wilkins; 2007.
3. Rosner R, Scott C. *Principles and Practice of Forensic Psychiatry*, 3rd edition. Boca Raton, FL: CRC Press; 2016.
4. Journal of the American Academy of Psychiatry and the Law. Bloomfield, CT.
5. Journal of the American Academy of Psychiatry and the Law. *Directory of forensic psychiatry fellowship programs*. 2016. http://www.aapl.org/fellow.php#US. Accessed July 16, 2016.
6. American Psychology-Law Society. *Resource Directory of Forensic Psychology Postdoctoral Fellowship Training Programs 2009–2010*. Washington, DC: American Psychology-Law Society; 2009.
7. Pritts J, Kayne K, Jacobson R. *Privacy and Security Solutions for Interoperable Health Information Exchange: Report on State Medical Record Access Laws*. Washington, DC: Agency for Healthcare Research and Quality; 2009.
8. Massachusetts Board of Registration in Medicine. Licensing and the practice of medicine. *243 CMR 2.07(13)(a)*. Boston: Commonwealth of Massachusetts; 2015.
9. Massachusetts Office of Consumer Affairs and Business Regulation, Division of Professional Licensure. Ethical Standards, Professional Conduct, and Disciplinary Procedures. *Ethical Standards and Professional Conduct*. Boston, MA: Commonwealth of Massachusetts; 2014.
10. National Association of Social Workers. *Social workers and records retention requirements*. 2010. http://socialworkers.org/ldf/legal_issue/200510.asp?back=yes&print=1. Accessed June 29, 2016.
11. American Psychological Association. Record keeping guidelines. *American Psychologist*. 2007;62(9):993–1004.
12. Massachusetts General Laws, §Title II, Chapter 234a, Office of Jury Commissioner for the Commonwealth (2016).
13. U.S. Department of Labor Wage and Hour Division. *Fact sheet #28G: Certification of a serious health condition under the Family and Medical Leave Act*. 2013. https://www.dol.gov/whd/regs/compliance/whdfs28g.htm. Accessed June 10, 2016.
14. Louie AV, Chan E, Hanna M, et al. Assessing fitness to drive in brain tumour patients: a grey matter of law, ethics, and medicine. *Current Oncology*. 2013;20(2):90–96.

15. Silverstein NM, Barton K. Medical review of impaired drivers and fitness to drive survey of stakeholders. *Transportation Research Record.* 2010(2182):55–61.

16. Gergerich EM. Reporting policy regarding drivers with dementia. *Gerontologist.* 2016;56(2):345–356.

17. Federal Gun Control Act of 1968, (1968). 18 U.S.C. §§ 922(d)(4), (g)(4).

18. An Act Relative to the Reduction of Gun Violence, Massachusetts General Laws, §Part I, Administration of Government Title 20, Public Safety and Good Order Chapter 140, Licenses Section 131, Licenses to carry firearms; conditions and restrictions (2016).

19. Norris DM, Price M, Gutheil T, Reid WH. Firearm laws, patients, and the roles of psychiatrists. *American Journal of Psychiatry.* 2006;163(8):1392–1396.

20. Price M, Norris DM. Firearm laws: a primer for psychiatrists. *Harv Rev Psychiatry.* 2010;18(6):326–335.

21. Brendel RW, Bryan E. HIPAA for psychiatrists. *Harvard Review of Psychiatry.* 2004;12(3):177–183.

22. Gutheil TG, Drogin EY. *The Mental Health Professional in Court: A Survival Guide.* Washington, DC: American Psychiatric Publishing; 2013.

23. *Rosenblitt v. Zimmerman,* 766 A.2d 749(New Jersey Supreme Court 2001).

24. Gross LE. Supreme Court rule 219: the consequences of refusal to comply with rules or orders relating to discovery or pretrial conferences. *Loyola Univ Chicago Law J.* 1993;24(4):471–496.

25. Greenberg LR, Gould JW. The treating expert: a hybrid role with firm boundaries. *Professional Psychology-Research and Practice.* 2001;32(5):469–478.

26. Greenberg SA, Shuman DW. Irreconcilable conflict between therapeutic and forensic roles. *Professional Psychology-Research and Practice.* 1997;28(1):50–57.

SAMPLE LETTER FOR STANDARD MEDICAL DISQUALIFICATION

[Date]

Office of Jury Commissioner
560 Harrison Avenue, Suite 600
Boston, Massachusetts 02118

Re: [Juror Name]
        [Juror Badge Number]

Dear Office of Jury Commissioner:

I am a physician treating [Juror Name] for [identify general nature of medical condition - specific diagnosis is not required.]. In my opinion, this medical condition prevents [Juror Name] from performing juror service.

Kindly disqualify [Juror Name] from the performance of juror service.

Sincerely,

[Physician's Signature]

[Physician's Printed Name]

SAMPLE LETTER FOR PERMANENT MEDICAL DISQUALIFICATION

[Date]

Office of Jury Commissioner
560 Harrison Avenue, Suite 600
Boston, Massachusetts 02118

Re: [Juror Name]
        [Juror Badge Number]

Dear Office of Jury Commissioner:

I am a physician treating [Juror Name] for [identify general nature of medical condition - specific diagnosis is not required.]. This medical condition is a permanent medical condition. In my opinion, [Juror Name] will never be able to perform juror service.

Kindly disqualify [Juror Name] permanently from the performance of juror service.

Sincerely,

[Physician's Signature]

[Physician's Printed Name]

SUBPOENA FORM

THE COMMONWEALTH OF MASSACHUSETTS SUBPOENA

_____, ss.

To: _____

_____

_____

_____

You are hereby commanded, in the name of the Commonwealth of Massachusetts, to appear before the _____ Court at _____ in the County of _____ on the _____ day of _____, in the year _____ at _____ am/pm, and from day to day thereafter, until the action hereinafter named is heard by said Court, to give evidence of what you know relating to an action then and there to be heard and tried between _____, Plaintiff, and _____, Defendant, docket number _____, and you are further required to bring with you _____

_____

_____

_____

_____

Hereof fail not, as your failure to appear as required will subject you to such pains and penalties as the law provides.

Dated at _____ the _____ day of _____, in the year _____.

_____

Notary Public – Justice of the Peace

RETURN OF SERVICE

I, _____, certify that I this day summoned the within named

_____

to appear and give evidence at Court as directed by the attached subpoena by delivering to

_____

in hand, - leaving at _____

a copy of the subpoena together with _____ fees for attendance and travel.

I further certify that I am not a party to the above entitled action and that I am not less than 18 years of age.

Signed under penalties of perjury this _____ day of _____, in the year _____

_____

INDEX

Note: Page numbers followed by italicized letters indicate *boxes* or *tables*.

treatment (*Cont.*)
  patient capacity to make decisions regarding, 94–95
  presentencing evaluation for, 283
treatment refusal
  in civil commitment, 33
  of electroconvulsive therapy, 165
  and patient-psychotherapist relationship, 87
  and treatment-driven model, 154, 155, 159
treatment refusal, antipsychotic medication
  addressing drug side effects, 161
  assessment and management of, 160–165, 166–167
  common reasons for, 159b
  in forensic settings, 157–158
  and involuntarily hospitalized patients, 153–154
  in nursing homes, 164–165
  opportunities presented by, 153, 160–161, 163, 166
  in outpatient settings, 164
  persistent refusal, 162–163
  prevalence and outcome of, 158–160
  procedures for adjudication of, 155t
  right to refuse treatment, history and legal criteria, 154–158
  treatment in emergencies, 157
trial courts, definition and use of, 5–6

Uniform Adult Guardianship and Protective Proceedings Act, 121
U.S. Constitution
  Bill of Rights, 3–4, 10–12, 17–18
  history and development of, 3–4
  and rights to fair trial, 10–12
U.S. v. Loughner, 157, 158
Veterans Administration (VA) disability evaluations, 300–301
vicarious liability, 173–174
violence, risk assessment for
  and access to firearms, 46–47, 51, 58
  approaches to violence risk assessment, 47–48
  and civil commitment, 23–24
  common errors in, 54–55
  demographic and historical factors, 42–43

example of, 51–53
frequently asked questions regarding, 58
interventions to modify risk factors, 51
involuntary hospitalization to manage risk, 50–51
liability issues regarding, 55–57
management of violence risk, 49–51
and mental illness, 43–45, 58
methods of assessing risk, 48–49
and monitoring symptoms, 51
as ongoing process, 55
and patient history of violence, 43
predicting violence risk, 41
presence or absence of specific threat, 55
presentencing evaluations, 283
protective and risk factors, 41–42
risk factors for violence, 41–47, 58, 88
settings and process of, 39–40, 57
social and environmental factors, 46
and substance abuse, 46
subtypes of violence, 40–41
violence, subtypes of, 40–41
Violence Against Women Reauthorization Act of 2013, 228
Violence Risk Appraisal Guide, 48, 283
virtue theory, of ethics, 342
voluntary admission, conditional, 28–30

warning labels on medications, and informed consent, 100
Washington v. Harper, 157–158
Williamson v. Liptzin, 178
wills and testaments, capacity to make, 124–128, 136–137
witnesses, types of in legal system, 8–9
Wollschlaeger v. Governor of Florida, 344
workers' compensation evaluations, 295–297, 312
workplace accommodations, 302
workplace safety, relationships with security personnel, 28
work-related trauma, 295–297

young adults, assessing risk of suicide in, 73–74, 89

Zinermon v. Burch, 29, 50